The West beyond the West
A History of British Columbia
Revised Edition

The critically acclaimed British Columbia history of choice has now been revised. Here is the story of Canada's westernmost province, beginning at the point of contact between native peoples and Europeans and continuing through 1995. Jean Barman tells the story not only by focusing on the history of BC's government but also on the roles that women, immigrants, and native peoples have played in the development of the province. She weaves together political, social, economic, and demographic events into an absorbing account that reveals the roots of contemporary British Columbia in all its diversity.

This new edition includes information from the 1991 census, and revisions have been made throughout the book, including the references, to bring it up to date.

JEAN BARMAN is a member of the Department of Educational Studies, University of British Columbia, and the author of *Growing Up British in British Columbia: Boys in Private School*. She is co-editor of several other books, most recently *First Nations Education in Canada: The Circle Unfolds*, with Marie Battiste, and *Children, Teachers and Schools in the History of British Columbia*, with Neil Sutherland and J. Donald Wilson.

The West beyond the West

A HISTORY OF
BRITISH COLUMBIA

Revised Edition

Jean Barman

UNIVERSITY OF TORONTO PRESS

Toronto Buffalo London

Canadian Cataloguing in Publication Data

Barman, Jean, 1939–
The West beyond the West :
a history of British Columbia

Rev. ed.
Includes index.
ISBN 0-8020-7185-6

1. British Columbia – History.   I. Title.

FC3811.B36 1996   971.1   C96-930429-3
F1088.B37 1996

Much of this book appeared originally in somewhat different
form in a course prepared for the BC Open University. Material
from that course is included by permission of the Principal of the
BC Open University.

University of Toronto Press acknowledges the financial
assistance to its publishing program of the Canada Council
and the Ontario Arts Council.

Contents

Preface

Growing up on a farm south of Winnipeg, I dreamt of British Columbia. Totem poles and snow-capped mountains symbolized the west coast province. I fell in love sight unseen with this west beyond the west. Only in adulthood was I fortunate enough to come to live in British Columbia. Two decades of residence have not diminished the attachment formed as a child. British Columbia continues to fascinate, in part because it so often presents an enigma. Reality and perception, the geographical entity and its social constructs, Vancouver as a cosmopolitan city amidst one of the world's last frontiers – they all intertwine into a mysterious, fascinating whole that is British Columbia.

This history of British Columbia not so much disentangles as it attempts to integrate the various strands that together make up the province's past. The interpretation is firmly centred in the scholarly literature. Margaret Ormsby's provincial history, now long out of print, has proven an invaluable beginning point. So has the research of a growing number of people interested in British Columbia's past. Yet many topics remain unexplored, and for that reason this interpretation interweaves the perceptions of contemporary observers and critics. Memoirs, fictionalized evocations, local histories, diaries, and letters have been used to evoke the rhythms of everyday life and to personalize general points. Emily Carr appears time and again. Her eye for detail remains unequalled among the men and women who have written about British Columbia. Carr is not alone, being accompanied through the pages of the past by such diverse observers as Hudson's Bay physician John Sebastian Helmcken, young Nova Scotia school teacher Jessie McQueen, Allerdale Grainger's logging fraternity, cowboy adventurer Richmond Hobson, and Howard White's raincoast chroniclers.

The text is organized on two levels. Chapters interpreting political and economic events overlap chronologically with topical chapters examining major areas of social change. Any general survey must be selective, and some subjects receive more attention. In some cases this is owing to the existence of extensive secondary scholarship, in others to the author's predilections. Conversely, a paucity of research has limited discussion of some important topics to general points. Among areas of deliberate emphasis are the demography of settlement, processes of work, everyday lives of ordinary British Columbians, the role of the school as an institution, and native peoples.

This history has three overlapping audiences in mind. The first are individuals without any previous knowledge about British Columbia or possibly about Canada as a whole. The text explains topics and issues as they are introduced. For readers having general knowledge about the west coast province through residence or interest, this history builds on that base. The third intended audience are students of Canadian history. The text's interpretation of the existing literature challenges some dominant perspectives and seeks to encourage new research.

It is only the unstinting assistance of innumerable individuals that has made this history possible. Through personal interviews and by correspondence, over two hundred men and women of diverse backgrounds have shared with me important aspects of their lives in British Columbia. Their observations and insights have been critical to my understanding, and I thank each of them. Time spent since 1984 teaching for the University of British Columbia in Vanderhoof, Vernon, Kamloops, Victoria, Prince George, and Chilliwack has measurably extended my understanding of the province as a whole. I am very grateful to these students, native and non-native, as well as to the many I have come to know at the University of British Columbia itself, for their considered reactions to concepts and ideas often not yet wholly formed.

The historical record of British Columbia has survived through the perseverance of countless archivists and librarians, many of them volunteers. I have received generous assistance in, among other locations, Kamloops, Kelowna, Merritt, Nanaimo, Port Moody, Prince George, Powell River, Vancouver, Vanderhoof, Vernon, and Victoria. Also helpful have been the dedicated professionals in the Provincial Archives of British Columbia, including its Oral History Division which oversees some four thousand recorded interviews with British Columbians of all backgrounds, in the Special Collections division of the UBC Library, in the Anglican Archives located at the university, and in the Northwest Collection of the Vancouver Public Library. I thank you all. I am especially grateful to the Social Sciences and Humanities Research Council of Canada for its support of the Canadian Childhood History Project, out of which some of the research finding its way into this history originated.

Good friends have been generous with time and encouragement. For helpful and detailed critiques of the manuscript, I am indebted to Celia Haig-Brown, Robert A.J. McDonald, George McWhirter, Richard Mackie, Patricia Roy, Neil Sutherland, J. Donald Wilson, Roderick J. Barman, and two perceptive press reviewers. The assistance of Gerry Hallowell, Laura Macleod, and Diane Mew of the University of Toronto Press has been invaluable. For cheerfully responding to queries and providing moral support, I also want to thank Jane Fredeman, Jacqueline Gresko, Irene Howard, Robert Kubicek, Elizabeth Lees, Norah Lewis, J.R. Miller, Claus Naske, Dianne Newell, Alice Niwinski, Alison Prentice, Keith Ralston, A.J. Ray, Letia Richardson, Peter Seixas, Nancy Sheehan, Veronica Strong-Boag, Duane Thomson, Alan Twigg, Peter Ward, and Howard White. Elizabeth Lees, Donna Penney, and Clinton Evans provided valuable research assistance. My husband Roderick and children Rod and Emily have been endlessly patient and understanding.

Parts of this history originated in a distance-education course written for the Open Learning Agency of British Columbia, and I want especially to thank Ian Muggridge for permission to build on that text and to use here the maps prepared for History 225. Penny Street gave invaluable support as course designer, as did Sharon Meen as senior tutor. Robert A.J. McDonald originally persuaded me to write the OLA course and served as course consultant. Without his generosity, unequalled expertise on British Columbia history, and wise counsel, there would have been no course and no history. To the extent a published work can be blessed with a godfather, it is Bob McDonald.

Any general history will inevitably contain errors of fact and omission. The responsibility for these and for misinterpretations or misrepresentations of others' research is mine. I have preferred natural language in the interests of a readable text. Where this has necessitated simplification of complex points, I also apologize for any offence so created.

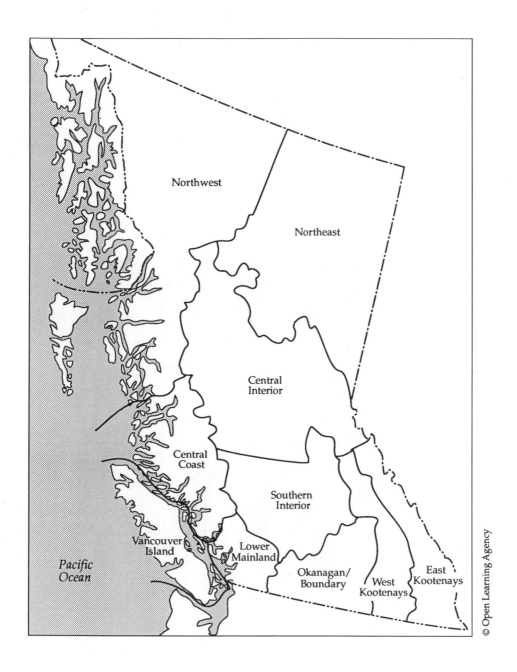

Map 1 Regions of British Columbia

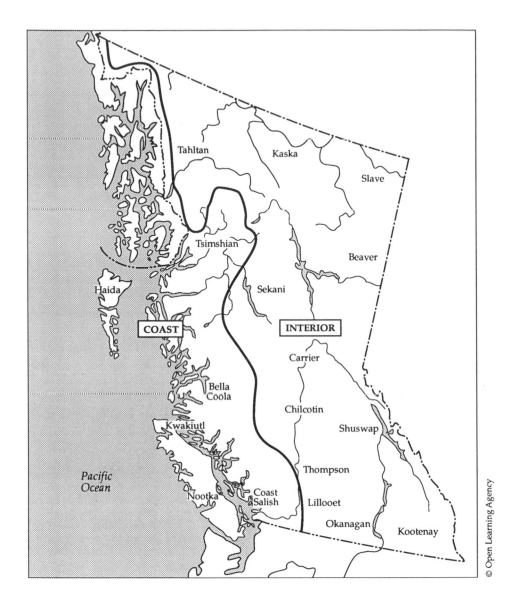

Map 2 Principal cultural divisions of British Columbia native peoples

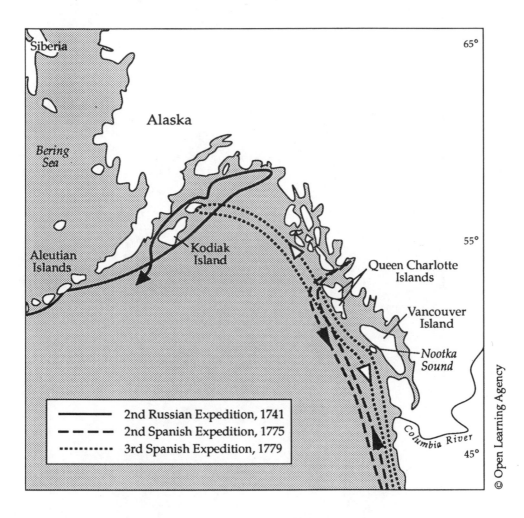

Map 3 Russian and Spanish exploration of Pacific northwest coast

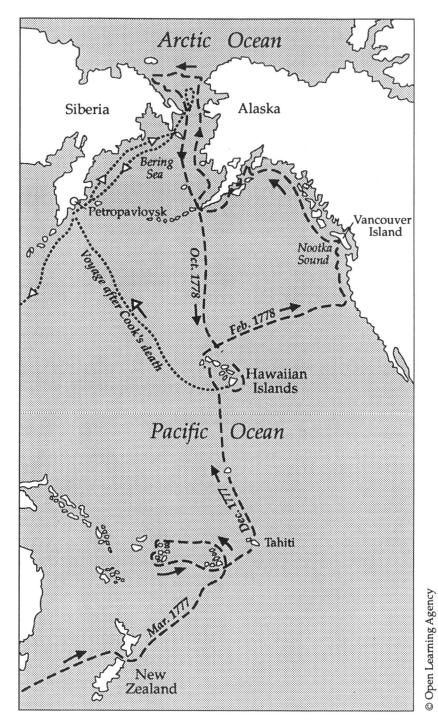

Map 4 British exploration of the Pacific northwest coast by James Cook

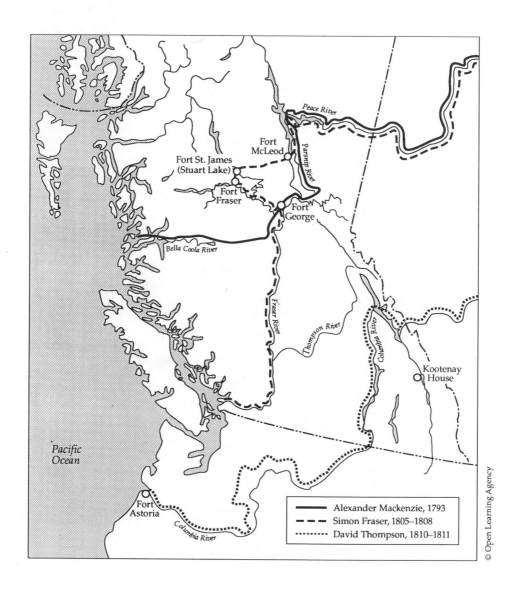

	Key
——	Alexander Mackenzie, 1793
- - -	Simon Fraser, 1805–1808
·····	David Thompson, 1810–1811

Peace River

Fort McLeod

Fort St. James
(Stuart Lake)

Fort Fraser

Fort George

Parsnip River

Bella Coola River

Fraser River

Thompson River

Columbia River

Kootenay House

Pacific Ocean

Fort Astoria

Columbia River

© Open Learning Agency

Map 5 Early overland exploration of the Pacific Northwest

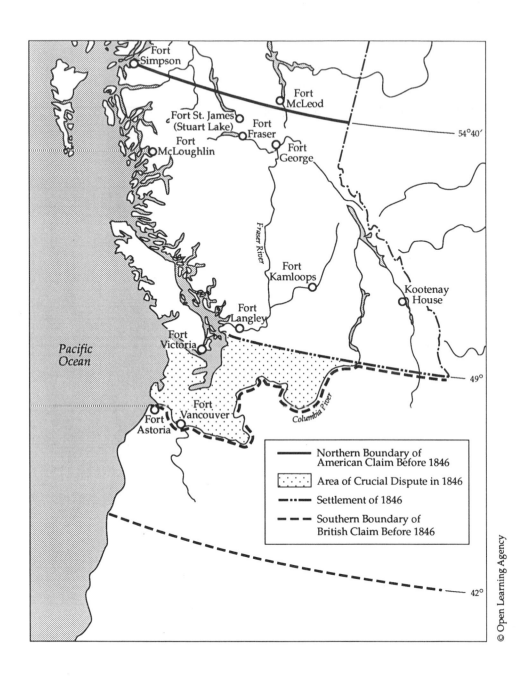

Fort
Simpson

Fort
McLeod

Fort St. James
(Stuart Lake)

Fort
Fraser

Fort
George

Fort
McLoughlin

54°40′

Fraser River

Fort
Kamloops

Kootenay
House

Fort
Langley

Fort
Victoria

Pacific
Ocean

49°

Columbia River

Fort
Vancouver

Fort
Astoria

Northern Boundary of
American Claim Before 1846

Area of Crucial Dispute in 1846

Settlement of 1846

Southern Boundary of
British Claim Before 1846

42°

© Open Learning Agency

Map 6 **The fur trade in the Pacific Northwest**

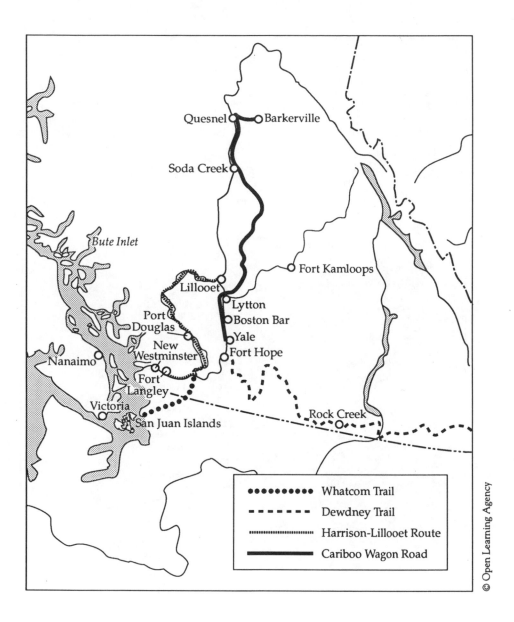

Map 7 Colonial British Columbia

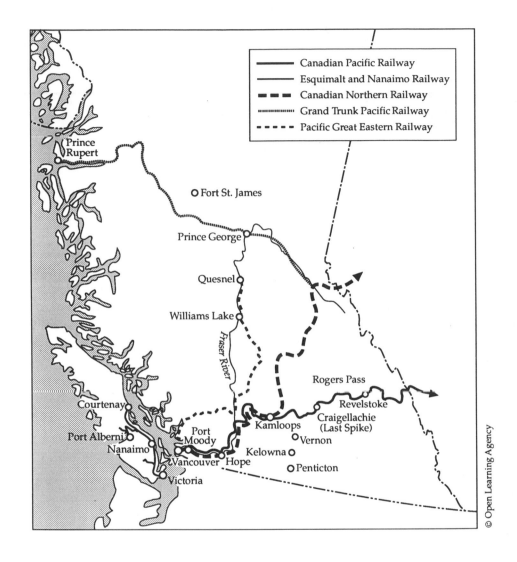

Legend:
- Canadian Pacific Railway
- Esquimalt and Nanaimo Railway
- Canadian Northern Railway
- Grand Trunk Pacific Railway
- Pacific Great Eastern Railway

Prince Rupert
Fort St. James
Prince George
Quesnel
Williams Lake
Fraser River
Rogers Pass
Courtenay
Revelstoke
Craigellachie (Last Spike)
Port Alberni
Kamloops
Port Moody
Vernon
Nanaimo
Kelowna
Vancouver Hope
Victoria
Penticton

© Open Learning Agency

Map 8 Major railway routes across British Columbia at the time of the First World War

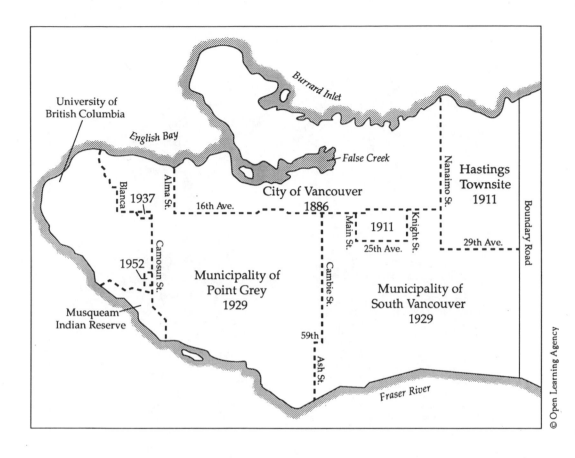

Map 9 Vancouver's expanding boundaries

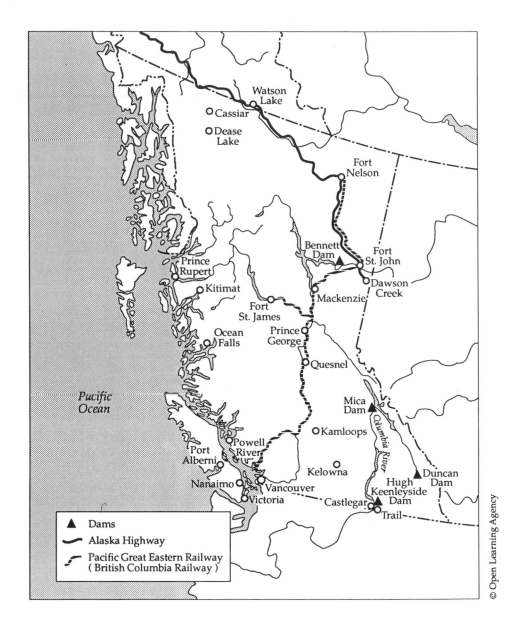

Map 10 Economic development of British Columbia from the time of the Second World War

The West beyond the West:
A History
of British Columbia

1

In Search of British Columbia

British Columbia presents an enigma. Its identity is elusive, yet images abound. Mountains and coastline offer powerful counterpoints. Sir John A. Macdonald's 'sea of mountains' vies with Margaret Atwood's 'postcard mountains' and George Woodcock's 'chains of mountains repeating each other time and again from the Rockies to the sea.' Jack Hodgins termed British Columbia's coast 'the Ragged Green Edge of the World.' Gwen Cash concluded that, 'along this amazing coastline, despite human courage and puny encroachment, nature is still largely untouched.'[1]

The visual often overwhelms. 'There is beauty here, at length, for the first time in Canada,' young Rupert Brooke mused as he approached the Rocky Mountains heading for the west coast. The protagonist in Ethel Wilson's *The Innocent Traveller* lamented on coming to British Columbia in middle age: 'It is so lovely ... that I feel I've wasted my life in not living here before.' Stephen Leacock is alleged to have quipped: 'British Columbia ... If I had known what it was like, I wouldn't have been content with a mere visit. I'd have been born here.' Only from time to time does a harder reality intrude, as reported by one early twentieth-century visitor: 'We raved about the scenery wherever we went, but, as we were sometimes reminded, "men cannot live upon scenery."'[2]

The importance of images cannot be underestimated, for British Columbia is no ordinary place, perhaps no single place. The indigenous population comprised many separate peoples. Early fur traders had shifting spheres of influence. The British crown originally created two colonies within the present-day province. Just five years after they were united as British Columbia, that colony joined the young Canadian Confederation. But the acquisition of a permanent political status did not denote internal cohesion. The new province contained extraordinarily difficult terrain, more often isolating settlers than drawing them together. *British Columbia Magazine* astutely observed in 1911 in an article entitled 'British Columbia's Fifty-Seven Varieties' that, 'while there is only one British Columbia, there are so many kinds of it that he is a brave man indeed who can say he knows the province and get away with it.'[3] The same topography responsible for the visual images so appealing to residents and visitors alike has not encouraged a strong sense of identity as a single province.

Any search to understand British Columbia and its past must begin with geography. British Columbia's history is integrally linked to its physical face. Thirteen hundred kilometres from north to south, British Columbia extends some eight hundred kilometres, from maritime coast to eastern mountains and prairie: the town of Atlin in the northwest lies over twenty-five hundred driving kilometres from Cranbrook in the southeast. British Columbia totals 948,600 square kilometres. Daunting even in the late twentieth century, the province's size and diversity long prohibited overall understanding or comprehension. Only in British Columbia's southwestern tip and in its far northeast is physical movement relatively easy. Asked by her husband to accompany him on his judicial duties in the Cariboo, a young Victoria matron of the late 1870s recalled her reaction: 'That vast, mountainous region of grand vistas, precipitous plateaus and hairbreadth highways was a mysterious, forbidding empire ... To a Victorian, it was pretty much like suggesting a trip to Tibet.' A 1914 brochure promoting the new northern metropolis of Prince Rupert made much the same point. 'Few indeed, even in our own Province, have the faintest conception of this great hinterland now at last ready for the farmer, the miner, and the lumberman.'[4]

While British Columbia's complex geology resulted in vast mineral deposits, it also put in place seemingly endless chains of mountains. The Coast, Skeena, Monashee, Selkirk, Purcell, and Rocky ranges are only some of those traversing the province from northwest to southeast. Their sharp peaks, steep slopes, and narrow valleys ensured that isolation would be a major motif for many of the province's inhabitants. These parallel ranges also created natural corridors running north and south, in direct opposition to the province's political status premised on links running east and west.

Apart from mountains, British Columbia's two most prominent natural features are a long coast line and a vast interior plateau. The coast has generated its own mystique, related in part to the sophistication of its indigenous peoples, in part to distinctive geography. Journalist Gwen Cash evoked 'deep fjords twisting between precipitous cliffs, glaciers glistening on mountainous horizons, dark forests, tiny bays, enchanted islands, tumultuous tides.'[5]

Characterized by a moderate but rainy climate, the coast's thick forests of cedar, fir, spruce, and hemlock are frequently shrouded by cloud and fog. Two days out of every three classify as 'wet weather.' Emily Carr recorded in her journal: 'October 11th [1935], Victoria. The first dismal rain of winter. Summer hanging between life and death. Everything shivering and dripping like the time between death and funeral.' For Ethel Wilson, the air of the British Columbia coast had its own character, being 'mild, soft and (to tell the truth) sometimes deliciously drowsy.'[6] The rain eventually stops. With brighter weather nearby islands rise abruptly and even precipitously out of the sea. Ethel Wilson's description is shared by many coastal British Columbians. 'Oldtimers of Vancouver, though a little weary of the rain, know always that when a glorious day breaks on the green ground and on the mountains, this rain will be forgotten in the brilliant air.'[7]

British Columbia's large interior plateau, bordered by the basins of the Fraser, Columbia, Skeena, and Peace rivers, is the northern extension of the great North American desert, much of it rocky and dry. A long-time inhabitant described it vividly: 'You have a hundred and fifty thousand acres of wilderness, 98 per cent of which will never – either today or tomorrow or one hundred years from now – be scratched by the share of a plough, since its soil is so stony and barren it is incapable of producing any other crop but the shrubbery and grasses and twisted scrubby timber that God put there in the beginning.'[8] This vast central plateau helps explain why, although over half of British Columbia is forested, very little of the province is suitable for agriculture; under 3 per cent of the province is arable or potentially so. Early arrivals quickly became aware of this. An 1884 settlement promotion warned that British Columbia's 'extremely rugged and mountainous character' rendered its 'agricultural areas comparatively small, far removed from each other, and difficult of access.'[9]

In climate as in agricultural potential, British Columbia differs from most of Canada. George Parkin considered one of the province's contributions to Canada was that 'it gave the Dominion a new climate, or, one might rather say, a variety of new climates, for between the summit of the Rockies and the shore of the Pacific there are more gradations of temperature and climate effect for both summer and winter as marked as between Norway and northern Italy.' Even single locations can be so affected, as in a somewhat perplexed Christmas 1858 report from gold-rush Victoria: 'For the last ten days our climate has exhibited a most variable character, marked by sudden alternations of frost, thaw, snow, sleet, rain, hail, heavy gales of wind, mingled with some mild fine weather at short intervals.'[10] In some locations away from the coast harsh extremes are seasonal fare. 'In winter weather was the master, we its slaves ... We seldom tried to buck weather, to quarrel with it ... Instead, we tried to get along with it, to understand it, and if possible figure out its shifting moods in advance.'[11]

British Columbia can be variously divided into regions. A fundamental division, and the one that characterizes its indigenous peoples, is between the coast and the interior. Wilson pinpointed the demarcation in *Swamp Angel*. 'Make no mistake, when you have reached Hope [at the eastern end of the Lower Fraser Valley] and the roads that divide there you have quite left Vancouver and the Pacific Ocean. They are disproportionately remote. You are entering a continent, and you meet the continent there, at Hope.'[12] Sometimes a further division is made. The interior is limited to the southern half of the province, to about the fifty-fourth parallel, or the city of Prince George. The remainder is the north. For historical purposes British Columbia is most usefully divided into ten regions used by the federal census during much of the twentieth century and in modified form for purposes ranging from weather forecasting to tourist promotion (see Map 1).

Moving from west to east and then south to north, the first of the ten regions is Vancouver Island and adjacent Gulf Islands. Descending from a mountainous backbone running north and south, Vancouver Island possesses rugged coast on the west but on the east some fertile lowland suitable for agriculture. Many of the earliest encounters between native people and Europeans occurred on Vancouver Island's west coast. The Hudson's Bay Company arrived on Vancouver Island in 1843 and within the decade fur-trade families had settled permanently at Fort Victoria. A large natural harbour at Esquimalt a few miles from Victoria served for almost half a century as the home base for Royal Navy operations along the Pacific coast.

A moderate maritime climate encouraged farming, particularly in southeastern Vancouver Island and on nearby Saltspring Island, the largest of 225 Gulf Islands in the Strait of Georgia. About 110 kilometres northeast of Victoria lies Nanaimo, whose European origins go back to the mid-nineteenth-century demand for coal to power the new steam-driven vessels of the Royal Navy. Vancouver Island became the seat of the provincial government on Confederation; thus references to Victoria are as likely to refer to the government as to the city itself.

For many Vancouver Islanders the island remains the centre of loyalty, a world of its own. British Columbians' widespread use of the term 'mainland' to distinguish the rest of the province continues a perception going back to the earliest years of European settlement, when the island ruled supreme. Poet Susan Musgrave, a descendant of a pioneer island family, made the point. 'My father, who never referred to the prairies as anything but "other parts of Canada" did not believe that mainlanders should be allowed on the Island ... In my father's opinion, "mainland drivers" only cluttered up the roads, and when the B.C. ferries began operating, increasing the volume of traffic to the Island, he blamed the hourly service for the rise in crime.'[13]

Immediately across the Strait of Georgia from Vancouver Island is the lower mainland region. Extending north to the Sechelt peninsula, it runs east along the Fraser River as far as the community of Hope. With the gold rush of 1858, the lower mainland became British Columbia's second principal area of non-native settlement. In explaining why the capital of the new mainland colony of British Columbia should be sited at present-day New Westminster, Colonel Moody of the Royal Engineers made clear the region's appeal. 'The entrance to the Frazer is very striking – Extending miles to the right & left are low marsh lands (apparently of very rich qualities) & yet f' the Background of Superb Mountains – Swiss in outline, dark in woods, grandly towering into the Clouds there is a sublimity that deeply impresses you. Everything is large and magnificent.'[14] The Fraser River's delta and valley, extending about 135 aerial kilometres east from the coast to Hope, is often referred to as the Lower Fraser Valley. Especially attractive to small farmers, it soon became – and remains – the most intensely cultivated part of British Columbia.

Just north of the Fraser's delta is a large land-locked natural harbour able to accommodate ocean-going vessels. Its existence determined the location of the western terminus of the Canadian Pacific Railway at what was named Vancouver in honour of the early maritime explorer. Vancouver rapidly became the dominant metropolis of the lower mainland, soon of the province as a whole. The city's linkages eventually extended into the prairies and towards Asia. Essentially a huge service centre, Canada's third-largest city has always lived – sometimes very well – off other people's money. From the 1920s the lower mainland region contained more than half the province's population. Thus, while the coast refers literally to a much greater geographical area, when used by British Columbians living in the province's interior it is often equated with the lower mainland or even just Vancouver.

Northeast of the lower mainland lies a major transportation corridor known as the southern interior. Long before the first Europeans arrived, Interior Salish and Chilcotin were using the rivers of the area as trading routes. The routes to the gold-fields of the Cariboo crossed the southern interior. From Lillooet distances on the journey were incorporated into the names of road houses, becoming such pioneer communities as 70 Mile House and 100 Mile House. Ethel Wilson repeatedly drew on the strong visual imagery of the central interior. For her, like many coastal residents, it was known as the upper country. The junction of the Fraser and Thompson rivers at Lytton was a powerful theme in Wilson's writings, caught most vividly in *Swamp Angel*.

Say 'Lytton Bridge' – and the sight springs clear to the eyes. There is the convergence of the two river valleys and the two rivers. The strong muddy Fraser winds boiling down from the north. The gay blue-green Thompson River foams and dances in from the east. Below the bridge where Maggie stood the two rivers converge in a strong slanting line of pressure and resistance. But it is no good. The Thompson cannot resist, and the powerful inexorable Fraser swallows up the green and the blue and the white and the amethyst. The Thompson River is no more, and the Fraser moves on to the west, swollen, stronger, dangerous, and as sullen as ever.[15]

Large stretches of open range and grassland make much of the southern interior suitable for raising cattle. Particularly in discussions of ranching but going back to the gold rush, the region has often been loosely equated with the Cariboo. Finer distinctions are sometimes drawn, the term Chilcotin being used to define the area that lies west of the Fraser River. The Cariboo is then limited to the area east of the Fraser and north of the Thompson, essentially between Lytton or Lillooet and Prince George. Whether the broader or closer definition be used, the Cariboo has generated strong visual images. For the London *Times* correspondent in British Columbia during the gold rush, 'views in Cariboo exceed anything he saw in Andes or Himalayas.'[16]

East of the lower mainland and southeast of the southern interior lies the Okanagan-Boundary region. Its central feature is Okanagan Lake running 130 kilometres north and south with subsidiary lakes at either end. Colonial governor James Douglas was enthusiastic about the region's possibilities, reporting to the Colonial Office 'the profusion of grass that covers both woodland and meadow, affording rich pastures for domestic animals, a circumstance which gives to this district an extraordinary value, as every part of the surface, whether hill or valley, may be turned to account and made available either for tillage or stock farming.'[17] For several decades the region attracted only a handful of settlers, mostly interested in ranching. But from the turn of the century the Okanagan Valley especially appealed to British immigrants and others who came to farm or grow fruit. Agricultural settlement extended into the Boundary area near the American border, where mineral exploitation also occurred.

East and northeast of Okanagan-Boundary are the mountainous West and East Kootenay regions. Rugged chains running from north to south are intersected by major rivers widening into lakes. The West Kootenays, bounded by the Monashees on the west and the Purcells on the east, centre on Arrow and Kootenay lakes. The East Kootenay region, which abuts on neighbouring Alberta, centres on the Columbia River. The geography of the two regions has encouraged separation from the rest of the province: the language spoken by the Kootenay nation prior to contact with Europeans has no close relatives, arguing that its culture developed independently. It was the discovery of minerals that opened up the Kootenays to extensive non-native settlement. In the 1890s high-grade deposits of silver, copper, lead, and other metals were brought into production, and for a time the two regions contained almost one-fifth of the province's population.

The four remaining regions of British Columbia are each far more isolated from each other and from the province as a whole than are their southern counterparts. British Columbia's coast lying north of the lower mainland divides into two regions: the central coast and the northwest. Extensive European penetration of the central coast has been restricted to cannery and logging communities, long-time company towns such as Powell River and Ocean Falls, and a handful of idealistic enclaves in the wilderness. In the travel classic *The Curve of Time*, Muriel Blanchet recounted inter-war summers spent exploring coastal coves and inlets with her children in a small cedar boat named the *Caprice*. As Blanchet quickly became aware, in spite of its pockets of settlement, the coast was still largely unknown, and commercial maps and charts paled before the detailed descriptions of Captain George Vancouver in the late eighteenth century.[18]

The northwest region extends from the southern tip of the Queen Charlotte Islands to the province's northern boundary at 60°, excluding the long coastal strip of the Alaska Panhandle. Accepting a clerical job at Telegraph Creek, a Hudson's Bay post located in the very centre of the northwest, a young Englishman rhapsodized in 1923: 'This was the North, Robert Service's land of abysmal loneliness, vast and untamed and beautiful, stretching away into endless distances of mountain and valley, river and lake, with places of solitude where no human had walked ... This sprawling land was the country of dreams ... It was also the frontier, raw and harsh, seductive and brutal by turn ... It was on this northern frontier, this wilderness of miners and trappers, Indians and whites, brawling rivers and silent valleys ... that I hoped to escape the pressures of the so-called civilized world.'[19]

Apart from a handful of intrepid individuals, the northwest has had little non-native settlement, the region's climate and mountainous terrain, intersected by forested plateau, being too forbidding. Now and again Europeans passed through, as in the abortive Collins Overland Telegraph project of the mid 1860s and the Klondike gold rush of 1898. For the most part they did not linger in this overwhelming wilderness. Among the most persistent were Christian missionaries, going back to William Duncan's arrival at the old Hudson's Bay trading post of Fort Simpson in 1857. Permanent settlements are still restricted to native people, a handful of resource-based towns such as Terrace and Kitimat, and the coastal port of Prince Rupert.

Inland from the northwest region is the central interior, the geographical centre of the province, part of the vast interior plateau which extends into the adjacent southern interior and Okanagan-Boundary regions. The central interior also possesses mountainous terrain and some river valleys suitable for cultivation. The region was known to the early fur traders as New Caledonia, and many of the first Europeans to live year-around in British Columbia did so at the trading posts of Fort Fraser, Fort St James, and Fort George, founded at the beginning of the nineteenth century. A century later a rail link west from the prairies to the newly established port of Prince Rupert opened up the central interior to agriculture. The central interior's southern third contains such gold rush boom towns as Williams Lake, Quesnel, and Barkerville, and forms part of the Cariboo.

The last of the ten regions into which British Columbia divides, the northeast, is on the far side of the Rockies, which otherwise form the province's eastern boundary. To the extent that this range has become a psychological symbol of British Columbia's separation from the rest of Canada, the northeast is left an orphan; it is, to quote Hugh Brody, 'not even a name but a geographer's indefinite description.' Its three worlds – foothills, muskeg, and prairie – long remained beyond Europeans' grasp.[20]

The agricultural potential of the northeast's southern third, named for the Peace River flowing east into Alberta, began to be realized during the inter-war years once it became accessible by rail from the prairies. Extremely hot in summer and cold in winter, the Peace presented both an opportunity and a challenge. The area north of the Peace, too climatically harsh for farming, was extensively penetrated by Europeans only with the American construction of the Alaska Highway during the Second World War. The post-war oil and natural gas boom extended settlement.

The differing topography, geological formation, and human habitation of the ten regions comprising British Columbia point up the complexity of the larger whole. The regions' distinctive attributes begin to explain why impressions of British Columbia are so diverse and, just as important, why the province's development has differed from that of other parts of Canada. The land and water mass brought together as a Canadian province did so through historical coincidence rather than any carefully considered vision. Long after British Columbia entered Confederation, some observers considered that the province lacked viability. Writing in 1881, a British colonial official dismissed British Columbia as 'a barren, cold mountain country that is not worth keeping. It would never have been inhabited at all, unless by trappers of the Hudson's Bay Company, had the "gold fever" not taken a party of mining adventurers here, and ever since that fever died down the place has been going from bad to worse ... Fifty railroads would not galvanize it into prosperity.'[21] While British Columbia disproved its critics by surviving intact and reasonably well economically over the next century and more, it did not do so as a cohesive entity. The trend to equate the province with one or more of its ten regions – most often Vancouver Island or the lower mainland – has repeatedly led to misconceptions and misunderstandings.

Any historical interpretation of British Columbia must be firmly grounded in the province's geography. Men and women – be they first peoples or later arrivals, long-time residents or visitors, members of the dominant society or of an ethnic minority – have each constructed a particular vision of British Columbia out of distinctive social, geographic, economic, and political circumstances. It is only by retrieving, respecting, and building on these images as they emerged and were redefined through time that the past acquires meaning.

2

First Encounters
1741–1825

British Columbia – the very name resonates with the authority of
Britain and empire. Names can be deceiving. British Columbia was
once a British colony, but its history was not formed by Britain alone.
During the first century of contacts between indigenous peoples and
Europeans, Russia, Spain, England, and the young United States
were all interested in the area at one time or another. Yet no country,
not even Britain, cared enough to draw the distant land mass into its
imperial orbit through a firm, unequivocal assertion of sovereignty.

The first encounters between seagoing explorers and local peoples
occurred as recently as the eighteenth century. By then the Europeans, in blatant disregard for indigenous populations with distinct
cultures, claimed to have 'discovered' most of the world. Among
areas lying off established sea routes was the Pacific Northwest,
extending from southern California to Alaska.

The peoples of the Pacific Northwest had had many thousands of
years to develop their culture. It is thought that hunters in pursuit of
game first crossed the Bering Strait from Siberia over what was
then a land bridge at least twenty thousand years ago. By about
12,000 B.C., as the late ice age receded, the numbers coming to North
America by land and sea grew. The oldest known archaeological site
in British Columbia, in the Peace River area, is about 10,500 years old.[1]
As glaciers melted, so the province's land mass took its present form
and human beings were adapting to the natural world we know
today.

Indigenous peoples living in what is now British Columbia were among the world's most distinctive. They spoke several complex languages, they were economically self-sufficient, and they boasted of cultures that were in many ways more developed than those of any other part of the continent north of Mexico.[2] Estimates of numbers are tentative. The anthropologist Wilson Duff worked from the first Canadian censuses of the late nineteenth century. Taking into account what is known about the effect of disease, war, and other such occurrences, he concluded that eighty thousand or more Indians lived in British Columbia in the late eighteenth century.[3] It has been estimated that at the time of the first contacts with Europeans, nearly half the native people in Canada lived in British Columbia.

Several factors explain the large numbers. Across North America people tended to concentrate along coastlines and river valleys where the natural resources could be most easily exploited. British Columbia possesses ideal conditions. Among preferred locations were Vancouver Island, the lower mainland, central coast, Queen Charlotte Islands, and major river valleys. About two-thirds of British Columbia's first peoples lived along or near the coast.

Population distribution reflected not only environment but also linguistic and cultural divisions (see Map 2). Some thirty-four distinct languages were spoken. The principal cultural groupings derived out of these different languages and their dialects. The early explorer Simon Fraser used the term nation to distinguish peoples of different languages and manners, as do some Indian groups. What are called tribes and bands were, in general, the social divisions utilized by the native peoples themselves. Tribe often referred to peoples who assembled during some part of the year, whereas a band lived together all the time.

The nations on the coast, moving from south to north, comprised the Coast Salish, Nootka, Kwakiutl, Bella Coola, Tsimshian, and Haida. The interior was home to three nations: the Interior Salish, made up of the Okanagan, Lillooet, Thompson, and Shushwap peoples; the Athapaskan nation, which encompassed the Chilcotin, Carrier, Sekani, Tahltan, Kaska, Slave or Slavey, and Beaver peoples; and the Kootenay nation which stood on its own (see Map 2).

Complex trading relations often developed between the different tribes, leading to surprisingly varied local economies. Through interpreters and middle men, such items as mountain goat skins were exchanged for abalone shells, lichen dyes for dried seaweed. It has been estimated that over fifty kinds of trade goods and twenty separate trade routes were in use by 1750 by just the ten thousand Tsimshian people living near present-day Prince Rupert.[4] Rivalry over control of trade goods and routes sometimes erupted into conflict and open warfare.

While interior peoples were similar in many respects to natives across North America, the cultures of Indians living along the narrow strip of land west of the coastal mountain range were unique. Their economies were based on the two bountiful staples of salmon for food and cedar for virtually everything else from clothing to dugout canoes. Most lived year round in long shed-like structures housing upwards of thirty families, each with its own cooking hearth, work space, sleeping benches, and storage area. Summers were given over to fishing and food gathering; rainy winters were passed more comfortably indoors. The Tsimshian, for instance, spent late winter and spring along the lower Nass River trading and fishing for eulachons, much prized for their oil. In late spring they moved to coastal islands to fish, hunt sea mammals, and gather seaweed. Summer and fall were devoted to salmon fishing in the Skeena River, as well as to trading, hunting and gathering. In late fall the Tsimshian returned to their tribal winter villages for ceremonial activities and socializing.

All of the coastal peoples lived within sophisticated social organizations based on the concept of inherited rank and on intricate patterns of sanctioned and prohibited behaviour. Kin groups might have their own houses with the right to special ceremonies, sacred goods, and designs, which were sometimes expressed in carved ceremonial totem poles. Each kin group controlled particular economic resources, such as a fishing station, a berry patch, a hunting territory. While these groups were often autonomous, with their own chief and system of justice, in most areas a number of groups came together to form tribes.

Nowhere north of Mexico were distinctions between individuals of high and low status so sharply drawn as on the northwest coast. Hierarchy within the kin group and, more generally, within the tribe was determined by descent. Marriages were family arranged, their purposes far broader than the two individuals' satisfaction. According to a Kwakiutl, 'it was through marriage that people got the rights to masks and songs and dances in those early days ... People who were high married into a high family.'[5] Particularly on the north coast, sharp divisions separated nobles, commoners, and slaves, who were often individuals taken in battle. The elaborate ceremonial and religious life that characterized the winter season centred on the potlatch, a highly regulated celebration held to confirm or assert status or to commemorate important events in the life cycle. Food and such valuable items as blankets, canoes, and 'coppers,' shield-shaped plaques symbolizing wealth, were presented to guests invited to witness the festivities and so validate the claim. Excess goods were available for redistribution because of the congenial physical environments, which also made possible leisure time devoted to artistic expression. Symbolic representations adorned not only totem poles but many items of everyday life.

Relationships between the sexes were varied. Along the north coast descent tended to be matrilineal, traced through the female line, while in the south patrilineality was stressed. Yet, as with the Haida nation living on the Queen Charlotte Islands, property passed through the female line did not automatically translate into women's superior status or authority. Women were subservient to their husbands and sometimes began married life in their inlaws' home. On the other hand, a Haida wife's consent was apparently necessary for finalizing trade deals. Women participated in ceremonial activities, and a few became chiefs. Conversely, among the Coast Salish property tended to be held by men and passed through the male line. Married women, if separated from spouses, usually left children with their father. Governing councils appear to have rigidly excluded women. In sum, it appears that although women had some influence and authority in native society, real power was almost always wielded by men.[6]

The cultures of the interior tribes were simpler than those on the coast. A harsher environment meant that greater effort had to be devoted to the economics of survival. Hugh Brody has emphasized how peoples had to remain flexible, material possessions often being more of a hindrance than a help. 'The Sekani became expert at the use of mountain resources; the Beaver specialized in the foothills and adjacent forests; the Slavey remained on the muskeg and along the river valleys of the Mackenzie drainage, where they made particularly extensive use of moosehide boats in summer and snowshoes in winter.'[7] Fish formed a diet staple, usually supplemented by land animals and whatever else could be secured from an austere habitat.

Living arrangements tended to be pragmatic. Among Interior Salish underground earth-covered houses sheltered several families each winter; peoples to the north lived in dome-shaped lodges of poles and hides, which were easily transportable from place to place. Social organization focused on small, localized kin groups or bands, possibly no more than two or three families who, though nomadic, lived together throughout the year. Interior peoples were in general far more egalitarian than their coastal counterparts.

All North Pacific peoples shared a concept of their relationship to the natural environment and the land. The goal was to live in harmony with nature. Kinship bands or other groups possessed exclusive rights to natural resources or to particular geographical areas, and in that sense aboriginal peoples 'owned' the land. 'The patterns of ownership and utilization which they imposed upon the lands and waters were different from those recognized by our system of law, but were nonetheless clearly defined and mutually respected ... Except for barren and inaccessible areas, which are not utilized even today, every part of the Province was formerly within the owned and recognized territory of one or other of the Indian tribes.'[8]

Indigenous peoples across British Columbia gave precedence to the group over the individual, to an ethic of sharing, and to a set of spiritual values which did not distinguish between the sacred and the profane. Supernatural beings pervaded the natural environment, and both animate and inanimate beings possessed spirits, whose power could either confer blessings or bring disaster. All aspects of life, from rites of passage to everyday activity, encompassed an element of ritual and respect. The education of the young focused on learning by example and by precept, be it daily behaviour or respect for the environment.

The need for contact with the Europeans did not emanate from British Columbia's indigenous population, but came rather from the seemingly insatiable demands of the whites. Since the late fifteenth century the nations of Europe have been moving ever farther afield in search of lands to exploit economically. The Orient exercised special appeal. The wealth of goods available in Asia, particularly the silks, porcelain, teas, and spices of China, first became known through Mediterranean intermediaries using overland routes. As maritime technology improved, it became possible to cut out middle men by establishing direct contact with the Orient. Portugal and Spain were early leaders in the search for sea routes to Asia. The Portuguese reached India by the end of the fifteenth century. In 1513 Vasco Núñez de Balboa crossed the isthmus of Panama and claimed the Pacific Ocean for the Spanish crown, including any shores it might wash onto, shores which extended into present-day British Columbia. Defeating powerful native states, the Spanish soon established a vast empire in the Americas as far north as Mexico.

While Portugal and Spain were searching out southerly routes to Asia, England and France each determined to find a northern route – in effect, a Northwest Passage. In 1577 Francis Drake set off around the world. It is known that he sailed along the west coast of North America as far north as San Francisco Bay, and some would like to believe that he reached Vancouver Island. Over the next century and a half England settled the east coast of the future United States. England also acquired indirect control over a major part of India through the East India Company, a joint-stock company given a trading monopoly east of the Cape of Good Hope. A parallel company, the Hudson's Bay Company, was created in 1670 to exploit the fur-trading potential of the lands of North America draining into the immense inland sea known as Hudson Bay. During these same years France took control of the area of North America known as New France, to be lost to England in 1760.

A fifth monarchy was also active. In the fifteenth century Tsar Ivan III began a process of political consolidation around Moscow. Russian territorial expansion had reached the Pacific Ocean by the early seventeenth century. As elsewhere, merchants' interest in new trade goods coincided with royal priorities, particularly after Peter the Great came to power in 1682. He was eager to discover whether the territory over which he ruled was linked by land to North America. To mount an expedition was no easy matter. Before ships could be constructed at Russia's Pacific port of Okhotsk, materials and men had to be moved many thousands of miles overland from the capital at St Petersburg. A first expedition was undertaken in 1728–9 under Vitus Bering, a Danish sea captain in the Russian naval service. When it concluded that Asia and North America were separate continents, a second expedition was ordered, also under Bering, to explore colonization possibilities.

The second expedition's two ships sailed from Okhotsk in 1740 and from Petropavlovsk on the Kamchatka peninsula the next spring. They then lost contact. The first reconnoitred islands off the North

American coast before returning to Petropavlovsk (see Map 3). Bering's ship, the *St Peter*, reached an island backed by snow-covered peaks on the saint day of St Elias, after whom he named both island and mountains. Since the St Elias range extends some way south, it is possible that Bering and his crew were the first Europeans to set eyes on British Columbia. Bering also undertook scientific investigations, and established some contact with local natives. Running aground, the crew of the *St Peter* were forced to winter on one of the islands, where Bering died from scurvy and exposure. His ship made it back to Russia in the spring, in its cargo several hundred pelts of sea otters killed for food over the winter.

Bering's expeditions had two consequences: it was finally determined that America was a separate continent, and for the first time a group of European merchants became aware of the Pacific Northwest's economic potential. The key lay in the pelts. The sea otter, which feeds off ocean kelp beds extending from southern California to Alaska, possesses a silky coat soon prized, particularly by the large Manchu upper class of northern China, to trim garments. Once the value of the pelts became known, Russian traders began making their way to the Aleutian chain of islands extending southwest from present-day Alaska. There the indigenous population was encouraged, at times coerced, to provide pelts. The Russian government began to exploit the trade through agreements with private companies, which were guaranteed sole trading rights to particular areas. Such a mercantilist arrangement was not dissimilar to that enjoyed by the East India and Hudson's Bay companies. Political and economic priorities intertwined.

Russian initiatives in the Pacific Northwest were soon paralleled by those of Spain. In 1759 an energetic new monarch, Carlos III, came to the throne. Although Spain nominally claimed the entire Pacific coast based on Balboa's proclamation of the early sixteenth century, little had been done to assert sovereignty north of Mexico. Subsequent exploration had reached somewhere north of San Francisco before lapsing; the area seemed to have few economic possibilities compared to Mexico. Now the Spanish crown established a thriving shipbuilding industry at San Blas on Mexico's west coast as a base for sending expeditions north. By 1770 plans were under way to set up outposts at Monterey, San Diego, and San Francisco.

Despite Russian attempts to keep their North American activities secret, Spain soon discovered it was not alone in the Pacific

Northwest. Carlos ordered the viceroy, the head of the Mexican government, to initiate exploration farther north than San Francisco. The purpose was quietly and secretly to take possession and establish sovereignty by planting twelve-foot wooden crosses along the shoreline. Statements of possession were to be placed in sealed bottles at their foot 'so that in the days to come this document may better be preserved and may serve as an authentic testimony.'[9] Three expeditions were eventually launched from San Blas, each with a combination of purposes. Scholars and priests were aboard with instructions to inquire of all peoples encountered concerning their numbers, customs, and religion. Much of what is known about British Columbia's indigenous population at the time of contact with Europeans comes from their detailed observations.

Using Russian maps, the first Spanish expedition departed in January 1774 under Juan José Pérez Hernández in the *Santiago*. Its instructions were to go as far north as 60° – in effect, to British Columbia's inland northern boundary parallel to the St Elias Mountains. Sighting land at 52°, the captain decided to replenish his fresh water supplies at what were later named the Queen Charlotte Islands. Some Haida paddled their canoes out to the *Santiago*, exchanging intricately woven blankets and sea otter pelts for clothing, beads, and knives. Scurvy among the crew forced the expedition to turn back, and on the way home the *Santiago* dropped anchor near the excellent harbour of Nootka Sound, halfway up the west coast of Vancouver Island. Although winds were too heavy to put up the wooden cross to claim possession, some trade was conducted on board ship before heading south. The Nootka apparently came away with, among other items, some silver spoons.

The viceroy was displeased that Perez had not claimed any territory. A second expedition, this time led by Bruno de Hezeta, was launched the next spring, in 1775. Accompanying the *Santiago* was Juan Francisco de la Bodega y Quadra on the smaller *Sonora*. Stops were made in northern California and at the northwest tip of Washington State to erect crosses. Farther north the two vessels lost contact. Less adventurous, Hezeta soon decided to turn the *Santiago* homewards. On the way south he came upon but did not explore 'the mouth of some great river,' which would be named the Columbia on its discovery seventeen years later by the American maritime trader Robert Gray. The *Sonora* continued north as far as 57°, halfway up the Alaska Panhandle. There a cross was erected, which the Indians almost immediately moved nearer to their dwellings. Bodega y Quadra noted hopefully in his diary that 'they made us signs with their arms giving us to understand that they would keep it there.'[10] Then bad weather and scurvy forced the tiny vessel to turn homeward.

Two years later a third Spanish expedition was ordered north with instructions to reach 70°, about two-thirds the way up Alaska. By the time it set sail in 1779, the expedition had as a larger purpose the consolidation of Spanish claims in the face of British interest in the Pacific Northwest. The ranking officer at San Blas, Ignacio de Arteaga, had charge on the *Princesa*. Once again Bodega y Quadra was second-in-command, this time captaining the *Favorita*. Crosses were planted at about 55° on the southern Panhandle and at 60° in sight of the St Elias Mountains, about the point reached by Bering coming south in 1741. The priests on board used the opportunity to acquire five children from local natives in exchange for trade goods, a transaction justified by Bodega y Quadra 'both because they offered them voluntarily and because the object was to make Christians of them, and free them from the wretched conditions in which their unfortunate lot had placed them.'[11] No record exists whether these children ever returned home.

This third voyage of 1779 would be the last Spanish expedition for some time, subsequent efforts being limited to establishing religious missions along the California coast and a military presence at Spain's northernmost settlement of San Francisco. Attention also turned to war with Britain, declared in response to the appeal of its thirteen American colonies for assistance in gaining their independence. The need to protect Spanish possessions in the Caribbean and elsewhere took precedence. In theory the three expeditions added a far-flung territory to the Spanish empire; in reality interest in the area north of California remained marginal. No systematic documentation was undertaken, no interest was expressed to settle in what was clearly considered too cold a climate. Despite acquisition of some furs, there seemed to be no recognition of the Pacific Northwest's economic potential. On the other hand, Spain believed that, with Russian activity centred on the Aleutians, it had taken sufficient steps to ensure its sovereignty over the coast as far north as the St Elias Mountains.

Just as Russian and Spanish interest in the Pacific Northwest grew out of larger political and economic considerations, so too did British involvement. For more than two centuries British ships had searched for a Northwest Passage to the Orient. Existing routes remained inaccessible or unsatisfactory. The Dutch controlled the Cape of Good Hope around the southern tip of Africa and the Spanish dominated the Panama isthmus, while the route around Cape Horn was too long to be profitable. By the mid eighteenth century the search had become so desperate that Parliament voted a reward of £20,000 – an enormous sum in those days – for discovery of a passage between Hudson Bay and the Pacific Ocean.

Britain turned to a national hero, Captain James Cook, to locate a Northwest Passage. Cook had already been the first European to visit New Zealand, Australia, and the Sandwich Islands, later renamed Hawaii. The eminently sensible plan was that, since attempts to find a route by sailing westward had failed, Cook should sail eastward. He was instructed to reach the west coast of North America from the Pacific at about 45°, but not to explore the coast in any detail before 65°, the latitude at which it was considered a passage most probably lay. By so doing, Cook would also ensure that he did not intrude on Spain's Pacific empire.

This was the third maritime expedition led by Captain Cook and once again he was in charge of the *Resolution* and the *Discovery*. He set sail in 1776 and explored the south Pacific before reaching the northwest coast in March 1778 at about 44° (see Map 4). Cook's first anchorage was near Nootka, where he discovered that the local people were already familiar with iron and other European metals. Among items Cook acquired from the Nootka were sea otter pelts and two silver spoons. These he considered to be of Spanish manufacture. They had probably come from the *Santiago* four years previous. By the time Cook reached 70°, two-thirds the way up Alaska, he despaired of finding a Northwest Passage. He turned away from the coast to winter at the Sandwich Islands, where he met his death at the hands of natives in February 1779. The next summer the *Resolution* and *Discovery*, commanded by Charles Clarke, undertook a second, equally unsuccessful search to locate a Northwest Passage.

The two ships turned homeward with stops, first at Petropavlovsk where crew members learned about the Russian trade in furs, and then at Macao. There the skins acquired at Nootka were sold at such a high price that the crews wanted to return immediately for more furs. However, the *Resolution* and *Discovery* continued on to England, arriving in October 1780. Almost immediately, information on the Pacific Northwest's economic potential began to spread. Within a year unauthorized accounts of Cook's voyages were circulating in England and on the European continent. The systematic knowledge of the Pacific Northwest which appeared in print for the first time even included precise directions on getting to the area. Even though Russia and Spain possessed stronger claims to its northern and southern coasts respectively, the various accounts created the impression that the Nootka area and, more generally, the Pacific Northwest had been discovered by the British.

The Russian traders had been able to keep their activity relatively quiet, but Britain's discovery of the same trade good – the pelt of the sea otter – set off a rush for furs in which native people willingly participated by exchanging skins for European trade goods. Over 170 separate ships from several nations traded in the Pacific Northwest during the peak years of exploitation between 1785 and 1825.[12] More than half of them stayed for more than a single season, or returned for a second or even a third or fourth trip. Friendly relations were thus encouraged with the local inhabitants who might well be encountered again the next year or on the next voyage. As the sea otter neared extinction in one area, so ships moved to another bay or inlet, there to bargain for pelts accumulated since the last visit by Europeans.

Four principal nations competed for control of the maritime fur trade: Russia, the United States, France, and Britain. Some seventy Russian voyages had taken place since Bering's time, visiting more and more of the Aleutian islands as the otter disappeared from areas nearer to Russia itself. One of the most intrepid of the traders was Gregory Shelikov, who decided to overcome the vast distances by establishing a permanent settlement on Kodiak Island northeast of the Aleutians. This would provide a base for going farther along the American coast, even as far as California. Local chiefs were given copper tokens with the imperial arms as symbols of Russian sovereignty. Together with his wife Natalia, who accompanied him on all his voyages, Shelikov oversaw construction of the settlement, which had living quarters for over a hundred permanent residents and a school to teach the indigenous children Christianity. Additional settlements soon followed.

Merchants from the newly independent United States also began making their way to the Pacific Northwest. After the end of the Revolutionary War in 1783 the young country suffered considerable economic dislocation and depression. New England merchants had traditionally relied on a triangular trade with the West Indies and England to acquire much-desired luxury goods from Asia. While they could now trade directly with China, little interest existed there in the few products available from the United States. The Boston traders thereupon turned to advantage a large merchant fleet built up during the war. Soon after the results of Cook's voyage become known, three ships departed via Cape Horn for the Pacific Northwest, to arrive the next summer, in 1788. Another thirteen followed in the next half-dozen years.

French interest was mainly political. In direct response to Cook's expedition, the French government sent the Comte de la Pérouse in 1786 to search out any areas not yet claimed and so establish a foothold. After various stops along the northwest coast, a detailed report was sent back by another vessel, fortunately so since Pérouse's ship was wrecked in the South Pacific, all aboard being killed. French interest subsequently waned as the country became caught up in revolution. Over the next three decades just three French ships traded in the Pacific Northwest.

Compared with Russia, the United States, and France, Britain appeared at first to have the undisputed edge. Its mercantilist policies of granting a monopoly to companies capable of exploiting the trade under the umbrella of the state were already in place. The South Sea Company had exclusive rights to British trade in the Pacific off the shores of North and South America, while the East India Company controlled British trade east of the Cape of Good Hope, including China. In reality, only a minority of the thirty or so British ships that made the trip to the Pacific Northwest in the first decade of concerted trade, 1785–94, possessed official licences to trade, granted on the understanding that they also examine the area's potential for permanent trade depots, similar to those that the East India Company maintained along the coast of India.

Most British traders came illicitly, circumventing the rules in the name of profit. One of the favourite ruses was to acquire another national flag under which to sail. Among such individuals was young Charles Barkley, whose voyage to the Pacific Northwest in 1787 under the Austrian flag was notable for including his seventeen-year-old bride, Frances. Barkley family tradition recalls how, just as Indians allowed on board their ship anchored at Nootka Sound were becoming dangerously aggressive, Frances emerged from her cabin, her long red-gold hair blowing in the breeze. The Indians fell down before her, convinced she was supernatural.[13]

One of the individuals persevering the hardest in the shadows of legality was John Meares. After a first trip in 1786–7 which openly disregarded established trading practices, he went into 'partnership' with a Portuguese resident of Macao. This permitted him, so he reasoned, to sail under a Portuguese flag and thereby legally flout British authority. Meares decided, not unlike the Russians and the East India Company, that the best way to develop the fur trade was from a land base. So on his next voyage, in 1788, he acquired some land at Nootka from a local chief and built himself a house.

At this point Spain again turned its attention to the Pacific Northwest. Indifference to the economic potential of the area remained as strong as ever, possibly because of an abortive effort to persuade Indians in California to collect pelts on Spain's behalf. But the threat of permanent settlement by other nations in an area over which Spain claimed sovereignty was taken very seriously. A 1788 Spanish voyage of reconnaissance to Kodiak Island came away convinced that the Russians intended to occupy Nootka the next year in order to counteract British activity in the area. The Mexican viceroy decided to take immediate possession of Nootka for Spain. He based the Spanish claim to sovereignty, not only on previous expeditions up the coast, but on British instructions to Cook not to interfere with Spanish claims and on Cook's acquisition of the two silver spoons, indicating an earlier Spanish presence. The viceroy decided to construct a fort at Nootka Sound.

The consequence was an international political crisis over Nootka, perceived as the gateway to control of the Pacific Northwest. For a brief period Nootka seemed to hold the key to control of all western North America north of San Francisco Bay. The Spanish arrived at Nootka in May 1789 to begin fort construction. Among ships soon turning up was a British vessel bringing artisans from China to build Meares's trading post. By this time the head of the Spanish expedition was aware that the British, not the Russians, were the real competitors for possession of Nootka. Artisans, officers, and crew were all captured and dispatched to San Blas.

Then, for reasons which remain obscure, instructions arrived from Mexico to abandon the fort at the end of the season. The viceroy may have lost his nerve, fearing that the government in Spain would not sanction his hasty initiative. Possibly there were not enough supply ships to support the Nootka fort permanently in addition to those at Monterey and San Francisco. The mere action of construction might have been perceived a sufficient basis for asserting sovereignty without ongoing occupation. In any case, at the end of the summer the fort was dismantled and crosses planted in its stead, documents at their bases detailing Spanish activity.

News of events at Nootka soon reached the outside world, in part through letters of complaint by the imprisoned British officers but principally through Meares's activity. Never actually at Nootka in 1789, Meares nonetheless turned up in London with a memorial detailing and embellishing his side of the story. On its presentation to Parliament, members became so incensed that they voted £2 million to prepare for war with Spain over control of Nootka. While the British viewed Cook's expedition as providing the first documented European claim to the area, much of the war talk was prompted by the frustrations of international politics, in particular by events in revolutionary France which was Spain's ally.

In the end diplomacy won the day. Spanish ships returned in the summer of 1790 to rebuild the fort at Nootka, but Spain also released its British prisoners. On 28 October 1790 Spain and Britain signed the Nootka Convention, which gave both powers the right to trade in areas of the Pacific Northwest so far unoccupied. Nootka Sound was to remain open to all European nations and Meares to have his property restored. Neither side obtained sovereignty in the Pacific Northwest. Spain relinquished any claim to exclusive control over Nootka and thereby to the Pacific Northwest, an area which had not in any case yielded appreciable benefit. In exchange Britain agreed to specific measures seen as respecting Spanish possessions elsewhere in the New World.

It took five years for the Nootka Convention to be implemented, in the course of which much of the coast was explored and mapped. Spain and Britain were each concerned to support their positions by acquiring as much precise knowledge as possible concerning the Pacific Northwest. Spain also constructed a second base on the Strait of Juan de Fuca, seen as a viable alternative northern boundary to its empire. The two countries each named as envoys men already familiar with the area. The Spanish appointed Bodega y Quadra, now head of the San Blas naval department, the British George Vancouver, who had visited Nootka as a young midshipman serving under Cook. Vancouver arrived in the spring of 1792 with two ships, the *Discovery* and the *Chatham*. While instructed to implement the Nootka Convention, in part through receiving restitution of Meares's property, he was also ordered to survey the mainland coast from 30° to 60°, that is, north from Baja California. Mapping Burrard Inlet, Vancouver encountered two Spanish ships anchored at Spanish Banks and so learned that both nations were engaged in much the same enterprise. The four ships jointly explored as far north as the Queen Charlotte Islands. There Vancouver met a British trading vessel which passed on the news that Bodega y Quadra had arrived at Nootka.

Negotiations at Nootka soon bogged down. Not only had the Spanish fort become a settlement of some four dozen dwellings, but dispositions collected from local people asserted that, contrary to Meares's emotional account, he had never actually been sold any land. Vancouver replied that he had not come to argue but simply to take possession as ordered. Quadra agreed, but requested the new base at Juan de Fuca be considered Spain's northern boundary, to which Vancouver countered that its most northerly settlement at the time of the controversy had been San Francisco. Quadra, for his part, interpreted the convention as giving the British access only to Nootka itself. Relations were further strained by the arrival of third parties: over the summer of 1792 at least fifteen ships were trading along the northwest coast. The presence of half a dozen American vessels, whose captains and crews had no love for the British, may have led Quadra to believe that he had the psychological advantage.

Differences were referred back to home governments. Vancouver wintered the next two years in the Sandwich Islands, returning each summer to survey the Pacific coastline as he awaited instructions to return to Nootka. In October 1794 a disgruntled Vancouver left for home, his report giving particular attention to the growing number of traders, particularly Americans, who were in his view all too willing to trade arms and stir up local populations against each other. Actual settlement of the Nootka incident came the next March when in a brief ceremony at Nootka the land where Meares had built his house seven years before was returned to Britain. Spain, which had already abandoned its fort at Juan de Fuca as unnecessary, now also withdrew from Nootka. A revised convention signed in 1794 stated that neither country would maintain a permanent base at Nootka, although their ships could visit. Britain and Spain pledged to keep any third country from claiming Nootka Sound.

While the Nootka agreement did not determine sovereignty in the

Pacific Northwest, it effectively removed Spain from contention. Spain now turned its attention elsewhere. This apparent indifference was largely pragmatic, since the nations of Europe, including Russia, were almost constantly at war until 1815. The Pacific Northwest's significance paled by comparison. In 1819 Spain formally surrendered any surviving claims by ceding to the United States all 'rights, claims, and pretentions' north of 42°, California's northern border. In exchange the United States promised to respect Spanish possessions south of 42°.

Britain's presence in the Pacific Northwest also declined. Private individuals soon discovered that their country's monopolistic trading policy was too firmly in place to be repeatedly circumvented, and trading within its constraints was not profitable. Licences had to be obtained from the South Sea Company to hunt in its territory and from the East India Company to sell in its territory. Even then furs could not be traded directly for goods but only for specie to be deposited with the company. Moreover, the thirty or more British vessels that made the trip during the years 1785–94 flooded the Chinese market with pelts, bringing down prices. Even the monopoly companies lost interest in licensing further ventures, much less establishing permanent depots on the northwest coast. Only in 1834 would the East India Company's monopoly end. By then the maritime fur trade had exhausted itself.

In these circumstances, the principal contenders in the trade became Russia and America. By the end of the century over forty separate Russian enterprises had made more than a hundred voyages and founded ten separate settlements. The character of Russian activity altered in 1799 when the quasi-official Russian American Company acquired monopoly rights. Directed by the powerful Alexander Baranov and headquartered at New Archangel in the Alaska Panhandle, the company became the principal Russian economic force. The song composed for the dedication of New Archangel, later renamed Sitka, made clear that the Russians still harboured territorial ambitions:

> Buildings are raised on New World ground,
>   Now Russia rushes to Nootka Sound,
> The Peoples wild are Nature's child,
>   And friendly now to Russian rule.[14]

In reality further expansion was hindered by several factors. Chinese closure of the nearest port of Canton made the trade more expensive.

Any single settlement could exist only until the nearby otter population was exhausted. Supply lines became longer and longer. Although a fort was established north of San Francisco at Rossiya, (Fort Ross) in 1812, the Russian offensive had become over-extended.

From the beginning of the nineteenth century the United States dominated the Pacific Northwest trade, serving a well-established Boston–Pacific Northwest–Canton route. Up to 1800 thirty American ships had made the trip; during the first quarter of the new century over eighty additional vessels entered the trade, compared with just eight new British ships. But by 1825 the sea otter was in decline, and Americans were searching out other products to fill their holds. Whales were taken off the coast, sandalwood purchased in the Sandwich Islands, and contraband goods acquired in Spanish California and Mexico.

Early European penetration of the Pacific Northwest coast, extending from the mid eighteenth into the early nineteenth century, embodied a reciprocal relationship with local peoples. The maritime trade flourished only because both Europeans and Indians considered it beneficial to their interests.[15] Ships' crews did not locate or trap animals, nor could traders compel local populations to trade. Just as the first Haida encountered by the Spanish paddled out on their own volition, so later Indians voluntarily exchanged sea otter and other animal pelts for a variety of European goods. On the other hand, the historical record reveals that ships sometimes fired on villages and brutalized hostages in the hopes of making local peoples more amenable.

Contemporary accounts make clear that natives used the control they possessed over the trade to their advantage. As one of the journals from Cook's expeditions noted, they 'are very keen traders getting as much as they could for anything they had; always asking for more.' In the view of a Boston trader, 'the Indians are sufficiently cunning to derive all possible advantage from competition, and will go from one vessel to another, and back again, with assertions of offers made to them,' which has no foundation in truth. Native peoples across great distances soon became aware just where and when to expect trading vessels: the early overland explorer Alexander Mackenzie was informed by local Indians while still some three hundred kilometres inland in 1793 how 'in the bay which the sea forms at the mouth of it, a great wooden canoe, with white people, arrives about the time when leaves begin to grow.'[16]

Trading conformed to native needs as well as to European priorities. The material sophistication of coastal peoples meant that the trinkets acceptable in some parts of the world did not compare with what they already possessed. Items made of iron and copper, particularly if sharpened, were early preferred. Sea otter pelts had traditionally been used as clothing; as they were traded away in greater numbers, demand grew for European blankets and wearing apparel. Alcohol, tobacco, and weapons also entered the trade. Europeans wanted to hurry up the process of exchange and be away whereas local people had unlimited time at their disposal. A more leisurely process became the norm which meant that ships were forced to spend months and even a year or more on the coast in order to secure a full cargo of furs. The use of middle men, already present in trade between coastal and interior peoples, meant higher prices.

At the same time, contact brought fundamental changes to the Indians' lives. Greater prosperity and new iron tools may have, according to some anthropologists, stimulated material culture, particularly carving. Greater access existed to more powerful weapons and to alcohol, previously unknown. For the indigenous peoples, the maritime fur trade began a process of adaptation that would irrevocably transform their ways of life.

Overall, it is tempting to conclude that the maritime penetration by Europeans into the Pacific Northwest was of little significance to the subsequent history of the area. Despite the fortunes made in the trade and increased scientific knowledge of the coast and its peoples, the Pacific Northwest remained at the periphery of European and American interests. Even events at Nootka, as important as they appeared at the time, might easily have been otherwise resolved had Vancouver or Bodega y Quadra made slightly different moves.

No European power considered the Pacific Northwest sufficiently important to make the effort necessary to secure exclusive sovereignty. The more important goal was to ensure that no other nation did so. The Spanish claim never acquired an economic basis. Interest waxed and waned, but mostly waned. The British government played only a limited role in events; like the Spanish, it viewed the Pacific Northwest principally in terms of larger goals. Its merchants were constrained by a monopolistic trading system, with the monopolies themselves soon concluding that the coastal trade possessed limited utility. The Russians had a longer-term interest but never established themselves comfortably beyond present-day Alaska. American traders were aggressive, but their government did not link such activity with a possible assertion of sovereignty. A century of maritime exploitation, during which the sea otter was nearly exterminated, had little effect on the eventual determination of sovereignty over the territory that would become British Columbia.

3

The Trade in Furs
1789–1849

European expansion into the Pacific Northwest by sea was soon complemented by penetration by land. About the time that maritime interest peaked economically in the scramble for sea otter furs and politically in the Nootka controversy, overland exploration began. This second phase would eventually have far greater impact on the native peoples and on British Columbia's development, but at first was as inconsequential as the seaborne exploitation. The Pacific Northwest as such occasioned little interest; its exploration was incidental to the search for better routes to provision a fur trade centred elsewhere. Only gradually was the area recognized as a major source of furs in its own right.

The North West Company, fur traders operating out of Montreal, was the first to initiate and develop a land-based fur trade in the Pacific Northwest. The origins of the inland fur trade went back to the first Europeans' arrival within the confines of today's Canada. The early informal trade in beaver pelts became lucrative once European craftsmen discovered that barbs in the beaver's underfur matted together into high-quality felt perfect for making men's hats. As wide-brimmed felt hats became the rage in Europe, so competition for furs grew. The Hudson's Bay Company was chartered in 1670 precisely in order to exploit that trade.

The Hudson's Bay Company was managed from London and was ultimately responsible to a small group of British shareholders, who selected a governor to act on their behalf. Many of its backers were influential men closely linked to those in political power, but the company was not an agent of the crown. The goal was private profit, not the extension of British sovereignty. Although the Hudson's Bay Company claimed exclusive rights to trade over the entire Hudson Bay watershed, extending west to the Rocky Mountains, its posts were mainly on Hudson Bay and competitors found it expedient to act as if the company controlled only the bay itself. Individual traders, based in New France, steadily extended their activities westward as animal populations declined nearer to home. By the mid eighteenth century the furs of a variety of small animals were being collected as far west as Lake Manitoba and the Saskatchewan River.

The British takeover of New France in 1760 brought fundamental reorganization of its fur trade. The colony, now known as Quebec, was opened to the outside world. Among new arrivals in Quebec's commercial centre of Montreal were enterprising Scots and Americans intent on sharing in the profits to be had from the fur trade. To reduce competition and thereby prices paid to the Indians for pelts, they entered into agreements with each other not to trade in the same area. Agreements became longer term and more comprehensive, culminating in the emergence of the North West Company in the years 1776–80 as the major competitor of the HBC.

The North West Company was essentially a loose partnership of equals, many allied by blood or marriage, who shared in annual profits. The company received no special privileges from government but also stood outside of official control. The North Westers' trade strategy, like that of their predecessors operating out of New France, was based on going where the furs were. As distances grew, a two-stage process evolved. Wintering partners lived year-round at small trading posts where they secured furs from the local Indians; Montreal partners marketed the furs and purchased supplies. The two groups rendezvoused each summer at a post on the northwestern shore of Lake Superior to decide on company policy and exchange furs for supplies.

North West practice thus differed fundamentally both from the maritime trade and from Hudson's Bay policy in the immediacy and continuity of contact with the aboriginal population. Sustained ties replaced the fleeting contact between Europeans on ships and Indians ashore or between Hudson's Bay Company traders in long-established posts on Hudson Bay and visitors come to sell furs. The North Westers depended on local men and women not just to acquire furs but for their very survival. Links extended through the entire range of human relationships from economic transactions to sexual liaisons.

The North West Company's trading tactics soon forced the Hudson's Bay Company to reconsider its policy. The North Westers, by going to where the pelts originated and establishing sustained relationships with local people, were obtaining the best furs. By the mid 1770s the HBC was being forced to establish its own inland posts as far west as the Rockies. The consequence was ever greater competition between the two trading companies to cut costs and locate new sources of pelts. In this rivalry, the HBC possessed the great advantage of a cheaper means for the shipment of furs and supplies. Ships could sail from Europe directly into Hudson Bay, located in the very heart of North America, whereas the North West Company had to rely on overland canoe routes to and from Montreal. The more the North Westers expanded geographically the more its profits were eaten away by the high cost of land transport. The ideal solution clearly lay in locating better supply routes, preferably a water route, from the interior to the Pacific coast, whence furs could be moved more economically by sea.

It was the search for routes, as well as additional sources of furs, that initiated overland exploration of British Columbia by three North West partners: Alexander Mackenzie, Simon Fraser, and David Thompson. To these men the fur trade was all-important. Each had entered the trade in his mid-teens and worked his way up through individual effort and ability. All three men were already familiar with the Indian peoples. In their separate travels through British Columbia, they willingly entered into relationships of trust with local natives, without whose assistance they could not have travelled on foot and by canoe through unknown terrain, particularly as difficult as is that of British Columbia. Their accounts underline how genuinely decent were Indian men and women, not just once or one group, but again and again. Natives shared food and lodging as well as advice in circumstances where they might as easily have done the explorers physical harm, even to the extent of killing them to acquire their possessions. This kindness was all the more worthy considering that the individualistic spirit which motivated the Europeans was alien to Indian culture.

Geographical knowledge of the northwest was limited to the coast, based mainly on Cook's and subsequent sea voyages. The advice and expertise of Indian guides and of local men and women encountered along the way largely determined the direction the traders took. Often traditional trade routes were followed. A Carrier informed Mackenzie in 1793 that the Fraser River's 'course is very extensive, runs toward the mid-day sun; and that at its mouth, as they had been informed, white people were building houses,' an apparent reference to Spanish activity under way at Nootka Sound. The next day another 'depicted the lands of three other tribes, in succession, who spoke different languages.' The natives assured Mackenzie that 'the way is so often travelled by them that their path is visible throughout the whole journey,' and indeed, Mackenzie was able to follow well-marked Indian trails as he made his way to the coast. Fifteen years later Fraser would note in his journal, 'I have been for a long period among the Rocky Mountains, but have never seen anything equal to this country ... We had to pass where no human being should venture. Yet in those places there is a regular footpath impressed, or rather indented by frequent travelling upon the very rocks.'[1]

Each of the men quickly became aware of the vast distances that the interior Indians regularly travelled. The natives were familiar with the courses of all the major rivers by which they acquired European trade goods such as iron and brass. An old man recounted for Fraser how he 'had been at the sea; saw *great canoes* and white men,' whose chiefs 'were well dressed and very proud.' A Chilcotin revealed how as a boy he had been to the sea, 'where he had seen men like us, who lived in a wooden enclosure upon an island.'[2] Thompson's relationship with the Indians was the most intimate; his wife, who sometimes accompanied him on his journeys, was the daughter of a North West wintering partner and an Indian woman.

The earliest of the three explorers, Alexander Mackenzie, undertook two journeys to find a brigade route to the Pacific, both starting at Lake Athabaska in the extreme northeast corner of present-day Alberta. In 1789 Mackenzie followed principally what was to be named the Mackenzie River and, as a consequence, reached not the Pacific but the Arctic Ocean. So as not to fail again, Mackenzie determined to improve his scientific knowledge and spent a winter studying astronomy and navigation in England. In the fall of 1792, Mackenzie again started out from Lake Athabaska. Wintering on the Peace River, he set out next May with a fellow Scot, six *voyageurs*, and two Indian interpreters and guides (see Map 5). Two and a half months later they reached the Pacific Ocean at the mouth of the Bella Coola River, roughly equidistant between the Queen Charlottes and Vancouver Island. 'I now mixed up some vermilion in melted grease and inscribed, in large characters, on the South-East face of the rock on which we had slept last night, this brief memorial – "Alexander Mackenzie, from Canada, by land, the twenty-second of July, one thousand seven hundred and ninety-three." '[3]

Despite the accomplishment of being the first European to cross the North American continent north of Mexico, Mackenzie was conscious that his second voyage was also a failure. The difficulties were such that the route possessed little practical utility for the fur trade. A trading post was established on the Peace River, making it the first non-native settlement on the British Columbian mainland. In the account of his travels published in 1801, Mackenzie affirmed the importance of an inland water route which he considered might lie via the Columbia River whose mouth had been sighted by the Spanish in 1775 and then discovered by the American trader Robert Gray in 1792. Mackenzie considered the river to be not only of potential economic importance but of strategic significance, and he urged the British government to establish a permanent presence at its mouth.

The importance of a viable overland route was heightened by stiffening competition. As well as the Hudson's Bay threat, American interests were beginning to intrude on territory considered by many to be under British or possibly joint British-Spanish control. In 1803 the United States purchased French claims to Louisiana, a vast unknown land mass extending from the Mississippi River to the Rockies. About the same time, President Thomas Jefferson read Mackenzie's published account of his travels and became aware of the strategic and economic potential of the Pacific Northwest, which abutted geographically onto the Louisiana Purchase. Jefferson dispatched an American expedition across the continent to explore his new territory and to establish a military post, if only temporarily, on the mouth of the Columbia River. Arriving late in 1805, Meriwether Lewis and William Clark built a cluster of log cabins, hoisted an American flag, and then evacuated the post the next spring.

The same year, an expanded and dynamic North West Company put Simon Fraser in charge of operations west of the Rockies, with instructions to trace the Columbia to its mouth and at the same time establish inland fur-trading posts. In the area he named New

Caledonia or New Scotland (in effect, the central interior region of British Columbia) Fraser set up headquarters on Stuart Lake. This became Fort St James with Fort McLeod, Fort Fraser, and Fort George soon constructed nearby. About the same time the older Peace post was moved to the main trail and another post named Fort St John's was established nearby. Over time the various interior posts would be moved or closed in response to the exigencies of the trade (see Map 5).[4]

Fort George stood at the junction of the Nechako and Fraser rivers, and it was from there that Fraser led an expedition in 1808 down what he thought was the elusive Columbia. He reached the river's mouth only to discover 'the latitude is 49° nearly, while that of the entrance of the Columbia is 46°20'. This River, therefore, is not the Columbia.'[5] Moreover, the river's course was far too perilous to become a trade route. Fraser turned back, frustrated and disappointed.

While Fraser was journeying down the river that now bears his name, David Thompson was exploring the Rocky Mountains in the hope of finding the course of the Columbia, a task made doubly significant with the establishment of the new NWC posts to provision west of the Rockies. In 1807 he reached the Columbia and then Lake Windermere, where he constructed Kootenay House as a trading fort. Each year Thompson explored a little farther, taking time to establish additional posts. Then he learned, probably in the summer of 1810, of renewed American interest in the Pacific Northwest. The American fur trade magnate, John Jacob Astor, had joined with several former North West employees to organize a maritime expedition. Its purpose was to establish a trading post at the site claimed for the United States by Lewis and Clark in 1805. Astor's ship arrived at the mouth of the Columbia in early 1811 to begin work on what would be the first European settlement along the northwest coast between the Russian posts of Fort Ross and Sitka since Nootka's evacuation by the Spanish over a decade and a half earlier. Construction was well under way at Fort Astoria on the south side of the Columbia by the time Thompson appeared in mid July.

The issue of political control was to be resolved, at least for the time being, by the War of 1812. The United States and Britain, including its remaining colonial possessions in eastern North America, were pitted against each other as a side effect of the conflicts in Europe. Late in 1813 the first supply ship sent out by the North West Company to provision its New Caledonia posts via the Columbia

River arrived. Its instructions were to seize the American fort of Astoria for Britain. The acquisition was short-lived; the treaty ending hostilities committed each side to restore property taken during the war. This, of course, included Fort Astoria. By the terms of a convention signed in 1818 Britain and the United States 'agreed, that any country that may be claimed by either party on the northwest coast of America, westward of the Stony [i.e., Rocky] Mountains, shall ... be free and open.'[6] In other words, the territory surrounding Fort Astoria was to be jointly occupied.

Astor had in the meantime lost interest in his venture; so the North West Company remained in effective control of Astoria, now renamed Fort George. The arrival of annual supply ships at the mouth of the Columbia from 1813 onwards firmly established the company as a trading presence in the Pacific Northwest. From Fort George supplies went by foot and canoe to the heart of its operations in New Caledonia and a new trading post, Fort Kamloops, was established at the junction of the South Thompson and North Thompson rivers. While some furs were sent out from Fort George by ship to China, others went overland by brigade.

These early posts were fairly simple enterprises, intended to further the trade. As far as possible they were expected to be self-sufficient, with gardens and livestock. Differences existed between locations. Everyday existence at Fort St James, Fort Fraser, and the other interior posts was austere. Typical of the traders was Daniel Harmon, who spent the years from 1811 to 1819 as a wintering partner in charge of New Caledonia. Harmon's regular company at Fort St James was limited to his wife of mixed Indian and *voyageur* descent, a handful of *voyageurs*, and Indians of the Carrier tribe with whom he traded. As Harmon's journal reveals, he soon discovered that Company business occupied only a small part of his time, leaving the remainder for meditation, reading and 'teaching my little daughter Polly to read and spell words in the English language, in which she makes good progress.'[7] Such isolation, however, was certainly no worse than that of comparable settlements at Kodiak Island, New Archangel, and elsewhere in Russian Alaska. In contrast, life for the partners stationed at Fort George on the mouth of the Columbia became comfortable and, on occasion, even luxurious. Men who had spent years in remote posts found themselves with a ready source of supplies arrived by sea and made up for past hardships by self-indulgence. Fine dining with delicacies imported from Spanish California and little gifts of jewellery, perfume, and even silk stockings for native companions were possible from time to time. Be the lifestyle austere or gracious, the North West Company had established an ongoing European presence in the Pacific Northwest.

Yet the North West Company's advance across the Rocky Mountains only worsened its economic difficulties. Company organization remained loose while supply lines lengthened. Moreover, in the years after 1810 the long-standing competition between the Montreal-based traders and the Hudson's Bay Company intensified. The Hudson's Bay Company became increasingly aggressive and for the first time intruded into traditional North West territory, establishing a post in British Columbia in 1820. Located in the Peace near the North West enclaves, it was intended to be a springboard for expansion into New Caledonia. At the same time the prices offered for furs escalated so rapidly that both the companies appeared headed for bankruptcy. Cooler heads prevailed, and in 1821 the North West Company merged into the Hudson's Bay Company. Henceforth, a single monopoly controlled the fur trade across British North America.

The amalgamated company, which continued to be known as the Hudson's Bay Company, took on the personnel and resources of its competitor. Its geographical domain became enormous when the British government granted it 'the sole and exclusive privilege of trading with the Indians' over all of British North America 'not being part of any of our provinces.' The new monopoly thus extended west from Hudson Bay to the Pacific Ocean, even though Britain possessed little or no political sovereignty over much of this immense territory.

The Hudson's Bay Company retained its administrative structure. The headquarters stayed in London with North American affairs to be resolved annually at a council of chief officers. Its British tradition of strict hierarchy between officers and servants continued. Officers were by definition gentlemen with the requisite education and social status. Their typical career was to enter the company as an apprentice clerk at age sixteen, rise steadily to be appointed a chief trader in charge of a major post or fort and nearby outposts and then hope to be made a chief factor of a department containing a number of posts. Servants included craftsmen, labourers, interpreters, and other contract employees. At the time of the merger they totalled about fifteen hundred men. Servants had traditionally been Scottish Orkneymen in the HBC and French-speaking *voyageurs* in the NWC. Increasingly, indigenous Hawaiians, known as Kanakas, were hired as servants.

The new Hudson's Bay Company incorporated critical features of the old North West Company, in particular its far greater recognition of the contribution made by men in the field. Officers were considered partners rather than being merely paid employees. The twenty-five chief factors and twenty-eight chief traders of the merged company were allocated 40 per cent of annual profits, each of the latter receiving a double share. Profit-sharing continued for several years after retirement. Amounts could be considerable, rising to as much as £400 a year for a chief trader, in addition to board and room. This was a great incentive for each officer to work as hard as possible to increase profits.

The quarter-century after 1821 witnessed relative stability in the land-based Pacific Northwest fur trade, in large part as a result of the man the Hudson's Bay shareholders appointed governor in North America. George Simpson, nicknamed the 'Little Emperor,' was what would today be termed an efficiency expert. He was a self-made man who combined tremendous energy and self-confidence with considerable analytical powers. As early as 1826 he was being commended by Hudson's Bay headquarters in London for his 'distinct businesslike arrangement, and ... indefatigable zeal and perseverance in making yourself master of all the minute details, as well as of the general arrangement of the business.'[8]

Simpson's three visits to the Pacific Northwest – in 1824, 1828, and 1841 – demonstrate both his ability to oversee even the farthest reaches of his vast enterprise and the singularity with which profit was pursued by the Hudson's Bay Company. At the time of the merger, some question existed among its leadership as to whether the area west of the Rockies should be retained, given that 'hitherto the trade of the Columbia has not been profitable, and from all that we have learnt on the subject we are not sanguine in our expectations of being able to make it so in future.'[9] While closing down the Peace River posts and Fort George in New Caledonia following the killing of several traders by Indians in 1823, Simpson was determined to make the trade economically viable. A trusted chief factor, Dr John McLoughlin, was put in charge of the Columbia Department centred at Fort George on the Columbia River.

Even before Simpson's arrival in the Pacific Northwest in late 1824, he was convinced 'that mismanagement and extravagence has been the order of the day at Fort George [on the Columbia]. It is now, however, necessary that a radical change should take place and we have no time to lose in bringing it about.' Cutting the department's manpower in half, he ordered posts to become self-sufficient in foodstuffs, to eat more locally available salmon and potatoes, and to cut down on imported 'Eatables Drinkables and other *Domestic Comforts.*' Simpson was more impressed with what he learned concerning New Caledonia and came away convinced that, overall, 'the trade of this side the mountain if sufficiently extended and properly managed I make bold to say can not only be made to rival, but to yield double that profit that any other part of North America does for the Amount of Capital employed.'[10] Some thought had been given to linking the New Caledonia posts overland with older HBC posts on the other side of the Rockies, but Simpson opted for a brigade trail to the Pacific via the Okanagan Valley and Columbia River.

Strategic considerations also underlay the 1824 visit. Looking to the future, Britain considered that some future boundary settlement with the United States might well divide the Pacific Northwest along the Columbia River, based on American claims to the river's south bank rising out of the Lewis and Clark expedition, Astor's activity, and the War of 1812. Simpson carried instructions from the British foreign secretary to move Hudson's Bay operations to the north side of the Columbia. The site selected for a new fort was some 120 kilometres up river (see Map 6). Fort Vancouver was not, however, to be the major depot for the Columbia Department. Simpson believed strongly that, despite Simon Fraser's negative assessment, the Fraser was navigable. Locating the Hudson's Bay headquarters at or near the mouth of that more northerly river would make it easier to provision the profitable New Caledonia posts. The result was the construction of Fort Langley, named for a governor of the HBC, on the Fraser River.

Fort Langley never achieved its intended purpose. Returning in 1828, Simpson first visited the New Caledonia posts. Their importance was if anything greater than at the time of his earlier trip. In 1825 Britain and the United States had signed a convention recognizing Russia's sovereignty over its existing trading territory. Russia's southern limit for claims was set at 54°40', which meant that New Caledonia no longer had to fear possible Russian expansion southward. Russia's eastern boundary would now follow the summits of the coastal mountain range, bringing into being what has become known as the Alaska Panhandle. Simpson then set off down the Fraser River and learned the hard way that navigation really was impossible. 'Frazers River, can no longer be thought of as a practicable communication with the interior; it was never wholly passed by water before, and in all probability never will again ... I shall therefore no longer talk of it as a navigable stream.'[11] Fort Vancouver under McLoughlin was accordingly designated department headquarters.

During the same visit Simpson decided to take a share of the remaining maritime fur trade away from the Americans. Now that the threat of Russian expansion was removed, it made good economic sense to introduce coastal trading vessels and establish trading posts along the northern coast. The most strategically sited was Fort Simpson, constructed in 1831 at the mouth of the Nass River across from the northern tip of the Queen Charlotte Islands and just south of the Alaska Panhandle. Two years later Fort McLoughlin was established adjacent to the Queen Charlotte Islands' southern tip. Fort Langley continued to exist, but as just one of a growing number of coastal and interior HBC posts.

Simpson's third visit in 1841 confirmed the success of the policy of using vessels, in particular the *Beaver*, a paddlewheel, coal-burning steamer able to enter narrow waterways. Indeed, the *Beaver* was doing such a fine job acquiring furs that Simpson ordered most of the coastal posts closed. That decision was also undoubtedly motivated by the fact that the HBC two years earlier had outmanoeuvred American maritime traders. By securing an exclusive contract to provision Russian American Company posts, previously undertaken by American ships on their way to collect furs, the Hudson's Bay Company deprived them of part of their reason for coming to the Pacific Northwest in the first place. The demise of the sea otter completed the rout.

The HBC increasingly realized that the land along the Columbia River was ideally suited to agriculture. It now turned its attention to growing a variety of crops, hoping to export such items as wool, tallow, hides, tobacco, and grain. After the governors in London pointed out a possible conflict of interest with the company's fur-trading mandate, a separate company was set up whose shares were sold only to Hudson's Bay officers. The Puget's Sound Agricultural Company soon established farms on the southeastern edge of its namesake, from where it implemented the provisioning contract with the Russians.

In 1841 Simpson made a crucial change in the Pacific Northwest fur trade by ordering the Hudson's Bay Company's headquarters moved farther north. Simpson had never much favoured Fort Vancouver and still considered it of questionable economic use. The precise extent to which its finances had turned around is difficult to assess, the HBC itself asserting in 1838 that, whereas the Columbia Department 'afford employment to about 1000 men, occupying 21 permanent trading establishments,' Fort Vancouver realized no profits worth mentioning.[12] The fort was a long way from profitable New Caledonia. It was situated too far upriver to be easily defended, and a sandbar at the mouth of the Columbia limited access for trading vessels. Health was also a problem; during the early 1830s the local native population had been decimated by a mysterious epidemic, only later identified as a variety of malaria transmitted by a mosquito that, fortunately, did not thrive any farther north. The result was a shortage of labour to acquire pelts, which were in any case declining as the area became trapped out.

Simpson preferred Vancouver Island about 240 kilometres north and dispatched James Douglas, two years earlier named a chief factor, to search out a suitable location. Douglas opted for Camosun, later named Victoria. It was strategically situated on the island's southern tip 'about half a mile off the main strait of [Juan] De Fuca, in a snug sheltered cove from 5 to 10 fms deep, accessible at all seasons to vessels ... The place itself appears a perfect "Eden," in the midst of the dreary wilderness of the Northwest coast, and so different is its general aspect, from the wooded, rugged regions around, that one might be pardoned for supposing it had dropped from the clouds into its present position.'[13] Construction of Fort Victoria began in 1843, using Indian labour paid at the rate of one Hudson's Bay blanket for every forty cedar pickets cut. That autumn livestock were brought north, and the next spring the first crops planted.

The Pacific Northwest land-based fur trade, as initiated by the North West Company and rationalized under George Simpson and the Hudson's Bay Company, went beyond economic exchange between Europeans and native people. Both the NWC and the HBC cared only for profits, which demanded the largest possible number of furs at the most reasonable prices. Local people congregated around posts and vied with one another for the best trade advantages. Employment by the Europeans became so prevalent that the practice would continue at Victoria long after its function as a trading post disappeared.

The natives' role in the fur trade extended into personal relationships. Such Indian leaders as the Carrier chief Kwah, who lived between 1755 and 1840 near Fort St James, established close ties with the handful of Europeans stationed across New Caledonia. While camped at Stuart Lake, Simon Fraser received much needed foodstuffs from him – 'about a dozen Beaver and a few Rabids [*sic*].' Kwah reminded Harmon of his equality with Europeans. ' "Do not I manage my affairs as well, as you do yours? You keep your fort in order, and make your slaves," meaning my men, "obey you ... When did you ever hear that Quâs [Kwah] was in danger of starving? When it is the proper season to hunt the beaver, I kill them ... I know the season when fish spawn, and, then send my women, with the nets which they have made, to take them. I never want for anything, and my family is always well clothed." '[14]

Kwah's leadership was indispensable, particularly in securing the thirty to forty thousand salmon needed annually to feed the men stationed across New Caledonia. About one-third were trapped, split, and sun-dried under his direction. As one of the traders noted, Kwah 'is the only Indian who can and Will give fish, and on whom we Must depend in great Measure. It behooves us to endeavour to Keep friends with him.' Kwah was sometimes singled out for preferential treatment, being given goods on credit and receiving special gifts from Simpson on visiting New Caledonia.[15] Such consideration did not diminish Kwah's shrewdness, as evidenced by his returning two high-quality guns a day after receiving them on the grounds that sixty beaver skins was too high a price to pay in exchange.

It was Kwah who in 1828 supposedly saved the life of James Douglas, then a young trader. Five years earlier a local Carrier had killed two Hudson's Bay clerks on discovering that one of them was having sexual relations with a woman the Indian considered his property. The Indian hid in Kwah's vacant house, which as a chief's home was in Carrier tradition a sanctuary. Not knowing (or possibly not caring) about the tradition, Douglas in his capacity as chief trader at Fort St James entered the house and killed the man. Kwah on his return led a gathering of outraged Carrier to the HBC post. His nephew drew his sword and asked permission to kill Douglas, but Kwah made it clear that he only sought an explanation. At this point the women at the post, including Douglas's young mixed-blood wife, apparently began throwing gifts at the Indians in compensation. Kwah convinced his men that satisfaction had been obtained and they went quietly home. But understanding went only so far: the Hudson's Bay Company blamed Kwah as intermediary and for several months he was not allowed to return to the post.

Indian women also played an important role in the land-based trade. As many traders' journals attest, native women provided far more than passing sexual gratification to the Europeans. Women prepared food and clothing, taught traders the methods of survival in a sometimes harsh climate, provided a modicum of personal life particularly when children were born, and acted as links with local bands in the actual trading of furs. Most Indian women probably gained from the relationship, acquiring higher status in the eyes of their band and having a physically easier life.[16]

The duration of liaisons varied greatly, most probably ending when a trader went to another post. Some women decided to stay with their band rather than follow their mate into a strange land. Over time it became possible to establish relationships with the half-breed daughters of earlier alliances, and these in general lasted longer. Many of the officers and servants of Fort Vancouver and the other posts across the Pacific Northwest had formed such long-term liaisons which were often formalized through some kind of ceremony before fellow traders and the woman's family. The private lives of Daniel Harmon and James Douglas provide examples of the strength of such links.

Loneliness made Harmon take a mixed-blood girl to live with him, which he rationalized in his journal as being 'customary for all the Gentlemen who come in this Country to remain any length of time to have a *fair* Partner, with whom they can pass away their time at least more sociably if not more agreeable than to live a lonely, solitary life.' The day of his union with fourteen-year-old Lizzette, Harmon stated firmly that he intended only 'to keep her as long as I remain in this uncivilized part of the world, but when I return to my native land shall endeavour to place her into the hands of some good honest Man, with whom she can pass the remainder of her Days in this Country much more agreeably, than it would be possible for her to do, were she to be taken down into the civilized world.'[17] Fourteen years later, Harmon took his leave of fur-trade country. What about Lizzette and the children? As Harmon himself put it:

Having lived with this woman as my wife, though we were never formally contracted to each other, during life, and having children by her, I consider that I am under a moral obligation not to dissolve the connexion, if she is willing to continue it. The union which has been formed between us, in the providence of God, has not only been cemented by a long and mutual performance of kind offices, but, also, by a more sacred consideration ... How could I spend my days in the civilized world, and leave my beloved children in the wilderness? The thought has in it the bitterness of death. How could I tear them from a mother's love, and leave her to mourn over their absence, to the day of her death?[18]

Daniel, Lizzette, and young Polly and Sally Harmon left New Caledonia as a family.

The experience of James Douglas, who would spend virtually his entire adult life in the Pacific Northwest, is equally instructive. Born in British Guiana but educated in Scotland, Douglas was the son of a Scots merchant and a coloured woman. In 1828, shortly before the incident with Kwah, Douglas took as his wife sixteen-year-old Amelia Connolly, the daughter of his chief factor in New Caledonia and an Indian woman. Sometime later he defended his action. 'There is indeed no living with comfort in this country until a person has forgot the great world and has his tastes and character formed on the current standard of the stage ... To any other being less qualified the vapid monotony of an inland trading Post, would be perfectly insufferable, while habit makes it familiar to us, softened as it is by the many tender ties, which find a way to the heart.'[19]

Although Amelia remained his lifelong companion, Douglas realized that, outside the areas dominated by the fur trade, native ancestry was increasingly to be disparaged. At Fort Vancouver, where he was stationed from 1830 till his transfer to Fort Victoria as chief factor, Douglas had to bear the disdain of the likes of the HBC's Anglican clergyman and his wife just arrived from England. The Reverend Herbert Beaver made no secret of the fact that he considered Indian and mixed-blood wives to be purveyors of 'vice and immorality.'[20] Official descriptions, particularly those published after Douglas became governor of Vancouver Island in 1851, tended to obscure Amelia's origins. Douglas cautioned their daughter Martha, when at school in England, not to emphasize her ancestry. 'I have no objection to your telling the old stories about "Hyass" but pray do not tell the world that they are Mamma's.' During Douglas's long tenure in power, his wife kept 'very much (far too much) in the background,' only infrequently being persuaded to see visitors.[21]

The stability of native-European liaisons in the Pacific Northwest received a boost with the HBC's consolidation into present-day British Columbia, initiated by Simpson in 1841. The problem of fur-trade families on retirement home to Britain was long recognized. The Red River colony provided one location where traders could, through their numbers, find social acceptability for their mixed-blood families. The establishment of Fort Victoria would create another.

Yet even as the finishing touches were being applied to Fort Victoria, the course of the fur trade in the Pacific Northwest fundamentally altered. International politics again intruded. The issue centred on ownership of the huge area west of the Rocky Mountains over which the HBC possessed trading rights. To the east a boundary between Britain and the United States had been set as far back as 1818 at 49°. In the next decades a powerful new ideology swept the United States, arguing that God, or 'Destiny,' was on the young nation's side. It was 'manifest' that the United States was 'destined' to rule the continent from sea to sea. Events such as the Louisiana Purchase and the Lewis and Clark expedition all pointed in that direction. In the early 1830s groups promoting westward settlement had turned their attention to the Oregon Territory, as the area of the Pacific Northwest south of the Columbia River was becoming known in the United States. The first Americans to arrive mingled with retired Hudson's Bay servants living near Fort Vancouver and survived largely through goods supplied on credit by the HBC. As numbers grew, the new arrivals began to assert a separate identity under the leadership of strong-minded Methodist missionaries.

The United States became increasingly possessive over the Oregon Territory. In 1838 a bill was introduced in the Senate calling for military occupation of territory west of the Rockies north to the Russian boundary at 54°40'. Three years later an American naval expedition visited the Pacific Northwest, supposedly for the purposes of scientific exploration but in reality to gather intelligence. Its report gave a detailed description of Hudson's Bay posts, including their defences, and urged military action to secure the entire area between California and Alaska for the United States. One of the 150 arrivals the next year held a commission signed by the US secretary of war appointing him sub-agent of Indian affairs west of the Rockies;

on that basis he confidently assured his fellow settlers that the American government intended to put them under its protection.

Events gathered speed. An army survey was dispatched to locate the most accessible mountain pass across the Rockies into the Oregon Territory. In 1843 several hundred settlers travelled by wagon train over the new Oregon Trail. The same year the Senate declared the Oregon Territory to be American. Letters from Methodist missionaries described a visionary land flowing with milk and honey, and newspaper accounts accused the Hudson's Bay Company of encouraging local Indians to massacre Americans. Perhaps not unexpectedly, many of the fourteen hundred arrivals in 1844 and the three thousand the next year were even more determined than their predecessors to oust the HBC.

The accusations were particularly ironic given the ambivalent position of Fort Vancouver's chief factor. John McLoughlin has been accused retrospectively, perhaps with some justification, of favouring the American position.[22] McLoughlin's primary concern was to maintain peace and harmony, as demonstrated by his ready assistance to early arrivals. Anxious over the course of events, Simpson had after his 1841 visit persuaded some Red River families to move west. McLoughlin then encouraged these men and women to merge with the growing community of Americans rather than establish a separate settlement. While McLoughlin's defenders argue that his policy was intended to ensure American support for the continued presence of the Hudson's Bay Company, detractors point to his having retired to the United States and become an American citizen. American texts consider him the Father of Oregon.[23] In any case, by late 1843 even McLoughlin was forced to take action and he wrote to London requesting the dispatch of British ships to protect Hudson's Bay property.

By the time a Royal Navy ship arrived, larger political considerations were overtaking events on the ground. The United States was in the midst of a presidential election. The Democratic party under James Polk looked to Manifest Destiny for its inspiration. Campaigning on the slogan '54°40' or Fight!' – and thereby asserting a boundary for the western United States extending north to the Russian frontier – Polk was swept into office. Tensions between the United States and Britain escalated. By 1846 it began to look as if military hostilities might break out off the Oregon coast.

Then, as was repeatedly the case in British Columbia's history, compromise triumphed. On 15 June 1846 Britain and the United States signed the Treaty of Washington, by which neither country obtained all its territorial claims. The boundary between the two nations was placed at the forty-ninth parallel as far west as 'the middle of the channel which separates the continent from Vancouver's Island, then southerly through the middle of the said channel, and of [Juan de] Fuca's Straights to the Pacific Ocean.' This gave all of Vancouver Island to the British. Property south of the border, including Fort Vancouver and the Puget Sound farms, was to be respected until it could be sold at a fair price. Britons retained navigational rights along the Columbia River on the same terms as Americans. By the Treaty of Washington the United States acquired all of the territory lying south of the Columbia River, the existing Oregon Territory. It also obtained the area north of the river to the forty-ninth parallel – still home only to a handful of Americans together with Hudson's Bay men and native peoples – which in 1853 became the Washington Territory.

Whether or not the Treaty of Washington be viewed as equitable, it is clear that British priorities were not centred on the Pacific Northwest. Direct intervention was used only as necessary to protect its national interests without resorting to the ultimate step of a formal declaration of sovereignty. From the perspective of Britain's vast empire stretching across the world, the treaty of 1846 counted for little. At the far edge of the North American continent, the Pacific Northwest appeared to possess minimal economic or strategic significance. Growing free trade sentiment in Britain meant that colonies were no longer simply assumed to benefit the mother country in the vague name of imperialism but were judged on their profitability.

Britain's principal concern was to maintain American goodwill at a time when relations with its European neighbours were strained. In one sense, the British government did no more than reinforce Simpson's earlier decision to move the Columbia Department's headquarters north to Vancouver Island. Any argument that might have been advanced by Britain concerning the strategic or economic significance of the Columbia River was muted, possibly negated, by that action. The treaty only extended west to the ocean the international boundary already in place east of the Rockies.

Even as the physical entity that would become British Columbia was receiving official acknowledgment, the fur trade that spawned it was in retreat across the Pacific Northwest. Some trade in furs continued, but its role as the sole basis for European interest in British Columbia had passed. The land-based trade, initiated by the North West Company and consolidated under the Hudson's Bay Company, had held sway in the Pacific Northwest for half a century. With the assistance of Indian peoples, explorers and traders had slowly penetrated the interior of the Pacific Northwest. Indirectly, a British presence was established. Europeans, albeit in tiny numbers, now resided year around in the future province.

The role played by the fur trade in determining the long-term character of British Columbia is not easily assessed. The Hudson's Bay Company cannot be dismissed, as one popular historian has done, as 'a great parasite over the country, draining and corrupting the original life without bringing any fundamental change or any positive development.'[24] It was North West Company traders who first found routes through the interior and demonstrated the feasibility of permanent European settlement in difficult physical and climatic conditions. The traders' presence gave Indian peoples some breathing space before having to face mass European settlement.

The fur trade's role in determining British Columbia's boundaries was principally indirect. The North West Company and the Hudson's Bay Company had little interest in the Pacific Northwest's long-term political development, nor should they have had. The NWC was a private partnership. It might well have withdrawn from the Pacific Northwest of its own accord had not the merger with the HBC ensued. No right existed for it to claim territory on behalf of Britain; the best it could do was advocate such a course to the British government, as Mackenzie did in the published account of his voyages.

Although the Hudson's Bay Company differed from the North West Company in being a mercantilist, monopolistic creation, in practice it also served its own immediate economic purposes rather than those of the British crown. By the mid 1820s Spain and Russia had each lost interest in the Pacific Northwest. Simpson was concerned to protect the HBC from a possible American threat and not, it must be stressed, to use the HBC as a bulwark to counter that threat on behalf of Britain. The decisions to move the principal trading post north of the Columbia River and then to Vancouver Island represented economic responses to a changing political reality. Simpson's policy was essentially short term, intended to increase profits. Underlying his decisions lay the likelihood that the HBC might withdraw from part or all the Pacific Northwest should the area be incapable of making a profit.

Once compelled to act by the course of international events, Britain's position was undoubtedly influenced by the HBC's presence. Without it negotiations might never have ensued and none of the Pacific Northwest survived in British hands. American settlers would simply have moved farther and farther north to occupy territory whose international status was in any case unclear. At the negotiations, the existence of the HBC may well have encouraged Britain to hold out against the more extravagant American demands. In the view of the historian John S. Galbraith, 'British Columbia became British rather than American or Russian largely because of the work of a small number of fur traders and of the capitalists they represented.'[25] Without the trade in furs Canada might well have lacked a Pacific coastline and the province of British Columbia not existed.

4

Impetus to Settlement
1846–1858

Once the international boundary had been negotiated in 1846, Britain again disengaged from the Pacific Northwest. The territory that it retained was handed over to the Hudson's Bay Company. The HBC, now headquartered in Fort Victoria, oversaw not only the fur trade but also economic diversification and non-native settlement. Population grew slowly, and it required an extraordinary event – a gold rush – to bring large numbers of men and women to the Pacific Northwest. Britain was finally forced to assert direct control over a territory that had for two-thirds of a century been within its sphere of influence.

As a result of the 1846 boundary settlement the Hudson's Bay Company had to find another way to provision the interior posts. New Caledonia remained an important source of furs. The market for beaver had collapsed because of changing European fashions in preferring silk to felt hats, but the price for marten, which flourished in New Caledonia, was rising. Even before 1846, the HBC had dispatched one of its officers to look for a new route from the coast to the interior.

By the next summer other factors gave urgency to the search. Although Britain retained navigational rights on the Columbia River on the same basis as Americans, the Hudson's Bay Company discovered that it was subject to American import regulations. This meant that duties could be levied on supplies brought by sea to Fort Vancouver for shipment to New Caledonia via the Columbia and also, at least potentially, on furs brought down the old brigade route.

Even more significant was the effective closure of the Columbia basin after bitter Indian-European warfare broke out following the Whitman Massacre of 1847, in which fourteen members of a Methodist mission at an inland post were killed.

By 1850, a new route to New Caledonia via the Fraser and Thompson rivers was put into operation. At the point of transshipment from water to brigade pack train a new post optimistically named Fort Hope was built. Fort Langley regained some of its earlier importance as a source of supplies for the New Caledonia posts. On the whole, the new route did not do much to alter the daily life of the inland traders, which remained tedious and often brutish.

The Columbia Department's move to Fort Victoria made sense only if the Hudson's Bay Company possessed authority over Vancouver Island. The company already held the exclusive right to trade with the indigenous population on the mainland west of the Rocky Mountains to the year 1859; it now requested jurisdiction over Vancouver Island in exchange for promoting colonization. The proposal raised a storm in Britain, reflecting growing public opinion in favour of free trade as opposed to restrictive trading monopolies. The East India Company's privileges had already been curtailed, and critics now pointed to the HBC's record, arguing that even at the Red River settlement it had not encouraged colonization or any independent form of government. Why should it do so on Vancouver Island? Apart from its value as a source of furs, the area appeared useless. Free traders also argued that colonies must be able to pay for themselves, and this it seemed highly unlikely ever to do.

A compromise was reached in early 1849 which effectively relieved Britain of direct responsibility. Britain handed over proprietorial rights to Vancouver Island to the Hudson's Bay Company for the next decade, subject to several conditions. It retained civil authority in the person of a governor appointed by the Colonial Office. The Hudson's Bay Company agreed, 'within the term of five years from the date of these presents, [to] have established upon the said island a settlement of resident colonists, emigrants from the United Kingdom of Great Britain and Ireland, or from other Our dominions.'[1] Ninety per cent of the moneys realized from the sale of land to settlers at the agreed price of £1 an acre was to be spent on infrastructure: roads, churches, schools, and the like. The grant would be revoked in five years without compensation if no colony had been created. In any case, the HBC's proprietorial rights to Vancouver Island, as well as its exclusive trading rights with Indian peoples west of the Rockies, would terminate in May 1859. At that time the company would be reimbursed for its property and for all expenses related to colonization. The move to Fort Victoria was completed by the end of 1849 although Fort Vancouver continued in operation through the next decade.

The move to Fort Victoria did not much change the actual management of the fur trade. The two worlds of the Hudson's Bay Company remained intact. As at Fort Vancouver, officers under the leadership of Chief Factor James Douglas formed their own closed society, centred on such rituals as dining in the bachelors' hall complete with china, silver, and crystal. News of the discovery of gold in California in 1848 did for a time threaten the HBC's contract labour force of Orkneymen, Kanakas, and Canadians. To counter the 'visions of California floating in their minds,' some men were given a six-month leave of absence to visit the gold-fields. Others simply departed, to be replaced by Kanakas and local Indians.[2]

The HBC's character was changing nonetheless. The fur trade was in retreat. Animals were being trapped out, and the company was developing into a general resource company.[3] The California gold rush, which continued into the 1850s, encouraged diversification. So little European settlement existed along the Pacific coast that California miners in search of supplies eagerly purchased whatever the Hudson's Bay Company was willing to sell, including lumber. A water-powered sawmill began operations near Victoria late in 1848; within the year a second mill was at work. Shingles and salted salmon were dispatched to Hawaii. Royal Navy ships, which had become familiar with the Northwest coast during the Oregon crisis, began to stop in at the port of Esquimalt about five kilometres from Fort Victoria to pick up fir spars for masts and other supplies. Their requirements expanded after 1854, when Britain was at war with Russia in the Crimea. The two nations agreed that their respective territories in the Pacific Northwest would be considered neutral, but the base at Esquimalt was nevertheless seen as pivotal in countering a possible Russian-American alliance.

The most significant of the new resources to be exploited by the Hudson's Bay Company was coal. Although rumours of deposits on Vancouver Island had circulated for some time, it was demand that spurred activity. An American mail route using steamships had been established between Panama and the Oregon Territory following resolution of the boundary dispute. Coal was at first imported from Wales but, on hearing that Vancouver Island possessed deposits, the mail company approached the Hudson's Bay Company.

In 1849 Fort Rupert on the northwestern tip of Vancouver Island was founded as a base for working nearby coal deposits. While local Indians first viewed its establishment with trepidation, they were soon assisting in its construction and then collecting surface coal. By mid-year native men and women had traded 750 tons to the HBC at a rate of one Hudson's Bay blanket for every two tons. The HBC did not, however, consider them sufficiently skilled to employ on a permanent basis and so recruited miners from Scotland. The new arrivals soon found conditions not to their liking, their principal complaint being summed up as too much fish and too little porridge. In the spring of 1850 some of the miners deserted to California on ships arriving to pick up coal. Others went on strike for double pay and improved rations. Ironically, the Hudson's Bay Company was able to fulfil its contracts because about eight hundred Indians kept on mining, using axes, hammers, and crowbars to pry coal loose from surface seams.

The inferior quality of Fort Rupert coal soon became apparent; at the same time the HBC learned of other deposits farther south on the island. The inadvertent messenger was an Indian using coal in his blacksmith forge at Fort Victoria. Questioned, he replied there was plenty more where that came from and, to prove the point, returned with a canoeful. By the end of 1852 a new mining centre was established at Nanaimo north of Victoria. Operations were closed at Fort Rupert, the remaining miners were moved to Nanaimo, and some two dozen others and their families brought out from England. Through the 1850s Indian labour was also employed at Nanaimo to mine surface coal, with both men and women carrying coal in buckets on their backs to the harbour. A work-force of mostly native women then transported it by canoe to waiting ships. As early as 1853 two thousand tons were shipped to San Francisco. Nanaimo took on permanence: by 1855 it contained forty-two houses and a European population of 150.

Except at Nanaimo, the HBC's efforts at attracting colonists from Britain met with little success. Several factors contributed. The company's traditional character was incompatible with encouragement of extensive settlement. As Douglas early recognized, 'the interests of the Colony, and Fur Trade will never harmonize, the former can flourish, only, through the protection of equal laws, the influence of free trade, the accession of respectable inhabitants; in short, by establishing a new order to things, while the fur Trade must suffer by each innovation.'[4] Simpson observed cynically that, even if HBC's grant was revoked after five years for failure to colonize, the 1849 agreement was worth while. The fur trade would be five years nearer its natural extinction.

Another obstacle to settlement was the HBC's perception of suitable independent colonists. In its view, they should be individuals who could not make a good living in England but who could still afford passage, land purchase, and such additional costs as bringing out labourers to work their property. The company's views echoed those of the theorist of colonization, Edward Gibbon Wakefield, who saw colonies as providing cheap raw materials for Britain and, in the person of their settlers, a market for British products manufactured from these same raw materials. The London secretary of the Hudson's Bay Company, in his instructions to Douglas, emphasized that 'the object of every sound system of colonization should be, not to re-organize Society on a new basis ... but to transfer to the new country whatever is most valuable and most approved in the institutions of the old,' including 'the same Classes' performing 'the same relative duties.' Admitting all sorts of people was only to chance 'the worst evils that afflict the Colonies' – a possible reference to the rebellion of the Thirteen Colonies which culminated in the independence of the United States.[5]

Advertisements placed by the Hudson's Bay Company in English and Scottish newspapers met with little response, not surprising given that the unsurveyed land in a far-away corner of the British empire had to be purchased at a fairly high price sight unseen. In sharp contrast, just next door in the United States land could be occupied prior to its purchase at one quarter the price. Despite the HBC's optimistic prognosis, most individuals interested in emigrating did so out of economic necessity, not because they possessed surplus capital to invest in land.

The trip itself, if you sailed round Cape Horn, took about five months. You could cut that time in half by taking the riskier and more expensive alternative of crossing the Panama isthmus, but there you might catch the dreaded yellow fever while awaiting first the train for the six-hour trip across the isthmus, then a ship on the other side. Once arrived, so Douglas warned, 'the first settlers in this country will have many difficulties to contend with, first the scarcity and quality of food, the want of society, – exposure to the weather, – and, generally, the absence of every thing like comfort.'[6] In the event, only three independent purchasers of over a hundred acres actually settled on Vancouver Island under the Hudson's Bay Company, and none of them profited from their interest in land.

Most of the settlement that took place into the mid 1850s was through either the Puget's Sound Agricultural Company or the Hudson's Bay Company itself. The former moved its operations north, establishing four farms near Fort Victoria, the best known being Craigflower. Each was to be managed like an English country estate with a resident gentleman bailiff and labourers brought out on five-year contracts. But of the first seventy-four labourers that came out, only nine were married and brought their wives with them. This only confirmed the suspicions of critics in Britain that the HBC, even through its Puget's Sound subsidiary, did not consider long-term settlement a priority. The results were not satisfactory. Bailiffs were quite willing to adopt the leisurely lifestyle of a country gentleman, all expenses charged to the Puget's Sound Agricultural Company. The labourers, on the other hand, refused to accept their inferior roles, particularly when they could become independent farmers, tradesmen, or miners in the nearby United States or on Vancouver Island. Those who remained at work did so primarily for the free land promised them at the end of their contract.

Settlement by Hudson's Bay men was more successful; both officers and servants bought land around Fort Victoria for their retirement. James Douglas set the example in December 1849 by acquiring several hundred acres of land. While he originally applied 'more as a speculation, than with any serious intention of settling, yet there is no saying what in the chapter of accidents, may come to pass.' Less than a year later he was building his family a fine house on a ten-acre site near the fort in the hope that 'these improvements will induce other parties to embark capital in the same manner, and will tend greatly to the progress of the Colony and to the advantage of the Company.'[7] Douglas's initiative encouraged fellow HBC men to do the same. Additional town lots as well as some seventeen thousand rural acres were taken up, most of it by half a dozen officers. In addition, about twenty servants were given twenty acres each.

The property thus acquired by the Europeans was obtained legitimately through treaties with native people. Douglas early became aware that, as settlement grew, so would competition for land. On consulting HBC officials in London, he was advised that natives should be 'confirmed in the possession of their lands as long as they occupy and cultivate them themselves.'[8] Beyond that, matters were left to Douglas's discretion. Douglas made fourteen treaties between 1850 and 1854 with Indians living in areas where Europeans wanted to settle. Eleven were in the vicinity of Fort Victoria, one at Nanaimo, and two at Fort Rupert. A tribe agreed to surrender all land in a designated area 'entirely and for ever' in exchange for a small sum of money. The wording of each treaty was identical and fairly straightforward. 'The condition of or understanding of this sale is this, that our village sites and enclosed fields are to be kept for our own use, for the use of our children, and for those who may follow after us; and the land shall be properly surveyed hereafter. It is understood, however, that the land itself, with these small exceptions becomes the entire property of the white people for ever; it is also understood that we are at liberty to hunt over the unoccupied lands, and to carry on our fisheries as formerly.' Douglas later explained this wording; 'As the native Indian population of Vancouver [Island] had distinct ideas of property in land, and mutually recognize their several exclusive possessory rights in certain districts, they would not fail to regard the occupation of such portions of the Colony by White settlers, unless with the full consent of the proprietary tribes, as national wrongs; and the sense of injury might produce a feeling of irritation against the settlers.'[9] In other words, Indians possessed proprietary rights that should, in Douglas's view, be extinguished by treaty prior to settlement.

No longer was Fort Victoria just another trading post in the wilderness. Used by both coastal Indians and the Royal Navy as a supply base, it and nearby Esquimalt had become the centre for the HBC's Pacific trade, which now extended along the coast from Alaska to San Francisco and reached westward to Hawaii. Victoria was, in the view of one early resident, HBC physician John Sebastian Helmcken, 'as civilized as any respectable village in England.' Familiar plants and flowers were fast replacing indigenous varieties, daisies and red currants being brought from California, seeds and bulbs from Britain. The two most basic social amenities, churches and schools, existed. As early as 1847 the Catholic church named as Bishop of Vancouver Island Father Modeste Demers, who had been active in missionary work in the Pacific Northwest for almost a decade and was the first priest to have visited New Caledonia. Reverend Robert Staines, sent out by the HBC in London, provided a Church of England presence. Arriving in March 1849, Staines and his wife opened a boarding school for the children of Hudson's Bay officers. Two years later Douglas requested 'the establishment, of one or two elementary schools in the colony to give a proper, moral, and religious training to the children of Settlers.'[10]

The livelihoods of almost all the settlers depended either directly or indirectly on the Hudson's Bay Company or its satellite, the Puget's Sound Agricultural Company. Nearly half the two dozen independent entrepreneurs engaged in lumbering or trade had begun their careers in the HBC, and their clientele were largely company personnel. Indeed, without the HBC's presence, only a handful of retired traders with their mixed-blood families would have survived economically, much less psychologically. In Helmcken's view, few places 'have been so solitary – so free from intercourse.'[11]

Everyday life revolved around the officers of the Hudson's Bay Company. The presence of the Puget's Sound gentleman bailiffs only reinforced the social structure of the Old World. Intermarriage created additional linkages: in 1850 two of the most prominent Hudson's Bay officers at Fort Victoria, William Fraser Tolmie and Roderick Finlayson, married daughters of retired chief factor John Work and his mixed-blood wife; two years later the young Dr Helmcken married one of Douglas's daughters. The docking of a Royal Navy ship at Esquimalt provided the impetus for social activities. As one naval officer recollected, 'All of the half-dozen houses that made up the town were open to us. In fine weather, riding parties of the gentlemen and ladies of the place were formed, and we returned generally to a high tea or tea-dinner, at Mr. Douglas's or Mr. Work's, winding up the pleasant evening with dance and song.'[12]

The appearance of social exclusivity almost inevitably generated dissatisfaction among those not included in its numbers. Richard Blanshard, appointed first governor of Vancouver Island, provided a ready audience. From the moment of his arrival from London in March 1850, Blanshard came up against the closed world of the Hudson's Bay Company, headed by Douglas as chief factor. As Helmcken put it, 'the former had all the authority, but the latter held all the power!'[13] Rather than the land grant Blanshard had incorrectly assumed to be his reward for taking on the job without pay, the ambitious young lawyer found himself without even a roof over his head, much less an independent populace to govern. 'It was nothing more than a fur-trading post, or very little more.'[14] Nine months later a disillusioned and disgruntled Blanshard tendered his resignation. He carried back with him to England – and likely helped draft – the first of several petitions signed by the few island residents not directly dependent on the HBC deploring its monopoly over economic life.

Before departing the Pacific Northwest, Blanshard acted on entreaties by the few independent settlers that he establish a three-man advisory council. Such a move also responded to standing instructions from the Colonial Office. Douglas in his position as chief factor was named the new council's head. The Colonial Office also appointed Douglas to succeed Blanshard as governor, thus tacitly acknowledging the effective political authority wielded by the Hudson's Bay Company. Under Douglas, government of the colony was informal and even ad hoc. When required to appoint a court judge, Douglas looked no further than his recently arrived brother-in-law. Accused of favouritism, since the man possessed no legal training, Douglas retorted that neither did any other person on Vancouver Island, so why not him. Petitions opposing the HBC's monopoly and Douglas's authoritarianism continued to make their way to the Colonial Office. Particularly contentious was his decision to impose liquor licences as a means to raise revenue and introduce a measure of social control. In London the petitions attracted sufficient attention, if not to oust the HBC, at least to secure a measure of electoral representation in the pattern already in place in such settler colonies as the future Ontario.

In 1856 Governor Douglas was ordered to establish a representative legislative assembly, even though there were only forty-three people in the colony who owned the twenty acres necessary to exercise the franchise. The area settled by Europeans was divided into seven districts. Only the Victoria constituency had enough interested residents meeting candidacy requirements – ownership of three hundred acres or comparable immovable property – for there to be a contested election. The seven members of the new assembly consisted of Hudson's Bay officials, gentlemen bailiffs, and independent entrepreneurs. Overall, they reflected the company's outlook as much as had their appointed predecessors: five of the seven were or had been linked to the HBC. The legislative assembly, which first convened on 12 August 1856 in the HBC's bachelors' hall at Fort

Victoria, enacted little substantive legislation and was hardly any challenge to the HBC's hegemony. As long as the Colonial Office maintained its hands-off policy and the Hudson's Bay Company considered the fur trade and related economic activities sufficiently profitable to maintain its presence in the Pacific Northwest, dramatic change appeared unlikely.

Settlement remained sparse. At the time of the first census, taken in 1855, the fort and village at Victoria contained about two hundred non-native inhabitants, with seventy-nine residences and a dozen shops. Some 350 men, women, and children lived on nearby farms, 150 of them on the three Puget's Sound properties. As well as the 150 settlers in Nanaimo, handfuls were scattered from Fort Rupert in the north through New Caledonia, at interior posts such as Fort Langley, and on the HBC's large sheep farm just east of Victoria on San Juan Island.

Yet, just three years later, the status quo was irrevocably shattered. In the spring of 1858 this tiny, isolated oasis of Europeans was inundated, almost overnight it seemed, by would-be gold miners and entrepreneurs in search of sudden wealth. The explanation lay in the unique character of gold. It is in part physical appearance, in part scarcity, that has always equated gold with wealth and status. Since ancient times, gold was prized for ornamentation and as a trading commodity. In 1821 Britain adopted a gold standard as the basis for its currency, to be followed by most other countries. A boom psychology developed, fuelled by the ease with which single individuals could extract the metal. This was particularly the case with placer gold hidden in the sand and gravel of river bottoms and in the crevices of surface rocks. It was possible to go from rags to riches overnight: all that was necessary was somehow to get to the location, stake a claim, and scoop up the gold.

The lure of gold enticed innumerable individuals to spend years in its pursuit. As one veteran wrote his family from the Pacific Northwest in 1858, 'I have spent the best portion of my life in chasing after gold which has unfitted me for any other occupation, and to throw away the present chance appears to me like sacrificing all my past years of toil.'[15] A compatriot in British Columbia's far northwest two generations later was equally captivated: 'It must have some mystical quality apart from its worth. It kindles a fire in the blood of men who find it ... Holding those nuggets in my hand there beside my lonely fire, I yielded completely to gold fever ... On a nameless creek, in what seemed at that moment a place a million miles from civilization, the dream of every prospector had come true for me. I had found the eternal treasure.'[16] During the nineteenth century, gold rush followed gold rush: California in 1849, Australia in 1851, the Pacific Northwest in 1858, and then the Transvaal in 1886 and the Klondike in 1898.

Comparatively, the gold rush occurring in the Pacific Northwest proved to be fairly small. Whereas about thirty thousand men and women headed for the British Columbia mainland in 1858, three times that number had reached California in 1849, the first full year of its rush. The numbers coming to British Columbia never again approached 1858's heady total, whereas they grew in California to over one hundred thousand the second year and continued high. The value of gold extracted in British Columbia approached $700,000 in 1858 and averaged $3 million a year over the next decade; the mean in California was about $40 million a year. At the beginning of the British Columbia gold rush the population of the principal supply centre of Victoria was under three hundred, and although it reached perhaps six thousand at the height of the rush, it only retained at most three thousand over the long term. California's supply centre of San Francisco had a population of about eight hundred in 1848, which climbed to forty thousand within a decade.

But when gold was discovered in the Pacific Northwest no one could know its eventual extent. Gold-seekers compared it to the most recent discovery, in California, where the money to be made was phenomenal. Many predicted that the Pacific Northwest would outstrip California, since each succeeding new discovery had been found farther north and proved to be larger. Thus, it was argued, the largest finds of all must be yet farther north, in 'this new, and much richer, El Dorado.'[17]

The nature of gold made it at one and the same time attractive and disquietening to the Hudson's Bay Company. Given the decline of the fur trade, any new source of wealth, including gold, was welcome in order to provide profits for the London shareholders. The Indians also sought to exploit this valuable trading commodity. At the same time, because gold was so easy to extract, exclusive control over its exploitation was much harder to maintain than with coal or lumber. It was only necessary for rumours to get out to lure men to use every means – licit and illicit – to reach its supposed location.

Secrecy, therefore, was imperative, and this both the Hudson's

Bay Company and local Indians maintained surprisingly effectively for nearly a decade. In reality the 1858 rush represented not the initial discovery of gold but a loss of control. When news of the California gold rush arrived in the Pacific Northwest, the HBC had begun to look for gold within its own territory. Officials at Fort Simpson on the northern coast procured some gold dust to show to local Indians, inquiring whether they had ever found anything similar. By the summer of 1850 Governor Blanshard was reporting to authorities in England that he had seen 'a very rich speciman of gold ore, said to have been brought by the Indians of Queen Charlotte Islands,' then an unclaimed territory lying across the strait from Fort Simpson.[18]

The HBC's desire to combine exploitation with secrecy was both hindered and helped by local Haida. The Indians were equally determined to maintain control over this valuable trading commodity and so convinced Hudson's Bay men arrived from Fort Simpson that non-native mining was not in their best interest. They also dealt effectively with two boat loads of Americans enticed north by rumours circulating in the Oregon Territory. When one of the vessels was accidentally driven ashore, it was looted and its occupants held up to ransom for five blankets each. Several vessels from San Francisco were similarly luckless, with either HBC officials or Haida preventing access.

In the meantime, Douglas impressed upon the Colonial Office the benefits of an official policy of exclusion. As well as economic advantages, there were political considerations. If American adventurers actually found gold on the Charlottes, 'it is said to be their intention to colonize the island, and establish an independent government, until, by force or fraud, they became annexed to the United States.' Roused to the situation, in September 1852 the Colonial Office gave Douglas administrative authority over the Queen Charlotte Islands and charged him 'to take immediate steps for the protection of British interests' by requiring licences of all prospective miners.[19] While the lure of gold on the Charlottes soon diminished because of native opposition and difficulty of access, important precedents were established. The licensing mechanism put in place was based on British practice in Australia; it was made official policy that all minerals found within British territory were subject to government regulation.

Even as events were winding down along the coast, attention turned to the British Columbia mainland. Although nominally under

Hudson's Bay control through its trading monopoly, the vast territory remained largely unexplored and unknown. From 1852 rumours of gold finds began to filter into HBC posts; the official in charge of Fort Kamloops in the southern interior even requested iron spoons so that the Indians could more efficiently scoop up the ore. By 1856 Douglas was documenting specific discoveries. 'Gold was first found on Thompson's River by an Indian 1/4 of a mile below Nicomin ... The Indian was taking a drink out of the river. Having no vessel, he was quaffing from the stream when he perceived a shining pebble which he picked up and it proved to be gold. The whole tribe forthwith began to collect the glittering metal.'[20] Douglas provided shovels, picks, and pans to encourage their efforts.

For a time the natives, with Hudson's Bay support, retained control. Douglas wrote to the Colonial Office in July 1857 that the Thompson Indians 'have lately taken the high handed, though possibly not unwise course of expelling all parties of gold diggers composed chiefly of persons from the American territories.' Not only do they 'desire to monopolise the precious metal,' but they have 'a well-founded impression that the shoals of salmon which annually ascend those rivers and furnish the principal food of the inhabitants will be driven off and prevented from making their annual migration from the sea.' In December Douglas observed approvingly that the Thompson, 'having tasted the sweets of gold finding, are devoting much of their time and attention to the pursuit.' They were, however, so 'destitute of tools for moving earth and washing implements for separating the gold' that they had to 'pick it out with knives [or] use their fingers for that purpose.'[21]

By the end of 1857 Douglas realized it would be impossible to keep prospectors out much longer. The Thompson and Fraser rivers' 'reputed wealth ... is causing much excitement amongst the population of the United States territories of Washington and Oregon, and I have no doubt that a great number of people from these territories will be attracted thither in spring.'[22] On his own volition Douglas proclaimed the British crown's authority over mainland gold deposits. All prospective miners were required to obtain a licence at Victoria. A single miner was allowed to claim twelve square feet (about one square metre), the maximum size later modified with the provision that claims not worked would be forfeited.

Douglas's prophesy was borne out early in 1858. Rumours began to circulate in California, where large companies were buying up the best claims and bringing in expensive equipment unavailable to individual miners. Few workable streams remained unstaked. British Columbia promised a return to a halcyon past, and prospectors began arriving from near and far. By March, so a Washington Territory newspaper reported, 'nearly all the French and half-breeds on the [Vancouver] Island had either started for this new El Dorado or were proposing to start. Fort Langley is sure to be entirely deserted – the chief factor being gone to the diggings with provisions, merchandise, etc., leaving but one clerk and a few Kanakas in charge. The company's blacksmith at Victoria is employed day and night in manufacturing picks, shovels, etc., for the mines.' By April shipping in Puget Sound was paralysed as crews abandoned their vessels. A description from California was evocative. 'The roads from the mountains were lined with foot-passengers on their way to San Francisco. Stage coaches came rolling into Sacramento, groaning under their living cargo of sturdy miners. The worm-eaten wharves of San Francisco trembled almost daily under the tread of the vast multitudes.'[23]

Boat after boat headed north from San Francisco: three with 455 passengers in April, another three with 1,262 in May, twenty-one with 7,149 in June, followed by thirty-five vessels with 6,278 aboard in July and four with 254 in August, for an official total of 15,398. But these figures probably represent the legal limits rather than actual totals. The vessels were packed to overflowing when they reached Victoria, and more than twenty thousand disembarked.[24] Others came by land or sea from Oregon and Washington territories. The logical overland route, the HBC's brigade trail to New Caledonia, was blocked by wars raging south of the border between Indian tribes and the United States army. The governor of Washington Territory attempted to create an alternative American-based route by building a trail northeast from Whatcom, the future Bellingham (see Map 7). A mini-boom swept Whatcom until reports began to filter back that the trip took two months. In the meantime Governor Douglas, underlining Victoria's status as the sole legal port of entry for miners, issued a proclamation in early May which threatened to confiscate any goods not imported through Victoria.

The gold rush captured the popular imagination in British North America, the United States, and Britain itself. Correspondents for such publications as the *New York Times* and *Illustrated London News* painted a rosy picture. Especially important was the London *Times* correspondent Donald Fraser, who hurried north from San Francisco and penned over two dozen dramatic dispatches describing the gold rush even as it was unfolding.

Overall perhaps thirty thousand men and women passed through British Columbia in 1858. One of the participants asserted, possibly accurately, that 'never perhaps was there so large an immigration in so short a time into so small a place. Unlike California, where the distance from the Eastern States and Europe precluded the possibility of an immediate rush, the proximity of Victoria to San Francisco, on the contrary, afforded every facility, and converted the whole matter into a fifteen dollar trip.'[25]

Victoria was transformed. A tent town rose overnight. Although coming from California, most of the gold seekers had originally made their way to that rush from elsewhere in the world. British subjects suddenly found themselves jostling native-born Americans, blacks, Chinese, Germans, Italians, Jews, and Spaniards on the streets of Victoria. Experienced entrepreneurs brought with them from San Francisco the stores of goods they knew would be needed by miners. The first large merchant house to compete with the Hudson's Bay Company was started by two American blacks, Peter Lester and Mifflin Gibbs. Within six weeks over two hundred buildings went up, most of them retail or wholesale establishments. Their sign-boards underlined the diversity of men and women making their way north: Ghiradelli, Antonovich and Co. (merchants), Hass and Rosenfield (wholesale clothiers), Ehrenbacher and Oppenheimer (auctioneers), Liciero and Stahle (barbers), Madam Pettibeau (private school).

Once a miner had gathered his supplies and obtained the necessary licence, his sole interest was to make it across Georgia Strait to the gold-fields. A contemporary wrote of 'parties of sober old miners, clad in blue or red shirts, with their "pants" tucked into knee boots, their belts showing the usual jack-knife and revolver, their heads crowned with wide felt hats, and their backs laden with small well put-up packs, consisting of a pair of blankets, enclosing a spare shirt and pair of socks.' Another described her fellow passengers, chiefly miners, on the Hudson's Bay steamer crossing the strait. 'Most of them had their pack of baggage, consisting of a roll of blankets to the cord of which was slung a frying pan, kettle & oilcan ... Every man had his revolver & many a large knife also, hanging from a leather belt. I should say that this mining costume in "highest style" consists of a red shirt (flannel), blue trousers, boots to the knee and a broad brimmed felt hat, black, grey, or brown, with beard & mustache ad libitum.'[26] While a lucky few secured passage on the steamer, others bought dugout canoes from local Indians or even constructed rafts. Later the crossing could be made more safely, if at sometimes exhorbitant fares, as enterprising Americans brought boats north to profit from the new bonanza.

Given these conditions, it is not surprising that many did not survive the passage, much less make their way successfully through the unmarked terrain of dense forest, rugged mountains, and treacherous bodies of water. 'We soon found ourselves in the quandry of not knowing where to go; one advised one thing, one another, and a third another, all equally certain to be "a dead thing," until we were fairly puzzled.' Another prospector mused concerning the Fraser River leading from Georgia Strait to the gold-fields: 'Will the number ever be known of those who met death in that dangerous river or on its inhospitable shores?'[27]

By June 1858 serious digging had begun on the Fraser River about five kilometres below Fort Hope. The focus was on the sand bars, some up to half a kilometre long, which tended to occur at river bends where erosion had washed gold out of ore-bearing rocks. Most of it existed in the form of fine dust or minute particles, although reports circulated of nuggets up to half an ounce (about fifteen grams) in weight being found. Gold lay anywhere from a few centimetres to almost a metre below the surface and extended through part or the entire length of a bar. Many experienced miners brought with them the picks and pans needed to separate placer gold from the sand and gravel. Others preferred to extract the metal with a rocker cradle or sluice box, readily constructed from wood at hand. A blanket spread with mercury was laid on the bottom of the cradle. One man shovelled in sand, gravel, and water while his partner rocked the device up and down to amalgamate the gold with the quicksilver while dislodging the excess sand and gravel. Whichever method was used, each day the average miner found about three or four ounces (about one hundred grams) of gold, at a value of some $50 to $65.

As the search for gold moved up the Fraser, so makeshift communities sprang up around existing HBC posts or at new sites: Fort Langley, Fort Hope, Yale, Boston Bar, Lytton (see Map 7). Everything had to be brought in by pack animals, and prices escalated with distance. A bag of flour worth $16 in Whatcom sold for $25 at

Fort Langley, $36 at Fort Hope, and $100 at the farthest gold diggings. While it cost just over $20 to dispatch a ton of freight from London to Victoria, the charge from Victoria to the farthest reach of the gold fields surpassed $200 by 1859.

The recollection of an 1858 Yale resident suggests that there were many temptations that worked to part the miner from any new-found wealth. 'A city of tents and shacks, stores, barrooms and gambling houses. The one street crowded from morning till night with a surging mass of jostling humanity of all sorts and conditions. Miners, prospectors, traders, gamblers and painted ladies mingled in the throng.' Donald Fraser of the *Times* 'found the place ... so filthy and unsavoury – so exactly like its inhabitants, in short, that we could not pitch our tents in or near it; so we shot across the river, shook the dust of this modern Sodom from off our feet, and camped.'[28]

The sudden influx of humanity disrupted life, for both the indigenous population and the Hudson's Bay Company. Having lost control over a valuable economic resource, Indians were not above scaring off or robbing miners. On the other hand, as Douglas thankfully reported, native people recognized the limits of their power, and a number accepted employment backpacking in supplies, especially over difficult stretches of the Fraser Canyon. Continued control was equally impossible for the Hudson's Bay Company. All that Douglas could do through his dual mandate as chief factor and governor was to effect a holding action. The presence of a Royal Navy ship at the mouth of the Fraser helped to enforce the crown's authority over the gold-fields, as did regulations that mining licences had to be carried on the person and produced on demand.

As the number of failed and disgruntled miners grew over the summer, Douglas determined to use their labour to construct a metre-wide mule trail across the land portages of the Harrison-Lillooet route, the principal road to the upper gold-fields. Five hundred men signed up for the work, in exchange for food and equipment. While the quality of the construction was slipshod, a Victoria newspaper lauded the project on its completion. 'Good boats are running on all the lakes, while farms have been taken up in many favourable locations, and numerous houses of public entertainment are open all along its line.'[29]

Douglas also had townsites laid out at Fort Hope and Fort Yale. While many of the miners returned south to the United States, some three to five thousand spent the winter of 1858–9 on the mainland, mostly between Fort Langley and Fort Yale. Their numbers were descried by a contemporary as comprising 'ENGLISHMEN (staunch Royalists) *Americans* (Republicans), Frenchmen, very numerous, Germans in abundance, Italians, several Hungarians, Poles, Danes, Swedes, Spaniards, Mexicans, & *Chinese*.' Others opted for the amenities of Victoria. One miner wrote his family, 'I have spent my time agreeably in this City having a Church to go to and some society makes it feel more like home.'[30]

By mid 1858 the British government finally realized that it must take direct responsibility for the situation on the mainland. The probable alternative was clear: the gold miners would provide a useful precedent for the United States to annex remaining British territory west of the Rocky Mountains. Since the Oregon Territory's official creation in 1848, Americans had begun to move north of the Columbia. Soon some of its several thousand residents petitioned to have a new territory of Columbia separated off from the Oregon Territory. Washington Territory, so named to avoid confusion with the District of Columbia, was established north of the river in 1853. Its first governor pursued an aggressive settlement policy. Military forts were established at strategic points, and Indians unwilling to surrender their land were brutally suppressed.

Many of the miners identified with the American presence. In the summer of 1858 they began passing resolutions: one from near Fort Yale helped persuade Douglas to increase the allowable size of claims. Miners' declarations could as easily be used by the United States as the pretext to assert sovereignty. The United States even rushed in a special commissioner to the gold diggings to protect its citizens from supposed harsh treatment by the Hudson's Bay Company. His report to the Congress declared it only a matter of time before both Vancouver Island and the mainland came under American control. Indeed, he considered the eventual outcome so certain that no special effort need be made in that direction, unless of course the government wanted to use evidence of Hudson's Bay harassment as a pretext for intervention.

The British government acted. While the HBC's grant over Vancouver Island had another year to run, its authority on the mainland was limited to the fur trade. In July 1858 a bill was introduced into the House of Commons to create a mainland colony of New Caledonia, comprising that part of the HBC's fur trade monopoly lying west of the Rocky Mountains. The name New Caledonia had to be abandoned when it was learned that the name had already been given to some French islands in the Pacific. The second choice of Columbia, honouring the Hudson's Bay department of the same name, could be confused with a region of South America. In the event Queen Victoria made the decision by tacking 'British' on to Columbia.

Royal assent for the new colony of British Columbia came on 2 August 1858. Douglas was named governor, with the provision that he avoid a possible conflict of interest by resigning from the Hudson's Bay Company. On 19 November 1858 a new government was installed at the provisional capital at Fort Langley. The weather ensured that the event was distinctly British Columbian. 'Yesterday, the birthday of British Columbia, was ushered in by a steady rain, which continued perseveringly throughout the whole day, and in a great measure marred the solemnity of the proclamation of the Colony.'[31] English civil and criminal law was extended to the mainland. When the HBC's lease to Vancouver Island expired, on 30 May 1859, Britain would take direct responsibility there, completing its assertion of sovereignty in the Pacific Northwest.

These decisions were not unanimously applauded in Britain. While the colonial secretary committed Britain to underwriting the military protection of the new mainland colony, he was adamant that British Columbia should otherwise pay its own way. 'Her Majesty's Government expect that British Columbia shall be self-supporting ... Any expenditure which the British Treasury shall have incurred on this account will have to be reimbursed by the Colony as soon as its circumstances permit.'[32] Critics wondered whether such a remote area would ever produce sufficient revenue to pay its bills, much less attract a substantial population. In reality it was only the threat of a take-over by the United States that finally forced Britain into declaring sovereignty over the Pacific Northwest.

The proclamations were accompanied by practical initiatives. Key officials for the two colonies were dispatched from Britain; responding to Douglas's concern over the lack of organized force to control the thousands of miners, the British government sent out a contingent of Royal Engineers. As well as keeping order and providing military protection, they were to be 'pioneers in the work of civilization, in opening up the resources of the country, by the construction of roads and bridges, in laying the foundations of a future city, or seaport, and in carrying out the numerous engineering works which in the early stages of colonization are so essential to the progress and welfare of the community.' On the Engineers' departure five years later, the colonial secretary summed up their contribution as 'to found a second England on the shores of the Pacific.' One of the Engineers' first actions was to choose a site for the new mainland capital on the first high ground reached up the Fraser River. 'It is the right place in all respects. Commercially for the good of the whole community politically for imperial interests & militarily for the protection of & to hold the country against our neighbours at some future day.'[33] Named New Westminster after its English counterpart, the capital was soon under construction. Once again Fort Langley was eclipsed.

If relatively small on a world scale, the gold rush of 1858 played a formative role in the development of British Columbia. For a decade a settlement had revolved around the Hudson's Bay Company, with the economy still centred in the fur trade. While the Hudson's Bay Company had diversified, none of its other activities were sufficiently remunerative to ensure its continued presence should the trade in furs drastically decline.

The events of 1858 changed all that. The non-native population increased greatly, and with the establishment of an independent government, the power of the HBC was eclipsed. Yet had the company not been in place, both as a fur-trading enterprise and as a nucleus of settlement, the outcome of the gold rush might have been very different. The transfer of authority from the Hudson's Bay Company ended a distinct phase in British Columbia's history. The British government had finally been compelled, by events not of its own making, to assume direct responsibility for a territory around which it had dallied, so to speak, for two-thirds of a century.

5

Distant Oversight
1858–1871

By the end of 1858 Britain had assumed effective control over the entirety of the Pacific Northwest where it held sovereignty. When the Hudson's Bay Company's lease to Vancouver Island expired a few months later, on 30 May 1859, the British government took over direct responsibility there. James Douglas became governor of both colonies. But Britain took few initiatives beyond immediate necessity. Douglas exercised almost total authority. By the time of his retirement in 1864, the gold rush had peaked and the long-term status of the colonies was put in doubt. The two colonies' union in 1866 as the single colony of British Columbia was an economy measure. Soon British indifference combined with economic recession to transform colonial into provincial status. In 1871 British Columbia entered the Canadian confederation.

The gold rush continued into the 1860s. As some miners departed, others took their place. Many came from farther away, and the diggings pushed increasingly inland. By 1859 the search was moving up the Fraser River to Lytton and the junction with the Thompson. The next year attention turned to the Cariboo, whence came reports of flakes and even nuggets as opposed to the gold dust common along the Fraser. Speculation mounted. '$400 Per Day to the Hand!' the *British Colonist* boasted in September 1860. Donald Fraser reported to the *Times* a year later. 'I have not written much on the subject of British Columbia of late because the accounts which reached us throughout the summer and autumn were of so glowing a character and gave so superlative a description of the wealth of the upper gold country as appeared fabulous.'[1]

The Cariboo rush of the early 1860s did offer great prospects but not in the same fashion as the Fraser River. While some nuggets were just waiting for the taking, much of the gold lay beneath the surface, making it necessary to sink shafts upwards of eighty metres to reach bedrock. A visitor summed up the situation: 'No surface gold in Cariboo; deep workings requiring capital; plenty of gold; therefore so many disappointed.' Technical expertise, managerial skills, and money became the keys to success. Some miners ended up as wage labourers or in other occupations, others simply despaired. 'Number of men on foot passed during afternoon, blanket on back, seeming halting & footsore, unsuccessful miners on way back I presume.' The wealth acquired by the lucky few disoriented many men, who, as Fraser related, 'wandered about the pathless wilderness "prospecting" for rich and yet richer "claims" which would contain the philosopher's stone and lost their time, and their strength and health in their restless wanderings and earned nothing.'[2]

The Cariboo rush created the boom town of Barkerville, which supposedly peaked in 1863 at upwards of ten thousand residents. A somewhat cynical observer described its style as 'neither Doric, Ionic, nor Corinthian, but decidedly Columbian.'[3] Most structures were raised on posts as protection against flash floods from the hillsides that were being denuded of trees for lumber. As would long remain the case in many communities, wooden plank sidewalks provided some respite from the seemingly everlasting mud.

Several minor booms complemented the Cariboo. In 1860 attention turned to the Boundary region just above the American border. Two years later reports filtered back from the central interior and the mouth of the Stikine River opposite the Alaska Panhandle. In 1865 miners headed for the northern Columbia River in the West Kootenays. Thereafter individual enthusiasm waned, although companies' operations continued to make gold the principal export. For single men to make a go, it was increasingly necessary to buy into an existing claim. Gold was 'played out,' to use miners' parlance. The value of gold being exported reached $2 million by 1860, just under $4 million in 1863, and then levelled off at $2 to $3 million a year.[4]

Effective administration was essential in the colony, but it was no easy matter. As Douglas himself acknowledged, 'to create a great social organization, with all its civil, judicial, and military establishments, in a wilderness of forests and mountains, is a herculean task.' In the view of Dr Helmcken, 'everything had to be done – established – commenced – new land regulations – education and what not – new franchise act.'[5]

The authority of Douglas as governor was in theory limited. The colony of Vancouver Island had an elected legislative assembly as well as an appointed council. The two bodies had to agree on legislation, and the council also acted in an advisory capacity to the governor. In sharp contrast, the 1858 act creating the colony of British Columbia gave the governor the right to rule by decree, an indication of the lack of confidence in the mainland's dominantly non-British, transient population. Douglas soon appointed an informal advisory committee which over the short term helped legitimize his acts. Small bureaucracies were established in each colony.

Some moves towards greater representation were made in the early 1860s. In 1861 Douglas requested that Vancouver Island's appointed council, which had become solely legislative in function, be reconstituted as a legislative council. He also urged the creation of a separate executive council, composed of heads of government departments. Both bodies were to be appointed by the governor. Two years later Douglas's request was granted not just for Vancouver Island but also for British Columbia. While the mainland colony still lacked an elected body comparable to Vancouver Island's legislative assembly, its legislative council was to have a gradually increasing proportion of elected members.

In spite of these budding institutions, Douglas relied primarily on his own judgment and authority. His three priorities were to protect the two colonies' boundaries, uphold law and order, and provide access to the gold-fields. On paper the boundaries were secure. To the west lay the Pacific Ocean, where the Royal Navy provided a comforting presence. The 1858 declaration of British authority over the mainland set an eastern boundary along the Rocky Mountains. A northern border with Russia had been established by treaty east of the coastal mountain range at 54°40′ as far back as 1825, a southern boundary with the United States by the 1846 Treaty of Washington. Since 1839 the Hudson's Bay Company had leased from the Russian American Company territory lying inland from the Alaska Panhandle between 54°40′ and 62°, known as the Stikine. In 1863, following the discovery of gold in the Stikine, the British Parliament quietly asserted sovereignty north to 60° and east to the 120th meridian. British Columbia's present boundaries were essentially in place.

All the same, American proximity created anxiety. By 1859 the Indians were crushed in Washington Territory, which was opened to settlement. Within the year its non-native population surpassed eleven thousand, doubling over the next decade. In early 1859 Colonel Richard Moody of the Royal Engineers predicted ominously that the mainland colony 'will be an American Country before long, if not neutralized by the presence of many Englishmen coming out at once.'[6] Despite Britain's assertion of direct authority, American miners could still become a spearhead for annexation, given that an experienced military force was near at hand.

Events in 1859 seemed to confirm the worst fears. The international boundary ran along the forty-ninth parallel west to Georgia Strait, then south through the middle of the channel separating Vancouver Island from the mainland. In reality not one but several channels existed through the San Juan Islands lying between Vancouver Island and the mainland. At first both countries apparently agreed on a boundary running east of San Juan Island, where the HBC maintained a sheep farm. Then the United States had second thoughts, giving its customs inspectors jurisdiction over all the San Juans. A boundary commission became deadlocked, and soon a series of minor events escalated into an international incident known as the Pig War.

The immediate origins of the fracas lay with disgruntled American miners who had retreated south to the San Juans to farm, one of whom had set himself down in the middle of the HBC's sheep farm. In the summer of 1859 he shot a pig that had got through his fence. When the Hudson's Bay Company demanded compensation, the American customs inspector so informed the military commander of the Oregon and Washington territories, a man still committed to '54°40' or Fight!' After visiting Governor Douglas in Victoria to discuss the matter, General William Harney reported to the commander-in-chief of the US army: 'The population of British Columbia is largely American and foreigners; comparatively few persons from the British Isles emigrate to this region. The English cannot colonize successfully so near our people; they are too exacting. This, with the pressing necessities of our commerce on this coast, will induce them to yield, eventually, Vancouver's Island to our government. It is as important to the Pacific States as Cuba is to those on the Atlantic.'[7] The energetic general encouraged San Juan residents to draw up a petition requesting protection against Indians. On this pretext he dispatched troops to take possession of San Juan Island for the United States even as a Royal Navy ship was planting the British flag.

In the event, the threat of hostilities was soon diffused. A senior British officer at Esquimalt persuaded Douglas to seek a diplomatic solution through London. The immediate result was joint occupation of San Juan Island by two separate garrisons of a hundred men each. And so the island remained throughout the 1860s, a visible and frequently discussed symbol of ongoing tensions between the United States and Britain in the Pacific Northwest. The issue was eventually referred for arbitration to the German emperor, who in 1872 decided for the United States.

An important consequence of the Pig War was a determination by the inhabitants of the two colonies to defend themselves. While the Royal Engineers were intended to protect the mainland, Vancouver Island's defences were non-existent except for the periodic visits of the Royal Navy. Voluntary militia units were quickly organized. The first initiative came from Victoria's black community, made up of several hundred men and women come north from California to escape racial discrimination. In April 1860 about fifty blacks received permission from Douglas to form the Victoria Pioneer Rifle Corps, known popularly as the African Rifles. Others formed similar groups in Victoria, Nanaimo, and New Westminster, spurred on by the outbreak of the American Civil War. During the war at least twelve British naval vessels were regularly stationed at Esquimalt, which became the British Navy's Pacific headquarters in 1862. From that time on there would be a permanent presence and greater security.

The Pig War underlined the necessity for law and order at the local level, Douglas's second priority. It was imperative, as the head of the Royal Engineers put it, that miners' 'eyes were opened ... to see that in the Queen's dominions an infringement of the Law was really a serious matter, & not a sort of half joke as in California.'[8] Building on precedents from the gold rush in the Charlottes, two levels of authority were established. Gold commissioners on the ground were to be buttressed by periodic visits from a travelling judge.

Appointed to specific jurisdictions, the gold commissioners' main function was to issue annual mining licences and to register claims. As Fraser reported to the *Times*, 'the Gold Commissioners are to keep exact records of the "claims" registered, are to make out every quarter lists of registered miners to be posted in the districts, and all the registers are to be open to the inspection of the public ... for the security and information of the miners.'[9]

The commissioners also acted as agents of everyday authority. One miner described a typical mining enclave as comprising 'the ordinary series of rough wooden shanties, stores, restaurants, grog shops, and gambling saloons; and, on a little eminence, the official residence, tenanted by the Gold Commissioner and his assistants, and one policeman, with the British flag permanently displayed.' The ten commissioners collected all forms of revenue, oversaw land pre-emptions, served as electorial officers, and acted as Indian agents. They could settle most mining disputes and make regulations for good governance in mining communities within their jurisdiction. An American miner reported home: 'The English officials are very strict, which is a good feature. It is astonishing with what skill and rapidity they ferret out any misdemeanor.'[10]

Gold commissioners gained credibility through periodic visits by a higher judicial authority. In 1858 the British government appointed Matthew Baillie Begbie to be Judge of British Columbia. Begbie's education at Cambridge University and experience as a London barrister gave him an immense self-confidence. One visitor came away impressed, describing Begbie as 'very fine, a fine tall fellow of 6 feet, well made & powerful, magnificent head, hair scanty and nearly white, with nearly black mustache & beard.'[11]

Begbie rapidly established the physical reality of British justice across the mainland. He relied on the traditional British practice of circuits, riding out to the people to try cases rather than holding his court at some central location. He spent at least half of each year away on circuit, and he reached every corner of non-native settlement, no matter how remote. Begbie would set up his tent, dress in the traditional robes, wig and black cap, and then conduct business. The proceedings would be held in the open if weather was good, otherwise in his tent or elsewhere indoors. In reality, most offences were fairly ordinary, resulting from drink, greed, or lust. Between 1859 and 1872 Begbie presided over trials by jury of just fifty-two murder cases. Five individuals were acquitted, nine found guilty of a lesser charge, and thirty-eight convicted. Of the twenty-seven who were hanged, twenty-two were Indians, one Chinese, and four white. To the extent anyone got a bad deal, it was, not surprisingly, Indian people. They possessed few if any means to defend themselves against the non-Indians who were inevitably their accusers, since disputes only between Indians were avoided.

If most of what Begbie ended up doing was fairly prosaic, no one at the time could have known it. British Columbians feared that the early miners from California would bring with them the lawlessness, vigilantism, and lynching which was said to prevail down south. Begbie's presence may have made a difference, so a traveller noted in his journal. 'Passed Judge Begbie on horseback. Everyone praises his just severity as the salvation of Cariboo & terror of rowdies.' Begbie's role was well summed up in 1870 by a speaker in the legislative council. 'Justice has been properly administered in the country; there has been absolute security to life and property.'[12]

An efficient transportation system was vital to economic development of the new colonies, and was one of Douglas's priorities as governor. As Fraser repeatedly observed, 'the most serious evil which British Columbia suffers from is the want of roads, and there is no possibility of removing this evil except by Government aid.'[13] Not only was it important for the economy that miners reached the gold diggings; it also mattered how they got there. Licensing alone would not ensure that miners passed through Victoria and New Westminster, thereby acknowledging Britain's authority and likely purchasing supplies from local merchants. American attempts to develop an alternative route through Whatcom had failed, but access was possible through the same north-south valleys that were used to supply the Hudson's Bay's interior posts. Douglas determined that politics and economics must override topography. Throughout the colonial period – and indeed into the present day – government policy encouraged the construction of roads and other physical infrastructure intended to unite the British Columbia mainland from east to west rather than follow the natural north-south geographical pattern.

The Royal Engineers were an important asset in this road-building policy. They broke a trail from New Westminster to nearby Burrard Inlet, already recognized as a fine harbour. They supervised the upgrading of the Harrison-Lillooet route into a six-metre-wide wagon road. They oversaw a major new route near the American border, pioneered in response to the 1860 discovery of gold in the Okanagan-Boundary region (see Map 7). A civilian surveyor, Edgar Dewdney, was contracted to construct a trail, which then fell into disuse once the diggings were exhausted. The brief 1865 rush to the

Kootenays brought the Dewdney Trail's extension, again to counter miners and supplies coming in overland through Washington Territory. The trail was thereafter little used, its eastern half being abandoned in the 1870s.

The Cariboo gold rush of the early 1860s generated the largest road-building project. Communications within the Cariboo and between it and the coast were deplorable. Douglas considered it critical that the new finds be linked to the Fraser River and thereby to New Westminster. He determined to establish a wagon route north from Yale, already linked by steamer to New Westminster (see Map 7). Limited government revenues forced Douglas to borrow part of the funds and encourage contractors to put up the remaining money in exchange for permission to levy tolls. The road when completed was five metres wide and over six hundred kilometres long. It ran from Yale to Barkerville and had cost the government well over one million dollars. Contemporaries were not surprised. 'Road must be expensive; frequently cut out of nearly perpendicular precipice overhanging river; rocky & rugged.'[14]

Not all attempts to provide access were so successful. Victoria business people were incensed when it was proposed to build the Cariboo Wagon Road with its terminus at New Westminster rather than Victoria. They resolved to finance an alternative route, which would involve going north from Victoria by steamer to Bute Inlet on the mainland (see Map 7), and then building a road that would run along the Homathko River to the Cariboo. Hopes ran so high that at one public meeting the audience pelted a speaker who dared to suggest the route's impracticability. The private company that began construction in 1862 soon ran into problems: the terrain was impassable and the local residents were hostile. Fearing that the newcomers were bringing disease in their wake, Indians killed thirteen of the road-builders in 1864. Understandably, the project was abandoned.

Governor Douglas's various initiatives in the new colonies were carried out by a variety of individuals, but there can be no doubt that the key factor in all aspects of government was the force of his personality. He was, so contemporaries' descriptions affirm, austere, distant, and overpowering.[15] A young girl meeting Douglas in 1860 was perhaps the most astute: 'A glove of velvet on a hand of steel.'[16] Although Douglas appeared to act within his legitimate powers, these were not so constraining as to limit his authority. He was accustomed to ruling as he wished, and this he largely continued to do. As governor, Douglas initiated most policies, and he was a master at overcoming the opposition, if any, of executive and legislative bodies. These policies were then implemented by a small bureaucracy, most of whom owed their appointment to Douglas and could be counted upon for their personal loyalty.

Douglas's overbearing style of governing encouraged opposition, particularly since he represented a past not shared by most of the recent arrivals. Douglas was strongly supported by fellow Britons, both long-time Hudson's Bay men and newcomers. But many settlers from within British North America, accustomed to its more representative political institutions, were exasperated by their lack of access to power. Entrepreneurs in the mainland capital of New Westminster, in large part Canadians, were particularly resentful. 'The fact that B. Columbia is governed by a Chief residing in Vancouver Is^d is a pill too bitter for the pride of a British Columbian!'[17] Douglas fuelled the flames. Although he took such needed measures as making New Westminster a port of entry to the mainland, opening up nearby land for sale, and making free grants to the major religious denominations, he made no secret of his personal preference for Vancouver Island. In 1860 he declared Victoria, along with nearby Esquimalt, a free port, thereby ensuring that external trade would continue to be routed through the island to the detriment of mainland merchants. In a letter written to English authorities in 1863 Douglas proudly asserted his unwillingness to 'cultivate the Canadian, in preference to the sound sterling English element in the Colony ... as I most thoroughly despise the whole of that contemptible clique.'[18]

Leading the political opposition were Amor de Cosmos and John Robson from their unique vantage points as sometime editors of the Victoria *British Colonist* and the New Westminster *British Columbian*. De Cosmos was a Nova Scotian who arrived in 1858 via the California gold rush, during which he had, for reasons which remain obscure, changed his name from plain William Smith to Amor de Cosmos, 'Lover of the Universe.' He turned to journalism for a living. In the press and from 1863 as a member of the Vancouver Island legislative assembly, de Cosmos repeatedly denounced what he termed a Family-Company-Compact controlling the two colonies. The phrase referred to the Family Compact that had long dominated Upper Canada's political and social order. It also harked back to Douglas's close ties with the Hudson's Bay Company. Ontarian

John Robson, who started the *British Columbian* in 1861, similarly used his paper as a vehicle for advancing the views of a Canadian minority which believed itself deliberately excluded from power. Such men strongly favoured representative political institutions in the pattern of Nova Scotia and elsewhere. De Cosmos in particular early became convinced that Britain's North American colonies from the Maritimes to Vancouver Island should join together into a single union.

By the time Douglas retired in 1864, times were changing. As early as 1862 the colonies' debt was almost $500,000, mainly a result of the feverish road building. It was still hoped that these construction costs would be recovered through rising revenues from customs duties, mining licences, road tolls, land sales, and a gold export tax. But debt mounted while revenues levelled off. By the time the Cariboo Wagon Road was completed in 1865 at a cost of well over one million dollars, the economic boom was coming to an end. The Hudson's Bay Company was visibly in retreat, having sold off its Nanaimo coal interests and much of its residential land at Victoria. In 1864 Fort Victoria itself was dismantled. The HBC's political influence, as exercised through Douglas, ended with the Colonial Office's appointment of two career administrators as the colonies' new governors.

The two men were minor colonial bureaucrats as much concerned with advancing their careers as with the particular circumstances of remote British possessions. Yet they each soon became strong defenders of their particular turf. Frederick Seymour, knowledgeably described as 'a well-meaning, easy-going mediocrity who seems to have owed his position to family influence,' eagerly put the final touches on the Cariboo Wagon Road.[19] Arthur Kennedy, while possessing considerable administrative experience, had not previously worked with an elected legislature such as Vancouver Island possessed. His time in office has been appraised as 'disheartening.'[20] Seymour's penchant for spending money became cause for worry, especially when the usual spring rush of miners north from California failed to materialize in 1865. To growing debt was added the Colonial Office's annoyance at the seemingly endless wrangling in the island legislative assembly over control of money matters.

The two colonies' political separation was short lived. On 19 November 1866 the two colonies became, through parliamentary act, the United Colony of British Columbia. The mainland colony effectively absorbed its island counterpart. The capital was to be at

New Westminster, and Seymour was named the new governor. Vancouver Island's elected legislative assembly simply disappeared, to be replaced by a single legislative council containing members from both the mainland and the island. Just nine of the twenty-three were popularly elected, the remainder either senior civil servants or the governor's appointees. Victoria lost its free-port status. The colonies' separate debts – the mainland's $1 million and Vancouver Island's almost $300,000 – were combined. The island-mainland rivalry initiated by Douglas's clear favouritism of Vancouver Island received new impetus as the mainland suddenly seemed to have acquired the upper hand. The antagonisms thus intensified would long plague British Columbian politics.

The creation of the united colony tacitly acknowledged another reality: the slowness with which a settler society was emerging. Gold alone was insufficient to ensure survival in the long term. The overwhelming majority of miners moved in and out of the Pacific Northwest with great rapidity. 'We meant to prospect the little creek which ran close to us in the morning, and if we failed to find anything, to get back as soon as we could and leave the country altogether to try our luck in Mexico or Australia, or any other place circumstances or our fancy might lead us to.'[21]

The one group most likely to continue mining were the Chinese. Arriving from California or directly from China, they also came to get rich but were more willing to labour long and hard towards that goal. Chinese together with local Indians worked the river bars below Yale and panned across the Cariboo for years after the majority of miners left in despair. A fellow miner praised their tenacity. 'This much-enduring and industrious race are generally to be found in little clusters, at work upon diggings deserted by the whites ... and will, doubtless, at the end of the year, by means of their frugality, save more than their white brother is likely to, in spite of his higher gains ... It is the fashion on the Pacific Coast to abuse and ill-treat the Chinaman in every possible way; and I really must tell my friends [that] ... they are hard-working, sober, and law-abiding – three scarce qualities among people in the station.'[22] Chinese persistence is perhaps best evidenced in the large number of mainland place names containing China, Chinese, or Chinaman. A minority of the four thousand or more Chinese present at the height of the gold rush were merchants competing for business in Victoria and elsewhere.

As time passed, individuals arrived from greater distances. For the 250 'overlanders' of 1862 who made the summer-long trek from Ontario via the Red River colony and Fort Edmonton, the journey with its very great personal hardships was not one they would have opted to repeat. One of the leaders concluded his narrative of the adventure with a warning. 'In thus pointing out these different roads across the continent, I do not wish to be understood as recommending, or in the least degree encouraging, the "Overland Route" as a means merely of reaching the gold-fields of British Columbia.' An overlander running a road house near Quesnel on the way to the Cariboo long regaled customers with 'a fearful account of hardships' experienced on the trip.[23] In some cases, non-material factors contributed to a decision to remain, as with Emily Carr's father who had originally emigrated from England to California. 'It irked Father to live under any flag other than his own.' So in 1863 he and his family set sail 'up, up, up the west coast of America till they came to the most English-tasting bit of all Canada – Victoria on the south end of Vancouver Island, which was then a Crown Colony.'[24]

Employment possibilities other than gold mining ranged from other forms of resource exploitation to administration, trade and entrepreneurship, the service sector, and agriculture. Some men and women came with such occupations in mind, as did European and Chinese merchants from San Francisco or government appointees from Britain. More often, prospective gold-seekers became disillusioned and looked around for other means of survival. Should they manage the transition, they might opt to stay a little longer; sojourners became settlers.

Gold's peculiar attraction tended to obscure elements of the economy put in place by the Hudson's Bay Company. Fraser pointed out to readers of the *Times* that 'mineral wealth besides gold abounds ... the soil and climate are good, healthy and genial; timber, coal, and fish abound without limit ... and as the country becomes better known to the world there can be no doubt that its advantages will be better availed of.'[25] While gold accounted for three-quarters of the value of exports through the end of the 1860s, lumber and fur each made up about 10 per cent and coal about 5 per cent. The fur trade continued relatively uninterrupted in the central interior and at some posts along the old brigade route. The earlier Peace River post of Fort St John was reopened in 1860. Nanaimo's coal mines, since 1862 owned by private British interests, continued to operate, surface

mining giving way to underground pits. By the end of the decade
Nanaimo's population was over seven hundred. About half the coal
was exported to the United States, the remainder sent to the Victoria
market or sold to the British Navy and to other steamship operators.

Lumbering was boosted by the gold rush, wood being used for
buildings, mine shafts, sluice boxes, and flumes sometimes kilometres long. The first sawmill on the mainland began at Yale in 1858.
Its lumber helped convert a tent city of some five thousand into a
more permanent community. Logging sites were generally near a
shoreline so that trees, on being felled and delimbed, could be slid or
rolled into the water. Short iron spikes with an eye on the end were
driven into some of the logs, which were then chained together to
create a boom for holding other logs. Booms were floated to a sawmill
sited by a necessary supply of waterpower. Among the thousands of
arrivals were experienced lumbermen such as Jeremiah Rogers from
New Brunswick, Sewell Prescott Moody from Maine, and Edward
Stamp from England. Through their and others' efforts, lumbering
operations proliferated. The Alberni Sawmill on Vancouver Island
opening in 1860 employed seventy men. Two mills producing wood
for export were established on Burrard Inlet: Moody operated on the
north shore at a site named after him, Stamp on the south side at what
became known as Hastings Mill. However, British Columbia lumber
faced a high American tariff and strong competition just across the
border in Puget Sound. For that reason, some exports, both of lumber
and of such related products as lathes and shingles, went to Latin
America, Australia, and New Zealand.

There was always the possibility of a government job to entice an
individual to the Pacific Northwest. Prior to 1858, virtually all
positions were filled by the Hudson's Bay Company, either directly
from England or through James Douglas's dual role as governor and
chief factor. There was no room for men who had not worked their
way up within the company, apart from such specialized positions as
physician, surveyor, or cleric. Once Britain took charge, new
opportunities opened up. Although the principal appointments,
such as that of Judge Begbie, were made in Britain, lesser posts were
filled in the colonies. Certain general qualifications held, including a
respectable social background and education, preferably at one of the
two established English universities, Oxford or Cambridge.

The gold rush's enthusiastic promotion in the British press
encouraged a number of reasonably well-connected adventurers to

catch gold fever. As one English publication explained in 1858: 'The competition for a livelihood amongst the educated and higher class of society in this country is so great that no one need disdain a colonial career. And to what more fitting place could they go than to that island which is pronounced on all sides to be the England of the Pacific?' The extensiveness of common knowledge is suggested by a letter written to the future novelist Samuel Butler by his father in August 1859. Giving consent to young Butler's desire to emigrate, he observed that 'Columbia is nearer than New Zealand and has a good prospect, but you are less fitted for it, for it is a newer country.'[26] Butler went to New Zealand, where some of his best-known novels were set.

Young men opting for the Pacific Northwest generally arrived with letters of introduction from the colonial secretary to Governor Douglas or other leading lights. These contacts often meant that a government job was waiting once realization dawned that mining was a tough proposition. The timing of events was such that many were straggling back to Victoria about the same time that the two colonial governments were making their original appointments. Paper credentials were often buttressed by marriage. One of Douglas's daughters had already married Dr Helmcken, who had become Douglas's chief ally in opposing de Cosmos and the Canadian contingent. Another married the HBC officer who in 1861 succeeded George Simpson as head of the Hudson's Bay Company in North America, a third an Anglican clergyman just out of England, and the fourth one of the bright young men lured by gold who was by 1859 safely ensconced within the bureaucracy. While some such individuals eventually returned to Britain or made their way to another of Britain's colonies, many remained, either as provincial administrators or in some similar occupation.

Other men and women turned to trade and entrepreneurship, soon realizing that more secure profits were to be made as saloon-keepers or butchers than in gold mining. Victoria's mayor in 1863 had, according to local gossip, 'commenced life here by borrowing 2 sheep from the H.B. Company & selling mutton retail in a tent.'[27] Most of the merchants who had come in 1858 soon returned to the United States, opening up opportunities for later arrivals. The North's victory in the American Civil War encouraged the departure of part of the black population, which had experienced some discrimination in Victoria, particularly from fellow Americans. Other

San Franciscans persevered: up to her death in 1870 Madam Pettibeau taught young girls of Victoria social proprieties and the rudiments of French.

Mainland opportunities were diverse. Overseers of pack trains included Mexicans who had come north from California. The completion of the Cariboo Wagon Road extended means of transportation. For about $100, Barnard's Express & Stage Line, known popularly as the B.X., took passengers between Yale and Quesnel in four days. By departing from Yale at 3 AM on Monday morning, it was possible to travel the Fraser Canyon by daylight and then reach Soda Creek in time to connect with the Thursday morning sternwheeler which docked at Quesnel later the same day. Distances to the gold-fields were often calculated from some central point, whence road houses along the way took their names. One set of travellers discovered that 8 Mile House was 'an Irishman's who gave us a very nice dinner. Chinaman cook.' Ten Mile House was kept by a German, 16 Mile House by a Scottish ship's carpenter. Most impressive was 150 Mile House consisting of 'a large square unfinished house; billiard room; lots of geese, ducks & chickens.'[28]

Entrepreneural successes were more than balanced by the many failures, especially as gold mining went into decline. Sometimes creativity ran amok, as when a Cariboo packer imported twenty-three camels, asserting that each could carry twice as much as a mule without the same feeding problems. The loaded camels became mired in the holes made by the mules' and horses' iron hooves, and soon were unable to move. Their sweat frightened other animals. In the end the other packers got a court injunction ordering the camels off the road. In disgust their owner turned them loose, and for years they appeared as apparitions, frightening interior travellers.

Another abortive project that for a time offered some men employment was the Collins Overland Telegraph. The electric telegraph was one of the great inventions of the mid nineteenth century; by 1861 the eastern United States had been linked to San Francisco. The greater challenge lay in tying North America with the rest of the world, particularly after a submarine cable across the Atlantic failed in 1858 within three months of being laid. Confidence wavered as to whether a replacement would be any more effective across that vast body of water. Russia's extension of its telegraph system into Siberia suggested the elaborate alternative of laying a line through British Columbia and Alaska and across the Bering Strait to Siberia. The existing cable was extended up the coast to New Westminster. Breakneck construction began in 1865 to beat competitors still pursuing an Atlantic link. Running along the Cariboo Wagon Road, the cable reached Quesnel by freeze-up. The next May some 150 men resumed work, moving northwest to Burns Lake and along the Bulkley and Kispiox rivers. Almost 650 kilometres of cable were laid, and fifteen log-cabin stations were constructed at forty-kilometre intervals. Then, forty kilometres up the Kispiox River, the project was abandoned on learning that a sixth attempt by the American entrepreneur Cyrus Field to lay an Atlantic cable had somehow beaten the odds and was functioning. Left in British Columbia was a completed line usable to Quesnel and, eventually, as far as Barkerville. Vast stores of supplies abandoned in the wilderness were soon used by native people for such innovative enterprises as a suspension bridge across the Bulkley River. For a few adventurous Europeans, the trail proved a useful means of access.

Farming was one of the most feasible means of making a living. Observers such as Fraser were sufficiently impressed to encourage individuals out from England with that goal in mind. 'Farming will pay first-rate anywhere within 300 miles of the mines.' Others were sceptical, asserting equally firmly that British Columbia would never be a good farming country. Negative images became so widespread that Fraser soon felt compelled to decry 'the fable, so pertinaciously circulated in England and in Canada that British Columbia possessed no fit lands.' 'Large quantities of grain and green crops have been put in and the extent of land under cultivation covers many thousands of acres.'[29] As with Hudson's Bay men turned farmers, few came with that intent. Yet by 1859 men and women were fanning out from Victoria as far north as the Cowichan Valley and Saltspring Island. When the Royal Engineers were disbanded in July 1863, the men were given the option of returning to England or receiving 150 acres. While all seven officers went back to pursue their military careers, 130 men stayed on with their families. Some opted for occupations in which they could use their skills, such as blacksmithing or surveying, but others became pioneer Fraser Valley farmers.

New land regulations for the mainland colony eased the transition to agriculture. Proclaimed in 1860, they gave any British subject or foreigner swearing allegiance to the crown the option of going anywhere except for a town site or Indian settlement and staking up to 160 acres. If the settler could demonstrate permanent improvements, he would receive the first right to purchase when offered for public sale at a price set originally at not above ten shillings an acre, a year later reduced to four shillings. If not already staked, adjoining land could also be purchased. During the 1860s over five hundred holdings were pre-empted in the Fraser Valley, many of them sufficiently close to a landing to make use of the steamships that regularly plied the river. The first settlers arrived in Maple Ridge in 1860, Mission in 1861, Chilliwack in 1862, and Sardis in 1863. By 1869 nearly three hundred farms existed.

To meet the needs of miners, thousands of head of cattle and sheep were imported from as far south as California, and the first cattle ranches appeared in the Cariboo by 1863. English visitors Walter Cheadle and Lord Milton were particularly struck by 'the "ranches" of the two Cornwalls; said to be Old Cantabs & men of some property who have take to stock farming out here; plain wooden houses, but much more finished than any we have seen.'[30] Over the decade ranching also began in the Okanagan, Thompson, and Nicola valleys. Tom Ellis was typical of the successful rancher. Arriving from Ireland in 1865, he became one of the first settlers in the Okanagan and one of its largest landholders, with grazing rights to over forty thousand acres extending south to the American border. Over the years the Ellis family created its own social structures, including an Anglican chapel where ranch hands were expected to attend morning prayers.

While most farms remained at the subsistence level, some grew enough produce to sell directly to consumers or for processing into such necessary staples as flour and beer. In the late 1860s Fraser Valley farmers were getting up to one dollar a pound for butter and cheese. Livestock, wool, tallow, ale and beer, flour, and vegetables were all exported to Britain, the Hawaiian Islands, and the United States. In spite of this expansion in the number of acres under cultivation, British Columbia remained a net importer of agricultural products, principally from the United States.

As more and more settlements sprang up in the Pacific Northwest, the need for familiar social organizations such as churches and schools arose. Early in 1858 four intrepid young nuns of the Sisters of St Ann made their way from Quebec to Victoria. They opened schools there, across the strait in New Westminster, and in more remote settlements. The Anglicans were soon in heady competition, determined not to be upstaged by 'the zealous Church of Rome.'[31]

Vancouver Island's legislative assembly provided some funding for common schools, but on the mainland it was individuals that took the lead. Jewish merchants established a synagogue in Victoria. Itinerant ministers such as John Robson's brother, the Methodist missionary Reverend Ebenezer Robson, travelled the gold-fields. 'At Hope, Yale, and the mining bars from Murderer's Bar to the famed Hill Bar, I visited the miners in their cabins and preached to all who would listen the glorious Gospel of Christ, often paddling alone, in my little canoe *Wesleyan*, through Hell Gate, and over Emory's Bar.'[32]

Voluntary activities ranged from theatres to fire brigades, from summer picnics on disputed San Juan Island to balls on visiting Royal Navy ships. Such organizations as the Cornishmen's Association, the St Andrews Society, and the Caledonia Society show the presence of ethnic divisions within the dominant group of British background. Not just in Victoria and New Westminster but wherever men and women were clustered together, a sense of community grew up. As early as November 1859 the Fort Hope Reading Room and Library opened with periodicals as diverse as *Punch*, the *New York Tribune*, and the *Alta California Bulletin*. A Cariboo Literary Society was founded at Williams Creek in the spring of 1863 so that 'men could meet and talk and once again feel themselves to be part of the world of music, books and the arts that had all been left behind on entering the gold fields.' By public subscription miners soon raised the one thousand dollars needed for a permanent library. A young man living in Barkerville in the mid 1860s reported being active in a literary society, a glee club, a library association, and a church choir. Within three years of arrival in New Westminster, the leader of the Overlanders, Thomas McMicking, had volunteered for its fire brigade, joined a hospital board and school committee, become an elder of the local Presyberian church, and was made president of a temperance group and a bible society.[33]

But a healthy settler society needs more than schools, churches, and voluntary associations to grow: it needs families. The communities that were springing up in the British Columbia of the 1860s were predominantly male. Outside of Victoria and New Westminster, women who were not wives or daughters were both rare and suspect, as in a reference to a 'white woman & negress, having spent the season in Cariboo (made fortunes).' A 'ball' held in the Cariboo to raise money for road building attracted 120 miners but just nine women. Columns in the *Times* repeatedly called attention to the situation. 'There is probably no country where the paucity of women in comparison with men is so injuriously felt ... Oh! if 50 or 100 should arrive from England every month until the supply equalled the demand, what a blessing it would be to us and the colony at large!' 'Without them the men will never settle in the country.'[34]

The Anglican church took the initiative. It realized that, much as it may disapprove of the European-native liaisons prevalent during the fur trading days and still widespread, these would inevitably continue as long as there were so few European women in the Pacific Northwest. On the other hand, England possessed a surplus due in part to the many men making their way into the empire. The two brides' ships that arrived in 1862 and 1863 were intended to do something about both situations by arranging for single, unemployed, poor young women to find husbands in the far British colonies rather than having to resort to public charity.

The sixty-two women arriving in September 1862 and thirty-six the next January were described in the *British Colonist* as 'mostly cleanly, well-built, pretty looking young women – ages varying from fourteen to an uncertain figure; a few are young widows who have seen better days. Most appear to have been well raised and generally they seem a superior lot to the women usually met on emigrant vessels.' A less flattering account termed the first group '60 select bundles of crinoline.'[35] Their arrival was cause for rejoicing. On the first occasion, all Victoria businesses closed. The most eager of the young men rowed out in order to have the first look. Officially, the women were to become governesses or servants, but everyone was aware of their intended destination.

It is difficult to follow the histories of all these women. A number married, one within three days to a man who had walked all the way from outlying Sooke to find a mate, another to a young homesteader on Saltspring Island. Husbands ranged from a Royal Engineer to a baker to a gold miner. Fraser reported several months after the ships' arrival that 'several of the girls are or are about to be married. Six such marriages were "proclaimed" in church the other day.' Others opened their own businesses or taught music. Some apparently 'went to the bad.' Yet others ended up bitterly unhappy: 'From the moment of landing I was disappointed. I saw nothing beautiful about the new country. I used to cry myself to sleep every night.'[36]

The ten thousand or so hardy souls who made their way in British

Columbia faced a deteriorating economic situation. As long as the wealth to be made from the gold-fields took precedence over all else, the political divisions appearing during Douglas's leadership were pushed into the background. But with the end of his authoritarian rule, coinciding as it did with a faltering economy, all these simmering tensions came to the surface. The two colonies' union did little to mitigate growing dissatisfaction; the united colony of British Columbia started life with a massive debt of almost $1.5 million and falling revenues.

Victoria was stagnant, its dream of rivalling San Francisco undone by the decline of what had proven to be a much smaller gold rush than was that in California. A newspaper report from January 1866 was frank. 'In Victoria I find the population reduced: a large proportion of buildings of every class unoccupied ... trade dull and diminished in amount.'[37] San Francisco's dominance as a manufacturing centre for the entire coast was undiminished, leaving Victoria, whose population had dropped below four thousand, as a distribution point. San Francisco was, moreover, much better sited, being directly linked with its hinterland rather than separated from it by a body of water. After bowing to pressure from the island's business community, the legislature decided in 1868 to shift the colony's capital from New Westminster to Victoria. Even this did little to improve the situation.

As the colony's economy worsened, British Columbians began to ponder on their future. They seemed to have three options: continuation as a British colony, annexation to the United States, and union with the new Dominion of Canada formed in 1867. Most Hudson's Bay men and later arrivals from Britain preferred the existing status. Long-time HBC physician Dr Helmcken 'wished the Colony to be let alone under HM Govt and to fight her way unhampered.' The Anglican bishop urged 'the closer union and protection of the mother country.' Such men shared a common background, including membership in the Church of England and a relatively high degree of literacy. Support was strongest in Victoria, which remained a British stronghold. 'The general tone of society and style of life' was, to quote a contemporary, that of England.[38]

Britain's willingness to take a strong position during the Pig War provided an optimistic precedent, as did the presence of the Royal Navy at Esquimalt. At the same time it was becoming increasingly clear that Britain did not intend to subsidize so remote a possession indefinitely, much less be held accountable for what were perceived as past extravagances. The indifference that had always character- ized British policy in the Pacific Northwest resurfaced with a ven- geance. Even Governor Seymour expressed dismay that British Columbia seemed to 'possess so little interest for the people of England.' The *Times* put the matter succinctly in an editorial whose very first sentence set the tone: 'British Columbia is a long way off.' What was unsatisfactory about the present position was that, 'instead of the Colonies being the dependencies of the Mother Country, the Mother Country has become the dependency of the Colonies.'[39]

The federation of the colonies of British North America – New Brunswick, Nova Scotia, Quebec, and Ontario – in 1867 to form the Dominion of Canada spurred into action those British Columbians who had come from Ontario or the Maritimes. A resolution urging British Columbia to join Confederation passed the legislative council, but bogged down over the practical question of how such action could even be contemplated in view of the enormous intervening land mass, at that time still under the loose authority of the Hudson's Bay Company. Many British Columbians knew little about British North America: 'Our trade was either with the u.s. or England – with Canada we had nothing to do.'[40]

Also working against British Columbia's entry into the Canadian confederation was the limited respect its supporters engendered among their counterparts of British background. Men and women of Canadian origin tended to come from relatively modest backgrounds and belong to one of the non-conformist denominations, such as Methodism, viewed by Anglicans as distinctly plebian. Helmcken later acknowledged that this opposition was based in part on prejudice. 'Canada was looked down on as a poor mean slow people, who had been very commonly designated North American China- men ... from their necessarily thrifty condition.'[41] In making the transition from sojourner to settler, residents from within British North America likely put down roots in New Westminster, the Fraser Valley, or in the southern interior, giving the mainland a distinctly Canadian ethos.

Most Canadians also shared a commitment to representative and responsible government. Legislators should be popularly elected and governments resign on losing the confidence of the elected body. British Columbia's legislative council was primarily government-appointed, its members so answerable. The campaign for representative and responsible government had reached a stalemate even as Confederation embodying those two principles was unfolding. De Cosmos and his allies turned to direct action. In May 1868 a Confederation League was founded. Four months later the league held a convention at Yale 'for the purpose of accelerating the admission of this Colony into the Dominion of Canada.'[42] In reality most minds were probably made up, in good part on a social and geographic basis. This became clear in the selection later in 1868 of the minority of members who were popularly chosen. All but one of the men picked on the mainland favoured Confederation, while all those from Vancouver Island were opposed. De Cosmos lost his Victoria seat. Opening the new session, Governor Seymour came out in favour of an elected body, only to be reminded by the Colonial Office that such a shift was not within his authority to enact.

As the two options of survival as British colony and confederation with Canada seemingly lost favour, so annexation to the United States appeared to gain momentum. While most early miners had departed, the minority who remained were reinforced by Southern refugees escaping the civil war. Everyday American practices were widespread. Baseball rivalled the British favourite of cricket; the fourth of July was cause for celebration in Victoria and, even more so, on the mainland; American stamps were used on mail sent to or through American territory. Dollars co-existed with pounds until 1865, when a decimal system of currency was officially adopted. The end of the civil war in 1865 again turned American attention outward. The consul in Victoria reported enthusiastically that 'the people of Vancouver Island, and of British Columbia, are almost unanimous in their desire for annexation to the United States.'[43]

On 30 March 1867, just one day after the British North America Act received royal assent in London, the United States purchased Alaska from Russia. Not only was Manifest Destiny reawakened but, more practically, British Columbia was now flanked on two sides by the United States. Secretary of State William Seward was convinced that 'our population is destined to roll its restless waves to the icy barriers of the north.' Indeed, among explanations advanced for the sale was Russian inability to maintain Alaska in the face of 'the feverish activity and enterprising spirit of Americans.' British Columbians were well aware of the implications of Russia's action, Helmcken later recalling how Americans 'boasted they had sandwiched B. Columbia and could eat her up at any time!!!' Nanaimo's newspaper became caught up, characterizing the British connection as a 'fast sinking ship,'whereas the United States was a 'gallant new craft, good and strong, close alongside, inviting us to safety and success.'[44] Britain itself may have been momentarily tempted to cede its Pacific Northwest colony to the United States. At the time of the Alaska sale Britain was negotiating with the United States over reparations for having permitted the South to build warships on British territory during the Civil War. The secretary of state proposed to take British Columbia as suitable settlement, but the British demurred on the grounds that the Royal Navy would be deprived of its Pacific base at Esquimalt. American claims were eventually submitted to international arbitration.

The American initiative was not thwarted. The railroad, one of the most significant practical consequences of the Industrial Revolution, reached the west coast in May 1869, linking San Francisco, British Columbia's gateway to the world, to the east. The Americans were, moreover, planning a second, more northerly, transcontinental railroad running just south of the border. In August Seward made a personal reconnaissance to Victoria, where he declared publicly that the Pacific Northwest's common interests would be best served by Oregon, Washington, Alaska, and British Columbia becoming partners. Back home he reported confidently that British Columbians were getting up petitions addressed to Congress in favour of annexation. In the end two petitions were dispatched, containing 104 signatures. Most of the signatories were Victoria merchants of Jewish and German origin, suggesting that economic stagnation may have played as large a role as pro-American sentiment. In the view of at least some business people, only the removal of tariff barriers with the United States would renew prosperity, and this was clearly most realizable through annexation. While the petitions were mentioned in the American Congress, no further action ensued and the surge abated.

Most importantly, Britain took action. Once Confederation became a reality in 1867, the Colonial Office concluded that its best course lay is joining its Pacific Northwest possession to the Dominion of Canada as quickly as possible. Britain assisted the new Canadian government to buy out the rights of the Hudson's Bay Company to the immense land mass lying between Ontario and British Columbia. The province of Manitoba was created out of the HBC's Red River settlement. If still caught between the Americans on the north and south, British Columbia was by 1870 bounded on the east by Canadian territory and at a distance by a new Canadian province.

Governor Seymour's death in June 1869 gave the Colonial Office the opportunity to appoint a new governor. Anthony Musgrave came with instructions to get the colony into Confederation through securing the support of its legislative council. Previously governor of Newfoundland, he was personally acquainted with the Canadian prime minister, John A. Macdonald. Musgrave was also acceptable to British-oriented politicians in Victoria, being, as one of them put it, 'gentlemanly in manner.'[45] The new governor was sent an official dispatch for immediate publication to the effect that Her Majesty's government considered British Columbia's political and economic interests best served through union with Canada.

Musgrave stated publicly his intention to get a formal proposal from the legislative council concerning its terms for agreement. He was well aware that support was limited, reporting to the colonial secretary at the end of October 1869 that 'the more prominent Agitators for Confederation are a small knot of Canadians who hope that it may be possible to make fuller representative institutions and Responsible Government part of the new arrangements, and that they may so place themselves in positions of influence and emolument.' The colony's Canadians, he added, have 'not contrived to impress their fellow Colonists with a prejudice in their favour.'[46] Shortly afterwards news of the annexation petitions surfaced, which furthered Musgrave's hand.

The pro-British faction was forced to choose between Canada and the United States. Some became so disheartened that they simply acquiesced to the inevitable rather than making a conscious decision. Their views seemed to count for naught. As the attorney general, Henry Pering Pellew Crease, put it, 'I believe England is sick of her Colonies and to be a Colonist whatever your POSITION & CHARACTER when at Home – is to lose Caste the moment you become a bona fide settler.' Those who, like Crease, held administrative appointments fretted over whether they would receive adequate pensions, and a few requested immediate transfer elsewhere in the empire. While Crease eventually threw in his lot permanently with British Columbia, he toyed briefly with a declaration of independence. 'What do you say to a large English Kingdom here west of the Rocky

Mountains ... If they despise us at home ... [can] we be the worse off as an entirely separate Country? ... All the armies in the World c^d not get into the Country if we defended the only passes ... I can readily imagine a great future.' For most of the pro-British faction their republican neighbour posed a greater threat than did a parliamentary dominion loyal to the queen. Expressions such as 'when we get Vancouvers Island' and 'when British Columbia belongs to us' remained commonplace south of the border, leading many to believe that only Confederation would prevent the colony from eventually falling into the hands of the Americans.[47]

Reservations were still strong during the legislative debate on Confederation held in February and March 1870. Helmcken, resident in Victoria for two decades, was well aware of the fundamental difference between colonial and provincial status. 'If we are united, or rather absorbed, everything will centralize in Canada, and the whole country will be tributary to Canada. The number of Representatives sent to Ottawa from other places would overwhelm the number sent from British Columbia. Even in the matter of appropriations, where the scramble always is, this Colony would be overborne ... The Tariff and Excise Laws of Canada will ruin the dominant interests of this Colony ... If we are Confederated with Canada we become its tributary.' Even de Cosmos, that unrelenting stalwart of Confederation, was convinced that any decision must be made, first and foremost, in the interests of British Columbia. 'I stand here not as a Canadian, but as a British Columbian; my allegiance is due first to British Columbia.'[48] The central issue rapidly became economic, how to counter stagnation and attract a large settler population.

Governor Musgrave's proposal to the legislative council of very bold terms for entry into the Canadian Confederation prompted its principal opponents to make the best of the harsh reality. The priority given economic over political considerations created ambivalence for men like de Cosmos who had hoped to see the inclusion of a demand for responsible government. The governor proposed that, not only should British Columbia insist that its debt be wiped out, but Canada must accept, for the purposes of a per capita grant along the lines of those given other provinces, a population base far higher than the actual number of persons resident in British Columbia. Colonial administrators adversely affected by the proposed union were to get adequate pensions. A principal demand was for a transportation link, to consist in the short term of a wagon road but to be eventually replaced by a transcontinental railway. On 6 April 1870 the proposed terms were approved.

A three-man delegation was selected to present British Columbia's demands to the Canadian government in Ottawa. It comprised a long-time pro-Confederationist from the Cariboo, Dr Robert Carrall; Joseph Trutch, a colonial official who had changed his mind in favour of Confederation since Musgrave's arrival; and John Sebastian Helmcken, who remained unconvinced but was without doubt the colony's most experienced politician. They departed in May 1870 by San Francisco on the new transcontinental railway, the trip from Victoria to Ottawa taking just twenty-four days. Helmcken's enthusiasm over the rail link may have helped to change his mind. More importantly, to their surprise, the Canadian government readily accepted the proposed terms, in part due to recent events in Manitoba. There, a brief rising by Métis, the settlers of mixed native and French ancestry, under Louis Riel had underlined how useful a rail link would be in maintaining order and communication across the vast dominion. The timetable for the railway was even pushed so far forward as to obviate the need for a wagon road, its promised completion date put at just a decade hence. All that remained were somewhat anti-climatic votes by the House of Commons in Ottawa and the legislative council in Victoria. On 20 July 1871 British Columbia entered the Canadian Confederation.

In less than a century the Pacific Northwest had passed through several political statuses and two economic booms, each based on a single resource. Fur and gold were equally transient – exploit and then move on. Yet in little more than a decade the area was not only consolidated as a political entity, but the nucleus of a settler society had emerged. Largely in response to the demands of gold, boundaries with the United States were affirmed, law and order established, and physical infrastructure put in place.

The contribution of James Douglas in shaping the future province should not be underestimated. Recognition came in his own lifetime in the form of a knighthood shortly before his retirement. At the same time Douglas's activity circumscribed options once gold ran its course. He alienated newcomers from Ontario and the Maritimes through his haughty demeanour and preference for Britons over Canadians. His passion for road-building left a burden of debt unpalatable to British authorities, who possibly should have reined in his enthusiasm earlier. Britain's long-standing indifference to the Pacific Northwest resurfaced. According to the dominant perspective, colonial possessions were advantageous only so long as they paid their way. This British Columbia seemed unlikely ever to do, much less absorb its debt. Thus, a third option apart from annexation to the neighbouring United States or confederation with Canada was removed.

If Douglas played a major role in determining British Columbia's course, so also did the gold rush. The events of 1858 ensured that both Vancouver Island and the adjacent mainland remained firmly British rather than possibly sliding into the United States' orbit through settlement gradually moving northward while that from Britain continued to stagnate. Over the long run, the gold rush may have been the singular event making British Columbia Canadian by virtue of telescoping developments. British Columbia was pushed more rapidly into Confederation than would otherwise have been the case and then kept there, along with western Canada, through the commitment to construct a transcontinental railway.

6

The Young Province
1871–1900

On 20 July 1871 British Columbia became a province of Canada. Of itself, entry into Confederation changed nothing; nor was there much reason for it to do so. The entity known as Canada was a long way away. The inhabitants of British descent, many of whom lived in Victoria, were quite satisfied with their domination of political, legal, and social structures. Men and women from other parts of Canada, living primarily on the lower mainland and throughout the southern interior, were still shut out from power.

The economic and strategic priorities bringing British Columbia into Confederation obscured the new province's fragility. The Dominion government was willing to grant British Columbia, for funding purposes, a population of sixty thousand; in actuality it contained under two-thirds that number in 1871, mostly native people.[1] A decade later British Columbia's population was still below its ostensible total at Confederation (see Table 5). The number of European-born settlers had doubled, yet stood at just seventeen thousand. It was from this limited pool that a provincial government and bureaucracy had to be formed, one strong enough to hold its own in dealings with the dominion government and with the rest of Canada. Against its four million inhabitants, the handful of people living in British Columbia became – as Dr J.S. Helmcken had worried aloud during the Confederation debate – largely irrelevant.

The demography of the young province reflected the depressed economic conditions that had persuaded Britain to encourage its

Pacific coast colony into Confederation in the first place; but it also demonstrated the determination of its inhabitants to make a living in difficult circumstances. Most Europeans lived on Vancouver Island. In contrast, over three-quarters of the Chinese were on the mainland, mostly prospecting for gold and, eventually, also labouring on the railway. British Columbia's Chinese population reached nearly four thousand by 1881; the number of blacks declined to under three hundred, as many made their way back to the United States. During the 1870s the number of natives fell to about twenty-five thousand. Among the adult non-native population there were still some three males for every female. Only in Victoria was the ratio about equal; in parts of the interior there was often just one woman for every ten men. The Chinese population was almost entirely male.

It was upon this very small population base that a province had to be constructed. On entering Confederation, British Columbia became subject to the provisions of the British North America Act, the British legislation which created the Dominion of Canada in 1867. Designed to ensure a strong central government, the act left to the provinces control only over matters considered of local significance: direct taxation within the province, appointment and payment of provincial officials, management and sales of public lands, development of physical infrastructure, education and health services, and administration of justice. All other matters fell within the purview of the federal government, and the decision-making powers over these subjects came principally through the parliamentary process. British Columbia was given three seats in the Senate and six in the House of Commons, such small numbers being further limited in their influence by distance, both real and psychological, from the national capital at Ottawa. A decision to run for Parliament was not taken lightly, for, as one of the participants in the 1870 Confederation debate foretold: 'Most men here are workers of some sort, and actively employed in their several professions and businesses, and we should have extreme difficulty in finding eight [sic] good men who would spare the time and expense to go to Ottawa.'[2] As a rule British Columbia's members of Parliament would not distinguish themselves on the federal level; certainly none of them would rise to national prominence.

Shortly after entry into Confederation elections were held for the six members of Parliament and for the new provincial legislature of twenty-five members. As in the other provinces, the Canadian governor general appointed a lieutenant-governor for the province. Acting on behalf of the British crown, he then requested one of the elected MLAS to form a government and so become premier. The first election returned such longtime activists as Amor de Cosmos and John Robson. Others, including John Sebastian Helmcken, had decided to retire from politics. Helmcken even turned down the lieutenant-governor's invitation to form the first provincial government. The honour went to John McCreight, a lawyer without previous political experience.

The provincial government's representative and responsible character, for which men such as de Cosmos had long fought, soon followed. Upon entering Confederation the British Columbian legislative assembly became entirely elective. Its representative character was extended with the introduction of full male suffrage in 1876. To vote it was no longer necessary, as in the colonial period, to hold property but only to be a white adult British subject resident in the province for a year and in the electoral district for two months. The manner of voting was changed shortly after entry into Confederation from open voting to the secret ballot.

The concept of responsible government was formally acknowledged when Premier McCreight resigned after losing a non-confidence vote in the legislature. It was confirmed in an exchange between the first lieutenant-governor and de Cosmos, who was asked to form a government in December 1872 on McCreight's resignation. The lieutenant-governor, Joseph Trutch, had been attending all cabinet meetings, leading to growing suspicions that he – and thereby the British contingent – was exercising too much control over what was meant to be representative and responsible government. According to British Columbia folklore, matters came to a head when de Cosmos refused to conduct cabinet business until the lieutenant-governor left the room, a principle that holds to the present day.

At the same time, even as men were congratulating themselves on their achievement of representative and responsible government, groups considered by them not to be part of the 'representative' process to whom government was 'responsible' were just as easily excluded. Voices urging the right of women to vote were being heard for the first time in British Columbia – the American suffragist Susan B. Anthony spoke in Victoria in 1871 – but female exclusion was total. In 1874 the right to vote in provincial elections was removed from the two most visible racial minorities, Chinese and Indians. However high-minded political leaders may have considered the principles for which they had so long fought, it must not be forgotten that their priorities were framed in their own image.

Through the end of the nineteenth century provincial politics revolved around loose coalitions of like-minded persons rather than the political parties that existed elsewhere in Canada and at the federal level in British Columbia. Common interests as opposed to formal political affiliation joined men together. Once asked to form a government, a potential premier named a cabinet from among sympathetic legislators, but not from within a political party with a formal structure and organization. The reasons were in good part pragmatic: not only were numbers of Europeans minute but the proportions participating in the political process even smaller. Only in the election of 1886 did the number of actual voters exceed seventy-five hundred. Just over forty men comprised all of the fifteen cabinets of the years from 1871 to 1903, when provincial parties were introduced.

While some alliances carried over from colonial days, others emerged in response to new circumstances. Most men probably remained loyal to the interest group that they originally joined, members of cabinet being asked to resign for public disagreement with enunciated government policies. Beginning with the second provincial campaign in 1875, candidates identified themselves in relationship to the group in power, using as labels 'Government,' 'Opposition,' and 'Independent.' These designations did not prevent some members once elected from changing loyalties for what were often personal reasons, such as having been dismissed from cabinet. The man who became premier acquired the position because he was best able to hold together a coalition of supporters long enough to get himself named to the top job.

Arrivals from elsewhere in Canada soon became aware of the peculiar character of British Columbian politics. 'The two parties here are not so distinctly defined as at home, and so far as I can make out, are somewhat mixed as to opinions,' so a young school teacher concluded in 1890 shortly after her arrival in the west coast province from the Maritimes. The poet and Canadian nationalist Charles Mair had been in the Okanagan for only six weeks in 1892 before reporting back to a friend in Ontario that 'there is no politics here.' Six months later he reiterated the point: 'Politics are unknown, that is to say Eastern party politics.' Mair was still perturbed two years later: 'Politics are very weak – the word "party" being seldom heard here.'[3]

Over time a certain continuity did emerge in provincial government. The historian F.W. Howay, writing in 1914 when the four decades since Confederation were still part of living memory, perceived two 'governments' having held power during most of the time period up to the appearance of formal parties in 1903.[4] The first, comprising four premierships, ran from 1872 to 1883 with the exception of two years in the mid 1870s when an 'Opposition' coalition governed. Men were joined by a primary concern to 'Fight Ottawa' in the interest of rail construction. Political calm then ensued under a second 'Government' extending from 1883 to 1898. During these years five different premiers had charge. The first three died in office, the fourth resigning on being appointed chief justice to replace the recently deceased Matthew Begbie (for details see Table 2).

Political tensions continued between Britons and Canadians and between what Premier George Walkem termed in 1882 'the adverse elements of Mainland & Island.'[5] Alignments could become complex, politicians with their livelihoods in the interior often perceiving advantages in identifying themselves with the small group of Victoria entrepreneurs who dominated the provincial legislature. Some families moved to Victoria to enjoy the capital city's greater amenities. Adding to the dissension was an agreement made at Confederation by which Vancouver Island was guaranteed twelve MLAS, the mainland thirteen. Gross inequalities between electoral districts favoured rural voters: in the 1878 election the Kootenays elected two members with fifteen votes, Esquimalt two with 160, and New Westminster two with eight hundred. While the total number of electoral districts was expanded from time to time, the island-mainland parity held.

Like most governments across the western world at that time, politicians did not see it as part of their mandate to encourage social welfare; they viewed the role of the state as laissez-faire, not interfering with businessmen pursuing their own self-interest. The principal social service for which the province had responsibility was education, and a system of non-denominational free public schools was established at the elementary level early in 1872. Children were expected to walk at most about five kilometres to school, and distances were enormous across areas of settlement. But under the strong leadership of John Jessop as superintendent of education, forty-five school districts were set up in just half a dozen years. Most often, parents took the initiative in erecting a school building and then securing provincial funding to hire a teacher. Over the next decade another sixty districts were established.

British Columbia's finances were never on very firm ground. Although the federal government's assumption of the provincial debt enabled British Columbia to abolish tolls on the Cariboo Road, the province's debt-free status was brief. The province was not spared the depression that hit the rest of Canada in 1873. Within the year the deficit reached $300,000, and soon the government was floating its first loans and reimposing tolls in an almost desperate attempt to secure revenue. The provincial debt doubled in 1875 when a program of pubic works was initiated to alleviate unemployment. The sole year without a deficit was 1881, and then only because no money was allocated to public works.

The biggest government initiative, both federally and provincially, was the promised railway. By the terms of union, the dominion government undertook 'to secure the commencement simultaneously, within two years from the date of the Union, of the construction of a Railway from the Pacific towards the Rocky Mountains, and from such point as may be selected, east of the Rocky Mountains, toward the Pacific, to connect the seaboard of British Columbia with the railway system of Canada; and, further, to secure the completion of such Railway within ten years.'[6]

Fears that the railway might not materialize in the specified time did not take long to surface. At first the dominion government blamed delays on the difficulty of surveys and inability to determine a feasible route across mountainous terrain. In 1873 the prime minister, John A. Macdonald, who had lent his personal prestige to negotiating the terms of entry with British Columbia, resigned over charges of corruption in awarding a contract for the line's construction. The Liberal party, which came to power under Alexander Mackenzie, not only had to deal with a depressed economy but lacked the Conservatives' national vision. In their view the west coast province was a spoilt child already given too much to cajole it into Confederation. The railway was the logical item to be put on hold until the economy revived, especially since it had become clear that no private company was about to undertake the venture and considerable federal funds would have to be expended.

Exasperation in British Columbia at the delay was heightened by the concern, shared by most politicians, to maintain Vancouver Island's pride of place as part of the rail package. Esquimalt was in 1873 named the line's western terminus, which implied a northern route by Bute Inlet. To encourage the decision the Confederation delegation to Ottawa in 1870 had even brought with them a map marking out the route of the earlier abortive road-building venture. From Bute Inlet a ferry or possibly a system of bridges would cross the islands of Georgia Strait to central Vancouver Island, a rail link going south from there to Esquimalt, where a large dry dock would, so it was argued, result in a port comparable to thriving San Francisco, with whom Victoria retained close ties.

Various tactics were used to goad federal authorities into action. There were repeated threats of secession. As early as 1875 Lieutenant-Governor Trutch reported to Macdonald, still out of power, that 'unless a change of policy be adopted toward us this community will become so alienated from its loyalty to Canada as to be a source of weakness to the Dominion.'[7] The next January the provincial legislature voted unanimously to petition Queen Victoria, outlining its grievances and threatening to secede. A vice-regal visit of that year was a deliberate attempt at pacification. The governor general, Lord Dufferin, went away impressed, but to no avail. The dominion government reminded him that it was not within his prerogative to interfere in internal Canadian matters.

Tempers again erupted when, in December 1877, Prime Minister Mackenzie confirmed growing suspicion that the railway would follow the Fraser River to Burrard Inlet as opposed to the Bute Inlet route favoured by Island promoters (see Map 8). The route would not only be cheaper to construct but directly compete with an American rail line being built just south of the border to Puget Sound. Once the Burrard Inlet terminus was confirmed, the provincial legislature again voted for secession. De Cosmos, who since 1871 had been a member of the dominion Parliament as well as a sometimes provincial legislator and premier, followed this up by moving a resolution in the House of Commons to provide for separation. Eventually a compromise was reached, an auxiliary line being promised for Vancouver Island. Even this then became unlikely, and in early 1881 secession talk returned.

Meanwhile, events began to move forward at the federal level for reasons largely unrelated to British Columbia. In September 1878

John A. Macdonald and the Conservatives were returned to power under the banner of the National Policy. The proposed policy looked towards nation-wide economic development through higher tariffs, immigration, and a transcontinental railway. The plan had its roots in the logic behind the act of Confederation. The provinces which came together in 1867 did so as separate and distinctive economic units, each believing that the act of union would somehow solve its own financial difficulties. For the Maritimes and central Canada the goal was to acquire new markets for their manufactured products. The National Policy echoed imperial ideology in viewing the role of the periphery, be it colonies or western Canada, as strengthening the economy of the centre through provision of raw materials later returned as manufactures. Value added in the form of jobs and industrial growth accrued primarily to the centre, be it Britain or Ontario and Quebec. Increased tariffs on most manufactured imports would encourage the growth of industry by keeping out cheaper foreign goods. Federal promotion of immigration was designed to attract into the west the agricultural settlers needed to produce raw materials and purchase manufactures, while the railway would transport newcomers onto the land and then the goods they needed to survive.

The National Policy provided the impetus for completing the transcontinental railway. Federal negotiations with a Montreal syndicate to construct the line with government assistance proved arduous, but in October 1880 agreement was reached with the Canadian Pacific Railway Company. In exchange for completion by 1891, the company received the seven hundred miles (over eleven hundred kilometres) of track already in place or under construction, tax and tariff exemption on all materials and equipment, a $25 million cash subsidy, alternative mile-square parcels of land on both sides of the railway to a depth of twenty miles (more than thirty kilometres) totalling twenty-five million acres, and a twenty-year monopoly prohibiting construction of a rival railway between the CPR and the American border. The thorny issue of the Vancouver Island line was resolved in 1884 by federal agreement to subsidize private construction of both a railway from Nanaimo to Esquimalt and the dock at Esquimalt.

Construction of the British Columbian portion of the CPR began in May 1880. The formidable section through the steep canyons of the Fraser and Thompson rivers was supervised by Andrew Onderdonk with his headquarters at Yale. The pace of construction soon accelerated from somewhat sluggish beginnings, and supply points like Yale experienced boom conditions. 'It was hammers and drills, picks and shovels, blasting night and day, and work for everybody who wanted it.'[8] The demand for services ranged from blacksmiths to saloons to enormous quantities of foodstuffs. Wood for ties, bridges, and scaffolding was often obtained locally. Hand labour was the rule, with reliance on machinery minimal. Workers willing to undertake dangerous tasks and be moved from place to place on short notice were in such short supply that Onderdonk was given permission to import Chinese labourers. Between 1881 and 1884 over fifteen thousand entered the port of Victoria, mainly from China and San Francisco.

By 1884 CPR directors were confidently predicting completion of the entire line well before the 1891 deadline. Late the next year, on 7 November 1885, the lines being built concurrently from the coast eastward and through the Rockies westward met at Craigellachie, near the divisional point of Revelstoke. Prime Minister Macdonald was informed the same day that 'the first through train from Montreal is approaching Yale and within four hours of the Pacific coast.' Its running time, including ordinary stoppages, was exactly five days. Two weeks later the first through freight reached Victoria after crossing Georgia Strait by steamer. The trip took 'fifteen days from England, a fact that must be hailed with delight by Englishmen and Canadians.'[9] The section over the Rockies did not at first permit full winter operation, which meant that it was 4 July 1886 when the first scheduled passenger train reached the CPR's western terminus.

Exactly where that western terminus should be had proved a difficult matter. Across the prairies and British Columbia, land speculation was an inevitable concomitant of rail construction. The barest rumours of a station's proposed location would be enough to set off a mini-boom. Such events paled in comparison to the drama surrounding the line's western terminus. The initial site had been Port Moody, and it was there that the first passenger train arrived in 1886. But by this time the Fraser Valley site had already lost its status. Its harbour was barely capable of handling coastal shipping, and could certainly not fulfil the CPR's growing ambition to extend its overland route by sea to Asia. The Canadian Pacific Railway had high hopes of diverting trade with the Orient away from the Suez Canal. On a more practical note, the cost of land at Port Moody had risen sharply through private speculation, and the CPR looked around for a cheaper site. They found it near the small lumbering enclave of Granville on the south shore of Burrard Inlet. Known locally as Gastown, Granville lay less than a kilometre to the west of Hastings Mill; an even larger sawmill lay on the north shore at Moodyville. While a handful of enterprising individuals had already bought up property, sufficient unalienated land existed for the provincial government to offer the railway six thousand acres in exchange for the line's extension. Most of the land was virgin forest situated on the far side of False Creek, south of the existing settlement. Local landowners, fully aware of how greatly they themselves would benefit from the CPR's change of heart, voluntarily donated a third of their lots to the company. As a result, the Canadian Pacific Railway acquired far more property than it would have at Port Moody. Over the wrath of Port Moody promoters, and of Victoria merchants enraged over the theft of their island's name, the new city of Vancouver was incorporated on 6 April 1886. The first scheduled train from the east arrived a little over a year later, on 23 May 1887.

The most obvious and immediate result of the line's completion was Vancouver's rise. The speculative cycle of growth that accompanied its first months rivalled Victoria's transformation at the beginning of the gold rush. In 1884 the shores of Burrard Inlet had a population of about nine hundred; within weeks of incorporation Vancouver alone possessed some eight hundred businesses and a population of two thousand. A bush fire which destroyed much of Vancouver in June 1886 did little to dampen enthusiasm. An 1888 visitor observed 'ever so many brick buildings in various stages of advancement ... So for the present at least, times are good in Vancouver ... Some say it will eclipse Victoria yet, but others that it will collapse presently.'[10] By 1891 Vancouver housed almost fourteen thousand people. Yet just a year later growth was stalled as a serious recession hit the province and the full extent to which the early expansion had rested on land speculation and CPR money was laid bare.

The influence of the Canadian Pacific Railway was everywhere visible in the city. A visitor of 1889 noted how, 'in Vancouver, it is the great thing to be connected with the real estate or the railway station; it assures your position in society, these being the two excitements of existence ... Everything in Vancouver is c.p.r.'[11] The Canadian Pacific soon extended its transcontinental service across the Pacific to

Asia, originally through the somewhat impromptu use of sailing ships and then steamships. The first ship arrived from Japan in June 1887 –just three weeks after the first train reached Vancouver. Two years later the CPR secured a contract to provide monthly mail service to Japan and Hong Kong. Three luxurious steamships were built especially to serve this route, the first of these sleek Empress liners going into service in 1891. What became known as the 'all-red route' – red being the colour accorded the British empire on maps of the time – now linked Britain with her Asian and Australian colonies. Passengers in transit between train and steamship could even remain safely esconced within CPR comfort by resting up in Vancouver in an elegant new Hotel Vancouver built under its auspices. Or they could relax at the nearby opera house, completed by the CPR in 1891 as a condition of receiving land grants.

The Canadian Pacific Railway's position as principal property-owner determined settlement patterns. The Hotel Vancouver, the opera house, and the railway station were all located in the core of its landholdings rather than farther east in the original business district in Granville. Similarly, CPR officials did not move into the existing residential area between Granville and Hastings Mill; they opted instead for what became known as the West End, where the CPR was a major property-owner. Even the city's infrastructure was directly intended to benefit the CPR. Using a system just perfected in the United States, an electric street railway was operating by 1891, running in a circular route through the fashionable new business district along Hastings Street, south on Granville as far as Broadway, along Broadway, then back on Main to Hastings. The Broadway section predated settlement and was part of an arrangement made by the CPR to attract purchasers into its holdings on the south side of False Creek: the street railway company was given sixty-eight free lots in exchange for constructing the line and guaranteeing service every thirty minutes.

The Canadian Pacific Railway was Vancouver's single largest employer. Numerous CPR officials established their own businesses, and they actively encouraged investment. One of the most successful enterprises was a sugar refinery founded in 1890 by an American, Benjamin T. Rogers, with, to quote from his wife's memoir, 'certain concessions of land, free water, and a few years' tax exemption from the city.'[12] The first melt, using raw sugar from the Philippines, took place in 1891. Eventually 'BC Sugar' was being sold as far east as Manitoba.

By 1891 the CPR accounted for upwards of one-quarter of city revenue and employed between five and six hundred workers as officials, trainmen, or labourers out of a total Vancouver work force of about five thousand. Vancouver's role as a service centre was already taking shape: about three-quarters of employed men and women were working in trade, clerical, or domestic work, the professions or transportation.

Vancouver took on a settled look. Since everyone came from somewhere else, they usually brought with them strong preconceptions of what a proper city should contain. Much of the enthusiasm had a strong boosterish quality, the residents recognizing that their own well-being was directly linked to Vancouver's appeal to prospective settlers. A newspaper editorial declared in 1887: 'We cannot afford to stand still, progress is our watchword, if we desire others to make their homes with us, we must give them streets and sidewalks, water and light, sewage and protection from fire, schools and hospitals.'[13] The city fathers acted on this exhortation; during Vancouver's first half-decade, one hundred kilometres of streets were cleared and graded. Schools were built for two thousand students. Stanley Park, near the West End, was officially opened in 1888, having previously been a military reserve laid out by the Royal Engineers. A year later the city acquired Hastings Park near Hastings Mill from the provincial government for an exhibition garden and race course. By the time recession temporarily curtailed growth, no question existed but that the upstart settlement had become a forceful presence within the province.

Vancouver's principal competitor was Victoria, where the CPR's hand was also evident. The British ethos remained strong there, but now the capital city boomed. Many of the houses and commercial buildings that had long stood vacant were occupied and the population more than doubled between 1881 and 1891. And fully 60 per cent of homes were reportedly owner-occupied by 1890, suggesting a strong commitment to Victoria's future.[14] The value of manufactured goods tripled as the good times generated by the railway gave a much-needed impetus for expansion.

During the 1890s Victoria slowed down economically even as Vancouver again surged ahead following the downturn earlier in the decade. The reasons bear examination. Late nineteenth-century Victoria presented an ambivalent image to the outside world. Visually the city exuded prosperity, being a pioneer in both street lighting and streetcar service. Victorians prided themselves on having more telephones per capita than any other city in North America. A new building code limited downtown construction to brick or stone buildings, and during the 1890s many of the city's deteriorating wooden structures were pulled down. Nearby, the seaside resort of Oak Bay was transformed into an exclusive residential suburb by a process much like that occurring in Vancouver's False Creek. A land developer offered acreage to the local street railway company in exchange for the line being extended. New home owners were then given free streetcar passes. Victoria's dominance seemed confirmed by the 1893 decision to erect imposing new legislative buildings.

Yet it was during these years that Victoria experienced an identity crisis, as its traditional economic base in maritime shipping and manufacturing came under increasing challenge. Concentration on the mainland of the growing salmon canning industry helped reduce Victoria's share of provincial exports from 85 per cent in 1892 to just half of the total four years later. So did the collapse of sealing, a locally based and operated industry on which the city had come to depend for revenue. But by the turn of the century jurisdictional disputes with the United States over overhunting doomed sealing. A few years later, in 1905, Victoria lost another source of maritime-based income when Britain, as part of a world-wide naval reorganization, closed its base at Esquimalt. Its replacement by a much smaller Canadian contingent underlined the larger shift occurring as the province moved from a maritime to a continental orientation.

Victoria underwent deindustrialization.[15] The value of manufacturing fell by half. The immediate cause was the depression of the early 1890s, which hit the city particularly hard. Over the long run local iron works, shipbuilders, and other companies were simply unable to compete with central Canadian enterprises. Ontario manufacturers, with their large population centres, could produce on a much larger scale, and they did not have to contend with the CPR's discriminatory rate structure. For instance, it cost more to send manufactures from west to east than vice-versa. The reason lay in the logic behind the CPR, which was intended to operate at a profit. Since the railway was perceived, by the very fact of its existence, as benefiting the west, it followed that the west should absorb as much as possible the costs of operation. Such reasoning was reinforced by the pragmatic reality that rates had to be held down in central Canada, where the CPR was in direct competition with other rail lines and with water transport. Only in the west, where the CPR held a monopoly, could rates be set at will. Among the victims was the Victoria-based Bank of British Columbia. In 1900 the bank's English directors sold out to the Canadian Bank of Commerce, headquartered in Toronto.

At the same time as Victoria was being forced to reshape its destiny, Vancouver assumed dominance over the province's economic life.[16] The CPR's control was loosened as businesses from central Canada, in particular banks and insurance companies, began to establish branch offices in Vancouver to service the city and its vicinity. As the city spread, the wealthy and socially prominent opted for West End addresses, leaving to working people the original residential area farther east and the Fairview and Mount Pleasant bluffs looking north over False Creek. Social status was often underlined by membership in newly founded clubs for gentlemen in the tradition of those already existing in older cities. Early supporters of the Vancouver Club included the mayor, CPR officials, leading businessmen, and land developers. Civic government became more self-confident, engaging in a series of confrontations with the CPR. Vancouver's council even dared authorize a $300,000 bonus to a competitor who proposed to build a railway from Vancouver to the American boundary. Although the line never materialized, the point was made.

Vancouver's independence from the Canadian Pacific Railway grew with the Klondike gold rush of 1898. In total some two to three hundred thousand men and women headed north, perhaps fifty thousand of whom reached their destination. While the main business of supplying and transporting miners fell to Seattle, a considerable volume passed through Vancouver and to a lesser extent Victoria. The CPR quickly put two fast steamers on a Vancouver to Skagway run and attempted without success to run vessels on the Stikine River in British Columbia's far northwest. Vancouver and Victoria wholesalers, shipping agents, hoteliers, lumber producers, and a host of other businessmen benefited.

By the end of the century Vancouver had surpassed Victoria in size; the 1901 census revealed Vancouver's population as just over twenty-seven thousand as against Victoria's twenty-one thousand (see Table 17). By the time the Klondike gold rush had run its course a few years later, Vancouver had entered a second boom, usurping Victoria's traditional role as the principal port of entry. The city dominated coastal shipping, whose growing importance was evidenced by the CPR's decision of 1901 to buy out an existing company and so extend its operations in that direction. To complement its ocean-going Empresses leaving every third week for Asia, the new coastal fleet took the names of princesses. Best known among the CPR's several competitors was the Union Steamship Company, incorporated in 1889 with British capital. Whereas the CPR served Vancouver, Seattle, Vancouver Island, and selected points north to the Alaska Panhandle, the smaller Union steamships were noted for their willingness to call in at any place, however small.

Canadian Pacific influence extended across British Columbia. Through the southern interior its rail stops evolved into settlements. In the tradition of the Hotel Vancouver, the CPR built luxury hotels at Sicamous, Revelstoke, and Field. They began as meal stops for train passengers, especially in the early years before heavy dining cars could operate through the mountains, but grew into resort hotels. Divisional points such as Kamloops, where train crews changed, became distribution centres. Roads or water transport usually ran out of CPR stations some distance in each direction. Many early roads were seasonal, most accessible by stagecoach or pack train during 'the dry season' or when frozen in winter. The CPR soon added branch lines to New Westminster, to Sumas just across the border in the United States, and in 1892 to Okanagan Landing near Vernon in the northern Okanagan Valley.

British Columbia's terrain, which encouraged settlement in narrow river valleys or by lakes, favoured water transport in the interior as well as along the coast. Here, also, the CPR was soon active. Sternwheel steamers, in use since the beginning of the nineteenth century on the Mississippi River and then in the California gold rush, became the favoured craft, their construction seemingly designed for British Columbia's inland waterways. Flat bottomed, with a draught of only fifteen to twenty centimetres, the sternwheelers bobbed like ducks on top of the water. They were powered by a single paddlewheel at the stern, making a wharf unnecessary: the bow simply nosed ashore while the stern remained in the water. 'It can lie right in with its snout on the beach like a crocodile and back out again into deep water.'[17] A plank walkway was all that was needed to unload and load cargo and passengers. Viewed from a distance, a sternwheeler resembled a packing crate. The bottom of its three decks was usually given over to the actual operation and to space for upwards to two hundred tons of freight. The main deck contained passenger cabins, a dining room, and an observation lounge holding perhaps two hundred people. The smaller upper deck held the pilot house and officers' quarters. The first sternwheelers appeared on the Fraser and other rivers during the Cariboo gold rush, and their numbers grew on the railway's completion. Overall, about forty sternwheelers operated over time on British Columbia's waterways.

Across the interior the Canadian Pacific's sternwheelers were in competition with a variety of pioneer enterprises. When the CPR's branch line to Okanagan Landing opened in 1892, there was the single sternwheeler somewhat nonchalantly plying Okanagan Lake. The prospect of regular CPR service initiated a spate of land speculation as pioneer ranches were hastily bought up. This in turn ensured the success of the CPR's sumptiously fitted *Aberdeen*, launched in 1893 and named after the governor general, one of the first individuals to subdivide ranch land for fruit-growing in the area. Connecting three times a week with the train at Okanagan Landing, the *Aberdeen* took passengers south as far as Penticton. A connecting stagecoach ran to the American border. The trip from Okanagan Landing to Penticton took about six hours, depending on the number of calls the *Aberdeen* made to deliver or pick up goods or passengers. A white flag was sufficient for a lone settler to ensure that the vessel stopped at his landing. The Okanagan Valley was soon transformed from ranching to intensive settlement utilizing irrigation for growing fruit and grains.

The Canadian Pacific Railway energized the province's economy, which was still based on the exploitation of natural resources with very little processing undertaken in British Columbia itself. The character of the particular staple helped determine the development of social structures. British Columbia's first century of European penetration had been moulded by furs, coal, lumber, and, of course, gold. The province's topography, encouraging isolated clusters of settlement generally based in a single resource, exaggerated the relationship between economic livelihoods and the character of everyday life outside the workplace.

The province's economy during its first three decades was based on several staples. Agriculture never acquired the significance it held elsewhere in Canada, where it long remained a major employer and source of income. In every other region, at least half of all employed males were working in agriculture; in British Columbia the proportion was under one-fifth. At the turn of the century proportions elsewhere ranged from 45 to 64 per cent, compared to 13 per cent in the west coast province. Over 80 per cent of British Columbia farms were owner-occupied.[18]

Agriculture developed in the Saanich peninsula and coastal valleys of southeastern Vancouver Island, on the Gulf Islands, and in the Lower Fraser Valley. Growth is clear from post office openings (Table 15). The acquisition of a post office meant that a group of settlers possessed sufficient commitment to the area to make the request in the first place and were considered numerous enough by federal authorities to warrant the service. The individual appointed postmaster often also ran a general store. The small community might have a school and one or two churches, and some social life, such as Saturday night dances in the school house. The number of post offices in the Vancouver Island and the lower mainland regions tripled from thirty-four during the 1870s to over one hundred in the next decade and then to twice that number in the 1890s. By the mid 1890s a dozen of the most populous Gulf islands had postal service. In almost every case, these communities were based in agriculture.

Across the Lower Fraser Valley upwards of half a dozen post offices opened annually as newcomers arrived, sometimes from the United States, but more often from Ontario or elsewhere in Canada. While some were older men and women looking for a fresh start, many were younger sons unable to obtain land back home who came west to farm. Such farming communities as Richmond, Surrey, Delta, and Langley each attracted between two and three hundred settlers. Most early farms were on lowlands next to the river, which gave the combined advantages of proximity to water transportation and fewer trees to be cleared off the land. A spring flood in 1894 caused tremendous damage, after which private dikes were replaced by a government-assisted system. This opened up additional lowland which was especially suitable for dairying. A bridge built across the Fraser River at New Westminster in 1904 encouraged agricultural development in the valley.

Cattle-raising increased on the large internal plateau extending from the Okanagan through much of the central interior. Ranches appeared across the Cariboo and Chilcotin, even as existing spreads in the Okanagan began to be subdivided for fruit growing. A description from a few miles west of Kamloops illustrates how many ranches got their start. 'He, like many others, did not find gold in the gravel and had gone into the freighting business on the Cariboo road from Yale. He had saved his money, and bought himself a few cattle which soon grew into a herd. Running them on free range was fine at the start, but he had bought land at Cherry Creek and, by 1886, had built up a pretty good outfit.'[19] While many ranchers were satisfied with two to three hundred head of cattle, some aspired to more. The Douglas Lake Cattle Company in the Nicola Valley was organized as a syndicate in 1882 to supply CPR construction gangs with beef. By 1886 it comprised twenty-three thousand acres running twelve thousand head of cattle. At Douglas Lake, as elsewhere, cattle were usually driven to the coast to market. By 1891 almost twenty-four thousand cows and calves were being slaughtered annually in British Columbia.

Following British Columbia's entry into Confederation, lumbering stagnated, owing both to limited internal demand and to a lack of external markets. Then railway construction gave the industry a needed impetus, and for a time demand for wood for ties, trestles, bridges, bunkhouses and stations seemed insatiable. The completion of the railway opened up new markets and sources of supply. Timber cut near the line could be moved by rail in either direction. Just east of British Columbia lay the Northwest Territories – the future Alberta and Saskatchewan – and then Manitoba. Their largely unforested terrain made them suitable markets for BC lumber, and totals dispatched doubled in the decade following the railway's completion. As settlement grew on the prairies, so BC mills pioneered new products, including prefabricated houses. Lumber also went to varied destinations in Asia, along the coast of South America, and in Europe.

As lumbering became more extensive and moved away from the most accessible stands along the coast, so work processes and social structures generated by the staple became more complex. Indeed, a guide to British Columbia warned newcomers that 'logging and saw-milling will never be industries much relied upon by newly arrived emigrants from Europe as the various descriptions of labour required are best carried on by persons who have had special training.' Novelist and forester Allerdale Grainger termed loggers 'skilled artists.'[20] Horse, donkey, or oxen teams dragged cut logs along greased skid roads resembling a railroad without rails to the nearest body of water. Trees were so large in British Columbia – cedar at forty-five metres high and up to three metres in diameter, Douglas fir at over sixty metres the tallest tree in Canada – that, in order to get above the swelling of the roots, springboards had to be jammed into notches a metre or more up the trunk. The springboards were then used as a platform while felling the tree itself. By the 1880s a crosscut saw held by two men and designed with special teeth to pull the sawdust out as the tree was being cut was replacing the earlier double-bitted axe swung by a single man on his own or by men in pairs.

While some operations grew in size, hand loggers – distinguished by their use of hand tools – continued to work on their own or in two-man partnerships. Hand loggers often lived alone in the woods for months on end, much as did mining prospectors near their claims. Necessary equipment for small-time gyppo loggers – named for a perceived tendency to want to get things on the cheap by 'gypping' others – was limited to a couple of axes and saws, some food, and a small boat to cruise the coast looking for suitable stands of timber. The three or four trees cut each day were kept in a boom to await a tug sent out periodically by a lumber company or sawmill looking for logs to purchase.

Just as lumbering created its own social structures, so the young industry of salmon canning brought a distinctive set of relationships into being. Salmon had always been valued as a food in the Pacific Northwest. Fur traders soon replaced the traditional pemmican with salmon as their diet staple, each man allowed so many dried fish a day as his food ration. The HBC pioneered the export of salted salmon in barrels to markets in Hawaii and as far away as London. Britain in particular was eager for any available food products. As a prime industrial country it simply could not produce the food necessary to feed its population. Yet salmon possessed limited commercial potential as long as preservation techniques were uncertain.

The solution became putting fish 'in tin boxes.'[21] Canning technology, a by-product of new industrial processes permitting very thin, uniform sheets of metal to be rolled out, began on a small scale in Scotland in the 1820s. Spreading across the United States, it reached the Columbia River by the 1860s. There commercial salmon canning was well under way by the time the innovation made it to British Columbia. It was first used by Alexander Ewen, a Scots entrepreneur who had been exporting salt salmon to England. In 1870 he dispatched three hundred cases from a cannery on the Fraser River; each case contained one hundred squat cans holding a pound (half a kilo) of salmon. Shortly after, a pioneer black British Columbian, John Sullivan Deas, opened a cannery on an island in the Fraser River subsequently named after him. In 1877 the first commercial cannery appeared on the Skeena River, followed by others on the Nass River and at Rivers Inlet. That year fifty-five thousand cases were exported from British Columbia. Almost all of them went to Great Britain, where tinned salmon quickly became a popular, primarily working-class food; when Emily Carr went to study painting in England at the end of the century, she discovered that a local Anglican clergyman was only interested to know 'how many cases of salmon British Columbia shipped in export each year.'[22]

Salmon canning was a risky business demanding an extensive outlay of capital over a considerable period. There are five species of salmon in the Pacific Northwest, of which sockeye was, and remains, the most popular because of its colour, flavour, and uniform size. After travelling long distances across the north Pacific, salmon return to the coast in late summer, where they head up river to spawn upstream. To be successful, fishermen had to be in the right place at the right time. Usually they gathered at river mouths to catch the salmon en route. The process was described by a fisherman born in 1887: 'Fishing is quite complicated and that's what is interesting. You have to find where to go and when to put in your net, you have to think how best to use it each time and place, for high tide and low tide, when the wind is blowing and when it's calm.' A fisherman's daughter explained: 'The net is rigged with surface floats and sinkers and hangs like a curtain in the water. The salmon swim into the mesh and are caught behind the gills, hence the name gill-nets.'[23] Most boats in the early years were gill-netters, their nets' mesh being big enough to allow free passage of undersize fish but small enough to capture salmon of the desired size.

Canneries had to be located near where the fish were caught in order to process them while they were still fresh. Salmon runs follow a variable two- to six-year cycle, so that the number of fish caught each season is unpredictable. Poet Daphne Marlatt evoked 'fortunes made & lost on the homing instinct of salmon.'[24] Moreover, the materials needed for canning were not easily acquired in early British Columbia. Tinplate had to be ordered from England, and it was not until 1882, when the Victoria *Colonist* began printing them, that the necessary coloured labels were available in the west coast province.

Canning was very labour-intensive and created its own hierarchy. Beginning about June each year, cans were cut, formed, and soldered by hand. The fish were butchered, the cans filled, soldered shut, processed by steaming in boilers, labelled, and packed, all manually. It was hard to find workers willing to be employed for two months of the year at most, particularly as most Europeans were loathe to do manual work unless absolutely necessary. Canners tended to employ Chinese and Indian labour. A young employee described working in a Fraser River cannery which in the particular year produced over fifty thousand cases of sockeye salmon. 'The cannery employed about 300 men and women, 150 inside and the remainder fishing. Chinese, hired on contract through a boss-Chinese, were the backbone of the canning operation – cutting, slitting, firing the retorts and during the winter, even making cans. Tsimshian, Salish, Kwakiutl, and other Indian women filled tins, and a handful of whites supervised, kept books, and managed the plant.'[25]

At a smaller Skeena cannery, 'a Chinese known as the "China Boss" held a contract at a certain price per case from the time the fish were delivered to the last stage of nailing up the cases ready for shipment.'[26] The China boss was then free to exploit his thirty-man crew at will. The men may well have had their fares paid from China by the China boss and were bound to him until they had repaid the money out of their very low wages. Contract or indentured labour was common.

Even when fish and work-force co-operated, an interval of eighteen months to two years separated the time tinplate had to be ordered and money was received from the product's sale in Britain. Although Victoria merchants with direct trade connections in Britain arranged bank overdrafts, the industry was soon in the doldrums. Railway construction enticed workers away, and prices fell after Columbia River salmon flooded the English market. Canneries changed hands repeatedly; some closed for a year or more. Only with the end of railway construction did labour become more available. Gradually new markets opened up.

The risky nature of salmon canning encouraged consolidation. For example, the pioneering Ewen and Deas enterprises each acquired additional canneries. New financing became more accessible. Victoria's decline as the province's financial capital coincided with growing quantities of external capital willing to invest in a growing economy. In 1891 Henry Ogle Bell-Irving, a Scots engineer who had worked on rail construction, arranged a major infusion of British capital to purchase eleven existing canneries, which were then incorporated in London as the Anglo-British Columbia Packing Company. By the end of the year five large companies dominated the industry. Exports reached $2.3 million, of which fully $2 million went to Britain, most of the remainder to Australia. In the peak year of 1901 over a million cases of salmon were produced. The next year saw further consolidation with the formation of British Columbia Packers, backed by a consortium of central Canadian and American financial interests and incorporated in New Jersey as a shareholding syndicate. Thus, in the course of three decades a series of locally based entrepreneurial ventures had largely passed out of BC ownership. Salmon canning had become an international enterprise externally financed and controlled, although to a considerable extent locally managed.

For all the expansion of lumbering and salmon canning, mineral production remained at the heart of British Columbia's economy. The almost mythical search for the perfect gold strike continued. Hundreds of prospectors, many of them Chinese, still followed every new rumour to distant corners of the province. Over time, as placer deposits were depleted, the actual production of gold became increasingly a large-scale company business. By the mid 1890s placer gold was being surpassed in value by lode gold whose process of extraction was far more technically complex and expensive (see Table 20). Mines had to be tunnelled into the earth and the gold-bearing rock hauled out by the ton to be refined into a few ounces of gold.

Coal production grew steadily, levelling out on Vancouver Island in the early 1890s at just over nine hundred thousand tons a year. Coal mining remained largely unmechanized until the beginning of the twentieth century. It was hard work, performed underground in dirty, dark, damp, and often hazardous conditions. Open lamps provided almost the only illumination by which holes were drilled and charges laid. The coal when blasted loose was loaded onto waiting cars drawn by mules to the nearest shaft and lifted to the surface.

The two companies exploiting the coal mines on Vancouver Island represented a stark contrast in management attitudes and working conditions. The Vancouver Coal and Land Company, to which the Hudson's Bay Company had sold off its interests, believed that profits were directly related to worker satisfaction. Nanaimo was laid out as a townsite based on independent freeholders. 'I have never seen coal-miners so comfortable placed as those of Nanaimo ... every miner has his own house and garden.'[27] The company donated land for a park and promoted cultural and sports activities, all of which gave workers a vested interest in the status quo. When, in the 1880s, two major mine disasters killed 170 workers, their widows and children were given free housing and fuel as long as needed. The company's concern to have contented employees meant that new mines were opened as older ones became depleted. Technology was kept up to date and a workers' union recognized in the late 1890s. By 1901 Nanaimo's population exceeded ten thousand, of which over two thousand were employed in mining.

The philosophy of the other, much larger company on Vancouver Island was very different. The company's origins lay with Robert Dunsmuir, one of the HBC miners brought out from Scotland to Fort Rupert. His reputed willingness to side with the company against the workers led to his rapid rise into management. Always looking for the main chance, in 1869 Dunsmuir discovered a new coal seam at what became Wellington and very soon put together a consortium of British naval officers to bring it into production for the San Francisco market. Dunsmuir, now joined in business by his son James, used contacts with that city's railway entrepreneurs to buy out his original partners. When they obtained the charter to build the Vancouver Island portion of the transcontinental railway, the Dunsmuirs received a large federal subsidy and huge land concessions – fully two million acres – containing additional coal resources. The Esquimalt and Nanaimo Railway was then used to transport coal, pushing profits even higher.

The Dunsmuirs' total concern with profit extended to their treatment of employees. The accommodation rented to workers was primitive, lacking even running water. Men and their families were forced to use the company store, which was notorious for its high prices. Death and injury were commonplace because of company negligence, yet no provision was made for dependants, who were liable to immediate eviction. Whereas the Vancouver Coal Company hired experienced miners from Britain, Dunsmuir & Sons sought workers least likely to rock the boat. Chinese were hired at the lowest possible wages, in some cases directly from China under agreements making them little more than serfs. Continental Europe was another prime source of supply. Knowing no English, newcomers could not communicate with other employees to fight against poor working conditions.

The consequence became open confrontation. When in 1877 miners went on strike after wages were cut by one-third, Robert Dunsmuir used his political contacts to persuade the provincial attorney general to order in troops. Both the government and a miners' committee proposed arbitration. Dunsmuir responded by threatening to shut down his mines for a year, which would have had such a detrimental effect on the sluggish provincial economy that the attorney general agreed to the eviction and arrest of workers. After four bitter months employees were forced back to work, whereupon they received a further punitive wage cut of 5 per cent. Dunsmuir won hands down.

The ruthlessness that characterized the 1877 confrontation set the pattern for employer-employee relationships. The passage of time only made the Dunsmuirs more visibly ostentatious in their personal lives. The family's ability to use the provincial government to their private advantage became even greater after 1882 when the elder Dunsmuir won election to the provincial legislature and almost immediately entered the cabinet. After his death in 1889, son James took charge of the company. A year later another confrontation erupted, ending some eighteen months later with the miners yet again being forced back to work by company and state acting in concert. In 1898 James Dunsmuir followed in his father's steps politically, being elected MLA. Two years later he became premier almost by default, more because of his financial status as the wealthiest man in British Columbia than because of his political stature. Even as he was ruling the province, his mines continued to maintain their justly deserved reputation as the most dangerous in the world, with a death rate three to four times that elsewhere in the British empire.

Mineral production in British Columbia received an important boost late in the century through the spectacular opening up of the East and West Kootenays regions. The exploitation of major deposits of silver, copper, lead, and gold related much more to shifts in the global economy and to changing technology than to events within British Columbia or even in Canada as a whole. Indeed, the impetus was thoroughly American, as were work processes. Hardrock mining was technically complex, demanding considerable seed capital. The key lay in smelting – that is, extracting by chemical or other means some desired metal from the parent rock or ore. The ore to be smelted came from deep underground mines. Miners working in extreme heat with water seeping down on them out of the rock removed large amounts of the ore by drilling and blasting. As in coal mines, elaborate systems of timber supports had to be used to prevent the dreaded cave-ins.

Hardrock mining began in the western mountain states of the United States as part of world-wide revolution in metal technologies occurring in the second half of the nineteenth century. As more and more rail lines were laid and copper-wire telegraph lines strung, so demand for metals grew. Once northern Idaho was linked to the rest of the United States by rail in 1883, prospectors began to move even farther north through the same interior valleys that two decades earlier had prompted construction of the Dewdney Trail, precisely in order to contain American influence. Encouraged by a sharp rise in the price of silver, hundreds of mining claims were staked across the Kootenays and mining companies floated.

While most of the discoveries only raised and then dashed hopes, leaving countless ghost towns in their wake, a few became long-term profit-makers. In a pattern repeated many times in the province's history, speculation was rife. From local settlers and prospectors to international syndicates, everybody suddenly believed their fortune would be made overnight. A lucrative find of 1886 led to the foundation of the West Kootenay supply centre of Nelson, to which the CPR then hastily built a branch line. The best-known of the East Kootenay mines, the Sullivan at Kimberley, was opened in 1892. In the West Kootenays one of the most important discoveries occurred in the summer of 1890 on Red Mountain, following which American mining companies moved north from Coeur D'Alene to establish what would become the community of Rossland. By mid decade numerous Red Mountain mines, in particular the lucrative LeRoi, were attracting much speculative attention: the number of claims staked in the vicinity of Rossland, mostly by Americans crossing over the border, grew from a hundred in 1893 to almost two thousand two years later. The LeRoi itself employed over 250 men.

Although ore could be smelted at a distance, profits were greater if processing occurred near the mines themselves. Smelters proliferated across the Kootenays, including one at Trail – named after the Dewdney Trail – which was then linked to nearby Rossland by rail. When the Trail smelter proved unprofitable owing to its inability to attract sufficient ore, its American promoter sold both smelter and railway to the CPR. It was this purchase of 1898 that permitted the rail giant to take the lead in integrating the Kootenay regions into the Canadian economy. The process was assisted by American speculators turning their attention to the Klondike and so selling out to British and Canadian syndicates. The Crow's Nest Pass agreement of 1897 was critical. The CPR agreed, in exchange for receiving a massive federal subsidy, to build a branch line through the Crow's Nest Pass between British Columbia and Alberta and to lower freight rates in the two areas of concern to central Canada: the movement of 'settlers' effects' heading west and of grain going east.

Confident of the assurance of profit built into the Crow's Nest Pass agreement, the CPR quickly completed the promised rail link from Calgary. A new round of speculation was unleashed, one account musing that 'within a radius of perhaps thirty miles from Cascade [a rail construction site] the intending investor can have his pick of lots in over a score of townsites, all as it were destined to be the future Rosslands or Johannesburgs.'[28] The CPR's smelter at Trail gained access to large coal deposits located near the Crow's Nest Pass, which were being mined by the turn of the century. By this date the total value of coal produced annually in British Columbia approached $5 million.

The Great Northern Railway, which had in 1893 completed a line across the extreme northern United States, was also busy building several extensions into the BC interior. Over the first decade of the new century Americans acquired direct access via the Great Northern to Crow's Nest coal, the market town of Nelson, Boundary copper, Lower Fraser Valley farms, and even Vancouver itself. In hot pursuit, the CPR bought up both competing lines and Kootenay mines, including the Sullivan. In 1906 the CPR's various Kootenay assets were brought together into the Consolidated Mining and Smelting Company, in which the CPR held just over half the stock. Five years later Consolidated Mining acquired control over the fabled LeRoi mine at Rossland.

Economic development in British Columbia thus continued much as it had since the fur trade and gold rush: at the end of the century fully half the total value of goods and services generated in British Columbia came from primary products or their manufacture (see Table 19). Just 7 per cent emanated from secondary manufacturing, the remaining 43 per cent from the provision of services. The value of commodities sent abroad from British Columbia, having risen slowly from under $2 million in the first full year following entry into Confederation to about $3 million at the railway's arrival, doubled to $6 million by the time of the worldwide recession of the early 1890s. By the end of the century the total value of exports from British Columbia had grown to $17 million. Most of this increase came from the phenomenal growth in production of Kootenay silver, lead, and copper, whose combined value now surpassed that of either coal or gold.[29]

Social structures reflected the continued dependence on staples. Patterns of settlement were so shaped, most notably the rapid opening up of southeastern British Columbia, leading to the incorporation of Nelson, Rossland, and Trail in 1897. During the last decade of the century the population of the East and West Kootenays regions grew tenfold to over thirty thousand. Wage labour was far more common than the entrepreneurship associated with agriculture and small manufacturing. The transient male labourer symbolized British Columbia just as the farmer still characterized much of the rest of Canada. As the companies exploiting the province's resources grew larger and more impersonal, so the gap widened between capital and labour.

Government continued to view its role as encouraging exploitation as opposed to asserting any measure of control. Political alliances centred on two common concerns: maintaining the economic dominance of Victoria and Vancouver Island, and dispensing patronage in the form of jobs, land, and other concessions. An 1893 observation from the Okanagan Valley made the point: 'The local politics are summed up in roads and bridges and opposition to the Island which through its capital, Victoria, rules the mainland very unfairly.'[30] Animosities ran so high that a provincial university proposed in 1890 was thwarted by disagreements over its location. All the same, the artificial balance in numbers of provincial legislators between Vancouver Island and the mainland, which had existed since Confederation, could not be maintained indefinitely. The 1891 census revealed that six out of ten British Columbians lived on the mainland, and shortly after, the electoral map was redrawn to reflect the changing population ratio between island and mainland. The new constituencies still favoured rural voters on the assumption that difficulties of communication made outlying areas of the province more difficult to represent. In the 1894 election it took seventeen hundred to twenty-five hundred votes to get elected in Victoria or

Vancouver compared to two hundred or less in some outlying ridings.

To the extent that provincial ministries governed it was principally to dispense patronage. Everyday administration lay in the hands of government agents and other local officials appointed in a tradition going back to James Douglas's preference for well-connected young Britons with letters of introduction in hand. Teacher Jessie McQueen's 1889 observation concerning a Nicola Valley acquaintance just 'home from Victoria this week in high glee' was typical. 'No more pitching sheaves for *him* – he'd got his position, and was going to lead a *gentleman's* life! ... His "position" is a government one-police constable, recorder and I don't know what all, for Nicola, Granite Creek and Similkameen, and it's what he has wanted ever since he came out here.'[31]

On the other hand, it is equally clear that, in a tradition going back to the colonial gold commissioners, many officials undertook an extraordinary range of activities very effectively. The commissioner appointed to oversee British Columbia's far northwest during the Klondike gold rush of 1898 'stood alone for law and order in what could well have been a lawless land ... He served as friend, father confessor, and adviser. He also served as lawyer and a stern but just and benevolent judge. I do not know on what legal foundation his authority rested, apart from matters concerning gold claims, but it was never questioned.'[32]

The most rampant abuse of authority centred on the policy of granting publicly owned lands and resources to private entrepreneurs. By the terms of Confederation, all of British Columbia's 234 million acres not legally transferred to individual owners remained the property of the provincial government, being known as crown land. Permission to purchase or lease crown land – be it for grazing cattle, cutting down trees, or mining – early became, and long remained, a principal form of patronage. Six short weeks after settling in the Okanagan Valley, Charles Mair lamented that 'a lot of political shysters at Victoria & old chaps who packed in over the mountains from Oregon and Washington have got hold of all the best land, both bottom and mountain.'[33] Robert Cail aptly summed up the disposal process: 'From the 1860's to the 1910's there was scarcely a public figure in British Columbia who did not acquire large holdings of agricultural, pastoral or mineral lands. As far as it is possible to trace transactions through official sources, these acquisitions appear legal, but, undoubtedly, information acquired as a member of the government, or as a confidant of such a member, would have had potential value.'[34] In some cases farms and ranches resulted, in others speculators were simply receiving their reward for having supported the government in power.

The terms by which timber lands could be leased from the provincial government were generous, the annual rental for leases as long as thirty years being a few cents an acre plus a small royalty on cut timber. In 1892, under a slightly more assertive premier, John Robson, the first restrictions were enacted. One of the most important limited the amount of surveyed crown land that could be purchased to 640 acres, or a square mile. One particularly attractive means of obtaining crown land was through railway construction, as the CPR had done. Since a proposed line would inevitably opt for a valley route, this land was particularly valuable. As a first step, it was only necessary to fill out a printed form with names of directors and terminus location, have a sympathetic MLA propose the appropriate legislation, and then persuade a cabinet minister to set aside a land grant extending to many thousands of acres. Cail documented the incorporation of eighty-seven railway companies during the 1890s, of which only five lines were actually constructed and received their promised land grants.[35] Nonetheless, even these five grants exceeded six million acres in a province whose potential arable acreage totalled six and one half million and where nearly fourteen million acres had already been alienated in connection with the CPR, another two million to the Dunsmuirs for the Esquimalt to Nanaimo line. Moreover, the additional millions of acres so rashly set aside for paper lines remained in limbo and inaccessible for years and even decades.

In general, the politicians provided precious little in the way of government. The few publicly funded institutions operated as much because of precedent as official encouragement. Education was a case in point. A high school was established in Victoria in 1876, but up to the end of the century there were secondary schools at only three other communities – Nanaimo, New Westminster, and Vancouver. A rigorous entrance examination further restricted the number of young British Columbians remaining in school beyond the elementary level to a tiny minority. And, unlike almost every other jurisdiction across North America, the province had neither a university nor a teacher's training college. Young people seeking professional status were forced to apprentice or to go elsewhere. While some returned, many were lost to British Columbia. The situation was not promising.

During British Columbia's first three decades in Confederation the Canadian Pacific Railway provided the principal motif. In the interlude during which British Columbians awaited their promised line, little changed. Once the railway was in place, the west coast province acquired a new ethos and a new vitality. Yet the dependency on staples continued unabated. In many ways British Columbia only remained a company province, the CPR replacing the HBC.

Interior of Nootka house, with salmon drying from the ceiling.
Sketch by John Webber of Captain Cook's 1778 expedition

The arrival of Captain Cook's ships
at Nootka Sound, April 1778

Victoria in the late 1850s,
with the Hudson's Bay Company fort on the extreme left.
Watercolor by Sarah Creese

James Douglas, Hudson's Bay Company factor
and later colonial governor

The main street of Barkerville,
the largest of the Cariboo gold rush towns

The Cariboo Wagon Road
opened up the interior to gold miners and settlers:
a freight train along the road in the 1860s

Salmon canning:
top, a seiner; *bottom*, the 'iron chink,' a mechanical device for gutting fish
which displaced Chinese labour

A Chinese laundry on Water Street in Granville, 1884

East Indian workers at
North Pacific Lumber Company, East Barnet,
in the early twentieth century

Native packers

A native family placer mining

A potlatch at Alert Bay about 1910
with housewares probably purchased for cash
being given away

OPPOSITE

Two young Indian women enjoying a break
at the Imperial Cannery at Steveston, 1913

Victoria at the time of the First World War,
with the Empress Hotel and the new Parliament Buildings

7

Population Explosion
1886–1914

Between the completion of the Canadian Pacific Railway and the beginning of the First World War in 1914 British Columbia underwent a demographic transformation. In less than three decades the province's non-native population expanded almost tenfold, even as the Indian people declined by one-third. A fragile settler society on the frontier of the western world became a self-confident political and social entity.

The population explosion occurred in two overlapping stages. With the coming of the CPR, settlers poured in from Ontario and the Maritimes. The second phase was promoted by the federal government's campaign to populate western Canada as the third prong of its National Policy. While intended primarily to settle the agricultural west, the initiative attracted thousands of men and women to British Columbia. Many of them came from Britain, restoring the province's earlier ethnic balance. By the time the First World War curtailed immigration, British Columbia's population reached 450,000.

As rail construction began in the early 1880s, British Columbia was home to under twenty thousand Europeans along with about twenty-five thousand Natives and four thousand Chinese. The trickle of arrivals turned into a steady stream once the railway was completed, and by the beginning of the 1890s the province was transformed. Whereas numbers of Chinese more than doubled the European population tripled. Both groups doubled once again over the last decade of the century, even as the native population was slowly declining (see tables 5 and 7). By the turn of the century British Columbia's population stood at almost 180,000.

The plurality of new arrivals came from within Canada. In 1881 just thirty-five hundred British Columbians – under one in eight – were born elsewhere in Canada; by 1891 the number had shot up to over twenty thousand, or almost one in three. Over the next decade the total doubled to more than forty thousand (Table 8). For the first time British Columbians born elsewhere in Canada exceeded the number born in Britain.

Various factors brought men and women to British Columbia. A shortage of agricultural land in longer settled areas of Canada, as well as in the United States, played a role; the rich land in the Fraser Valley was a magnet for enterprising Ontarians and others. Chain migration often occurred, family members following in the wake of an adventurous individual. Within months of arriving from Pictou, Nova Scotia, the young teacher Annie McQueen found her sister Jessie a job in the neighbouring school in the Nicola Valley. When Annie married a year later, her sister cajoled a childhood friend out to replace her. Lured by the much higher salaries in the west – in the case of the McQueens in 1887, $60 a month compared with $60 for six months in a similar Nova Scotia school – many Maritimers came out to teach in British Columbia's fledgling schools.[1]

British Columbia's staples economy was particularly conducive to male migration. Throughout the 1890s British Columbia contained just one non-native adult female for every three males. Table 11 makes the point, as does Jessie McQueen's exasperation: 'Oh I'm just sick of the faces of men.' Moreover, as an elderly male settler complained, 'they are all young men.'[2] As a consequence, men tended to marry later in British Columbia than in any other province, while women's mean age at marriage was the lowest at twenty-two years (see Table 12). Not surprisingly, the fertility rate in British Columbia was among the highest in Canada (see Table 13).

British Columbia was finally becoming Canadian, or so it seemed. The Canadian Pacific Railway had wrought its magic in joining the scattered provinces together. Sporting contacts proliferated: lacrosse, an Indian game long ago taken over by Canadians in the east, was enthusiastically adopted on the west coast. Canadian intellectual George Parkin visited western Canada in 1892–3 and summed up the railway's function as 'to draw those provinces out of their own narrow circle and give them the sense of a larger citizenship' to complete and round off a national conception. Two early provincial histories highlighted the CPR's role in finally bringing British Columbia into Confederation. American Hubert Howe Bancroft, who based his 1887 work on many interviews with pioneer British Columbians, considered the province's conditions and prospects most closely linked 'with the Dominion of Canada.' Alexander Begg termed the railway the 'Union of East and West.' Somewhat later, the historian Walter Sage concluded that, as a consequence of the rail line, 'by 1901 east and west in Canada were really joined and "the West beyond the West" had become Canadian.'[3]

Some Canadian travellers took a certain satisfaction in ridiculing British Columbia's lingering British ethos. A visitor at the turn of the century found Victoria 'delightfully old-timish' ... 'Where are the stocks and dunking-stool, I wonder?' The future lay in emulating Ontario. 'Ontario is in many respects the progenitor of British Columbia, and from Ontario's broad shoulders the lusty and vigorous child has looked on to the future.' While still a young province, 'he gets more like his dad every day.' As the century drew to a close Henry Crease, in many way the prototype of Victoria's pioneer British settlers, admitted to a colleague that, despite all of his efforts to maintain his children's heritage through such financial sacrifices as sending them back to school in England, 'While you and I talk of the Old Country as "Home," all our children call Canada "Home." '[4]

In many ways British Columbians were not so much emulating social structures in Ontario or the Maritimes as they were developing a sense of self, influenced certainly by the rest of Canada. Just six weeks after settling in the Okanagan Valley in the early 1890s, Charles Mair was making unfavourable comparisons. 'These people know nothing of Canada. In fact they deride everything Canadian ... It will be a very rich Province, but it must be *Canadianized*. It is not that yet.' Put another way, British Columbians were creating their own traditions. Such accepted features of daily life as 'the cannon that went off at Esquimalt for people to set their watches by every night' took on ritualistic significance.[5]

British Columbians' growing pride in their pioneer heritage was evident. The first published histories began to appear, and a government librarian was appointed to 'collect and compile data relating to the history of the Province.' The change was equally visible on an everyday level. Emily Carr recalled of her Victoria childhood how 'Sometimes Mrs. Cridge [wife of a colonial Anglican clergyman], Mrs. Mouat [possibly the widow of an HBC sea captain], Doctor Helmcken, and some of Sir James Douglas' daughters, all of whom had lived in the old Fort, would start chatting about old days, and then we young people would stand open-mouthed thinking it must have been grand to live those exciting experiences.'[6]

Social life took on a certain unique quality, even when building on practices elsewhere. On Queen Victoria's birthday on 24 May, in Victoria, 'we wore our Summer frocks for the first time.' On Mayne Island, 'afternoon events, featuring foot races and water sports, were followed by a dance in the evening.' Settlers in the Nicola Valley celebrated with a grand picnic: 'three hams, half a sheep, six chickens, chicken pies, beef-steak pies, corned beef and a *turkey!*' were followed by 'all kinds of cake, buns, bread, pies, & puddings' and 'ice-cream, candies, nuts, oranges, ginger beer etc etc.' Activities included a football match and a tug of war. A photographer 'set up his apparatus on the grounds on conditions that he shared profits with the managers of the picnic.'[7]

Fall fairs and harvest festivals became popular, giving support, both symbolic and real, to a growing sense of community. Neighbours competed in displays of their handcrafts and produce, as if to convince themselves and others that all the hard work had been worth while. By the late nineteenth century camping had become a favourite pastime for families of all classes. Mair, aged fifty-seven in 1895, went camping at Kalamalka Lake with his wife. He then took the entire family, including his daughter and new husband, to 'pitch tents down the Okanagan.' The same year a Victoria judge completely reassembled his household on Cordova Bay beach into 'a long line of tents – about dozen, each with a crossed British and Canadian flag at the top, and a two plank side walk in front of the line.' Included were a dining tent, a cooking tent, and a separate tent for the family's Chinese servant. By then the camping craze was so widespread that some beaches were entirely covered. Evenings were given over to sitting around the camp fire, fuelled by the plentiful driftwood, and listening to roving 'amateur musicians.'[8] Pioneer Vancouver families transplanted themselves to the beaches along English Bay, both immediately adjacent to the West End and along the bay's south side extending west to the cliffs of Point Grey.

Social barriers in the young society responded to British Columbia's particular mix of peoples. A certain ambivalence existed towards the groups in the middle, neither members of the dominant society nor so visibly different as were Chinese and native people. The several dozen Kanakas who had opted not to return to Hawaii fished on the Fraser, worked as millhands on Burrard Inlet, or farmed on Saltspring or a nearby Gulf Island. While the first generation mostly wed native or part-native women, many of their children, especially daughters, married Scandinavian, German, and other European farmers and loggers.

The Spanish-speaking packers, who had arrived from Mexico during the gold rush, had similar experiences. Those who turned to ranching in the Nicola Valley were given the right to vote and considered 'residents' but yet not quite 'white.' The 1876 British Columbia directory made clear their intermediate status: 'Population of Nicola District up to December 31st, 1876. White male adults, 55; white female adults, 24; white children, 40; Mexican male adults, 8; half-breed children, 24. Total population bona fide residents, 151.' As with the Kanakas, some wed native women, many of the children then marrying Europeans.

Attitudes towards the Chinese were far less conciliatory. They, along with native Indians, for long went unnamed in the annual provincial directories that otherwise listed every adult male or family head across the province. Although individually enumerated in the census, as were some Indians, the Chinese did not really much matter. Names in census rolls were routinely simplified, occupations identical for pages on end, and ages rounded off to a convenient 0 or 5. Many of the Chinese brought in to work on the railway were simply assigned the surname of Ah.[9]

Judge Begbie aptly summed up the general view of the Chinese in his observation that 'they are generally abused, and yet everybody employs them.' Since the earliest days of the gold rush the Chinese, together with the native peoples, were indispensable to the economy. A German visitor quickly observed that, 'besides the Indians, the Chinese are the most important working class element.'[10] Many came as indentured labourers, popularly termed coolies. Money for travel was advanced in China, the worker being bound to the lender until its repayment. The contractor, often a Chinese who spoke English, made arrangements with prospective employers, such as cannery or sawmill owners, to supply so many workers for a season or other specified period. Most Chinese ended up being paid one-third to one-half less than Europeans in the same job, which extended the time before they could save sufficient money to venture out on their own.

Promises were not always kept, as in the apparent commitment to repatriate labourers brought to work on the CPR. No one was willing to shoulder the financial responsibility and the men were left to shift for themselves wherever they happened to be working last. Some set up locally in jobs that no one else was willing to undertake, becoming laundrymen, market gardeners, and owners of small stores and restaurants. Virtually every British Columbian community acquired its Chinatown. Others turned to placer mining or worked in lumbering, salmon canning, coal mining, or agriculture.

Both Victoria and Vancouver were from their beginnings home to a large number of Chinese immigrants, several hundred of whom worked as house boys. The middle-class practice of relying on Chinese servants went back to the colonial years, when female domestic help was scarce. A Victoria matron was so grateful that she wrote a friend, 'God, I'm sure sends such Chinamen as all good things come from Him.' Another's comment was similar: 'Life here for a women depends, my dear, a good deal upon the Chinese ... If you are lucky, and treat your Celestial well, he seems to me to be a treasure beyond price.' The Vancouver West End household of social reformer Helen Gregory MacGill survived on a day-to-day basis through Gong's talent for 'creating a happy comfort with his good cooking, good housekeeping and good nature.'[11] A census taken in Victoria in 1886 found that almost one in three residents were Chinese. The Chinese accounted for one in five non-native British Columbians in 1881 and one in ten through the end of the century.

As numbers of Chinese grew, so attitudes hardened. The dominant society institutionalized discrimination, which appeared to many, not just in British Columbia but across the western world, to be 'scientifically' justified. Charles Darwin's Origin of the Species, published in 1859, was perverted into a concept legitimating racism based on biological characteristics. Out of the inevitable struggle to exist, so the adherents of social darwinism argued, the fittest survived, be they animals or human beings. To determine which of the races was the fittest, it was only necessary to compare western technological achievements and the growth of capitalism with the rest of the world. What became known as scientific racism argued that the peoples of the world were arranged in a hierarchy with whites at the top, a theoretical perspective that also seemed empirically demonstrated by

European colonizing exploits. In the extreme case, non-whites were deemed biologically perverted and not even within the bounds of humanity.

As early as 1873 an anti-Chinese society was formed in Victoria to curb competition in the workplace. The next year Chinese and native Indians were provincially disenfranchised. In Victoria and elsewhere bylaws and regulations supposedly intended to raise health and sanitation standards were in reality directed against Chinese entrepreneurs. In 1878 the provincial legislature banned Chinese from government employment.

The provincial government repeatedly enacted poll taxes or entry restrictions only to have them disallowed by the courts on the grounds that, under the British North America Act, only the federal government had the power to regulate immigration. British Columbians quickly concluded that central Canadians did not understand their situation given that, as of 1881, over 99 per cent of all Chinese in the country lived in British Columbia. Comparisons were made with the United States, which in 1882 passed a Chinese exclusion act denying entry for ten years to Chinese labourers lacking certificates of residence. As a compromise, a federal Royal Commission on Chinese Immigration was established in 1884, followed a year later by parliamentary disenfranchisement of Chinese and the imposition of a $50 head tax on new arrivals. Such measures did relatively little to satisfy opposition, increasingly led by trade unions convinced that the Chinese offered unfair competition in the workplace.

The reality was that many Chinese, because they were used to poor living conditions in their homeland, were willing to accept lower wages and harsh conditions of employment. Most were from a small rice-growing area in southeastern China where overpopulation and a shortage of land gave priority to increased productivity. Irrigation and fertilization demanded capital, provided by young men going abroad to work and sending money home. The social structure was based in the extended family. Surplus males could leave secure in the knowledge that their families would be cared for until their return. Men's willingness to do so was reinforced, as historian Paul Yee has pointed out, by religious beliefs. 'Confucianism taught that in a harmonious society, all people accepted their station in life.'[12] Originally these temporary migrants, or sojourners, had gone to southeast Asia, but increasingly North America was considered the best possibility.

Until about 1900 most Chinese came as contract labourers; thereafter they were more likely to arrive to join family members. Once a Chinese male earned the money needed for the fare home, he would go for a visit, returning with a young nephew or other relative who would then begin the chain anew, possibly also with a wife. The long-term goal of earning sufficient money to return home permanently did not necessarily change. Alternatively, if death came unexpectedly, it was the custom to have one's bones sent back to China. Carr described the practice in Victoria. 'On the far side of the cemetery the Chinese ... lay in rows in front of unpainted headboards with only Chinese characters written on them ... When there were bones enough they would all be gathered together from the graves and shipped back to China.'[13]

The consequence was a vicious circle: the circumstances by which Chinese came only exacerbated racism on both official and everyday levels. The mood was caught in a letter written from British Columbia concerning an acquaintance who bought goods locally rather than sending for them by mail order. 'She hasn't as much of the Chinaman in her as I have and doesn't think it fair to take all the money she can get here and spend it somewhere else.'[14] Because many Chinese came as sojourners, they were not interested in long-term integration into Canadian society but rather sought, while temporarily away from home, to maintain so far as possible a familiar lifestyle. Most Chinese immigrants were male, and they tended to keep to themselves and form communal and clan associations which encouraged such traditional leisure activities as gambling and opium smoking. Language and dress heightened differences with Europeans. As Carr, one of the least racist of her generation of British Columbians, observed: 'The Chinese kept themselves entirely to themselves like rain drops rolling down new paint – learning our ways, keeping their own. When work was done ... off they went to Chinatown to be completely Chinese till the next morning. They learned just enough of our Canadian ways to earn Canadian money – no more.'[15]

Other newcomers to British Columbia set themselves off by choice from the dominant society. The desire for an isolated lifestyle underlay several group ventures of the late nineteenth century. Bella Coola Valley on the central coast was settled by about 150 Norwegians, Cape Scott on the northern tip of Vancouver Island by a colony of Danes, and Sointula on Malcolm Island off northeast Vancouver Island by some hundred Finns. In the case of the Norwegians, their idealism was reflected in the constitutional provision that 'every member of this colony must abstain from import, manufacture, export or in any other way whatever the use of intoxicating drinks.' Having earlier emigrated to the American Midwest, they soon became unhappy with its poor economic conditions and an unfamiliar prairie landscape. By comparison, as the Lutheran minister prospecting the west coast for a new home enthusiastically reported back, 'in this Bella Coola Valley you have many features of your beloved homeland of Norway,' including a long fiord and steep mountains.[16] A block of land acquired from the provincial government was divided by lot with many tasks shared out in common. School teacher Ivar Fougner wrote in his diary on 5 August 1894 before leaving northern Minnesota: 'The present is occupied by building air-castles about British Columbia. Of course they will never become real, but anyhow they serve to bright that present ... *Idealize* the *Real* if you can't *realize* the *Ideal*.' At first disappointed, Fougner wrote two years later: 'I can't leave the colony without a great sacrifice – I love her too well for that.'[17] Some of the original settlers soon departed Bella Coola but others took their place. While the remoteness of their settlement would defeat the Danes and internal dissension split up the Finns, the Norwegian colony at Bella Coola survived largely intact as an ethnic community well into the twentieth century.

Yet, even as distinctive identities were emerging, British Columbia was again being demographically transformed. The province's population doubled over the first decade of the new century to almost four hundred thousand. While part of the growth was due to natural increase, most of it resulted from a federal immigration campaign launched in 1896. Critical to the National Policy's success was the west's growth through mass settlement. As the minister of finance put the case at the turn of the century: 'The best way you can help the manufacturers of Canada is to fill up the prairie regions of Manitoba and the Northwest [the future Saskatchewan and Alberta] with a prosperous and contented people, who will be consumers of manufactured goods of the east.'[18]

A decision to look abroad for population made good sense. For over two centuries most European countries had more people than their economies could support. Surplus population had already fanned out to European colonies, indigenous populations often being displaced, as in the case of Canada, to make room for the new arrivals. So long as the United States offered free homesteading land, little incentive existed to head farther north to an area less conducive to agriculture. But in the mid 1890s several factors came together in Canada's favour: the transcontinental railway opened up the country; the American west was filling up; and hardier wheat strains and dry-farming techniques suitable for the Canadian prairies were coming into use. The depression of the past few years began to lift about the same time as a more dynamic federal government came to power under Liberal Wilfrid Laurier.

Some sixty million acres of prairie land were opened for homesteading, and another eighty million put up for sale by the CPR and private entrepreneurs. The application process for immigration was speeded up and an advertising campaign launched in Britain, continental Europe, and the United States publicizing Canada as a land of promise, particularly for hardy farmers able to withstand cold prairie winters. The federal thrust was complemented by the initiatives of a growing number of interested parties, ranging from community boosters and land speculators to the CPR concerned to fill its trains and sell its land.

Between 1896 and the First World War the face of Canada – and particularly that of the west – fundamentally altered. Canada's population mushroomed from five to eight million, the proportion living west of Ontario rising from a tenth to a quarter. At first it seems a bit unclear why the campaign for more settlers should have affected British Columbia. It was aimed at prospective farmers, and the province possessed a limited number of fertile valleys suitable for agriculture, even with irrigation. Unlike the prairies, where land could be had for free, it had to be purchased either from the provincial government or, increasingly, from private speculators at market prices. British Columbia was, quite simply, not a province for the poor homesteader.

Yet men and women headed for the coastal province. Some came unaware of the poor outlook for farming. Others were persuaded by a milder climate or by ready work in resource industries. Overall, British Columbia attracted a different mix of immigrants than did the prairies. There the preponderance of settlers arrived from continental Europe or the United States. In British Columbia that proportion was under one-third. The majority – over half in 1911, 60 per cent by 1921 – came from Britain or its colonial possessions (see Table 9).

Overall, about 175,000 Britons arrived in British Columbia during the immigration boom. The consequence was to drive up the number of British-born in the non-native population from one in five to one in three. The proportion born elsewhere in Canada dropped back to one-fifth, that from continental Europe being just over 10 per cent. The earlier preponderance of Britons was returned.

There were several reasons. The province so optimistically thought to have been Canadianized by the transcontinental railway was in reality more complex. Contemporary perceptions of British Columbia differed greatly depending upon the beholder's assumptions and disposition. While some writers at the turn of the century were struck by a growing Canadian orientation, others emphasized the province's traditional Britishness. Its mostly mild climate, breathtaking scenery, excellent opportunities for shooting and fishing, and long-standing everyday social practices, such as driving on the left, were all remarked on. The British travel literature of the day was replete with such observations as 'it is very curious how the British Columbian prefers the Englishman to the Canadians of the Eastern Provinces,' and 'the nearer you approach to the Pacific the greater are the influence of English example all around.'[19]

Britain's foremost author of empire, Rudyard Kipling, became caught up in the rhetoric, declaring, 'were I rich ... I would swiftly buy me a farm or a house in that country for the mere joy of it.' Like many contemporaries, he began to believe what he wrote. The sales pitch to buy property that was made to him on his first visit to Vancouver in 1899 was irresistible. 'I give you my word it isn't on a cliff or under water, and before long the town ought to move out that way. I'd advise you to take it.' So he did, spending about $500 for two lots in Vancouver's Mount Pleasant neighbourhood. Returning in 1907 Kipling noted approving that their value had risen to about $2,000 and decided to hold on. He eventually sold out in about 1929.[20] Britons who by choice or force of circumstance opted to emigrate had ample reason to feel comfortable heading for British Columbia.

As more British immigrants arrived, so a renewed British ambience attracted yet others. Even Vancouver, born of central Canadian business interests, found its proportion of British-born residents doubling over the first decade of the new century. A visitor mused that, although the city was the province's most distinctly Canadian town, 'in Vancouver and to a certain extent all over British Columbia, the typical Ontario man would not feel at first quite at home.'

Historian Norbert MacDonald has pointed to such ordinary – and sometimes overlooked – aspects of everyday life as 'the prevalence of British accents among its store clerks, school teachers and police-men – the number of British papers in newsstands, the abundance of Tudor houses, and the popularity of flower gardens.' For thousands of Britons, many of very modest backgrounds, the west coast province beckoned. While some became part of the large transient labour pool that underwrote the resource economy, others soon took on the trappings of respectability. A British traveller reported 'a wonderfully large number who a few years ago left England or Scotland as clerks or artizans, and are now in a flourishing condition in Vancouver, doing a big business and living in large residences in the far-extended suburbs.'[21]

The British presence was particularly striking in the case of middle-class settlers, about twenty-five thousand of whom migrated to the west coast province during these years. The image of the remittance man surviving on periodic injections of cash from home – money sent in some cases precisely in order to ensure continued absence from Britain – was so widespread that it became a popular literary device. Saki's Bertie 'had gone to grow tea in Ceylon and fruit in British Columbia, and to help sheep to grow wool in Australia.' He had 'just returned home from some similar errand in Canada,' novelist H.H. Munro here following the British practice of continuing to distinguish between British Columbia and Canada.[22] While British Columbia attracted its share of young adventurers, others were older, often with a career in the military or the colonial service behind them. A desire for companionable surroundings encouraged resi-dence in Victoria or some other area amenable to a genteel lifestyle. Favourite places evoking the England countryside were the Cowichan Valley, the Gulf Islands, the Okanagan Valley, and the Kootenays. Often buttressed by a pension or other small income, the newcomers genteelly farmed or grew fruit.

Whatever the locale, middle-class Britons sought to re-create familiar class-based institutions, ranging from social clubs to private schools on the British model. Underlying their actions was the same assumption of superiority over the host society that had a half-century earlier been exhibited by many colonial Victorians towards Canadians. A preference for a leisurely lifestyle further divided many middle-class Britons from industrious Canadians imbued with the Protestant work ethic. A writer of 1912 explained, 'Canadians are critical of the English fruit-growers, as they say that they spend many a working hour playing tennis, and by no means come up to the dour ideal of "all work and no play."' Freya Stark described her father, who had gone out to the Kootenays to grow fruit prior to the First World War, as 'an incarnation of leisure, for his business depended on the seasons, whose movements encouraged no feelings of hurry except at harvest-time ... *The Times* came to him regularly, and he had a small shelf of books which he read over and over, admitting a newcomer now and then, after much deliberation.' Common affiliation with the Church of England, or Anglican church, encouraged superiority. As one woman put it as late as 1925, although personally she 'would greatly prefer Anglican to Presbyterian, on account of the beautiful service, ... the Anglicans often think they own the earth.'[23]

In retrospect it is clear that this generation of Britons exercised influence beyond their numbers. They entrenched a British Columbia regional accent which was widely accepted until well into this century. 'Many acquired the English accent without having set foot in England, or for that matter, travelled farther than Seattle or Vancouver.' As far back as 1882 Princess Louise had approvingly observed 'that the English language was spoken in old country accent & not like Canada.' A Victoria visitor over half a century later, in 1938, 'had always heard that it was very like an English town, but truly it almost *is* English, and so is the prevailing accent.'[24]

The social institutions that these immigrants transplanted soon extended into society as a whole. Private schools on the British model became favoured by many Canadian families. Men and women who made their fortune in the golden west sought for their sons and daughters, not the shared experience offered by the public school, but rather the attributes of social exclusivity inculcated by its private counterparts. Over the first half of the twentieth century about a hundred private schools on the British model of class-based privilege were founded across British Columbia. While some were small private ventures enduring a handful of years, others became major boarding institutions enrolling a hundred or more boys or girls. Their common consequence was to reinforce social and economic divisions in British Columbia from the top down.

The welcome extended to immigrants largely depended on their place of origin. The racism that legalized discrimination against Asians was extended, in varying degrees, to all arrivals. In the sense that British Columbians of the dominant society were racist – and indeed they were – they did not restrict their antipathies and prejudices. Visible minorities were but the tip of a much larger iceberg. It was the almost universal assumption, held not just in British Columbia but across English Canada, that immigrants should learn to conform to an Anglo-Protestant stereotype which those in positions of social and economic power equated with themselves and with them to the prestige and pre-eminence of the British empire.

General agreement existed that newcomers from Britain, elsewhere in Canada, the United States, and Protestant Northern Europe would make the best British Columbians. Some distinctions applied. English immigrants from poor or working-class background were often disparaged. For a time 'No English Need Apply' signs were commonplace in parts of British Columbia. Arrivals from elsewhere in Canada probably found their warmest welcome in the lower mainland, already extensively settled by people from Ontario and the Maritimes, or in newer areas of the province. Newcomers often clustered together, in part through the actions of land developers, in part by choice. Across the Okanagan, enclaves of middle-class Britons in the Coldstream area and near Kelowna were interspersed with Manitobans at Peachland, Summerland, and Naramata, Saskatchewaners at Rutland, French Canadians at Lumby, and Swedes at Mabel Lake.

There was a greater ambivalence towards continental Europeans, particularly if they were poor, swarthy in appearance, or Catholic. The adult generation, while necessary across western Canada for 'much of the rough work of nation-building,' was often written off for the purpose of assimilation.[25] In the case of British Columbia, the rough work translated into railway construction, coal mining, and such large resource projects as the smelter at Trail and pulp and paper mills being established up the coast at Ocean Falls and Powell River. Large numbers of Italians in particular worked at Trail and Powell River, mostly as brute labour. On the other hand, considerable hope was held out that the second generation would, through attendance at public school, become good Canadians.

Even though, seen through the eyes of the dominant society, continental European ways were to be disparaged, men and women somehow managed to survive and in some cases actually flourished. A Lower Fraser River settlement was a case in point.[26] Gradually over the years the river's south arm, extending from New Westminster to the coast, became filled with scow houses – floating homes on rafts. Those at Brownsville were occupied by northern Norwegians. The nearby canning centre of Annieville was home to southern Norwegians. Beyond lived a third group from the middle of Norway, all fishermen. To quote a contemporary, 'just below them, at Sunbury, were Finns, and several miles further down, at Deas Island, there were Greeks [who] nearly all came from one island.' 'They generally had what they called lutes ... and they had their sing-songs and dances under the trees.' 'A bunch got around in a kind of a semi-circle and held hands and just danced around.' Below Deas Island were some Basques, often heard 'talking about sheep in the old country' and, just as did the Greeks, about going back home once they made some money. Adriatic Islanders settled at Port Guichon. Unlike the others, they had 'brought their wives and families with them from the old country, and [so] they decided to become Canadians right away.' Fraser River fishermen in their modest scow homes were building community.

So were other continental Europeans. The gardens of proud Italian families were soon the envy of neighbours, be it in Cumberland, Powell River, or Trail. As early as 1900 Italian miners in Extension, soon also at Nanaimo and Cumberland, formed their own self-help society. In exchange for dues of one dollar a month, benefits were paid in case of injury or sickness of one dollar a day up to one hundred days and then fifty cents a day for another year. The society's dances, banquets, and group picnics encouraged ethnic solidarity.[27] Through mid century Trail was filled with Italian organizations and shops, with 'women going about their shopping who might have come straight from Naples; they still spoke Italian among themselves, and some of the older men had hardly any English.'[28] For these men and women British Columbia was just as much home as for their contemporaries of British background.

Among continental Europeans arriving during these years and after the First World War were new groups seeking separation from fellow British Columbians, notably Doukhobors and Mennonites. The two religious groups each grew out of Protestant Reformation traditions emphasizing the church as a community of the saved as opposed to a means to salvation. Because the dominant society was secular, its authority was unacceptable, be it swearing an oath or bearing arms. The two groups shared a common background of oppression, the Mennonites first in Germany and then in Russia, the

Doukhobors in Russia. Mennonites began leaving Russia in the 1870s fearful of the introduction of conscription, which ran counter to their pacifist beliefs. About seven thousand headed for the Canadian prairies where they were later joined by around twenty thousand brought out of Russia in the mid 1920s. Some 7,500 Doukhobors departed Russia for Saskatchewan at the turn of the century, under the spiritual leadership of the charismatic leader Peter Verigin. There dissatisfaction soon built up over demands that homesteaded land be registered individually, which ran counter to Doukhobors' belief in authority being vested only in the community as a whole.

The Doukhobors and Mennonites who moved on to British Columbia did so as intact communities strongly opposed to contact with the host society. Between 1908 and 1922 some five thousand Doukhobors communally purchased over twenty thousand acres in the West Kootenay and Boundary regions. Living on farms in houses with up to fifty people each, families re-created the austere, self-contained lifestyle and economy they had known in Russia. Mennonite families began arriving in British Columbia after the war, mainly from the prairie provinces. One group settled near Prince George in 1922. At Yarrow in the Lower Fraser Valley, where Mennonites took up land in 1928, they probably came closest to maintaining traditional ways of life. The village was physically patterned after its Russian counterpart, with narrow frontages and deep rears to houses. The everyday language was German. Local government comprised a council and schulze, or mayor, and the church formed the centre of social life. Mennonites maintained themselves as an intact group by buying farms or lots as close together as possible. As numbers grew during the inter-war years, so self-sufficient Mennonite settlements came to dot the Fraser Valley and to a lesser extent the central interior.

Doukhobors in particular kept relationships with other British Columbians to a minimum, particularly in the case of their extremist wing, the Sons of Freedom. The institution generating most tension was the public school, viewed as assimilating children away from their traditional culture. 'Just as soon as the person reached read and write education, then within a short time leaves his parents and relations and undertakes unreturnable journey.' The absence of a written holy book gave no meaning to literacy. 'We adopt our children to learn at wide school of Eternal Nature.'[29] Provincial regulations requiring compulsory attendance from age seven were met by Doukhobors with alternating semi-compliance and confrontation. For their part, Mennonites sent children to the local school and also to Saturday school to learn the German language and study Mennonite traditions. As Mennonite communities became more economically secure, so private schools were opened. For Doukhobors and Mennonites it was long possible to live in British Columbia without becoming part of British Columbia.

Even less desirable as immigrants were the Asians, not just Chinese but also Japanese and East Indians who began to arrive in growing numbers. The Asian presence continued to be far greater in British Columbia than anywhere else in Canada. In 1901 the province contained almost twenty thousand out of the twenty-two thousand Asians resident in Canada, by 1911 over three-quarters of the total of almost forty thousand.

The Chinese remained by far the dominant group. The small minority of women who arrived – some one to two hundred annually – often fared worse than did their male counterparts. While some became wives, others were brought over on contract as prostitutes, servants, or wage labourers. Some Chinese, particularly the minority that had married, were no longer sojourners. Alongside a Chinese-language school, their children attended public school. Scattered but unsuccessful attempts were made to segregate them.

Japanese began arriving in the 1890s. Although not identifying with the Chinese or seeing themselves as having common interests, the Japanese were generally viewed by white British Columbians as part of a single 'Oriental menace.' In 1895 the Japanese together with East Indians, then arriving only in minute numbers, were provincially disenfranchised. Like the Chinese, the Japanese were mostly single men. Principally fishermen, they favoured such areas as Steveston on the Fraser River. Near the canneries that provided their livelihood, they lived, as evoked by the poet Daphne Marlatt, in 'wooden houses jammed on pilings, close together, leaning, with wooden walks & muddy alleys, laundry, & dry marsh grass that stutters out of silt the dykes retain, from a flowing ever eroding & running river.'[30] Numbers grew, particularly at the turn of the century when a quarantine in Hawaii, another favoured destination, encouraged over eleven thousand Japanese to land in Canada. Some headed for the United States, others remaining in British Columbia.

Numbers of East Indians also grew. What contemporaries termed

'Hindoos' but were in reality Sikhs from the Punjab began trickling in at the turn of the century, principally to go into logging which in India was largely a Sikh occupation. During the peak years of 1905 to 1908 about five thousand came. As was the case elsewhere in Asia, they were pushed to emigrate by overcrowding and a surplus of male labour. Coming as sojourners, they were, like other Asians, concerned to maintain their customary lifestyle while temporarily residing abroad. Sikh religious dress of turban and beard, short trousers, and sword made them, if anything, more visible than the Chinese. This was particularly the case with the small minority who ended up begging on Vancouver streets. Despite living mostly in logging camps and sawmills, Sikhs acquired a reputation for quarrelsomeness, in part a carry over of Indian communal disputes.

Tensions heightened, even though immigrants from Asia declined as a proportion of the population. Actual numbers doubled to forty thousand by 1921, and it was this situation that renewed the ongoing dispute with the federal government over the knotty issue of putting controls on Asian immigration. A new round of discriminatory acts was passed provincially and then disallowed federally. In 1902 the head tax on Chinese coming into Canada was raised to $100 and another royal commission established. After it concluded that Asians could not be assimilated but that Japan at least seemed willing to restrict emigration, the head tax on male Chinese was raised in 1903 to $500. In 1908 the manufacture and sale of opium was banned in Canada.

Open racism repeatedly erupted. In the fall of 1907 rioting broke out on the streets of Vancouver. An Asiatic Exclusion League, which had been formed as a working man's association to protest what were perceived as unfair labour practices, scheduled a mass meeting on hearing rumours that another boatload of Asians was about to arrive. The evening was hot and sticky as a parade wound its way through Chinese and Japanese sections of the city, singing 'Rule Britannia' and shouting anti-Oriental tirades. Eventually seven thousand men and women were jammed outside city hall with another two thousand inside, all listening to inflammatory rhetoric. The crowd drifted back into Chinatown, less than a block away, and then towards the Japanese area. Window-breaking heralded four hours of rioting. Much damage was done, although, as Prime Minister Laurier later reported to the governor general, 'the Japs showed fight, turned upon their assailants and routed them.' The ambivalence of many

Canadians was clear from his very next line. 'This is at once a cause for rejoicing and for anxiety; rejoicing because the rowdies got a well deserved licking; anxiety because this may make the Japs very saucy, and render an adjustment of the trouble more difficult.'[31] The federal government was forced to respond. A diplomatic agreement with Japan limited emigrants to Canada to four hundred a year. The next year immigration from Asia was restricted to continuous passage from country of origin to Canada in order to keep out the growing numbers arriving in stages by way of the Hawaiian Islands, whose sugar economy relied on contract labour.

The new law precipitated a second major outbreak of racism on the west coast. A wealthy Sikh, who had made a fortune by importing BC lumber into Asia, determined to challenge the new restriction by hiring a Japanese steamer to take 376 prospective Sikh and Punjabi Moslem immigrants to Vancouver via Hong Kong, Shanghai, and Japan. The *Komagata Maru* was forbidden to land on its arrival in the summer of 1914 and sat in Vancouver harbour for two months while its backer argued for the illegality of the 1908 continuous passage legislation. In the end the act was enforced, and the ship returned to Hong Kong. The only subsequent concession was a 1920 ruling that East Indians already in the province could bring over their families, which reduced tensions.

The reasons why the dominant society in British Columbia reacted so strongly against individuals of Asian origin have concerned historians. The economic argument is persuasive. Willingness – or rather the necessity – to work for lower wages threatened both jobs and rates of pay offered other employees. Trade unions long opposed Asian immigration on the grounds of unfair competition, and it is probably a fair generalization that working people were at the forefront of popular opposition. Many middle-class British Columbians may have been less racist only because it was to their advantage to rely on cheap labour. Yet economics alone do not explain the virulent anti-Asian feeling extending across so much of the European population. Many jobs that were unpleasant and low-paying, such as those in salmon canning, very early on were done by Asian immigrants together with native men and women. Asians were legally excluded from many occupations, in some cases through government insistence. Both BC Sugar in Vancouver and the Powell River Company had stipulations in their agreement with the city and province respectively prohibiting the use of Oriental labour in their mills.[32]

In *White Canada Forever* Peter Ward considered the explanation to lie in white British Columbians' yearning for a racially pure society. 'Heterogeneity would destroy their capacity to perpetuate their values and traditions, their laws and institutions.' Patricia Roy has emphasized a variety of concerns: 'Some whites based their antipathy to Asians on real or anticipated economic conflicts; some were inspired by notions of racial differences; most had a number of reasons, both real and irrational, for their hostility and would have had difficulty in ranking their objections.'[33] Members of the dominant society wanted to believe that they belonged to a superior race yet doubted their ability to compete economically with Asians, all other things being equal. No single explanation suffices to explain the antipathies that so long existed.

The differing treatment of newcomers by the host society should not be allowed to obscure the human dimension of settlement. Whatever individuals' ethnicity or race, the actual process of adjustment was never easy. The daughter of a middle-class British couple arrived in the Okanagan after thirty years in India recalled her mother's initial reaction: 'And she looked at all of us. And she never said anything: she only said to my Father, "If you excuse me, Falkland, I think I'll go to bed" ... and she cried herself to sleep. She said, "Thirty years I've travelled with your father, and this is what we've come to: a wooden table, benches to sit on." '[34] Finding work was often far more difficult than anticipated. Some were forced to be always on the move from one casual job to another; others were transients more by choice. Ivar Fougner, a founding settler of Bella Coola, caught the mood in a diary entry made shortly before joining the idealistic venture: 'Oh, for a home of my own. A place where I should stay and be content; Give it me, and the peace of mind, dearer than old! ... Wanderer in life, where is your goal?'[35] Work in the various primary industries was frequently short term. Men moved time and again before finally securing a job to their liking – or perhaps more accurately to fulfilling the demands of an employer able to pick and choose from a large itinerant labour pool. Grainger's protagonist in *Woodsmen of the West* epitomized the wanderer. 'From the time when, as a boy of sixteen, he revolted against the grinding monotony of the little farm in Nova Scotia, to the present day, ... as Carter of Carter & Allen, loggers, Coola Inlet,' his wanderings took him far and wide. Beginning in eastern logging camps, Carter became a trapper in the Cariboo. He moved to Seattle and then to a Montana mine. The Klondike gold rush enticed him briefly. He left there to fish for a Skeena cannery before becoming foreman of a pick-and-shovel gang on the railway. After running a saloon in a Kootenay boom town, Carter spent 'a few weeks lying round Seattle, drunk most of the time' before moving up the British Columbia coast. Asked why he moved on time and again, Carter merely replied: 'I kind of got tired of that town and the people.' Yet, while frequenting 'saloons and dance-houses along with the boys, having a hot time,' Carter ruminated over whether he should have married and settled down. 'It's kind of cheerful for a man to come home from work and find the shack all tidied up, and a fire burning, and supper all ready cooked, and someone to wash his clothes and look after him.'[36]

Even men possessing some attributes in the form of job skills, schooling, or finance floated. On arriving from London in 1908, respectable young Arthur Shelford spent his first month with pick and shovel on a railway gang, moved onto a road crew, and then to a stint as a rough carpenter before deciding 'to try work in the coast logging camps.' A year later, on pre-empting land near Ootsa Lake in the remote central interior, 'my inward nature searching for the mode of living which would best suit me' he was finally satisfied.[37]

Journalist Bruce Hutchison recalled the experience of his reasonably well educated father, dispatched from England as a young man. Failing in real estate in turn-of-the-century Cranbrook in the East Kootenays, he became a reporter for the local newspaper, attempted to start his own paper in a nearby smelter town, grew plants for sale, and then simply abandoned his family for several years before turning up about 1910 in Merritt in the southern interior as 'John Hutchison, Limited, Notary Public, Real Estate, Mines, Investment.' According to young Hutchison, the supposed firm was 'apparently limited to him, since no associate ever appeared in the office.'[38] It was through political pull that Hutchison eventually secured a permanent position as a government clerk in Victoria.

The population explosion beginning with the Canadian Pacific Railway and culminating with the First World War transformed British Columbia. First seemingly becoming a Canadian province and then reverting to a British orientation, in reality British Columbia had a way of making newcomers its own. Geography and the economy helped determine patterns of settlement which were unlike the rest of Canada.

British Columbia's location at the end of the line, literally and figuratively, brought together peoples that might not otherwise have shared a common space. At the same time topography combined with the prejudices of the day to encourage distinctive ways of life. To the extent a sense of community emerged it was often equated with the locality – a Gulf Island or a coastal inlet, the Nicola Valley or the Kootenays. Some arrivals – Chinese, Doukhobors, Mennonites, middle-class Britons – sought to maintain their old ways. Discrimination isolated British Columbians the one from the other. The entity known as British Columbia largely remained a political abstraction.

8

Disregard
of Native Peoples
1858–1945

The difficulties of discussing the native peoples' role in early British Columbia are almost as great as understanding their lives at the time of initial contact with the Europeans. The written record continued to come largely from a single perspective, that of Europeans, who viewed aboriginal populations from a predetermined set of assumptions. Nonetheless, just as ships' logs contain useful observations, so subsequent accounts are often more revealing than originally intended. Brought together and disentangled, these sources show the fundamental change British Columbia's first peoples underwent as a consequence of European settlement. They also demonstrate the tenacity with which native men and women maintained their dignity and ways of life.

Adaptation did not begin with the Europeans' arrival, nor was it one-sided: just as Indian lives altered through contact, so did those of Europeans. Bands and tribes had long borrowed new practices or behaviours from trading partners. Indians never existed as in a museum in some perfect, idyllic state; adaptation to changing circumstances was an accepted part of everyday life. What altered was the speed with which change occurred and Indians' lack of control over its onset and direction.

Events in British Columbia were only one small part of a world-wide transformation of indigenous populations. 'By the end of the Victorian period hardly a people remained on the face of the earth whose social structure, culture, and basic way of life had not been more or less violently disrupted.'[1] Almost everywhere numbers were decimated. This stark reality in no way excuses events in British Columbia, but it does provide a useful reminder that the damage done was not particular to the province. Compared even with events in neighbouring Washington and Oregon, Europeans behaved less brutally than they might have done. The province experienced none of the prolonged wars waged around the world, be it south of the border or in other British colonies such as New Zealand and South Africa. Nonetheless, the native population in British Columbia was devastated, reaching a low point of about twenty thousand men, women, and children in the early twentieth century.

Indigenous people were easily shunted aside. They were sometimes perceived as nuisances, particularly in their persistent demands to retain land. Overall, the dominant motif of the Europeans was disregard rather than conquest or elimination. As a consequence, native peoples in British Columbia were never completely stripped of their self-respect or dignity. They were able to retain elements of their earlier ways of life while adjusting to the new social and economic order.

The fur trade may have eased the way. Maritime traders' expectation that they might return to the same place the next year to collect pelts encouraged friendly relationships. Land-based traders were dependent on local men and women not just to acquire furs but for their very survival. Linkages extended through the entire range of human relationships. Indians responded. At the time of the move to Vancouver Island, James Douglas observed that Europeans had no enemies. 'Instead of thirsting for their blood, the Natives are not only kind and friendly, but ready and willing to share their labours and assist in all their toils.'[2]

Douglas believed in the essential good will of most Indians. Unlike the United States where crimes by natives brought indiscriminate group punishment, persons accused of illegal acts against Europeans were treated as equals before British law. Douglas thus argued against a punitive expedition undertaken by Governor Blanshard on the grounds that 'in all our intercourse with the Natives, we have invariably acted on the principle that it is expedient and unjust to hold *tribes* responsible for the acts of *individuals*.'[3]

But change was in the air from the moment gold was discovered on the British Columbian mainland. Practical exigencies turned Douglas's attention elsewhere even as Indians came into contact with

Europeans far less considerate of native rights than fur traders had been. Most arrivals brought with them assumptions about other, supposedly inferior, peoples not tempered by personal contact. In 1861 Amor de Cosmos, then editor of the *British Colonist*, could write: 'Shall we allow a few vagrants to prevent forever industrious settlers from settling on the unoccupied lands? Not at all ... Locate reservations for them on which to earn their own living, and if they trespass on white settlers punish them severely. A few lessons would enable them to form a correct estimation of their own inferiority.'[4] For de Cosmos and many other recent arrivals, land became 'occupied' only when settled by their own kind.

No further treaties were negotiated after the first fourteen. Once the Colonial Office took over from the Hudson's Bay Company, Douglas requested funds to acquire additional property for European settlement, only to be told that it was not a priority. Land purchases were a purely colonial responsibility not to be borne by the British taxpayer. Douglas did include in the proclamations establishing land policy in the two colonies clauses prohibiting the pre-emption of Indian settlements. His intention was that Indians should select the land they wanted for their reserves. In practice, land policy became chaotic after 1858, and little surveying took place.

Douglas's departure brought a complete policy reorientation. His successors, appointed from England, accepted the popular prejudices of the day. The Bute Inlet incident of 1864, one of the few bloody encounters between Indians and Europeans in British Columbia, strained relationships. The roadbuilders' deaths were met by utter disbelief in the Victoria press. How could 'strong robust fearless' Europeans allow themselves to be killed by 'cowardly savages'?[5] A posse not unlike those in the American west was organized. While tempers eventually cooled, a precedent was set for mass reprisal and for Indian inequality before the law.

A perception of natives as untrustworthy was reinforced by administrators' advice coming increasingly not from an aging generation of traders but from self-interested settlers and land speculators. In their view the treaties negotiated by Douglas did not establish a precedent. Payments made to the different tribes had been 'for the purpose of securing friendly relations between these Indians and the settlement of Victoria, then in its infancy, and certainly not in acknowledgment of any general title of the Indians to the land they occupy.'[6] Much of the land allocated by Douglas was taken away. On the reserves that were set up, families were allotted a maximum of ten acres. By comparison, individual Europeans could pre-empt 160 acres and then purchase up to 480 more.

The legal position of British Columbia's indigenous population was fundamentally altered in 1871 when the colony joined Confederation. Section 91 of the British North America Act made Indian peoples the responsibility of the federal government. Control was exercised through laws and regulations known collectively as the Indian Act. Originally promulgated in 1869, an 1880 revision of the Indian Act established a separate Department of Indian Affairs. The department's goal has most often been viewed as assimilation but, at least in the case of British Columbia, its policy was primarily intended to ensure that the native peoples did not challenge the dominant society. Parsimony was the order of the day: other branches of government received far greater attention and comparatively more funding than Indian Affairs ever did.

The federal government's Indian policy in British Columbia reflected several critical misconceptions concerning native peoples. The first assumed their inferiority. Social darwinism was based on a belief in white superiority. Europeans' ways were by definition civilized. Europeans were also committed to the capitalist ethic which was grounded in individualism, private ownership of property, and the profit motive. They simply could not understand how those societies that espoused alternative philosophies could be anything but inferior. This view was admirably caught by Ethel Wilson in her description of 'the usual Indians standing leaning against the corners of the wooden [train] station' in Lytton on a hot summer afternoon prior to the First World War. 'The Indians always looked as though they had nothing to do, and perhaps they had nothing to do.'[7]

The second misconception built on the first. Europeans had for centuries cultivated the land, whereas the native peoples used it for hunting and gathering. To Europeans land was not 'owned' until settled and used for private gain. Indians simply roamed the face of the land, which was, to quote an observer, 'lying waste without prospect of improvement.' Land could, so the argument went, be justifiably claimed for Europeans' higher purposes. The 'indolent, contented, savage, must give place to the bustling sons of civilization & Toil.' New Westminster's newspaper claimed that 'according to the strict rule of international law territory occupied by a barbarous or wholly uncivilized people may be rightly appropriated by a civilized or Christian nation.' In the view of an 1882 visitor, 'it is an injustice to the whites who desire and need the land for homes and cultivation' to allow bands to retain even their reserves if not put to 'profitable use.'[8]

This misconception, prevalent in British Columbia, ran counter to British policy as it had been enunciated in the Royal Proclamation of 1763. By its provisions the crown prohibited settlers from occupying territory until its formal surrender by representatives of the indigenous population. Title to land had to be extinguished prior to its occupation by non-natives. At the time British Columbia entered Confederation treaties already existed in long-settled areas of Canada, and negotiations were under way on the prairies. Only one of these treaties would extend into present-day British Columbia: Treaty No. 8, signed in 1899, included the northeast region east of the Rocky Mountains. Lands were ceded in exchange for reserves averaging 128 acres per person, a small annual sum of money, and Indians' 'right to pursue their usual vocations of hunting, trapping and fishing throughout the tract surrendered' except where taken up for other purposes such as settlement.[9] While largely imposed by the Europeans, these treaties recognized the principles of indigenous ownership and of distinctive cultures.

The third misconception viewed Indian ways of life as detrimental to the Indians themselves. The complex social organizations that distinguished bands and tribes held no meaning for most Europeans. Typical was the exasperation of a provincial official that as late as the 1930s Indians in the northeast 'are roving and have no permanent place of abode; they have been allotted their reservations, but do not live on them except during a short time in the summer to receive their treaty money ... Their whole existence is the killing of game.'[10] Whereas indigenous peoples looked to the needs of the group as a whole, Europeans viewed the individual or possibly the family as the fundamental unit of society and made no attempt to understand any other perspective. Elements of matrilineality were at odds with European patriarchal assumptions and simply disregarded. Cultural activities such as the potlatch were interpreted by European standards and denounced.

Finally, many Europeans believed that indigenous peoples were going to disappear in any case, regardless of how they were treated. On one level, this misconception was the ultimate extension of Europeans' belief in their own superiority. An extreme interpretation of survival of the fittest viewed all indigenous peoples around the world as physically doomed. As one visitor to the Pacific Northwest mused, 'a succession of races, like a rotation of crops, may be necessary to turn the earth to the best possible account, and consequently the Indians must be removed to make room for others.' Even some Indians began to believe in their own eventual destruction. The pioneer ethnologist James Teit wrote in 1900 concerning the Thompson of the southern interior: 'The belief that they are doomed to extinction seems to have a depressing effect on some of the Indians. At almost any gathering where chiefs or leading men speak, this sad, haunting belief is sure to be referred to.'[11] From this perspective, it made little sense to spend great sums of money or even to take much care of Indian peoples.

This misconception had some basis in reality. The horrendous effect of European infectious diseases, compounded by alcohol, was obvious to contemporaries. The worst of several smallpox epidemics, in 1862–3, killed some twenty thousand of British Columbia's native population, already down to about sixty thousand. As soon as smallpox broke out in Victoria, infected Indians camped nearby were sent back home and so spread the disease along the coast and through the interior. Well into the twentieth century tuberculosis was responsible for many deaths. The nadir was reached, according to census data summarized in Table 5, in 1911 when the total number of Indian people in British Columbia dropped to 20,200. Periodic counts made by the federal Department of Indian Affairs differed; by their calculations the low point came in 1929 with 22,600 Indians resident in British Columbia. The decline was accentuated by the tremendous growth in the non-native population, from 30 per cent of all British Columbians at entry into Confederation to over 95 per cent by the First World War.

It was from these four misconceptions that federal Indian policy was implemented in British Columbia. The two principals were Indian agents and Christian missionaries. So that the Department of Indian Affairs could exercise its mandate, provinces were divided into districts, or agencies, each with its own Indian agent. British Columbia eventually contained twenty such agencies. Within each jurisdiction the Indian agent had the authority to settle disputes, encourage appropriate economic activity, and dispense welfare. Some agents were friendly with Indian people; others generated a very different response: 'for ordinary day-to-day needs, the Indian Agent was the last person we asked for help.'[12]

The authority of the agents was often reinforced by Christian missionaries. They were the foot soldiers in the government's efforts to manage indigenous peoples. By the time the first Europeans reached the Pacific Northwest the missionary impulse had become extremely powerful not just in North America but around the world. The conversion of heathens, as indigenous populations were termed, extended beyond belief in Christianity to acceptance of the European social order of which Christianity was an integral part. The very use of the term civilization to define that society underlines the extent to which Europeans had come to see themselves and their faith as inherently superior to aboriginal peoples.

The early efforts of missionaries in the Pacific Northwest met with middling success until Indians' numbers began to fall and traditional authority to weaken – a circumstance the missionaries then attributed to the Indians' sinfulness. One of the earliest missionaries in British Columbia was William Duncan, an Anglican lay minister who for over three decades ministered on the coast. Duncan put the obvious logic to prospective converts: 'Tsimshian are not happy but poor – miserable and diseased. Why so? Because their way is not God's way. You *see* misery follows sin here? Why do you stick to your sins then?'[13]

Most missionaries sought a complete reshaping of the Indians' lifestyle. Duncan arrived at the old Hudson's Bay post at Fort Simpson in 1857, and with a self-confidence that sometimes bordered on arrogance, set out not only to convert but totally to obliterate existing ways of life. Appalled by the detrimental consequences of Indians' contact with European traders and miners, in 1862 Duncan moved his Tsimshian followers twenty-five kilometres away to Metlakatla, to what Jean Usher Friesen has termed 'the city on the hill, the utopia in the wilderness.' Explaining why native people should have so readily acquiesced, Friesen has concluded: 'Duncan was offering them a set of rules to follow and the promise of eternal life if they followed him, and this was no doubt attractive to a disoriented people.'[14]

By the time British Columbia entered Confederation, virtually the entire province had been divided up between the various religious denominations. It was understood that where one missionary group had already established itself a competitor would not intrude. There were, to put it crudely, enough Indians to go around. The result was a number of little Victorian enclaves over which a Catholic, Anglican, or Methodist missionary or family exercised supreme authority.

Trusted converts became assistants, particularly in the Catholic Oblate system developed by Father Paul Durieu in Oregon Territory. A single priest kept control over a large territory through a carefully structured hierarchial system of native chiefs, catechists, and police-men who ensured that traditional practices were not resumed between his visits. For two decades Father Adrian Morice, from his headquarters near Fort St James, oversaw fourteen separate settle-ments of nominal Catholics spread across New Caledonia. As his biographer has shown, Father Morice built 'a veritable kingdom for himself' premised on complete control over his converts.[15]

The efforts of Duncan, Morice, and their counterparts were furthered by the popular appeal of the missionary life. For women, missionary work was one of the few occupations outside of the home open to them. While accepting the European racist view of the inferiority of aboriginal peoples, Christian missionaries still believed in their potential to be saved and civilized by European standards. The inconsistency between the two halves of the equation caused anguish in some minds, but the dilemma was most often simply set aside in the interests of conversion as a feasible first step.

Federal policy towards Indian peoples, as implemented by Indian agents and missionaries, sought to reorder the three fundamental components of natives' lives: their relationship with the land, their unique social structures, and the way they educated their young. Article 13 of the terms of union committed the federal government to 'a policy as liberal as that hitherto pursued by the British Columbia Government.' As part of that policy, 'tracts of land of such an extent as it has hitherto been the practice of the British Columbia Government to appropriate for that purpose' were to be conveyed 'to the Dominion Government in trust for the use and benefit of the Indians.'[16] It is possible that the federal government assumed that the prairie precedent of extinguishing land title by treaty would hold, but from the British Columbia perspective it was the government's colonial policy that was confirmed. The difference was considerable, for on the prairies a minimum of 160 acres per family was being reserved. When in 1873 federal officials suggested allotments of half that size, the British Columbia government countered with four acres and then offered a short-term compromise of eight. Negotiations simply broke down.

By the mid 1870s even the Canadian governor general acknowledged that it had been a mistake not to have recognized aboriginal title. By then the existing policy was too firmly in place to be easily reversed; for one thing, the cost of compensating Indians for land already alienated would be too great. As a compromise, the federal government established a land commission to draw up boundaries for the reserves, which generally comprised village sites, hunting grounds, and fishing stations. At first the province stalled, but growing native dissatisfaction in the interior forced a degree of co-operation. Hostilities were defused when Indians were allowed to address the commission, which expressed some sympathy for their cause. But the commission's work was soon neutralized by provincial intransigence and a change of chairman. Thereafter it responded almost entirely to setters' desires, operating up to 1910 without fully settling the land issue.

A successor body was intended finally to resolve the problem. In reality, the royal commission set up in 1913 to adjust acreage of Indian reserve land only gave an official stamp to the earlier body's actions. Commissioner J.A.J. McKenna summed up its attitude in a speech to interior chiefs, where he asserted that 'a strong race had supplanted a weaker ... Indians must accept the inevitable. Progress and development could not be stopped.'[17] The recommendations of the McKenna-McBride Commission, as it is generally known, removed forty-seven thousand acres of mostly good land from reserves in return for eighty-seven thousand generally poor acres. The value of land taken away was three times that added to reserves. Reserve policy became a vehicle for pushing the Indian peoples as far out of sight as possible. For example, the Songhees reserve on Victoria's inner harbour was bought out in 1911, its residents moved to a more isolated location. Much the same occurred with Indians in the Okanagan and those who had for a long while been living in what was becoming 'the white man's town' of Prince George.[18] Indian people were left with 843,000 acres as reserves. This represented less than 0.4 per cent of the province. There the matter rested.

The second prong of federal policy sought social reorganization. Reflecting the Indian Act's growing coerciveness, the revision of 1880 permitted the replacement of traditional leaders by individuals acceptable to federal officials. The complex social organizations of the coastal bands and tribes were ignored. Social structures were also redefined through the classification of a person's 'status' which was made the criterion for determining who was an Indian and therefore allowed to live on a reserve, receive government services, and be otherwise subject to the act's provisions. Status Indians comprised men initially so registered in 1886, with their wives and children. Non-native wives automatically acquired status. Conversely, in provisions based on the patriarchal assumptions of the day and revised only in 1985, any woman marrying a non-status Indian or a non-native lost her status. The woman's children were denied the right to acquire status, even if the marriage was subsequently dissolved.

Indians' traditional ceremony of potlatch created particular offence. The notion that a social event could occur apparently only in order to give goods away was utterly alien to Victorian standards of sobriety and thrift, with pride of place given to materialist, capitalist accumulation and to private as opposed to public display of wealth. Indian agents witnessing men and women working for years on end to be able to afford a potlatch denounced the institution as 'foolish, wasteful and demoralizing.' Missionaries believed it to be 'by far the most formidable of all obstacles in the way of the Indians becoming Christians, or even civilized.'[19] In 1884 federal legislation made it a misdemeanour, subject to imprisonment, to engage or assist in a potlatch. A rash of arrests followed, but the main effect of the prohibition was to create greater tensions in an already uneasy relationship. The continuation of potlatching was generally acknowledged among Europeans in contact with native society.

During the First World War the Indian agent at Alert Bay initiated a sustained effort to apply the potlatch law. Kwakiutl were given the option of surrendering 'all their masks and regalia and everything they owned from the Indian way' or being arrested. Those who refused were brought into Alert Bay and tried. In the case of one Kwakiutl, 'the time I have a potlatch when my brother died, I was arrested for it about three months after ... I was sentenced for three months.' Over twenty Kwakiutl were convicted and jailed, their material culture shipped off to the National Museum in Ottawa. A young Kwakiutl witnessed the event. 'The scow came around from the cannery and put in at the village to pick up the big pile of masks and headdresses and belts and coppers – everything we had for potlatching ... Our old people who watched the barge pull out from shore with all their masks on it said: "There is nothing left now. We might as well go home." When we say, "go home," it means to die.'[20] More than ever Indian agents became policemen rather than the advisers they were intended to be.

The third emphasis of federal policy was on schooling. Missionaries soon became convinced that, while adults could be converted, they were less readily 'civilized' than were members of the younger generation. Duncan early set up a classroom where he emphasized Scripture reading in English and familiarity with European ways. Missionary activity coincided with federal commitments. Treaties negotiated across Canada included clauses promising to establish schools on request, a commitment extended to British Columbia despite its paucity of agreements. But although the federal government assumed responsibility for schooling, it was not over-generous with the funds it made available for the purpose. In the 1880s the Department of Indian Affairs agreed to subsidize schools operated by local missionaries or other religious personnel, a far cheaper proposition than opening its own schools for Indian children.

Common assumptions governed the nature of schooling. The missionaries' early day schools had only limited success in keeping the young away from the old ways. Therefore the emphasis was placed on boarding schools, where children would be separated from their families for months and years on end. All instruction was to be in English, children prohibited from using their native languages at any time. 'What I could never understand, we weren't allowed to speak our language. If we were heard speaking Shuswap, we were punished. We were made to write on the board one hundred times, "I will not speak Indian any more."' There was little in the way of academic studies; girls spent part of each day learning how to become European-style homemakers, boys were taught farming and manual skills. This emphasis reflected European norms of what constituted civilized occupations and promised greater control over traditionally nomadic peoples. A half-day program was adopted in most residential schools, in the afternoons often the pupils doing little more than provide the manual labour necessary for institutions' survival. Because most schools were kept short of funds, many an Indian girl 'washed, cooked, cleaned, and mended her way through residential school.'[21]

By 1900 British Columbia possessed fourteen residential and twenty-eight day schools, enrolling some 40 per cent of Indian children across the province. By the end of the First World War most attended school for at least a year or two. This achievement was somewhat misleading. Whereas virtually all pupils in provincial schools completed the elementary grades, the overwhelming majority of Indian children never got beyond grade one or two. In 1940 just 6 per cent of native pupils reached grade six or higher. Even as late as 1947 the federal government was spending $45 a year per Indian pupil in day school compared with about $200 spent by the provincial government per pupil in public school.[22] Salaries for teachers in Indian schools were far below their counterparts in provincial systems. The goal of federal policy remained a little literacy on the cheap together with sufficient inculcation of European ways to keep the coming generation acquiescent and quiescent.

As federal policy became explicit in the decades following British Columbia's entry into Confederation, so Indians responded in a myriad of ways. They certainly did not accept passively the paternalistic, discriminatory treatment meted out to them. British Columbia's natural resources played a role. The continued availability of the traditional staples of salmon, cedar, and game animals meant that Indians never experienced the wrenching despair and utter dependency that befell their prairie counterparts on the disappearance of the buffalo in the 1870s. An 1884 description of British Columbia promoting migration and investment made the point: 'The intending settler may depend on finding the Indians peaceable, intelligent, eager to learn and industrious to a degree unknown elsewhere among the aborigines of America.' Moving to the interior from the prairies early in the next decade Charles Mair was struck by how 'the Indians differ *toto caelo* from the North West plains Indians. They are very well off.'[23]

British Columbian Indians demonstrated, in the view of political scientist Paul Tennant, 'an absence of the passivity, fatalism and lethargy evident among indigenous groups elsewhere.' Peoples in New Zealand and British Columbia were unique in 'the early appearance and continued presence of the response of political adaptation,' that is, in individuals using skills and knowledge acquired from the dominant society 'to lead their own people in maintaining a collective identity.' Historian Clarence Bolt has argued persuasively that the very act of religious conversion, that cornerstone of supposed European dominance over native peoples, was a deliberate act premised on the assumption 'that by forsaking their past they would acquire full Canadian citizenship along with its material, political and social rights.'[24]

Some missionaries encouraged native initiatives. Spending years of their lives among a single group of people – for Duncan sixty-one years, for Anglican W.H. Collison and Methodist Thomas Crosby forty-nine and forty-five years respectively – created close personal relationships. Missionaries often developed genuine sympathy for native positions on such critical issues as land rights and helped them express their views in letters and petitions. In the Okanagan in the 1870s the Oblate priests repeatedly voiced concern over ranchers acquiring and then fencing off virtually all good pasture previously used by Indians for raising stock. Natives made their views known in no uncertain terms to land commissions. 'We had been living before the whiteman came … it is our mother and father … We got our living from our land and our land is getting dry because the whiteman has taken the water and the land will not produce the living we used to get.'[25]

Among the most vigorous opponents of federal policy were the Nishga, part of the Tsimshian peoples living along the northwest coast. From the first years of European contact to the present day, they vigorously pressed their land claims, both through missionaries and directly. For the most part nobody listened. The Nishga nonetheless held to their claims, powerfully evoked in an old man's spontaneous interjection during an official government visit to the Nass Valley in 1887. 'I am the oldest man here, and can't sit still any longer and hear that it is not our father's land. Who is the chief that gave this land to the Queen? Give us his name. We have never heard it.'[26]

The Nishga were not alone in speaking out for their land. In 1906 Squamish chief Joe Capilano went to England to present a petition to Edward VII concerning aboriginal rights to the land. Three years later twenty tribes petitioned the king. Many natives did not approve of Treaty 8, negotiated in 1899; in fact the bands of the northeast did not at first want to sign. 'Their chief objections were that their country was too big to sell for a few dollars, and that they could make a good living in the bush without the aid of the Government.' A Kwakiutl born in 1905 recounted his father's efforts to resolve land issues. 'When I was around eleven years old, my father started going down to Victoria with other chiefs on the coast to let the government know that we own these lands and water. My father was told, "The interior Indians get big reserves because they need the land for ranching and trapping, but you get small reserves because you need the water for fishing."' Following the McKenna-McBride recommendations in 1916, Indian spokesmen asserted that the 'real position of the

Government of Canada is not that of a guardian protecting our rights, but that of an interested party ... seeking to take away our rights.'[27]

It was not just adults but also children that became involved. A pupil at a residential school in the central interior has recalled: 'The boys often rebelled and I didn't blame them. They were supposed to be in Lejac to get educated, but instead they were unpaid labourers, living on poor food and no more freedom than if they were prisoners in a jail. When the principal explained to them that they were being trained to be agricultural workers, the boys laughed.' The emphasis on farming made little sense to many young Indians. What was the use of any long-term commitment to a particular plot of land when you had no legal title to it? In any case, most land in British Columbia was unsuitable for farming, the marginal areas meted out for reserves even less so. Pupils repeatedly refused to accept treatment deemed unfair and discriminatory, continuing to speak their own language and, in cases of desperation, running away. 'Some were successful and managed to reach their parents' traplines, but more often, they were caught by the Mounties, brought back and whipped.' Conversely, parents seeking offsprings' schooling beyond the elementary level faced tremendous obstacles. 'I wanted my boys to go to high school, so I went to see the Indian agent, M.S. Todd, and told him so. He said to me, "Nothing doing!" I asked him, "Isn't it for everybody?" and he answered me, "Not for you people."'[28]

Many Indians managed to survive independent of European ways. A Nootka born in 1908 in a traditional longhouse on the west coast of Vancouver Island recollected growing up in a world little changed from before the coming of the Europeans. Emily Carr's verbal portrait of a coastal village around the turn of the century might have described the sketches made by John Webber, a member of Captain Cook's expedition:

On the point at either end of the bay crouched a huddle of houses – large, squat houses made of thick hand-hewn cedar planks, pegged and slotted together. They had flat, square fronts. The side walls were made of driftwood. Bark and shakes, weighted with stones against the wind, were used for roofs ... Each of the large houses was the home of several families. The door and the smoke-hole were common to all, but each family had its own fire with its own things round it. That was their own home.[29]

At the same time key resources were being usurped and native peoples were repeatedly forced to adapt. Soon after the turn of the century canners began pressuring the federal government, which exercised jurisdiction, into eliminating interior salmon fishing, particularly in the major spawning areas of the Skeena and Fraser river systems.[30] In 1905 the Carriers' customary fish weirs and traps were summarily seized and destroyed. Repeated Indian protests led to a compromise, whereby natives were given nets in exchange for their weirs. As the numbers of salmon acquired through netting fell far below that needed to survive the winter, the Carriers improvised. Moose, which had recently begun to migrate into the region, became a staple for both food and clothing.

Much of the same occurred with trapping. As the number of trading posts proliferated, enterprising Europeans, half-breeds, and some Indians 'traded food, dry goods and various other articles to the Indians for beaver, mink, muskrat, marten and fisher pelts' and sold supplies, in some cases at a healthy profit. Growing European settlement from the turn of the century increased the threat of disruption to the Indians' traditional way of life, particularly since settlement coincided with a substantial increase in the prices of furs. As a consequence, more and more non-natives looked to trapping as a source of cash income. As explained by a pioneer who combined subsistence farming with winter trapping: 'All Indian families had definitely fixed areas which were respected by all families. With the advent of the white man this whole system went by the board as the white hunter respected no such boundaries. The Indian had treated his hunting-ground as a farm and had not over-trapped it so as to leave plenty of breeding stock, but now the whole balance was upset and the size of the animal fur catch diminished.'[31]

Concern to maintain order and to protect wildlife from excessive harvesting brought government intervention. Registered trap-lines were introduced, whereby an individual acquired exclusive rights over a particular area. In the 1920s the young Englishman Eric Collier was given sole trapping rights over some one hundred and fifty thousand acres of wilderness in the Chilcotin. As graphically detailed in his adventure classic *Three against the Wilderness*, he knew the risks. 'We expected trouble from our Indian neighbours, to start with anyway ... Game was their only road to survival and if that road were denied them they and their kind must vanish from the face of the earth.' After directly confronting 'poachers' in the form of disgruntled natives continuing to trap in familiar territory, the Collier family survived by trapping for over thirty years, eventually managing some six hundred traps.[32] As the Depression attracted more and more newcomers into trapping, some Indians retreated behind the advancing colonial frontier by 'moving deeper into the woods and hills, beyond the intruders' reach.'[33] By the end of the Second World War fully half of the three thousand registered trap-lines in British Columbia were held by non-natives.

Other Indians chose to participate directly in the dominant economy.[34] The Europeans' disregard of native peoples has obscured the many ways in which they contributed to the economy of British Columbia, but there is much anecdotal evidence to support this. In 1892 Vancouver's recently opened BC Sugar refinery attributed cash flow problems to a smallpox epidemic. 'The smallpox has considerably interfered with our sales here this summer, but it is now about over and I hope for a brisk business – the Indians however are very much afraid of the disease & *may* not come down from the north for supplies as usual, if they do not, it will make considerable difference, as they are our most voracious consumers.' Native people clearly possessed very real purchasing power, and it came through paid work. As the federal government acknowledged in 1910, the Indians were 'of considerable industrial importance as a labour factor throughout the province.'[35]

Wage labour was often seasonal and would be combined with traditional pursuits such as fishing, trapping, and berry picking. A Haida born in the early 1880s worked as a commercial fisherman, also ran a trap-line, and for a time was a logger. The skills needed to enter the outside world were not those taught in the white man's school. With a Kwakiutl who ran a steam donkey, 'he didn't know how to read and write but he was a great engineer who knew everything about diesel, gas, and steam engines.' Indians and half-breed cowboys and cowhands early became – and remained – indispensable to the interior ranching economy. Despite the best Okanagan land being taken over by large ranches, natives raised stock as well as hunting, fishing, and gathering. In the Kamloops-Okanagan Indian agency the average Indian income peaked in 1910, the height of the pre-war boom, at just over $100 per capita or $400 per family. [36] Whole families harvested hops each summer in the Fraser Valley or nearby Washington State, enjoying the communal life that went on in the camps in the evenings.

Salmon canning was a favourite occupation along the coast, entire native villages moving to the canneries each summer. 'My wife and children all go, and we stay in the shacks that they built for the cannery people.' Men and boys usually fished. 'I was only ten years old. I had been out on fishing boats before but this was my first job on a fishing boat where I was a member of the crew.' In the new century, many saved up and put engines in their gillnetters or other boats. The Easthope engine, named for its Vancouver inventor and manufacturer, became a staple of coastal life. 'My father bought the first gas boat here at Cape Mudge in 1912. Within two or three years everybody here at Cape Mudge had been able to buy a gas boat with money we were paid for our fish ... That way our people grew up in this fishing business and always kept ahead and are successful in it.'[37] In 1922 new federal regulations permitted Indians to operate seiners. Purse seiners were an advance on gillnetters; in this method large nets were set up around schools of fish, then closed off with a purse-line rather like the tie to a pouch handbag. In other words, fish were scooped up as opposed to being individually caught by their gills. On the eve of the Second World War Indian fishermen comprised over one-fifth of the province's fleet. When the federal government decided in 1958 to put a seiner on the new Canadian $5 bill, the vessel selected would, appropriately enough, belong to a Kwakiutl fisherman.

Indian women worked inside the canneries. 'Chinese men slit, gutted, washed, and sliced the fish and our women selected the slices that had to be put together in one can and wrapped the fish in a tight fit with no gap at the centre ... Later machines replaced some of the work of slicing the fish and making the cans, but no machine could replace the work native women did in the canneries.' Visiting a cannery during the interwar years, coastal traveller Muriel Blanchet 'watched the fish leap from the packer onto the endless belt, onto the moving tables where the Indian women waited with sharp knives, and then into the tins ... so fast that you still seemed to sense some life in the labelled tins.'[38]

Indian women were vital to the survival of families and communities. Carr, who lived repeatedly in native communities while painting, believed that it was 'the Indian woman who shouldered the burden.' Missionaries found it easy to condemn the small proportion who turned to prostitution as the most viable means to support themselves, families, and kin groups, but in reality far more undertook such mundane work as salmon canning or becoming house helps. Jessie McQueen lamented how the family with which she boarded in the Nicola Valley 'has no help, hasn't even been able to get a washer-woman this week, for all the Klootches [Indian women] are away gathering huckleberries.' In what was a vigorous household economy, many women prepared wool and knit sweaters, an activity introduced by early missionaries. Others made baskets, described by Carr as 'beautiful, simple-shaped baskets, woven from split cedar roots, very strong, Indian designs veneered over the cedar-root base in brown and black cherry bark.'[39]

Ingenuity was sometimes the key to survival. As a child a Coast Salish born in the early 1930s was kept too busy ever to go to school, being taught such skills as shearing the family sheep and then washing, carding, and spinning the wool. As a teenager, she supported herself by picking berries, plucking turkeys, and working in a laundromat and café. Then came gillnetting with her husband, while also picking berries and digging clams for sale. Eventually the mother of nine children, she combined household responsibilities with spinning wool and knitting sweaters sold to a wholesaler for $4 each. 'Mom sent her children to school and when the two oldest were in grade four they had to show Mother how to sign her name. If she could sign her name she would receive Family Allowance, which was $6.00 for them.'[40]

Writing at the turn of the century, pioneer settler Susan Allison lamented that 'the white man has much to be ashamed of in his treatment of the rightful owners of the land.' Allison's memoir underlines how, on the frontier, everyday relations long remained close. Without Indian labour and companionship the Allisons would not have survived years on end in remote areas of the interior. A similar relationship is evident in the diary of a naturalist-adventurer living in northern British Columbia during the late 1930s. 'We invite nearly every Indian who arrives at our cabin to come in for hot tea and bannock ... Wherever we have gone in this country these people have been invariably generous about offering to share their homes and food with us. In this respect, at least, they are more hospitable to the white man than the white man is to them.'[41]

Other Europeans sought contact for less commendable purposes, such as gathering up Indians' heritage for the museums of the world, a process in which some natives willingly participated. Emily Carr related the comment of one woman concerning the sale of an 'ole eagle pole': 'Five hundred dollars for a old good-for-nothing thing like that! Ha, ha!' In 1929, when Carr returned to the sketching grounds of her youth, she became fully aware of the change wrought to Indian people over the past decades. 'Everywhere I saw miserable change creeping, creeping over villages, over people. The Indians had sold most of their best poles. Museums were gobbling them.'[42]

The persistence of everyday relationships between Europeans and native peoples is embodied in Chinook. Emerging out of early contact, the Chinook jargon possessed at most seven hundred words derived in approximately equal proportions from the powerful Chinook Indians of the lower Columbia River, from the Nootka of Vancouver Island, and from French and English. Grammar was sparse.Words acquired specialized meanings depending on tone of voice and gestures. Although it is difficult to carry on a lengthy conversation in Chinook, the patois provided 'an important vehicle of communication for trading & ordinary purposes.'[43] With a knowledge of Chinook Europeans were able to communicate with native peoples speaking very different languages. For example, James Douglas often spoke in Chinook when addressing Indians, a local native then translating his words into the local tongue. Bishop George Hills and other early Anglican clerics did the same when preaching. Chinook was the language of instruction in the school for Indian children that Hills established near Victoria in 1860. Judge Begbie was knowledgeable.

Chinook was widespread across British Columbia, for a time being possibly spoken and understood by more people than any other single tongue, including English. A miner whiling away the winter of 1858 in Victoria wrote his parents that he was passing the time 'studying the Chinook Jargon and can now converse with the Indians.' A beginning clerk in the Granville general store in 1884 was handed a Chinook dictionary, his pronounciation 'in the second language of the area' being repeatedly corrected by his employer. Again, the purchasing power of native people is underlined.

Between 1891 and 1904 a Catholic missionary priest at Kamloops published and widely circulated among local Indians the newspaper *Wawa* – Chinook for talk –with parallel columns in Chinook and English. According to a Kwakiutl born in 1905, in coastal canneries Chinook 'was all that was spoken in dealings between Indian and non-Indian people.'[44]

Chinook entered the dominant society. The summertime camps of late nineteenth-century Victorians 'were nearly all given rather fantastic and often facetious names: "The Three Black Crows" or something a la Chinook, i.e.: IKUM-UKUM.' A popular cheer at the young University of British Columbia during the First World War ran:

> Kitsilano, Capilano, Siwash, Squaw
> Klahowyah tillicum skookum wah,
> Hi yu mamook mucha zip
> B.C. Varsity, rip! rip! rip!
> Varsity, Varsity![45]

It was only at mid century, when almost all Indians adults had learned basic English in school, that everyday use of Chinook died out in British Columbia.

The disappearance from polite vocabulary of the term half-breed has obscured another important historical reality testifying to widespread contact. The long-standing sexual imbalance in the settler population combined with the realities of life on the frontier to encourage both short and long-term liaisons between European men and native women. Offspring were almost universally known, both by themselves and by others, as half-breeds, possibly breeds, but almost never as Métis, the prairie term for the descendants of Indian women and French-Canadian fur traders.[46] In some cases few marital options existed, as with men at the margin of social acceptability such as the Kanakas and Mexican packers. But the practice was far more widespread, liaisons with natives being for a time commonplace on the Gulf Islands and in the southern and central interior, particularly for men of continental European background. Almost all the numerous unions on Mayne Island were 'permanent until the death of one of the partners.' Similarly, two early settlers in the Nicola Valley who originally arrived during the gold rush, German-born William Voght and Mexican-born Jesus Garcia, married Indian half-sisters, Theresa Clama and Mary Kroventko, by whom they had large families. Of the fourteen children attending the local school in the mid 1870s, at least twelve had Indian mothers.[47]

In her letters home to Nova Scotia during the late 1880s, Jessie McQueen repeatedly revealed the ambivalence of the dominant society towards half-breeds. Referring to the four Garcia girls,

McQueen observed that 'they have attended schools for years but in spite of that they still have the squaw looks & manners.' On the other hand, 'Tena Voght is a half breed too but she is clever & pleasant & just like white folks ... The mother is a neat little thing but she keeps out of sight when there is company.' Writing about the upcoming wedding of one of the Voght daughters, McQueen commented that, although 'the girl is a half-breed ... I think she is far too nice for the man she is getting. He is old enough to be her father, and had a Kloochman for a wife once.' Being teased romantically about a young half-breed, she observed a bit coyly, 'I was ever so glad it was no worse – if it had been any white man I suppose I'd never hear the end of it.'[48]

With the passage of time half-breeds became outcasts. Europeans, Indians, and even some of the breeds themselves grew unwilling to acknowledge such an identity. A Skeena pioneer observed how 'children of mixed blood seldom had a place in a white man's society.' Yet they were legally prohibited from living on reserves, and native people sometimes scorned them. 'That was the only bad thing in those very early years of my life – some of the [Indian] village people, especially the children, treated me as a person apart, different in some way from themselves.' A Shuswap woman who married a half-breed shortly after the turn of the century discovered that while he had been allowed to go to the Indian school at the local mission, their own sons were refused admission on the grounds that they were 'taxpayers' children.' The frustration was summed up by a half-breed born in 1904, who went through life as neither one or the other. 'Not white and not Indian but we look Indian and everybody but Indians takes us for Indian ... It has been a complicated world.'[49]

Half-breeds tended to 'go white' or 'go Indian' depending on the marital decision of the second and third generations. As a rule, it seems that male offspring were more likely to be absorbed into native society, female siblings sometimes marrying Europeans. One of the premiers of the province, Simon Fraser Tolmie, whose mother was a quarter-breed, no longer identified (or was identified) with his native ancestry going back to the fur trade. Alexander Coutlee, who came west from Quebec to California and then to British Columbia, where he ran roadhouses first at Yale and later in the Nicola Valley, married an Indian woman. According to a family biography, a daughter and son then married whites. Their children again married Europeans thus diminishing the native background. The other two Coutlee children married native girls, as did their children. 'Thus the young Coutlees of the Nicola Valley are native.'[50] Far more British Columbians than generally acknowledged share a common ancestry.

By the early twentieth century the majority of Indian people had probably reconciled themselves to the changing social and religious mores being imposed by Europeans. Most children went to school, their families at least nominally Christian. Indian agents and missionaries managed local disputes. More and more Indian men and women chose, once again to quote Carr, 'to live as white people did.'[51] As a consequence, some educated young Indians sought to participate in the dominant society. Their efforts were largely unsuccessful because, ironically, they were pursuing the very integration that supposedly was the goal of federal Indian policy.

The realization that native people might be capable of participating as equals within the dominant social and economic order only heightened racism in the province. Clifford Sifton made the point extremely bluntly in his observation in the House of Commons that 'we are educating these Indians to compete industrially with our own people, which seems to me a very undesirable use of public money.' To the extent that racism had in the past been overlaid with a patina of paternalism, this was no longer possible as some young people overcame the limitations inherent in residential schools and attempted to move out into the larger society. 'It has to be carefully considered how far the country can be properly burdened with the cost of giving them superior advantages.'[52]

Local Indian agents were sometimes sympathetic and through their reports made clear that an important shift was occurring in British Columbia by the early twentieth century. A report from the Queen Charlottes in 1912 stated: 'We have men, who were raised in the boarding schools and some who had only a day school education, who are as shrewd as any whites.' Yet they and their children had to remain wards of the government in order to retain their land and home associations. A young man or woman seeking to enter the dominant society was most often repulsed. 'When applying for work outside of the reserve he is often refused because white men are as a rule unwilling to work alongside of Indians,' ran a typical agent's report.[53]

As if such discrimination was not sufficient to rebuff ambitious young Indians, official policy was altered to ensure their return to the reserve. By the time of the First World War the handful of British

Columbian public schools that had quietly admitted local native children were mostly closed to them, often as a direct consequence of the demands of white parents. The academic component of Indian residential and day schools across Canada was altered better 'to fit the Indian for civilized life in his own environment … To this end, the curriculum in residential schools has been simplified, and the practical instruction given is such as may be immediately of use to the pupil when he returns to the reserve after leaving school.'[54] The reasoning was conveniently circular, the official argument being that schools were becoming too expensive for the results obtained. A more flexible response would have seen Indian men, women, and families encouraged (or at the least permitted) to pursue voluntary integration on their own terms rather than being deliberately prohibited from so doing through legal and other barriers.

The full extent to which a federal policy supposedly promoting assimilation disguised a holding action was even more visible in official reactions to native peoples' early attempts to join together in order to seek better conditions of everyday life. Indian agents and the federal government had long been petitioned, not just by the Nishga but by a growing number of tribes and bands, on a variety of issues from the potlatch to land claims. Repeated rejection led to more systematic organization. Unintentionally, residential schools with their long absences from home and enforced learning of English played a role in socializing students away from their particular band or tribe and towards a common identity as Indian people. So did the racism pushing young men and women back on to the reserves. Early political leaders such as the Haida Peter Kelly, an ordained Methodist clergyman, and the Squamish Andrew Paull were products of the missionary school and its unintentional encouragement of a pan-Indian outlook.

Even though most early organizations proved ephemeral, by 1927 federal authorities considered it prudent to amend the Indian Act to prohibit the solicitation from or receipt of money by an Indian 'for the prosecution of any [land] claim.' According to Tennant, this prohibition 'was aimed directly at the British Columbia Indians and was intended to suppress political activity.'[55] The first long-lived association, the Native Brotherhood of British Columbia, was formed in 1931 through the efforts of Kelly and others, primarily Tsimshians, to represent the interests of coastal fishermen able to communicate with each other by boat.

At the same time native people did not abandon or forget traditional ways. Practical accommodation in the interests of survival did not equate with rejection of practices and beliefs that had bound peoples together for generations on end. Two missionaries revealed to Blanchet on one of her interwar adventures along the coast that, 'just when, with the help of the nursing and the religious teaching, they thought they had the feet of the village well on the road to civilization, they would come across something that made them realize that, below the surface, the Indian trails were still well trodden.'[56] The published autobiographies of four high-ranking Kwakiutl and Haida argue persuasively for adaptive continuity.[57] Not only were marriages still arranged, but stages in the life cycle retained their significance. 'One of the main reasons that my relatives wanted me to marry Flora Alfred was because of the high position that her family had as well as the Indian wealth that went with those positions.'[58]

Following the crackdown on the potlatch, alternatives were improvised. A Kwakiutl sentenced to three-months' imprisonment for having held a potlatch soon after gave a wedding feast for his daughter at which everyone danced 'in the white man's way and played games.' He then invited the guests to a special Saturday night show where he distributed 'fifty boxes of apples, ten boxes of oranges, five pails of candy and cakes, and soft drinks, chewing gum.' When a younger daughter came of age, his wife gave a potlatch privately. 'That was done by sending people out to go around with money. One is carrying the money, and one is carrying a book where the names are written and how much is coming to them.' At the same time he lobbied hard for the restriction's removal 'so the potlatch and payment can be done in the right way.'[59] The concession would only come at mid-century.

Traditional foods retained their attraction. 'Two kinds of moose stew, venison steaks, and a bountiful supply of bannock' prepared by the women of a northeast reserve for visiting government officials in the late 1970s might have fed European fur traders a century and a half earlier. Not only moose, venison, and dried salmon but such natural products of the forest as the soapberry have remained staples of the diet to the present day. Carr's description could as easily refer to the late twentieth century: 'One day after work I found the Douse family all sitting round the floor. In the centre of the group was Lizzie. She was beating something in a pail, beating it with her hands;

her arms were blobbed with pink froth to the elbows. Everyone stuck his hand into Lizzie's pail and hooked out some of the froth in the crook of his fingers, then took delicious licks. They invited me to lick too. It was "soperlallie," or soap berry. It grows in the woods; when you beat the berry it froths up and has a queer bitter taste.'[60]

Despite European imposition, Indian people continued to exercise a presence in British Columbia. If from the perspective of many in the dominant society they were conveniently out of sight and thereby out of mind, Indians did not disappear. While some natives maintained the old ways, others sought participation and even integration. On Vancouver Island, across the Fraser Valley, up the coast, and through the interior and the north many natives participated in the paid labour force. Racism determined the character of everyday relationships, but it did not prevent these relationships from coming into being and long continuing. Both Europeans and native peoples adapted. In part because of the very disregard exhibited by the dominant society, native peoples were, if daunted, in no way subdued.

9

Growing
Self-Confidence
1900–1918

As the nineteenth century became the twentieth, British Columbians whose memories went back to the 1860s had reason to be amazed by the transition that had occurred in the three decades since entering Confederation. Yet the years preceding the First World War would bring even greater change. A new dynamism was unleashed. Self-confidence grew. Political life in the province stabilized with the introduction of parties. An individual far more able as a politician than had been his predecessors acceded to power. Economic good times helped to give the office of premier new importance during the tenure of Richard McBride. The provincial government intervened in the economy by promoting railways much as James Douglas had done roads a half century earlier. Dependence on staples grew. So did corporate concentration. British Columbia's principal city of Vancouver surged ahead. It took a recession and then the First World War to curtail the euphoria that epitomized the McBride years.

Political parties entered the provincial arena in 1903. Population growth and an expanding economy made British Columbian life more impersonal. The number of voters had risen dramatically from some three thousand in the mid 1870s to forty-four thousand by the 1900 provincial election. The voters were tired of being governed by a small clique and by premiers whose prestige rested on their personal contacts and who were unable to exercise power effectively. By the end of the nineteenth century ministries fell so frequently that potential investors were being scared away. Of the five men who served as premier between 1898 and 1903, the longest was coal-mining magnate James Dunsmuir, who survived two years. The shortest stayed in power little more than three months. Clearly, government based on personal and group alliances no longer functioned.

The introduction of party labels and loyalties began to be discussed seriously around the turn of the century. Among the most vigorous supporters was young Richard McBride. Born and bred in New Westminster, McBride had received a law degree at Nova Scotia's Dalhousie University and then practised for a time in Atlin, a northwest mining centre. First elected to the provincial legislature in 1898, he soon demonstrated as MLA the combination of self-assurance, poise, and ability needed to exercise leadership.

To contemporaries, powerful arguments existed for and against parties. The localities were perceived as the principal losers, since individual legislators would have less freedom to pursue the demands of their constituents. On the other hand, parties minimized individual self-interest through necessary acceptance of party policy and party discipline. They also brought British Columbia in line with practice elsewhere in Canada. Most important, parties promised greater stability. McBride became premier in June 1903 under the banner of the Conservative party. When his opponents banded together as the Liberal party in emulation of federal practice, parties became a fact of life in British Columbia.

Once in power, McBride faced a legacy of unattended problems. Considerable malaise and self-doubt existed as to British Columbia's future course. To many, the heart of the problem lay in a difficult financial condition. As the provincial debt mounted – reaching $7.4 million by 1898 and $12.5 million five years later – so did the realization that such borrowings could not continue indefinitely. Many British Columbians maintained that the revenues the province was able to generate would always be insufficient to meet necessary expenditures. Therefore British Columbia could not carry on the ordinary business of government under the original terms of union with Canada.

The result was a quest for 'better terms' with the federal government. The argument, as put forward by McBride and the Conservatives, had several prongs. British Columbia's physical geography and scattered population made for exceptionally high routine costs of administration. The distance from commercial and administrative centres in Ontario and Quebec was very great. A lack of secondary manufacturing obliged British Columbia to import a larger proportion of goods and so contribute excessively to the federal treasury through tariffs and import duties. Forced to buy Canadian goods at high protected prices, the province had nonetheless to sell its chief products – minerals, fish, timber – on world markets in direct competition with goods from all other nations. Contrary to good business practice, British Columbia was forced to buy in the dearest market and sell in the cheapest. After much posturing the province reached a compromise with the central government. In exchange for a short-term annual federal subsidy, the McBride government agreed to raise taxes and reduce expenses in an attempt to balance the provincial budget. There matters rested until the end of the First World War.

The apparent ease with which the quest for 'better terms' resolved itself was deceptive. To a considerable extent the issue of provincial debt was set aside because the other half of the equation – greater revenue from resource exploitation – seemed for a time to offer a solution. Boom conditions gripped the province and Canada as a whole in the decade preceding the First World War. In 1905 British Columbia's annual surplus surpassed $600,000. In 1910 it peaked at $2.4 million. Over the seven years from 1905 to 1911 the surplus totalled $10 million, as a consequence of which the net provincial debt fell to $9 million. Economic growth, based on world demand for British Columbian products, seemed unending in its potential for filling provincial coffers. McBride both exploited and became caught up in the boom sweeping British Columbia and Canada as a whole. To quote Margaret Ormsby, 'more than anyone else he typified the spirit of the age: the optimism which verged on recklessness.'[1]

The rapid growth of settlement during these years led almost inevitably to government spending on a better physical infrastructure. Communication within British Columbia was still limited. The Cariboo Wagon Road and the Canadian Pacific Railway and its branch lines were complemented by sternwheelers and a variety of trails and roads, many only usable seasonally. Additional rail lines came to be viewed as some magic potion. Whereas during the 1890s entrepreneurs had been promised land, now they were given cash subsidies. Well over one hundred schemes were floated with such prepossessing titles as the Hudson Bay Pacific and the Mid-Provincial and Nechako.[2] Of the handful actually constructed in whole or part during the McBride years, the most significant were the federally sponsored Grand Trunk Pacific and the provincially subsidized Canadian Northern and Pacific Great Eastern lines (see Map 8).

During the 1904 federal election campaign the Liberals proposed a second transcontinental railway, supposedly to encourage immigration. This extension westward of Canada's oldest railway, the Grand Trunk, was intended to open up the central interior to European settlement. Entering British Columbia some 240 kilometres north of the CPR, its terminus was planned for an undecided site on British Columbia's northern coast. Much of the enthusiasm for the Grand Trunk Pacific was little more than short-term speculation. Promoters intended to make their money through the sale of lands granted the company in exchange for the commitment to undertake construction. McBride benefited in several ways, including a pandering to anti-Asian sentiment by obtaining an agreement that, unlike the CPR, only white labour would be used to build the new line.

In 1910 the GTP's construction began across the fur-trading area of New Caledonia. The Bulkley and Nechako valleys through which the line passed were occupied by a sprinkling of trappers, traders, and adventurers, along with Indian people. For a time everyone believed (or wanted to believe) that, once opened up to settlement, 'the central interior's history will be that of Ontario, Manitoba and other parts of Canada' where agriculture held sway. 'They who would flee from slave earning wages ... will find natural gifts here that can be pre-empted' at minimal cost. 'He who has the courage to break away from old surroundings and make new friends among new surroundings in a new land, will find the right kind of conditions for his happiness and independence. Like the history of the older and more settled districts of the sunny Pacific, history will record here in the Nechaco [sic] Valley an endless chain of romance, happiness and fortune building.'[3] For a time boosterism seemed to know no limits.

Townsites, arbitrarily chosen and mathematically laid out without any consideration of actual topography, were each promoted as infinitely more superior than their competitors down the line. As an advertisement aptly put the case for Fort Fraser, the old Hudson's Bay post, 'The price paid for a Fort Fraser lot is not paid for land alone – it is paid for opportunity.'[4] Whose opportunity became the question. In the case of a nearby site, also in the Nechako, the benefit went directly to a railway official from Chicago. Herbert Vanderhoof even named the townsite in his own honour. He hired a Chicago firm that had recently won a prize in Australia for laying out Canberra and this same design was adopted, down to its clubhouse, park, and artificial lake. Often competitors vied over location: one puzzled arrival at what would become Prince George discovered three separate sites being developed, 'each one claiming to be the greatest city of the future.'[5] Most important of all was the decision on the Grand Trunk's terminus. Possessed of an ice-free harbour, the new town of Prince Rupert was destined to become, its boosters asserted, a metropolis rivalling and even surpassing Vancouver further south along the coast. Almost overnight, so it seemed to one young man, 'workers, speculators, small businessmen, tinhorns, pimps, and prostitutes' invaded the wilderness he had known as a child, creating on muskeg and rock the future Prince Rupert.[6]

The promise of the Grand Trunk Pacific was insufficient to meet the agenda of McBride, who became totally committed to railways. In 1909 he determined to construct a rail line across British Columbia paralleling the CPR. The Canadian Northern Pacific Railway would enter the province farther north through the Yellowhead Pass and then run along the Thompson and Fraser rivers to Vancouver. The plan would piggyback on an enterprise already under way. The Canadian Northern had originated as a settler railway across the prairies financed by two small-town Ontarians, William Mackenzie and Donald Mann. McBride's offer of bonds and subsidies would simply extend the line farther west. Construction of the British Columbia section began in 1910.

Mackenzie and Mann expected to profit heavily, a goal they encouraged by investing widely in British Columbia industries to ensure future rail traffic. Not content to buy out Dunsmuir's coal interests on Vancouver Island, which they did in 1910, Mackenzie and Mann also purchased timber lands on Vancouver Island and in the Fraser Valley and then their own tugboat company to move the logs. A sawmill acquired at Fraser Mills just east of New Westminster was reorganized and modernized into a company town. Run with an experienced labour force brought out from Quebec, the mill was one of the most highly mechanized – and for many years the largest – in the British empire. Other resource industries were not immune from their seemingly never-ending investment dollars.

Innumerable additional lines were proposed by equally zealous entrepreneurs – so many that at one time four railways would have terminated at the tiny Norwegian settlement at Bella Coola on the central coast. Although most enterprises never left the drawing board, there were exceptions. During the 1909 provincial election campaign, McBride announced a cash subsidy to the CPR to build the Kettle Valley Railway. Running through the Boundary region, it would link the Kootenays to the CPR and thus to the coast. Three years later the provincial government guaranteed the bonds of a proposed Pacific Great Eastern line to run from North Vancouver to Prince George, there connecting up with the Grand Trunk Pacific. In theory the project made some sense, for it would give the central interior direct access to Vancouver.

Complementing the provincial government's encouragement of rail construction was its promotion of external investment, both from within Canada and from abroad. The growth that could be generated by local capital was limited: there simply were not many extra dollars around. The sequence of events that had already overtaken the salmon canning industry was repeated again and again as dollars, pounds, marks, and francs flooded British Columbia in expectation of easy profits to be made from resource extraction. Local entrepreneurs encouraged outside investment; they mobilized funds and in many cases remained largely in control of expenditures within British Columbia. They often directly influenced government policy, whereas shareholders in the United States and elsewhere had at best a distant voice. Nonetheless, companies based outside of the province possessed the ultimate decision-making powers, which made the interests of the people of British Columbia secondary. As foreign investment expanded, so also did British Columbia's dependence on the international marketplace.

Mackenzie and Mann's diverse investments were typical of the growth of capital coming into the province from other parts of Canada. As well, coal mines in the Crow's Nest Pass area of southeastern British Columbia were Canadian-financed. Much land speculation was capitalized from within Canada; subdivided properties were often sold to prospective settlers from the same province that had financed the project in the first place, as with the southern Okanagan communities of Summerland, Peachland, and Naramata, developed by Manitoba money. The CPR continued to invest in the province. A major thrust by the company to develop the West Kootenays as a tourist centre was only aborted by the war.

The penetration of international capital into British Columbia was part of a larger shift overtaking Canada as a whole. Between 1900 and the First World War foreign funds invested in Canada tripled, two-thirds of it coming from Britain, most of the remainder from the United States. In British Columbia, as across Canada, British pounds tended to be relatively unintrusive, often being in the form of portfolio investment in government-guaranteed bonds underwriting physical infrastructure or public utilities. Considerable sums also arrived with settlers, to be invested principally in land for farming and fruit-growing on Vancouver Island, in the Okanagan Valley, and in the Kootenays. Much smaller amounts coming from continental Europe included German marks put into real estate and Belgian francs into northern Okanagan fruitlands. The plentiful American dollars flowing into the province were likely to be directly invested in specific industries, particularly lumbering. Dollars underwrote the copper industry in the Kootenays and Boundary regions, whose value of production shot upward (see Table 20). Copper along with coal and gold set the pace for mineral production.

The two staple industries that most altered during the pre-war years were lumbering and salmon canning. What occurred in lumbering was a process of leap-frogging as experienced American entrepreneurs, mostly from the midwest, transferred their bases of operations from logged-out areas nearer home to the seemingly unlimited resources of the Pacific Northwest. From 1905 Washington State led the United States in lumber production, a status it retained almost unbroken for over thirty years. The Canadian province's appeal rested in part on proximity and in part on the growing accessibility of timber stands via the CPR, the Crow's Nest Pass Railway, and then the new interior lines.

The British Columbia government, in its concern to attract investment and generate revenue, was willing to offer very attractive terms on timber leases. The security of a transferable twenty-one-year term with the right to renew for another twenty-one years could be had for minimum rent and a small royalty on cut timber. The relatively simple process for staking claims was described by Allerdale Grainger in his classic novel of the British Columbian forest, *Woodsmen of the West*, published in 1908. 'A man could go anywhere on unoccupied Crown lands, put in a corner post, compose a rough description of one square mile of forest measured from that post, and thus secure from the Government exclusive right to the timber on that square mile, subject to the payment of a rent of one hundred and fourteen dollars a year ("No Chinese or Japanese to be employed in working the timber"). Such a square mile of forest is known as a "timber claim".' Crown land was alienated during these years on a grand scale. Investors and speculators rushed in, particularly after 1905 when the United States government withdrew much of its timber supply for new national forests. In 1902 just 9 per cent of the BC budget came from forestry revenues; six years later over 40 per cent of a much larger provincial budget did so. The situation reached such proportions that, according to Grainger, loggers and ordinary men 'talked freely of "graft" and "political pull." '7

Growing concern over the allocation of timber leases led to the establishment of a provincial Royal Commission on Timber and Forestry. Its report of 1910 urged greater government control through initial surveying, competitive bidding, and establishment of a forestry service. Grainger wrote much of the report, which included some frank passages. 'Everywhere in the early development of lumbering, cheap stumpage is seen to have been accomplished by butchery of wood; for human nature is careless of anything of low commercial value, especially when the supply seems inexhaustible and waste costs nothing to the waster ... We are of the opinion that the time is now opportune for the enactment of regulations that will prevent the misuse of the public estate.'8 Legislation enacted in 1912 ended the worst of the abuses, but the damage was done. By 1911 over eleven million acres, or approximately 80 per cent of crown timberland, had been leased. While a minority was held by small-holders, most of it had fallen into the hands of large syndicates.

The lumber industry grew phenomenally as a component of the provincial economy. Prairie markets for BC wood were seemingly inexhaustible. At the turn of the century three-quarters of the lumber exported from the coast still left the province in traditional fashion by water, a decade later two-thirds of coast lumber was heading east by rail, and on the eve of the First World War the proportion stood at fully 90 per cent. Interior mills, which came to account for one-third of the lumber produced in the province, sent almost all of their output east by rail. Very often mill owners in British Columbia established their own lumber yards near the tracks in prairie towns and so obtained additional profits from retail sales.

The industry diversified. Some entrepreneurs moved into wood-processing, in effect adding value to lumber by turning it into such items as shingles. An extremely strong building material known as plywood began to be made at Fraser Mills in 1913. Thin sheets of wood were glued together with the grains of alternate layers going at right angles. In 1900 total investment in BC timber stood at about $2 million; by 1914 it had reached $150 million, of which American investment comprised $90 million. Three years later British Columbia surpassed every other Canadian province in lumber production.

Forestry's expansion encouraged more sophisticated technologies. 'The Pacific Coast logger is no mere beast of burden. He is master of an intricate technique as applied to the handling of enormous timbers by powerful and complicated machinery. The B.C. woods is no place for the sluggish of brain or hand.'[9] Logging railroads were constructed into the bush. Animal teams gave way to 'donkeys,' steam-powered engines mounted on sleds that used long cables winched in on spools. Steam donkeys were used to yank logs out of the woods either onto rail cars or into the water.

Jobs became more specialized. The high rigger was responsible for delimbing, topping, and then equipping the spar tree; the bucker sawed felled trees into standard length logs; the chokerman attached the cable to the butt end of logs – in other words, he 'choked' the log – the donkey puncher or engineer operated the machine, while the whistle punk gave the signals telling who to do what how fast in order to move each log as rapidly as possible. Sometimes this was done by a signal wire, sometime with a whistle itself. The scene was described by a fictionalized bucker: 'The woods around him resounded with the clink of axes, the whine of steel cable in iron blocks, the shrill tooting of donkey whistles, the shudder and thrash of great machines spooling up half a mile of twisted steel rope on revolving drums, dragging enormous logs as if they were toothpicks on a thread, shooting them down to salt water, whence by raft and towline they passed to the hungry saws of the town mills.' As remembered by one long-time logger, a hierarchy existed: 'I was 14 when I got a job punkin' whistle … 15 when I started firing donkey and by the time I was 16 I was running the machine.'[10] Whatever the job, the work was dangerous and accidents common. Six long blasts on the punk's whistle announced an injury, seven a fatality.

Most logging camps were primitive affairs with straw mattresses and only such bedding as each man provided for himself. Work was seasonal and men came and went with great rapidity. Some of the more permanent and better constructed camps were built on floats because so much of the shore line was too steep to make land bases practical. 'All the buildings of the camp were built on rafts made of huge cedar logs – the bunk-houses, the cook-house, the office and store, and numerous small buildings. In this way, when the timber in one area was logged off, all the rafts would be strung together by short cables and towed to a new site by our little steamer.'[11]

Some loggers were ambitious to save and better themselves; others were eccentric characters primarily concerned to escape from the larger world except for a periodic trip to town. Loggers' hangouts along Cordova Street in Vancouver were graphically described by Bertrand Sinclair in *The Inverted Pyramid* as 'a region of Semitic clothing stores, cheap hotels, employment agencies where the woodsmen flocked in hundreds, gathered in groups along the sidewalk, rioted in the bars, or sought a job with empty pockets.' Money spent, men caught the next steamer back, possibly pawning some possession to get the fare. Alternatively they could wait around a hiring hall until jobs demanding their particular skills were posted: '50 axeman wanted at Alberni – 5 rigging slingers $4 – buckers $3 1/2.' One logger praised his occupation as 'a man's work.' 'And what did I have to show for it all? Some broken bones, some eating money, some drinking money, a good family of course, knowing a hell of a lot of good men, having a hell of a lot of fun and the thing inside that a man lives with that tells him he has done his best with what he had to do it with.'[12]

The salmon canning industry also saw changes. The annual pack in good years remained fairly stable at about a million cases. When the Anglo–British Columbia Packing Company was formed in 1891, it established its head office in Vancouver rather than Victoria. Other companies soon followed. Channels on the Fraser River were deepened to permit sea-going ships to come alongside cannery wharves. No longer did exports have to pass through Victoria. The business community that had built up the industry was bypassed.

Unlike forestry, the changes in the canning industry arose not from expansion but from the introduction of new technology to achieve economies of scale. Fishing became more complex. As more and more fishermen added Easthope or other engines to their boats shortly after the turn of the century, so they could travel farther with their haul. Gillnetters were increasingly challenged by larger seiners, which often had living quarters to enable them to go greater distances in search of fish. Other fishers trolled, a fishing technique used to catch higher-quality salmon intended to be sold fresh or smoked. Trollers had poles attached whose lines were trailed (trolled) behind the vessel at various depths. Fish were pulled in separately as they struck the hook on the lure, immediately dressed and packed in ice. Limited quantities of halibut, sold fresh, were caught by a process similar to trolling known as longlining. Hooks were regularly spaced on a line periodically reeled in.

Work processes altered in the sixty to eighty canneries operating along the coast during any particular year. The Chinese workers who performed much of the unskilled labour began to look for higher wages in a tighter labour market. To counteract this, owners began to look towards mechanization to lower costs. An automatic butchering machine invented in Seattle early in the century quickly became known as the Iron Chink in acknowledgment of the labour it displaced. By means of rotating knives and brushes, fish were decapitated and cleaned at the rate of one per second. About the same time hand-soldering of cans gave way to an automatic double-seaming process. The consequence of the first innovation was to cut a butchering crew of twenty-five to fifty down to two, of the second to reduce the number of workers needed to fill a thousand cases a day from over one hundred to just twenty-five.

While agriculture continued to be a poor cousin in the provincial economy, it also expanded. The population explosion was the trigger. While the majority of newcomers headed for Vancouver or Victoria, others sought the independence which many considered came only through ownership of land. Migrants of the first generation, attracted west by the CPR's completion, often came with farming expertise acquired elsewhere in Canada or in the United States. Likely settling in the Fraser Valley, or possibly on southern Vancouver Island, they understood the sacrifices necessary for long-term survival and were fortunate to acquire land suitable for agriculture.

The same was less true for many later arrivals. By the end of the century the Fraser Valley was almost completely filled up. Individuals with enough money to buy five or ten acres of improved or irrigated land for fruit-growing and then wait five or more years for the trees to come into production were often attracted as much by an area's natural beauty and social amenities as by practical considerations. The Okanagan's success encouraged unbridled speculation in other areas of the province less suitable for growing fruit, ranging from the West Kootenays to the south and central interior.

Among the best known of the marginal enterprises was Walhachin in the arid southern interior, promoted among the English aristocracy as much for its amenities as the quality of its soil. A Cariboo rancher described the many men and women cajoled onto grassland much like that at Walhachin: 'they came with all their savings wrapped up in the countless settlers' effects, full of great hopes and dreams and about all they ever raised was a hell of a big dust.'[13] Walhachin deteriorated once its young adventurers marched off to the even greater challenge of the First World War.

Poorer individuals determined to be independent had fewer alternatives. Some pre-empted land in remote areas, a deceptively simple process. 'To get land, you just searched around to find a suitable piece and then, if there were no other stakes visible on it, you put in your own stake' before rushing off to the nearest land office to record the location of the chosen 160 acres. As one adventurer exalted, 'We've found our country ... a place that will be all our own ... Our neighbours will be the wolves. Our music the call of the loon. Our beds will be the earth.'[14] Coastal British Columbia became dotted with tiny enclaves of settlement, as were areas of the southern and central interior accessible by sternwheeler, small boat, or some kind of transportation.

Many long persevered; one pioneer titled his memoirs, *Bacon, Beans 'n Brave Hearts*. Even poor farmland usually provided subsistence, which was then supplemented by some paid work outside, such as seasonal employment at a logging company, sawmill, or cannery. Stump farmers hacked ties for the railway; since the ties had a relatively short life span this became a common winter activity. Tie hackers were paid on a piecework basis for the forty or more ties cut in a day. Others hand-logged or prospected, oblivious to, or possibly scornful of, technological advances which favoured large corporations with plenty of capital resources.

The challenge of 'taming the land' – clearing a plot by toppling large trees and blasting their stumps – enhanced property's appeal. Long after it became clear that agriculture was not viable, men and women held on. As recollected by a Bulkley pioneer, often 'available land was away from the valley floor, difficult of access, and heavily timbered and was generally unfit for farming.' But men and women 'had burned their bridges behind them and so had to dig in and make the best of it.'[15]

Most dreams were eventually undone by the harsh BC landscape. Like many others, I wanted my own land – farmland. Land for raising cattle and growing crops and bringing up a family ... I wanted a farm as I remembered farms to be in England ... Well, it's green here all right, but by God, it's fierce ... it seemed the very nature of the land was against us. Was it hostile, I don't really know what it was, but even when timber was cleared, the land somehow still seemed to belong to the forest ... I *wanted* that land. I built a house near the sea and worked the land: clearing, then going out to [logging] camps to make money for food, then returning to clear the land some more. I was determined ... but as a farmer I could not succeed. Too much rain, or not enough sun, or early frost, or too much wind. It just would not go![16]

Overall, agriculture expanded as a component of the British Columbian economy. At first the growing demand for foodstuffs generated by an expanding population made the province a large net importer – $2 million worth by 1905 – of agricultural products. Widespread settlement on the land then helped to make the province self-sufficient. In 1911 the value of home production for the first time exceeded imports. The value of fruits and vegetables produced in British Columbia, almost nil at the turn of the century, reached fully two-thirds that of livestock.

Manufacturing remained marginal to the province's economy. Where not an extension of resource production, as with case of sawmilling, fish canning, or smelting, it was intended to supply local needs with such essentials as sugar, bread, and beer. Secondary manufacturing accounted in 1910 for just 8 per cent of the total value of goods and services produced in British Columbia, or gross domestic product (see Table 19). Of that, almost 30 per cent came from staples exploitation, 11 per cent from primary manufacturing, and the remaining half from the provision of services.

The importance of services as a component of gross domestic product was related closely to the phenomenal growth of Vancouver and to a lesser extent that of the provincial capital of Victoria. Vancouver's growing supremacy over Victoria was based on its unique location between water and rail and on lack of competitors. Two principal causes for urbanization exist. The first is the need to be close to opportunities for mass employment. While British Columbia's primary industries had differing labour demands, none were capable of creating large population centres. Mineral speculation resulted in innumerable boom towns in the Cariboo and across the Kootenay and Boundary regions, but only a handful flourished for any length of time. Even the most permanent of these – for example, Rossland and Trail – were limited by the particular staple's potential for creating jobs. Lumbering and salmon canning were not conducive to urbanization, owing to the transient and seasonal nature of employment. Because most British Columbian communities were built around a single staple, size was further limited.

Urbanization can also be fostered by the need for service centres or market towns. For this to develop a pivotal location is necessary, often where goods are transferred from one means of transportation to another, such as rail to road or water. Victoria and New Westminster vied for this role during the gold rush. Canadian Pacific construction sites such as Kamloops and Revelstoke became market towns for nearby miners, farmers, and ranchers. Vernon and Kelowna functioned similarly in the Okanagan. Across British Columbia service centres' size was almost always limited by difficult topography.

Yet, as soon as large-scale immigration began with the arrival of the cpr, British Columbia leapt to the fore as the most urbanized province in Canada. By 1891, 43 per cent of British Columbians lived in incorporated cities, towns, and villages of one thousand or more; this compared with 35 per cent in Ontario, 29 per cent in Quebec, 23 per cent in Manitoba, and 19 per cent in the maritimes. If only the non-native population is considered, proportions were even higher. In 1891 over 60 per cent of non-natives lived in the four coastal towns of Vancouver, Victoria, Nanaimo, and New Westminster. While the number of urban centres of one thousand or more rose over the next two decades in every province, at 51 per cent British Columbia just maintained its lead over its next rival, Ontario.[17]

The explanation lay in the character of urbanization in British Columbia. Elsewhere in Canada it evolved through the emergence of numerous communities. By 1911 Ontario possessed thirty-nine cities and towns of five thousand or more inhabitants, Quebec eighteen, the maritimes fifteen, and the prairies thirteen. British Columbia in 1911 still contained just five: Vancouver's suburb of North Vancouver and Nanaimo with just over eight thousand each, New Westminster with thirteen thousand, Victoria with almost thirty-two thousand, and Vancouver with one hundred thousand. The rise of a single metropolis underlay urbanization in the west coast province.

Vancouver functioned as a service centre to an ever expanding hinterland. Business opportunities ranged from importing supplies to processing to exporting the commodities themselves. During the pre-war years Vancouver acquired branches of major Canadian firms with head offices in central Canada. From Vancouver they serviced an area extending through the Fraser Valley or even into the prairie provinces. Older companies originating in Victoria established branches in the mainland city, often soon transferring their head-quarters there. Vancouver became home to most new British Columbian companies capitalized from outside the country. This was especially true in the rapidly expanding lumber industry which replaced the CPR as the city's largest employee. Vancouver emerged triumphantly as the province's undisputed metropolis with the opening in 1907 of its stock exchange, whose principal function became the raising of venture capital for resource exploitation.

By the time of the First World War Vancouver's chartered banks cleared nearly three times the amount exchanged in Victoria despite its being the provincial capital. Indeed, the Kootenays were the one hinterland area that eluded Vancouver's grasp. Even though integrated into the Canadian economy, its hardrock mining industry turned eastward to Calgary and Winnipeg and south to Spokane, owing in part to geography and in part to freight-rate discrimination.

Vancouver's physical face was transformed. The annual value of building permits reached a high of almost $20 million in 1912. An English visitor expressed amazement how 'everyone seemed to be greatly excited about "real estate" and men made fortunes in a most remarkable way.'[18] The business district, dominated at the turn of the century by three- and four-storey frame or stone buildings, by 1914 was distinguished by eight- to fourteen-storey stone, brick, and concrete structures. Some office blocks were erected by speculators to rent to small companies, but numerous insurance and shipping companies, banks, hotels, wholesalers, and retailers built their own quarters. The imposing edifices of Woodwards, the Hudson's Bay Company, and Birks became city landmarks. New public buildings included the court house, post office, and Carnegie library. An industrial area took shape along False Creek, where settlement had stagnated since the depression of the early 1890s.

Urban amenities developed apace. English Bay, not far from Stanley Park, prided itself on its pier, dance pavilion, bandstand, and beach overseen by the black lifeguard Joe Fortes. Vaudeville theatres such as Pantages vied for patrons with the Salmonbellies, nearby New Westminster's world-champion lacrosse team. Civic authorities gave encouragement. Despite a general belief that city government should be run like an efficient business, Vancouver's council responded to a growing sense of public needs by buying up private lots along English Bay and elsewhere to expand public recreational opportunities. The biases of the dominant society were evident in their concentration on the city's more prosperous West End and West Side.

Expansion outward became inevitable as up to a thousand persons a month arrived in Greater Vancouver. The electric street railway quadrupled to nearly two hundred kilometres of track by 1914. New lines criss-crossed Vancouver itself, and linked the city with the nearby communities of South Vancouver, Point Grey, and Hastings Townsite (see Map 9). In 1905 North Vancouver, on the far shore of Burrard Inlet, was connected by ferry, a streetcar then running north along Lonsdale Avenue. Hastings residents voted a year after the streetcar's arrival in 1909 to amalgamate with Vancouver; South Vancouver and Point Grey would remain separate municipalities until 1929, North Vancouver to the present day. The Lulu Island line, constructed in 1902 by the CPR, ran south across the Fraser River to the fishing village of Steveston and later from there to New Westminster; by 1911 the line had become circular with an extension back to Vancouver through neighbouring Burnaby.

Vancouver's real estate market was still dominated by the CPR. Thus, while the Lulu Island line originally depended on the fares of Steveston cannery workers, very soon the CPR was selling off property along the tracks in Point Grey in what would become the sedate community of Kerrisdale. The CPR benefited even more by developing Shaughnessy Heights as an exclusive residential area noted for its curving streets and large lots. Popular Victoria architect Samuel Maclure was repeatedly lured into constructing yet another of his elegant tudor mansions, making ample use of native woods. The construction in Shaughnessy of palatial 'Hycroft' by a business associate of Mackenzie and Mann helped initiate an influx of élite families out of the West End.

House construction was evident everywhere. Elsie MacGill, who was only a child then, recalled how 'in the residential sections roads were macadamized, roadside ditches and raised wooden sidewalks were disappearing, vacant lots were fewer.'[19] Few blocks were developed as a unit. More frequently, small parcels were sold in an unimproved state to individuals who built at most two or three houses, likely in the same design. Undeveloped lots or farms often separated clusters of new homes, which were usually located within walking distance of a streetcar line. It was supposedly possible to travel from Vancouver's central business district to anywhere in a twelve-kilometre radius in twenty-five minutes. Greater Vancouver neighbourhoods, not just Kerrisdale and Shaughnessy but Kitsilano, Collingwood, Cedar Cottage, and others, took on distinctive characters. South Vancouver was dotted with the small bungalows of working people, Point Grey with somewhat larger residences more suited to their middle-class owners. North Vancouver contained the modest homes of English immigrants for whom its rural atmosphere held particular appeal.

The poor, who were often non-English-speaking, tended to cluster in the city's original residential area. Lying between Granville and Hastings Mill, it became known as the East End. Many of the East End's large homes were turned into boarding-houses for recent immigrants and seasonal workers in the resource industries. Most of the city's three to four thousand Chinese lived in Chinatown in the East End. Many were in the service industry, as laundrymen, houseboys, and restaurant or small shop owners. A few had become very wealthy, the Chinese as a group owning some $2 million of real estate in Chinatown, another million elsewhere in the city.

Vancouver's immediate hinterland extended beyond Greater Vancouver into the Lower Fraser Valley. Under the aegis of BC Electric Company, a British-owned enterprise that controlled the streetcar and electric light systems of Vancouver, North Vancouver, and Victoria, the existing inter-urban line to New Westminster was extended into the Fraser Valley. By 1911 the farming communities of Abbotsford and Chilliwack were in easy reach of New Westminster and thereby of Vancouver. Frequent 'milk runs' moved one of the valley's principal commodities to the metropolis. Even such outlying enclaves as Ladner near the mouth of the Fraser were linked by steamer to New Westminster and so to the rest of the lower mainland.

Vancouver's dominance was confirmed when it was selected as the site of the provincial university. The first step was Vancouver high school's affiliation with Montreal's McGill University. In 1899 the Vancouver School Board received permission to offer first-year courses, students then transferring east to complete their degrees. In 1903 Victoria high school followed suit. The same year Vancouver added second-year courses. The government soon felt compelled to establish a separate provincial university. A commission was set up to determine the best location. Its first choice was the high ground overlooking Point Grey, perceived as offering both the rural atmosphere needed for contemplation in a true university and access to urban amenities. In September 1915 the University of British Columbia opened in temporary facilities at Fairview. Because of construction delays, the move to the university's permanent home on the Point Grey cliffs came only after the First World War.

The capital city of Victoria, while losing out in the university stakes, in 1920 acquired a two-year UBC affiliate known as Victoria College. More generally, the business of government was becoming central to Victoria's economy. Complementing the legislative buildings, erected at a cost of almost $1 million, were a new provincial library and archives. No additional industrialization occurred; to the contrary, over the first decade of the century the number of enterprises declined by one-third. The other component of Victoria's economy became tourism. Increasingly, the city consciously built on its British ethos to attract visitors. Not only was a Tourist Development Association organized, but the Canadian Pacific Railway was persuaded, by promises of free land and a fifteen-year exemption from taxes, to build a major tourist hotel. The Empress, designed as had been the legislative buildings by the fashionable architect F.M. Rattenbury, opened in 1908 to become a Victoria landmark. Its construction transformed the city; on what had previously been mud flats traversed by a wooden bridge set on piles was now an imposing hotel fronted by an elegant sea promenade.

Like Vancouver, Victoria benefited from the immigration boom. The city's genteel image appealed in particular to middle-class Britons. As Emily Carr put it, 'from London dock to Empress Hotel door was one uninterrupted slither of easy travel.' Kipling reported enthusiastically, on visiting 'that quite English town of beautiful streets,' that 'on a thousand [pounds] a year pension a man would be a millionaire in these parts, and on four hundred he could live well.' *The Times* of London considered Victoria 'the most "English" of the towns in Canada.'[20]

Victoria grew, but Vancouver grew faster. As the 1911 census showed, its population of one hundred thousand was over three times that of Victoria. Another twelve thousand were scattered in Victoria's immediate suburbs and on the nearby Saanich peninsula. On the other hand, Vancouver's adjoining municipalities now housed more people than did the capital city and its environs together – almost fifty thousand. With Vancouver filling up, the momentum of growth was shifting into its immediate hinterland. The Lower Fraser Valley contained an additional thirty thousand men and women.

British Columbia had become at one and the same time the most urban and least urban province in Canada. By 1911 half of all British Columbians lived in the lower mainland region, another 10 per cent in Greater Victoria or on the nearby Saanich peninsula. While some of the remaining 40 per cent lived in one of the province's handful of resource communities and market towns, many existed on or near the frontier. The wide dispersion of this minority of British Columbians is indicated most clearly by the proliferation of post offices, which virtually doubled to over seven hundred during the first decade of the century. More than a thousand post offices existed over the next decade extending across the First World War, and three out of every four were located outside of the populous lower mainland region (see Table 14). Geography and resource dependency combined to bring two very different British Columbias into being.

Most members of the dominant society identified with the province's urban face, and it was this British Columbia that became increasingly visible. Across North America the priorities of urban society in such areas as education and social services were assumed to fit equally well in resource communities, market towns, and frontier conditions. When they did not it was often the residents of these areas who were castigated for somehow not living up to expectations. In reality, services assumed to be the norm in Vancouver and Victoria were most often non-existent. Access to health care, to schooling, to professional expertise varied tremendously. Whereas Greater Vancouver and Victoria possessed electric street railway systems that were among the most sophisticated in North America, in only one other British Columbian city – the West Kootenay mining town of Nelson with its steep slopes – was there even a pale reflection.

British Columbia's integration into the larger world became especially evident as the boom ran its course. From 1912, even as rail construction surged forward and money continued to flow into the province, clouds appeared on the horizon. The deteriorating political situation in Europe played a role. So did realization that much of the dynamism and self-confidence was little more than the rhetoric of boosterism. Outside capital began to pull back. In 1913 the annual value of building permits in Vancouver dropped by half to $10 million and then to just $4 million in 1914.

The deflation in real estate values both occasioned and was epitomized in the collapse of the Dominion Trust Company in 1914. The project to construct Vancouver's first skyscraper, a thirteen-storey building billed as the tallest in the British empire, originated with a group of local businessmen who borrowed money using real estate as collateral. While the building itself was completed on the corner of Cambie and Hastings in 1910, the collapse of the real estate market made the trust company's failure inevitable. Unhappy depositors blamed the provincial government for not sufficiently examining Dominion Trust's finances before issuing its charter. The débâcle underlined the extent to which the city had grown faster than the economy warranted. Hundreds of buildings stood empty, lots worthless.

The promise of railways became a fading vision. For a time construction spurred on the provincial economy, just as the provincial economy fuelled construction. In 1912 McBride boasted that the various companies were committed to spending $100 million in British Columbia, somehow overlooking the fact that these same companies were underwritten by $80 million of provincially guaranteed railway bonds. The bonds begin to lose their appeal on the London market, as construction costs soared. Much of the supposed prosperity was underwritten only by speculation and greed. As late as 1914, 144 syndicates were still flogging land along the Grand Trunk Pacific and Pacific Great Eastern lines.

The provincial government became especially worried about the Canadian Northern and PGE projects for which it had guaranteed the bonds. The railways for their part needed more money if they were to be completed, but such assistance would mean further indebtedness. In 1914 the symbolic last spike of the federally funded Grand Trunk Pacific was driven at Fort Fraser: Canada's second transcontinental link had made it to completion. The Canadian Northern also survived; the first train reached its terminus at Vancouver a year later. The Kettle Valley Railway was completed by the CPR in 1916, by which time the Kootenay boom it was intended to promote had collapsed. The PGE, wreathed in charges of scandal and corruption, became too expensive. In the end two sections were constructed: one ran along the north side of Burrard Inlet between North Vancouver and Horseshoe Bay; the second went from Squamish, about fifty kilometres by steamer north of Horseshoe Bay, to Clinton, replacing pack brigades and stagecoach as the principal means of transport.

The completed railways did not live up to their promise. Anticipated traffic did not materialize. The province now possessed almost eighteen hundred kilometres of track, excluding logging railways. This was far too many for the economy to support. In the case of the Grand Trunk Pacific, so the line's boosters argued, its terminus at Prince Rupert was much closer by water to Asia. This meant, conversely, that the northern city was almost 180 kilometres farther away from Winnipeg and central Canada. Rupert's port was never to achieve its projected status as a viable alternative to Vancouver. More imminently, bond issues were becoming due.

The various railways had to be brought under direct government control or allowed to collapse. The federal government took over the Canadian Northern in 1917, British Columbia the Pacific Great Eastern a year later, federal authorities the Grand Trunk Pacific in 1920. The GTP, Canadian Northern, and other lines were consolidated in 1923 as the Canadian National Railways. The abortive PGE line was extended as far north as Quesnel, still some 130 kilometres short of its intended destination of Prince George. The British Columbia government ended up paying interest on the $80 million of bonds it had guaranteed, ensuring a new era of deficit finance. From $400,000 in 1912 the deficit grew to $3 million the next year and to over $5 million in 1914.

By the time of the First World War British Columbia had finally begun to push outwards towards its political boundaries, expanding north in particularly dramatic fashion. While Fort Fraser did not become the Edmonton of British Columbia or Vanderhoof the Canberra of Canada, as promised by their boosters, nonetheless these communities, like so many others strung out along the new rail lines, did struggle into existence as home to a handful of settlers. The central interior quadrupled in numbers, other regions at least doubled (see Table 14).

Along British Columbia's long coastline and on its many islands population so proliferated that by 1911 Union Steamships' red-and-black funnelled vessels had over one hundred ports of call each week. A mix of canneries, resource towns, logging camps, native communities, holiday destinations, and small enclaves of settlement extended as far north as the mining town of Stewart and across to Vancouver Island. 'Carrying passengers and groceries into virtually every nook and cranny on the B.C. coast, ships of the Union fleet provided a tangible link from southern "civilization" to the far northern suburbs.'[21] Every week the line's eight ships covered a total of three thousand kilometres. Its principal competitors, the CPR's Princesses, added some forty ports of call along the west coast of Vancouver Island. Vancouver's phenomenal expansion overshadowed these important shifts in the province's social demography.

Across the province political and social structures continued to be dominated by the nature of the economy. Company towns provide a graphic example. The visual image was powerfully evoked by poet Pat Lowther. 'First and always foreground the mill like an experiment in the logic of ugliness pins down the town, billowing smoke steam white-grey, grey-white into the low sky ... Then the neat wooden houses strung between mountains ... each with a lush old-fashioned garden (nourished perhaps by steam).'[22] The advantages of a dependable labour force in remote areas brought a growing number of similar settlements in industries such as sawmilling, smelting, and pulp and paper that could expect to continue in the same location over a period of time. The provincial government adopted a hands-off policy towards communities such as Fraser Mills, Britannia Beach, Powell River, Ocean Falls, and Trail. Usually unincorporated, with housing and community facilities owned and controlled by the company, they were immune from provincial regulations. The company that owned the town exercised virtually unlimited authority over the lives of workers and their families.

The consequence was a paradox. Companies' interest in long-term stability sometimes resulted in material benefits far superior to those available in comparable frontier communities: for example, amenities such as electricity and indoor plumbing, sports and leisure facilities, the most modern schools. Employees of different ethnic and racial groups were usually housed separately, to the satisfaction of the dominant society. Powell River, where Asian workers were prohibited by terms of the water use agreement signed with the provincial government, possessed a 'Balkan Village' and, for Italian families, a separate cluster of small company homes on the other side of the dam from the main community.

Yet, for all these benefits, company control limited worker independence. Purchases often had to be made at the company stores: 'You could buy anything you wanted so long as you had coupons. At the end of the month some people's cheques were only for a dollar or fifty cents because they'd couponed themselves to death at the store.' Unions were prohibited. Pro-labour newspapers mailed to subscribers were, so it was charged, 'destroyed by the postmaster, who had set himself up as a censor, and in conjunction with the village policeman ... decided that working class publications were not fit to be distributed ... So far as personal liberty was concerned,' company towns were 'nothing but slave encampments.'[23]

From time to time officials expressed concern over the potential for abuse. As lands minister Duff Pattullo acknowledged in 1917, companies sometimes 'exercised autocratic powers in the way of administration' by the 'refusing of entry to persons other than those they [were] willing to admit.'[24] A provincial Company Towns Act was passed in 1919 which, while granting public access, did not allow the residents such generally held rights as the holding of public meetings. Through the inter-war years company towns would remain worlds unto themselves, their circumstances reflecting the deference of the provincial government towards capitalism in its various guises.

Britain's declaration of war against Germany at the beginning of August 1914 fundamentally altered all aspects of life in British Columbia. Since Canada's takeover of the naval garrison at Esquimalt, consensus had grown that the west coast's defences were being neglected. As hostilities were about to break out, Richard McBride played the hero and on his own initiative purchased two submarines recently constructed in Seattle for the Chilean navy. The submarines, then a newly invented craft, arrived in Esquimalt on 5 August, the very morning that war was declared. Three days later the federal government took them over and arranged for their transfer to the Admiralty. McBride – and through him British Columbia – had made clear the great concern over defences as well as the province's commitment to the war effort.

Patriotism now became the order of the day. 'If ever there was a righteous war, this is one,' a prominent cleric intoned.[25] British Columbia had the highest per capita volunteer rate in Canada at just over ninety per thousand population compared with about seventy-five in Ontario and across the prairies, just over fifty in the maritimes, and half that in Quebec.[26] While British Columbia's uneven sex ratio played a role, so did the province's British character. Yet men of all backgrounds volunteered. On Mayne Island many were half-breeds, elsewhere native Indians. The Japanese and Sikh communities offered to raise troops. Just under two hundred Japanese eventually fought for Canada in Europe. By war's end 6,225 British Columbians were dead and over thirteen thousand wounded.

British Columbians contributed to the war effort in such large numbers that the social and economic structures of some small communities were irrevocably weakened. This was particularly the case with recent settlements where both the young and middle-aged marched off – more likely took the train – to war, many never to return. Wives, children and the elderly persevered so long as they could but many eventually gave up and returned to their country or province of origin, leaving an empty farm or vacant shop. Stern-wheeler service across the interior, already adversely affected by the extension of rail lines and of roads, further declined. The *Aberdeen* was retired in 1916, although other sternwheelers would continue service through the Second World War. Many volunteers had worked as wage labourers, and their departure created serious problems of supply. Women, married and unmarried, joined the work-force in large numbers. Fortunately for British Columbia, the stagnation of international trade caused by curtailment of shipping was soon offset by growing domestic demand. Not only were the province's staple commodities critical to the war effort, but a new industry of shipbuilding was stimulated. Massive federal subsidies assured the construction of needed vesels, and both Victoria and Vancouver benefited from the largesse.

It was during the war that McBride's premiership finally came to an end. A combination of factors, ranging from ill health to growing charges of patronage and corruption, brought his resignation in December 1915. The extent to which McBride and his allies person-ally benefited from their long tenure in power, while generating considerable speculation, has not been systematically examined. No question exists but that the Conservatives used patronage in the form of employment, contracts, and other benefits to consolidate power.

The value of the introduction of party politics was nonetheless confirmed. The two mainstream parties, the Liberals and Conserva-tives, had between them garnered the overwhelming proportion of the vote in the four provincial elections held during McBride's years in office (see Table 4). Parties and groups on the left never received more than one-sixth of the count. On a personal level McBride had, as the first British Columbian-born premier, inspired a kind of warm familiarity, and was at the same time able to evoke a forceful image as a 'distinguished silver-haired gentleman.'[27]

McBride's long tenure was a logical consequence of pre-war prosperity, his years in office underwritten by the splurge of spending on railway construction and other enterprises with which McBride identified himself and his Conservative party. By the time of his departure the economy as well as the province's physical face had altered. The boom had been fuelled by a combination of new settlers, improved access within the province, and increased investment capital. While such factors could not have in any case continued indefinitely, McBride's enthusiasm intensified the bust following the boom. He had encouraged and even subsidized over-expansion. While it might have been possible to justify two major railways spanning British Columbia, in no way was it possible to argue for the number that were supported financially, much less the many others proposed and in some cases actually considered by the provincial government. From 1912 British Columbia became caught up in international economic and political circumstances over which the most determined premier could have had no control. Nonetheless, the precarious state into which the province's finances were then placed rested in part on government initiatives taken during the boom years. Historian Patricia Roy has neatly summed up: 'By the end of 1915 Richard McBride was no longer a railway builder nor a politician extraordinaire but the victim of the end of prosperity which had permitted his success.'[28]

Politics over the next years were largely an addendum to McBride. Less than a year after becoming premier, his successor William Bowser was defeated by the scandals emanating from McBride's tenure. The Liberals, coming to power in November 1916, successfully projected themselves as the party of reform, clearing the air and beginning anew. Like the Conservatives, they then governed for a full dozen years. In their case, three men would serve as premier, owing to the death in office of the first two: Harlan Brewster in March 1918 followed by John Oliver in August 1927. Only with Oliver's ascendancy in the 1920s would McBride's formidable shadow begin to lift from the provincial political scene.

The years of early century, dominated by McBride and his politics brought a new dynamism to British Columbia. Self-confidence grew. Yet events were in many ways only more of the same compressed in time. While new arrivals were more diverse than their predecessors, the dominant society's continuum of acceptability still placed the same groups at the bottom and, of course, themselves at the top. Larger numbers only confirmed Vancouver's role as metropolis to an expanding hinterland. Party politics helped to maintain Richard McBride in power, but it was also the force of personality that buttressed his authority. The Canadian Pacific Railway may have lost its hegemony, but only to a mix of strong companies for the most part centred outside the province. Their authority often held supreme within a particular industry or segment of an industry. Staples still held sway and entrepreneurial capitalism reigned.

10

Reform and Its Limits
1871–1929

The tremendous expansion of capitalism in Canada during the late nineteenth and early twentieth centuries had an enormous impact upon the lives of individual British Columbians. Some became wealthier, but others were pushed to the margin, shut out of an expanding economy. Changing patterns of employment and residence heightened inequalities in conditions of work, remuneration, and the quality of life. As enterprises grew larger, so did the distance, both actual and psychological, between employer and employee. Urbanization of the province's southwestern tip made the poor more visible. The population explosion of early century heightened perceptions of differences between ethnic and racial groups. Events came to a head in the aftermath of the war.

Two parallel strands of reform emerged in British Columbia: agitation to improve conditions of work and a desire for social reform. For the most part the two strands acted separately and perceived their roles as distinct. The labour movement was essentially male and working class and was directed almost solely towards the workplace. Social reform was primarily concerned with life beyond the workplace and received its principal support from middle-class women and from Christians, both male and female, adhering to the social gospel.

The common goal of both movements was to raise minimum standards of everyday life, in the one case economically for workers, in the other socially for all British Columbians. Radical elements in the labour movement sometimes espoused revolutionary change to overturn the capitalist status quo, but even such individuals continued to operate on a pragmatic, day-to-day level, attempting to alter the existing society. The two groups' common goal – the reform of existing structures and attitudes – was conservative in that change was encouraged only so far as it embodied the norms of the reformers themselves. The proponents of social reform were determined to remould society into their largely middle-class Anglo-Canadian image of respectability. Working-class counterparts were equally concerned to organize wage-earners into the trade unions to which they themselves gave allegiance and which they just as strongly equated with respectability. In neither set of circumstances was much consideration given to whether individuals on whose behalf they worked wished to be 'reformed.'

While each of the reform thrusts achieved some successes, the efforts of these advocates of change often ended in stalemate or failure. Reform was limited, first, by the willingness of those being reformed and, secondly, by the attitude of government. In some instances, as with prohibition and the move to create one big union, the reformers' zeal ran ahead of general acceptance. Governments for the most part did not support reform. To the extent that they intervened, it was most often to defend the interests of those already in positions of power. Politicians' other priority was to ensure their own continued rule. Sometimes these goals conveniently coincided, as when the Liberals embraced social reform during and after the war years in order to garner votes.

To understand the importance accorded reform, it is necessary to consider Canada as a whole. Initiatives taken in British Columbia, while often responding to events on a local level, were influenced by larger circumstances. The combined effects of industrialization, urbanization, and immigration had caused alarm in nineteenth-century Ontario and Quebec at a time when British Columbia was still a frontier society. Montreal was home to 115,000 people by 1871, Toronto and Quebec City each half as many. The National Policy encouraged Montreal's growth to almost half a million by 1911, a pace matched only by Toronto whose population approached four hundred thousand.

By the first decade of the twentieth century the image of the self-sufficient farm family as society's backbone had lost its force. Some individuals were pushed off the land as the limits of agricultural settlement were reached, others departed eagerly for what they considered to be better opportunities in the west or the big city. Many worked in manufacturing or resource industries, joining a growing number of immigrants of diverse backgrounds. The laissez-faire attitude that individuals in a society should make their own way in the world or suffer the consequences of not so doing began to lose its hold. Social ills long a part of the human condition – workers stopping off for a drink on the way home, neglected children, prostitutes plying their trade, petty crime, juvenile delinquency – became more visible in crowded urban conditions. The prevalence of low wages and poor working conditions made working men and women ready candidates for the rhetoric of union organizers. They also soon aroused the interest of Christian activists.

The social reform movement was in its origins a largely female and middle-class enterprise. Traditionally women's lives were much more circumscribed than those of men. Even the minority who managed to acquire a higher education were not expected to put it to practical use. Some women had always been in the workforce, but usually only out of economic necessity or prior to marriage. Thereafter the male ruled supreme. The relationship between the sexes was summed up in Emily Carr's description of her parents: 'Mother was Father's reflection … No one dreamt of crossing his will. Mother loved him and obeyed because it was her loyal pleasure to do so.'[1]

A few women, particularly those whose husbands could afford labour-saving devices for the home or domestic help, had some leisure. It became a status symbol signifying membership in the middle class that a wife did not have to do her own house work or care full-time for her children. Women needed to legitimize – in terms of society's assumptions about their proper role – any move out of the home. The imperative within Christianity to do good works provided a rationale, in effect clothing women who dared to walk the streets without a male escort with the respectability of the church. In the case of organized reform movements the public leader was generally the local minister or another respected male; women provided management behind the scenes. Another justification for social reform grew out of the traditional perception of women's function as the physical, emotional, and spiritual nurturer of the next generation. Women's special role within the home was simply extended outward to encompass the entire community, a shift that has been dubbed maternal feminism.

The social reform thrust received a powerful impetus from the rise of the social gospel. The changes overtaking Canada in the mid and late nineteenth century challenged the churches' hegemony. Urban dwellers were less likely than their country and small-town brethren to go to church or even to observe the Sabbath. Immigrants brought with them their own faiths, some not even Christian. No longer was it sufficient to reconcile individuals into accepting their earthly burdens in anticipation of better conditions in the next world. The earlier obsession with theological dogma gave way to meeting the physical and social needs of parishioners. Methodists, who came out of a long tradition of social awareness that had already translated into leadership of the movement to establish public schools, were in the forefront in applying Christ's teachings to the economic and social problems of the day.

This social gospel exercised tremendous appeal within the Christian community. Conservative elements sought to restrain the human impulse for evil and guide the individual towards salvation, which remained for them the principal goal of Christianity. The other theological extreme, sometimes involved in the trade union movement and in the emergence of left-oriented political parties, viewed the social gospel as justification for complete reconstruction of an exploitative social order. The centre looked to broadly based reform, including social services and better conditions of employment. Social justice was the common goal.

While some working people became caught up in the social gospel and more generally in social reform, it was conditions of employment that mainly interested them. The federal Trades Union Act passed in 1872 did legalize the mere act of combining, but it did not force employers to recognize the organizations through which workers came together to press their demands. Dissatisfaction over lack of safety or low rates of pay was from time to time expressed in strikes, but usually to no avail. Supported by government, employers refused to recognize, much less negotiate with, representatives of their employees.

As a consequence there was a growing credence given to Marxist theory, especially its interpretation of the central role of capitalism and class in determining relationships between individuals within a society. The concept of class has been interpreted variously, but refers most generally to the mix of economic and social attributes by which individuals distinguish themselves and are distinguished by others. Karl Marx argued for the inevitability of conflict between a capitalist class, or bourgeoisie, and a working class, or proletariat. According to Marxist theory, working people were forced to sell their labour below its true value so that capitalists could make the profits upon which both their personal well-being and the emerging industrial order depended. Marx believed that, as working people became conscious of their systematic exploitation and organized themselves into trade unions, capitalism would be violently replaced by a more equitable, socialist order. For a time, in the late nineteenth and twentieth centuries, such a concept made eminently good sense to many working people in Canada and elsewhere.

In British Columbia, as elsewhere in Canada, local circumstances shaped the particular course reform took in and out of the work place. Class distinctions were particularly strong in the west coast province. The attitude of colonial Britons towards Canadians embodied a strong sense of superiority. Dunsmuir's actions during the 1877 coal miners' strike on Vancouver Island presented an extreme case of class consciousness being encouraged from the top down. The passing comment from the East Kootenays in 1901 concerning a local worthy was not untypical. 'Mr. Jones is most indignant at the workmen on the c.p.r. *daring* to strike, no matter how badly they are paid. According to him, the world is made for the rich, and the poor are to work for them and be grateful for the privilege.'[2]

Class tensions were aggravated by the lack of an independent middle sector in the form of farmers and their small-town suppliers, as existed across much of Canada. In British Columbia such middle groups were most often linked to resource exploitation. As a preponderance of small locally based enterprises gave way to much larger companies likely capitalized from outside of the province, as occurred earlier in Vancouver Island coal mines and then in the Kootenays, relationships between employer and employee became more impersonal. Growing awareness of common attributes and common needs heightened working people's consciousness of themselves as a class apart. The nature of mining, lumbering, and other forms of staple production meant that workers were thrown close together. Often, their places of livelihood possessed little appeal, as in an early description of Fernie with 'the atmosphere laden with coal-dust, the whole place dingy with coal-dust, and the people with countenances smeared with coal-dust.'[3] Rates of pay were uncertain. Most hard-rock miners were paid on a sliding scale pegged to the world market price of the metal being mined, coal miners on a contract basis. Neither practice made any provision for changes in the cost of living.

The concept of class as it emerged in British Columbia was also moulded by widespread immigration from countries with a strong tradition of labour organization, most particularly Britain, the United States, and northern Europe. British immigrants gave British Columbia's largest city, so Norbert MacDonald has argued, 'a somewhat more formal, structured, class-conscious quality.'[4] Some newcomers brought with their commitment to socialist ideology a preference for radical tactics and direct confrontation. 'Coming from an immigrant English family who had all signed up to work for the coal company [in the Crow's Nest Pass] I was always reminded by my parents, aunts and uncles that the only way these conditions of food, clothing and shelter would be changed to give everyone a break would be a complete change of the system ... As a little boy I remember my parents going to a "party" every month. I always wished I could go with them as I had never been to a party and they always seemed so happy on this special evening. The party was a Socialist Party meeting.'[5]

Notions of class were also shaped by the presence of racial minorities willing – or forced by circumstances – to work for lower wages than most workers of European descent. Overt racism divided individuals who on the basis of occupation might otherwise have joined forces to improve their material conditions. It also heightened consciousness of exploitation as a principal motif of the work place in British Columbia. As exploitation (or a perception of exploitation) became overt, so unions were seen as the best means of improving working conditions.

The opposition of employers to trade unions meant that early organization had to be clandestine. One of the first unions to appear in British Columbia was the Knights of Labor, which spread from the United States in the mid 1880s. Like most early unions, the Knights performed several functions. While the organization of a union at the local level often originated in confrontations over wages, the local then played a social as well as an economic role. Knights' locals acted as mutual benefit societies, members contributing a small sum on a regular basis to protect themselves against the unexpected costs of illness or death. The regular contact thus engendered often brought together disparate peoples into what has been called a working-class culture.[6] The Knights' appeal, strongest among coal miners and railway workers, rested in part on its opposition to Chinese labour. Indeed, the Knights' major confrontation began not as a strike but as a campaign to drive Asians out of Vancouver by painting large 'x's on businesses run by or having any dealings with Chinese. About twenty locals existed in British Columbia prior to the Knights' decline at the end of the 1880s, caused mainly by the rise of craft unionism.

Skilled workers such as miners and typographers preferred unions organized by occupation. By late century about 130 craft unions had locals in British Columbia. A trades and labour council bringing together craft locals was formed in Vancouver in 1889 and in Victoria early the next year. The various councils across Canada soon formed a Canadian Trades and Labour Congress. A certain conservative outlook predominated. Members were generally more concerned to protect their relatively privileged position within the working class than to promote improvements benefiting all working people at the possible cost of mass confrontation with employers.

The ballot box exercised appeal. The Knights encouraged members to stand for election. Growing numbers of working-class British and American immigrants brought with them long traditions of political involvement. In 1890 two pro-labour candidates from the Nanaimo area were elected to the provincial legislature. In 1893, a decade before the two mainline parties emerged in British Columbia, a labour party centred in Vancouver elected three MLAS, three years later a member of the federal Parliament. The 1898 provincial election brought successes by moderate candidates backed by Kootenay and Vancouver Island miners as well as by Vancouver workers. The three men found themselves holding the balance between the two major coalitions in the provincial legislature, split nineteen to seventeen, and were able to get legislation enacting an eight-hour day in metal mines and excluding underground employment of Chinese in coal mining. A few years later, in 1902, the government was persuaded to pass a workmen's compensation act, the first in Canada. By then the concept of candidates for political office being backed by unions and giving priority to the concerns of working people was accepted in British Columbia. The achievement was considerable.

Early efforts at social reform were shaped, just as in the workplace, by imperatives unique to British Columbia. The small number of females, and more specifically of servants, played a role. So did the demands of everyday life. Even the lucky few able to afford a Chinese house boy or Indian washerwoman faced a wide range of responsibilities. They routinely cared for kitchen gardens, preserved food to last the winter, oversaw occasional or regular boarders, and gave midwifery or medical assistance as needed. Chickens and cows were as common in West End Vancouver as on the frontier, their daily care falling on women and children.

Change came slowly. That incredible labour-saving device of the later nineteenth century, the sewing machine, was much prized as a household possession. Particularly in isolated areas, mail order catalogues from Eaton's and Vancouver's Woodward's stores were a boon. For a pioneer family near Ootsa Lake in the central interior, 'Eaton's catalogue was like the family Bible – it was read every day and all clothing was ordered from it.' With a northern Vancouver Island family, 'the great thing about Woodward's was we could buy hay, oats, chicken feed, groceries and clothes all in the same order.' In addition, as emphasized in an early catalogue, 'we carry a large stock of Umbrellas specially adapted for use in our British Columbia climate.'[7]

As was the case across Canada, the first reform groups were organized within the church. Religion's hold in the west coast province may have been less firm than elsewhere, possibly heightening the apparent necessity for reform among the committed. Early clerics were forced to spend as much time in an ongoing struggle to survive financially as in administering to congregations strung out across vast distances. A family in the Okanagan improvised, making do on Sunday with Bible reading in their home. Visitors from elsewhere in Canada expressed surprise at an apparent lack of religious observance. 'This has been a most glorious day, not a bit like Sunday though. It might have been any day of the week from the way we kept it. I am getting completely demoralized.' Visiting Vancouver, the same young Ontarian penned in her diary, 'people don't seem to worry much about churches out here.'[8]

Most Protestant denominations acquired social auxiliaries that were intended to appeal particularly to female parishioners. A branch of the Women's Christian Temperance Union was started in Victoria in 1882 following a visit by Frances Willard, head of the American WCTU. Shortly after, the Young Women's Christian Association began. British Columbians who were religiously committed, like Vancouver's Malkin family, evoked so perceptively by Ethel Wilson in the The Innocent Traveller, practised their faith with a vengeance. Herself a Methodist Malkin, Wilson considered that it was almost impossible to be young. 'Such an upbringing, even if transplanted to British Columbia, carried with it a terrific sense of duty and personal responsibility. I used to feel a little personal responsibility if rain fell on Dominion Day, a slight sense of guilt.'[9]

Among the most widespread, effective, and least intrusive of reform groups were Farmers' and Women's Institutes. Farmers' Institutes had spread from Ontario to British Columbia by the turn of the century. Intended to improve agricultural practices, they also provided an impetus for rural men and women to get together on a regular basis. Women's Institutes reached the west coast province in 1909 and soon became a welcome feature of rural life. Their mandate – 'study of home economics, child welfare, prevention of disease, local neighbourhood needs, of industrial and social conditions' – encompassed the issues agitating social reformers across North America.[10] Farmers' and Women's Institutes were supported by the provincial Ministry of Agriculture, which provided information and financed travelling lecturers.

Two of the issues which aroused social reformers, as much in British Columbia as across North America, were temperance and female suffrage. They were frequently linked. Women were perceived as more likely than men to support prohibition at the polls if given the vote. Advocates attributed to alcohol, and more particularly to the supposed inability of working people and immigrants to restrain themselves in its use, all the ills of a growing society. Various means of temperance were proposed, ranging from legislation to school courses. While the latter soon entered the provincial curriculum, the former proved more difficult to achieve.

Prohibition was a complex issue. British Columbia was still very much a man's province. Through the First World War its non-native adult population, despite expanding almost forty times since British Columbia's entry into Confederation, contained over twice as many males as females. For workers in resource industries or other forms of wage labour, an hour or two in the local bar constituted one of life's few pleasures. Emily Carr recollected from her childhood how 'on almost every street corner in Victoria there was one saloon or more. There were saloons in the middle of every block as well ... There were saloons, too, every few miles along the driving roads. These they called roadhouses.' While favouring temperance, Jessie McQueen embodied a certain ambivalence. The local Nicola hotel was doing mischief, yet 'it's the only place for the young men to gather, & as nearly every one is away from home, they must have *some* where they can meet and have a good time.'[11]

Nearby Merritt's appearance early in the new century brought 'a cluster of dingy houses' where 'red lamps burned over every front door.' As remembered by a delivery boy of these years, 'the ladies of these establishments, whom I had already seen on the streets, gorgeously attired, now wore daytime kimonas and shawls, their hair unbrushed, their faces pale and surprisingly wrinkled, I thought.' Vancouver's red-light district was explained away to inquiring young children as a place where 'bad men and women met,' their purpose for so doing being left to the imagination.[12] Virtually every community, whatever its size, housed equivalent enterprises.

Class and religion complicated matters. Even as largely middle-class reformers sought to rid the province of a menace perceived to be threatening working people, many continued themselves to use alcohol. The diary of Mary Isabella Rogers, wife of BC Sugar's founder and a leading Vancouver matron, contains such cryptic observations as 'the "at home" improved later when the WCTU gang left.'[13] To the extent that the campaign for prohibition was a religious movement it was dominated by social gospellers, particularly Methodists and Presbyterians. In British Columbia their influence counted for less in ruling circles than did that of the Anglicans, who favoured moderation as opposed to a complete ban. Consistent with the province's renewed British influence, the number of Anglicans shot upward to one in four by 1911, almost one in three a decade later. Elsewhere in Canada it ranged between one in seven in the maritimes to one in five in Ontario. One in three British Columbians belonged to one of the other mainline Protestant denominations: Presbyterian, Methodist, or Congregationalist; about one in six were Catholic (see Table 10).

The equally difficult campaign for female suffrage went back in British Columbia at least as far as 1871 when American suffragist Susan B. Anthony told an enthusiastic Victoria crowd that 'the present condition of women is similar to that of slavery before the [Civil] War.'[14] Eight months later the first of numerous unsuccessful bills to give women the vote was introduced in the provincial legislature. Support came from middle-class reformers and from moderate elements within the labour movement: as early as 1878 a Workingman's Party based in Victoria included a female suffrage clause in its by-laws. From the 1880s the WCTU repeatedly petitioned for the vote. Change came slowly. Late in the century women secured the right to vote for local school boards, an area of public life considered within their realm of expertise. A turn-of-the-century bill for a provincial franchise was supported by a petition signed by some twenty thousand British Columbian men and women and nearly received legislative consent.

By the beginning of the new century recognition of the need to improve the existing social and economic order was widespread across British Columbia. Attempts to effect gradual change, be it in conditions of everyday life or in the workplace, seemed to have had few results. The dramatic expansion of British Columbia's resource economy challenged organized labour's reformist orientation. Historian Carlos Schwantes explained the changing circumstances in the American Pacific Northwest, where similar conditions existed. 'Because many unskilled or semiskilled workers headed west expecting to achieve personal success, they easily became disappointed and outraged by anything that prevented them from claiming the rewards promised by western opportunity ... Time after time clashes between unrealistic expectations and harsh reality gave rise to radical crusades, militant unions, and violence.' A BC labourer echoed the sentiment: 'By the time I had worked a couple of years in the sawmill and logging industry under the most deplorable conditions, I became a dedicated socialist.'[15] Much debate raged over whether fundamental change was possible through the political process or must necessarily occur, as Marx argued, through direct confrontation. Differences in perspective, intensified by political developments in Russia and elsewhere in Europe, fractured the unity that working people might have achieved. Not only did the members go off in all directions; they then expended much energy condemning all those daring to act in opposition to their own views.

The tactics of socialist parties grew far more confrontational. Indeed, socialism in Canada as a whole might be said to have originated in the 1901 foundation of the Socialist party of British Columbia, out of which a national party emerged three years later. Dissatisfied coal miners and others became convinced that capitalism could not be reformed but must be overturned, although in practice they still accepted the electoral process. The provincial election in 1903 brought the Socialist party victory in two Nanaimo area constituencies with concentrations of radical miners. Shortly after, labour again held the balance of power. The two MLAs were able to get an eight-hour day in coal mines as a concession from Premier McBride. Although moderate reformists also continued to run for office, the momentum had shifted to the left.

As population grew and British Columbia's resource industries depersonalized, activity in the workplace expanded. Membership in trade unions reached over twenty-two thousand, or 12 per cent of the non-agricultural labour force by 1911. Increasingly, moderates were challenged by supporters of industry-wide action. Reflecting the changing orientation of their members, trades and labour councils across British Columbia came into increasing conflict with more conservative national associations tied to craft unionism.

The American-based Industrial Workers of the World represented this new, more radical outlook. The IWW, or Wobblies, offered a simple message proclaiming the self-worth of workers toiling for low pay in difficult conditions without any security of employment. A handful of locals appeared in British Columbia in early century, mostly attracting unskilled workers, often recent immigrants. Asserting working peoples' critical role as the basis of the economy, the IWW emphasized their power to stop the wheels of production if only they united into a single group. The Wobblies differed from most other workers' groups of the time in that they truly believed in egalitarianism and in the organization of workers of all races, including Chinese, into a single industrial union. Like the Knights, the Wobblies supported a range of social amenities, and this heightened their appeal. Union halls doubled as dormitories, mail drops, and employment agencies. The peak of IWW influence in British Columbia came in the summer of 1912 when thousands of railway construction workers staged largely unsuccessful strikes for better wages and conditions. Economic recession and then wartime restrictions brought the Wobblies' decline.

In the early twentieth century more strikes broke out in British Columbia than in any other province. The two resource industries most affected were coal mining and the fisheries. Conditions in the mines were still harsh, and labour unrest extended from Vancouver Island to the Crow's Nest Pass. The most extensive confrontation involved almost seven thousand Island miners, cost the North American trade union movement $1.5 million, and lasted two years, from 1912 to 1914. The paternalistic Vancouver Coal and Land

Company had been sold in 1902 to a San Francisco concern that was considerably less liberal in its treatment of workers. Elsewhere Dunsmuir's legacy endured, despite his company's sale in 1910 to Mackenzie and Mann. In 1909 a gas explosion killed thirty-two Dunsmuir miners. The subsequent investigation pointed to dangerous working conditions and, more generally, to employer willingness to gamble with lives in the interests of profit. Employees responded by forming locals of the United Mine Workers.

Confrontation erupted in the summer of 1912 after the company refused to recognize a complaint of dangerous conditions made by a workers' gas safety committee whose existence was sanctioned by provincial legislation of the previous year. Management fired the complainants whereupon some three thousand fellow workers voted to take a 'holiday' until their reinstatement. Chinese and other non-union labour kept the mines in partial production over the winter, but the following April a general strike was proclaimed. Tensions built up during the summer of 1913, heightened by the news in August that one of the companies intended to resume operations. Riots broke out. As in 1877, the provincial attorney general dispatched troops to the company's assistance. This act seemed to many to offer clear proof of government's alignment with big business, in particular with one of the biggest capitalist enterprises of them all, Mackenzie and Mann. In the brutal confrontation that ensued, over 250 miners were arrested. Some were subsequently sentenced to as much as two years' imprisonment.

Even though strike-breakers, known disparagingly as scabs, kept operations going over the winter of 1913–14, the miners held on. Financial support came from the United Mine Workers' international strike fund to which every unionized miner in North America contributed fifty cents to support the Vancouver Island miners. Premier McBride tried repeatedly to get a settlement but, because the employers' proposal did not include union recognition, workers rejected the offer he negotiated in June 1914. Two months later they were forced to accept it, owing to the desperate need to feed their families and to the outbreak of war earlier in the month. While the agreement shut out the union, the two companies agreed to conduct future wage negotiations with employee committees. Although they may have lived up to this clause, they apparently reneged on a promise not to blacklist by refusing to take back some of the strikers. Some left permanently, others joined the army. For those who stayed, as Lynn Bowen's reminiscences of miners, *Boss Whistle*, makes clear, enmities generated by the strike long continued.[16] Even into the late twentieth century some scab families were still being scorned by those whose families had held out.

Unrest among fishermen was heightened by racial enmities and corporate concentration.[17] Canneries on the Fraser River, which up to the First World War accounted for over half the province's production, had joined together in the 1890s to control prices and output. The price paid for fish equated to a wage scale, but one particularly unpredictable owing to the salmon's variable cycle. As European and native fishermen found themselves competing with growing numbers of Japanese, so direct action ensued. A union was formed, soon followed by a strike for better pay. Japanese fishermen were hired as strike-breakers. Despite pressure from cannery operators and the local Indian agent, native fishermen and female cannery workers held out even after European fishermen began to capitulate. Nonetheless the union collapsed. Displacement by Japanese fishermen accelerated: by 1901 Japanese held almost two thousand out of just over forty-seven hundred fishing licences issued in the province, as well as most of the thousand licences allotted to canneries.

Renewed union organization by Europeans and Indians was countered by the formation of a Japanese benevolent society under the patronage of the Japanese consul in Vancouver. Strikes for higher prices in 1900 and 1901 each involved upwards to eight thousand fishermen and allied workers. While at first all three racial groups co-operated, open conflict soon erupted. Europeans and Indians were again pitted against Japanese who, faced with language difficulties and discrimination, were in a weaker bargaining position. Three weeks after the 1900 strike began, martial law was declared at Steveston in order to permit Japanese workers' unimpeded return to the waters. Compromise came a few days later. The next year's work stoppage saw the union equally unable to cope with Japanese strike-breaking.

Then the situation came full circle. In a 1913 protest against a mid-season price cut it was the Japanese, according to a newspaper description, who were 'completely organized, with union halls and officers.' By comparison the Europeans, 'being of all nationalities besides English-speaking,' favoured compromise.[18] So did the Indians. The violence, intimidation, and property damage were reminiscent of earlier strikes, only the protagonists' positions were reversed.

The next years brought quiescence, apart from a rearguard attempt by the New Westminster Board of Trade to drive out the Japanese on the alleged grounds that they remitted earnings abroad rather than spending the money in British Columbia.

As the experience of coal miners and fishermen demonstrate, several factors limited the success of strikes, whatever the industry. Many early unions were transitory, even fragile entities. Lacking permanent organization and a firm financial base, they disintegrated in the face of strong employer opposition. Strikers were sometimes left to fend for themselves without the moral, much less financial, support of a larger body. It is in retrospect amazing – and indicative of the appalling working conditions existing in some sectors of the economy – that workers were willing to gamble what modicum of job security they possessed to remain weeks, months, even years without any wages coming in to support themselves and their families.

Immigration, so critical in promoting union activity, was used also to undermine direct action by the workers. A West Kootenay mine manager's private letter is illuminating. 'In all the lower grades of labour and especially in smelter labour it is necessary to have a mixture of races which includes a number of illiterates who are first class workmen. They are the strength of an employer, and the weakness of the Union. How to head off a strike of muckers or labourers for higher wages without the aid of Italian labour I do not know.' One of the characters in Allerdale Grainger's novel *Woodsmen of the West* observed how 'railroad foremen treat their men like dogs, as the saying is; the men being, for the most part, Galicians [Ukrainians] and Polacks [Poles] and Dagos [Italians] and such-like that cannot stand up for themselves.'[19] Asians were particularly vulnerable to exploitation, both as a source of cheap labour and as strike-breakers.

Especially important in containing strikes was the government's willingness to act in concert with employers to get workers back on the job without granting demands. After railway employees and coal miners struck unsuccessfully in 1903 to secure recognition of newly formed unions, a federal Royal Commission on Industrial Disputes in British Columbia was established. Fears existed that the work stoppages, which generated widespread sympathy strikes, were part of some larger socialist conspiracy emanating from the United States. Despite overwhelming evidence to the contrary, the commissioners came to precisely that conclusion. The American unions supporting British Columbia's workers were described as revolutionary socialists, their leaders as, 'not trade unionists, but foreign socialistic agitators.'[20]

Responding to labour unrest across Canada, Parliament soon acted. In 1907 an Industrial Disputes Investigation Act was passed, providing for the appointment of a conciliation board, and if necessary compulsory arbitration. During the process direct action in the form of strikes or lock-outs was prohibited. The legislation, which up to the Second World War provided the main basis for settlement of labour disputes, favoured employers by putting no restraints on them not to fire or blacklist workers suspected of harbouring union sympathies.

The failure of direct confrontation may have contributed to the fragmentation of political initatives even though they seemed for a time to be the more fruitful avenue for workplace reform. Only in British Columbia were labour or socialist candidates elected provincially or federally prior to the First World War. All the same, from 1910 the Socialist party lost supporters as class unity gave way to internal dissension. Pitted against each other were eastern European immigrants, who were pure Marxist socialists, and British workers, who came from a more moderate socialist tradition. The Social Democratic party, formed as a socialist splinter group in 1907, won two coal mining seats in 1912. In that election the Liberals were eliminated by McBride and the Conservatives, which made the two socialists the only opposition. But defections and disarray would reduce opportunities for election under the socialist banner in the future.

In the years of early century the ferment in the workplace was matched by demands for social reform. Individual women began to step into leadership positions. Among activists were Helen Gregory MacGill and Helena Gutteridge, who represented two very diverse strands among female reformers. MacGill epitomized the Canadian establishment, Gutteridge the enterprising working-class immigrant. MacGill, born into the Ontario élite, settled in Vancouver with her lawyer husband in 1901. As recalled by her daughter, 'in the age-old fashion of dutiful women she had followed in a husband's wake, accommodating her life to his plans, his wishes, his whims, ready to fashion a new role for herself from whatever material came to hand.' But for Helen MacGill this conventional role was not sufficient. She soon became involved in a range of voluntary activities, and was quickly made aware that the legal status of women and children was 'outmoded, harsh and morally repugnant.'[21] On becoming a colonial possession, the future province had acquired the laws then in force in England, which remained in effect in their mid-nineteenth century versions until actually repealed or modified in British Columbia even though more liberal legislation had been passed in Britain itself. For some three decades better protection under the law for women and children was MacGill's principal concern.

Helena Gutteridge stood in sharp contrast. A single working woman until well into middle age, she was a committed activist before her arrival from England in 1911. While everything involving womens' interests concerned Gutteridge, it was 'particularly those things that affect women out in the labour market' that mobilized her into action. Becoming secretary of the Vancouver Trades and Labour Council, Gutteridge helped organize female workers and campaigned for a minimum female wage and a pension for needy mothers.[22] Despite their different emphases in reform, MacGill and Gutteridge stood together on the central issue of female suffrage.

The long-standing campaign for suffrage, as for temperance, was gathering momentum. In 1910 the first of several new suffrage associations was formed, their female and male memberships from across the province sharing the one goal of securing women's enfranchisement. Delegations were organized, petitions circulated, public meetings held, and support secured from such diverse organizations as the WCTU, labour groups, and the Liberal party, then in opposition provincially. The provincial Liberals first backed women's suffrage at their 1912 convention, seeking to take advantage of growing public sentiment. The impetus to success came out of the war. Across Canada patriotism on the home front was perceived as a fight to eradicate the ills of society. Many social gospellers believed that the war represented the final struggle to establish God's kingdom on earth. The stalemate was broken nationally when in 1915 Manitoba gave women the vote, followed in short order by Alberta and Saskatchewan.

Backed by a broad coalition of reform groups, British Columbian Liberals made prohibition and suffrage part of their successful 1916 election campaign. The ballot included referendums on the two

issues and both were approved. Acts soon went into effect prohibiting the sale of liquor except for medical prescriptions and giving
women the right to vote and be elected to the legislature. Women
received the franchise federally in two stages, war nurses and
immediate relatives of military men in 1917, followed by all women
on the same basis as men the next year.

The First World War also fundamentally altered relations between
management and labour in British Columbia. A penchant for
confrontation was superseded by a generally shared interest in
promoting the imperial cause. Then, as hostilities dragged on,
working people grew restive. High inflation reduced what were
already modest wage packages. The introduction of national registra-
tion late in 1916 was followed by federal conscription legislation the
next August. Opposition was widespread. French-speaking Canadians in particular were outraged. So were many farmers and wage
labourers, convinced that they were being forced to do more than
their fair share in the war effort. They believed that 'the conscription
of wealth, and the means of wealth production and distribution'
should accompany any conscription of men.[23] Fears were heightened
by rumours that the government was considering industrial conscription, which would have the effect of curtailing trade unions.

In July 1918 the federal government issued a war labour policy
giving workers the right to organize, while prohibiting strikes and
lock-outs for the duration of the war. It also banned the most radical
of the workers' organizations, including the IWW and the Social
Democratic party. These actions may have served temporarily to
contain labour unrest, but they did so at the cost of raising tensions in
the long run. Working people in western Canada were particularly
vociferous in their opposition to the federal initiatives, and unrest
was strongest among the Crow's Nest Pass coal miners and Vancouver shipbuilders.

About the same time British Columbia obtained a martyr in the
person of Albert 'Ginger' Goodwin, a socialist organizer active earlier
among Vancouver Island coal miners. Declared physically unfit for
military service, he resettled in Trail. There he helped lead a 1917
strike at Consolidated Mining's smelter to obtain the eight-hour day
for all workers. Soon after Goodwin found himself reclassified as 1A,
an action that those aware of his poor health were convinced was
politically motivated. Rather than be conscripted, Goodwin, like
many others, headed for the hills, in his case to central Vancouver

Island. Killed in July 1918 by a constable hunting him down who asserted that he had acted in self-defence, Goodwin became a cause célèbre for the province's union movement, which claimed that he had been murdered. A twenty-four-hour general strike called in Vancouver was broken up by returned soldiers organized by city businessmen. These events only served to polarize further the divergent groups in the society.

By war's end in November 1918 reform was again on the agenda. The cost of living across Canada had risen by 8 per cent in 1916, 18 per cent in 1917, and 13 per cent in 1918. High rates of inflation – some 30 per cent between 1916 and 1917 – inflicted great hardship. Compared to Canada as a whole, inflation was almost 10 per cent higher in British Columbia, while the unemployment rate was one and a half times greater. Union membership in British Columbia rose from a low of under eleven thousand during the war to about forty thousand by 1919. This represented about 22 per cent of the province's non-agricultural labour force.

The scene was set for what in retrospect can be seen as the culmination of the labour thrust of the previous two decades. Two separate, overlapping initiatives occurred. The concept of One Big Union, a single union of all workers, was coming to the fore in Australia and being organized across western Canada even as a general strike broke out in Winnipeg in May 1919. Much as was the case in British Columbia, class relations in Winnipeg had become polarized before the war. They were then intensified by inflation and the conscription crisis. Thousands of returning soldiers in search of jobs presaged unemployment, while the Russian Revolution heightened the appeal of socialist and communist rhetoric, particularly among Winnipeg's large immigrant community. The Winnipeg Trades and Labour Council's call for a general strike originated with skilled Anglo-Saxon craftsmen, but it soon encompassed many others, including unorganized immigrants. Radical social gospellers made the church one of the rallying points for protesters. At its peak, some thirty-five thousand workers, or one-fifth of Winnipeg's population, were on the streets. Although essential services were maintained, the city was paralysed.

Sympathy strikes were soon under way across Canada. Support in British Columbia was boosted by a general strike the previous February in nearby Seattle. The first in the United States, it lasted four days before its sixty thousand participants were forced back to work.

Activity in British Columbia ranged from interior logging camps to Rossland and Prince Rupert to Victoria and Vancouver. Nearly twelve thousand men and women left work in Vancouver, though as in Winnipeg, they maintained essential services. But support for the strike was never complete, and as time passed men and women across the province drifted back to work.

Opposition to the general strike mounted. Employers across Canada had been as hard hit by inflation as had their workers, and they, too, narrowed their vision to immediate self-interest. The economic downturn occurring at war's end only heightened employers' antagonism towards men and women daring to strike for higher wages. The perspective was vividly caught by the novelist Bertrand Sinclair in recounting one young businessman's visit to an exclusive Vancouver men's club. 'These worthy gentlemen over their wine and cigars affected to believe the State, the home, the nation, reeled to ruin before union wage scales. The rancor in their voices when they spoke of working-class demands amazed Rod sometimes. But, as he listened, he perceived ... that this uneasy spirit lay in the fact that the sweeping tide of war prosperity had slacked suddenly where they had childishly believed it would surge on to greater heights, – and that this slackening was unprofitable.' These men might well have included BC Sugar's B.T. Rogers, who in response to a 1917 strike for union recognition and higher wages retorted, 'I will have nothing to do with any union or union man, and I will not have a union man at work in the refinery. I will discharge whoever I want to and employ whoever I want to, without reference to any union ... The men have the right to work or quit work as they see fit, and I insist on my right to employ or discharge who I see fit.'[24] The strike at BC Sugar soon collapsed.

Some in Canada went even further, fearing that the general strike which had begun in Winnipeg as a wage issue was becoming an attempt at revolution. The workers' enthusiasm for events in Russia, including the Victoria TLC's open endorsement of the Soviet system, underlay growing anxiety. The Seattle general strike was widely interpreted as the beginning of a Bolshevist revolution. There dozens of immigrant workers were rounded up and deported as alien subversives. A rash of anarchist bombings against prominent American political figures contributed to Canadian willingness to use repressive measures if necessary to counter the perceived threat of insurrection. A citizens' committee working closely with government brought an end to the Winnipeg general strike on 26 June after six weeks of confrontation. Some Vancouver workers held out longer, hoping to secure the release of BC union leaders arrested in Winnipeg. Others remained off the job for more specific reasons, including telephone operators protesting supervisors' replacement by strike-breakers. In the end the operators were forced back on the company's terms and within the year their union collapsed. In total over one million person-days of work were lost across Canada.

Even as the Winnipeg general strike continued, the constitution of a proposed One Big Union was being written, to be shortly adopted by various trades and labour councils across western Canada. By the end of 1919 the OBU had a reported membership of over forty thousand, almost half in British Columbia. As numbers grew, so did opposition. Employers and governments feared a socialist revolution. Premier John Oliver termed the OBU a Bolshevist plot and ordered various union officials arrested, their offices searched. Consolidated Mining and Smelting's general manager locked out miners carrying OBU cards. Established international unions saw their memberships being drained away and withdrew the charters of locals supporting the OBU concept. In the post-war recession the resource industries whose workers provided the OBU's backbone of support were hit particularly hard; increasingly the men were concerned just to hold on to their jobs, let alone improve conditions of employment. As more and more OBU supporters were unable to pay dues, the split between traditional unionists and OBU supporters was decided in the former's favour. After 1920 the One Big Union in Canada became a shadow of its former self.

Organized labour's post-war thrust proved equally unsuccessful at the local level. The case of the loggers is a good example.[25] Lumbering's transient and seasonal character had long made union organization almost impossible. Yet a very ambitious campaign launched in January 1919 by members of the Socialist party soon attracted eleven thousand of the estimated fifteen thousand loggers at work in the logging camps across the province. Inflation levels far in excess of wage increases, the growing impersonality of the industry, and poor living conditions in logging camps all contributed to the success of the campaign to organize. Logging's rapid unionization created, almost overnight so it seemed, strong militancy. From no strikes in 1917 and 1918, the number rose to thirty-one in 1919 and fifty the next year. Demands, while concerned with wage and work issues, centred just as much on 'single bunks' and companies' provision of blankets.

Yet within two years union offices were bankrupt and membership negligible. Two principal factors defeated the loggers' cause. The first was internal dissension over whether short-term strategy should emphasize direct action in the workplace through strikes or self-education to prepare for the worldwide revolution expected shortly to overthrow capitalism, as had already occurred in Russia. Secondly, employers vigorously counter-attacked. Industrial councils were established, better recreational facilities provided, and union leaders blacklisted. Growing recession sealed the fate of the loggers' unions.

Labour's offensive failed for several reasons. The Winnipeg general strike made clear that the brute power of the state in support of capitalism was superior to that which could be marshalled by the working class, even under favourable material conditions. Established unions were often more concerned to protect their existing interests than to promote genuine class-based action such as underlay the One Big Union concept. The OBU remained a regional phenemonon, centred in western Canada. Even there its appeal was relatively limited and short-lived.

It might be argued further that the post-war initiative failed because it did not comprehend the reality of working people's lives. Workers were, quite simply, not sufficiently conscious of themselves as a single entity or class. Although many immigrants, in particular in western Canada, were working class by background and by occupation, they had not come to Canada to identify themselves permanently with other such individuals, but rather to improve themselves. They sought to rise in status, possibly becoming employers themselves. Carpenters wanted to become contractors, skilled workers the owners of their own small businesses.[26] Like the father of the British Columbian politician Cyril Shelford, many immigrants brought with them a dream of wealth and freedom, determined to escape an existence 'where generation after generation worked in the coal mines or the textile industry with no hope of ever improving their lot in life.' So long as that dream was possible, they were willing 'to endure many hardships to establish that new life.'[27]

Even where individuals survived only on the margin, many remained incurably optimistic that improvement was just around the corner 'next year.' 'Life is pretty much what we make it for ourselves and for others. So what is the use in letting our burdens get us down.'[28] With the passage of time some acquired a stake in the future, often through marriage and children. 'I was now married and wanted to get established somewhere in my line of work, as I was no stump rancher.' Women were concerned, so one working man's wife lamented, to settle down. 'I wanted a place we could call home. I have had enough of continual moving from pillar to post.' Acquisition of material possessions and the passage of time tempered willingness to chance job loss through direct confrontation. 'If you had a job you felt safe at the time, and when you were out of work, you were too busy trying to stay alive to worry about the system.'[29]

The limits to reform confronted by the labour movement were paralleled in social activism, particularly in the case of prohibition.[30] The end of the war spelled its death knell in the west coast province. Many returned soldiers were as unhappy about a lack of beer as about job prospects. Ordinary men and women resented a law that seemed to violate common notions of justice and make criminals out of respectable people. The law was openly flouted and probably unenforceable. Bella Rogers observed how, following a social event at the Vancouver Club, 'several members came here [to her home] afterwards to counteract the grapejuice.'[31] Thousands of prescriptions were written every month prescribing alcohol for supposed medical conditions. A leading provincial politician expressed mock astonishment that it was only after prohibition that whisky was found to be the best medicine for innumerable diseases.

A moderation plebiscite was held in 1920 and passed. This made British Columbia the first province of English Canada to repeal prohibition, just a year after Quebec's turnaround. In its place were strictly regulated government liquor stores – which then provided an excellent opportunity for rampant patronage in their oversight and operation. British Columbia would over the next decade become the source of much of the liquor smuggled illegally into the United States on coastal rum-runners during that nation's much longer period of prohibition extending to 1933. Vancouver's 'rum row' had nearly sixty yachts, steamers, schooners, and other vessels berthed between runs up and down the coast, the largest able to carry sixty thousand cases of alcohol. Products obtained legally in Canada were supplemented by moonshine. To the north, at such remote locations as Pocahontas Bay on Texada Island, seemingly endless numbers of stills turned out thousands of gallons for the American market. Without doubt this was how some of the eighty-three millionaires reportedly living in Vancouver in 1929 acquired their fortune.

More generally, the post-war years witnessed a consolidation of social reform gains. To quote Helen MacGill's daughter, 'the drive for social legislation was now so steady and continuing a force that it and the other benefits due to the women's voting potential were accepted as natural features of the social landscape.'[32] It was now accepted that certain minimum standards of life were necessary in a modern society, such as Canada considered itself. Social reform through voluntary effort could accomplish only so much; it was the duty of the state to ensure that basic amenities were extended to all individuals. Paid professionals increasingly replaced the dedicated amateurs of an earlier day in public health, child care, and social welfare. Laws as opposed to private advocacy regulated such diverse areas as garbage collection, school attendance, police and fire protection, and provision of pure water. On both the provincial and federal levels Liberal governments caught the reform mood and enacted a spate of legislation: civil service reform, workmen's compensation, provisions for neglected children, minimum wage for women and girls, establishment of public libraries.

Many of the reforms for which MacGill, Gutteridge, and others had long fought were realized. In 1917 British Columbia became the first province to enact an equal guardianship and custody law. Pensions for needy mothers were legislated in 1920, causing some British Columbians to ponder the timing: the impending provincial election would see women voting for the first time. British Columbia again became a national leader in 1927 on passing enabling legislation which put into effect a federal old age pension act passed the same year. The parliamentary initiative, which responded to the lobbying efforts of labour and other groups, represented a major departure. It was the first sustained intervention in Canada into provision of social welfare. Based on a means test, the cost of the pensions was shared between the federal and provincial governments. The attitude of British Columbia's governing Liberals towards social reform incorporated a certain cynicism –'progressive legislation reasonably assures contented labour and operates as an insurance policy for Capital' – but nonetheless the deeds were done. As summed up by Elsie MacGill, 'in one gigantic stride British Columbia quit her earlier and unenviable position as the most backward province to emerge as the leader in social legislation in the Dominion.'[33]

The one area of reform where the limits continued to be pushed outward was in schooling. The reasons lay in the coincidence of interests between the two reform strands. Middle-class British Columbians' concern over the quality of schooling extended beyond their own children to the the well-being of working-class and immigrant families. Post-war labour militancy gave priority to measures intended to conciliate a potentially dangerous group within the society. In the logic of one social reformer, 'the bolsheviks of today are mainly the neglected children of yesterday.'[34] Working people were equally interested in their children's future, if for somewhat different reasons. Despite the failure of the labour offensive, many men and women retained some of the self-confidence achieved as a consequence of earlier efforts by organized labour. Wages were higher because unions had struggled into existence. Now the quality of life outside of the workplace, not just in the present but for the next generation, took on importance for many working people across British Columbia. Moderate labour leader Angus McInnis, active in Vancouver during the 1920s as school trustee and in other civic capacities, made the point succinctly in his observation that 'knowledge is essential for universal progress but fatal to class privilege.' Education's function was no more and no less than 'the emanicipation of the working class.'[35]

Concern over the welfare of children grew. Public health measures were intended to ensure a minimum level of care for all families. Mothers were showered with the advice of 'experts' on how best to raise their children. The Child Welfare Association of British Columbia was launched in 1918. By 1922 over two hundred thousand copies of *The Canadian Mother's Book*, published by the Child Welfare Division of the federal Department of Health, were in print across Canada. Voluntary organizations for children and young people such as the Boy Scouts, Girl Guides, and church-related groups became firmly entrenched. New laws prevented older children and young people from being used in full-time paid employment. Supervised playgrounds, pure milk legislation, and compulsory immunization were introduced.

Much attention was accorded schooling, which encompassed an ever greater time in children's lives. Since the first free, non-sectarian common schools were mandated by law in 1872, the school-leaving age had been raised from twelve to fourteen. By the 1920s most children remained for the full term of public schooling.

They were also more likely to attend regularly, day after day, than a few decades earlier when children were kept out of school to perform household tasks, farm chores, or work for pay to assist the family economy.

Equality was a different matter. On the frontier, as educational historian J. Donald Wilson has emphasized, conditions of schooling remained simplistic or even primitive.[36] In the interior and the north and along much of the coast, one-roomed log or wood structures erected by volunteer labour were still the norm. Some families were so isolated that they lacked access to any school at all, and it was during these years that provincial correspondence education was introduced. British Columbia was a world pioneer, being in 1919 the first jurisdiction after the state of Victoria in Australia to implement such schooling at the elementary level. A decade later it was the first in Canada to put in place its secondary counterpart. Lessons were pre-planned so that children could undertake them on their own with parental assistance, then send responses in to their correspondence teacher for a detailed written reply. In some cases the option actually encouraged families to move to the frontier, as in one father's decision of 1920 to pre-empt land along the central coast. 'He was simply brimming over with fine plans for the future. He said he had it all mapped out – everything. Once I interrupted him to ask where I would be going to school and ... he said I would get all the education I'd need by mail. The government sent correspondence lessons to kids out in the woods.'[37] Over three thousand students were enrolled in correspondence courses by the mid 1930s, some five thousand by the beginning of the Second World War, this out of a total provincial school enrolment of between one hundred and fifteen and one hundred and twenty thousand.

The school as an institution took on additional responsibilities. Urban schools in particular expanded their horizons to include occupational training, viewed almost wholly in gender terms. Boys received technical education, girls instruction in what was known as domestic science or home economics. As the terms suggest, both areas built on the more general interest of the early twentieth century in scientific management of everyday life. As one observer commented approvingly on visiting a British Columbian home economics class, the work was 'performed with almost military promptness and precision, each dish in each girl's cupboard being in its exact place, and even the knives, forks and spoons being ranged like a row of little soldiers.'[38] By the end of the 1920s three out of four female students were being taught homemaking skills whose machine-like standard-ization, reliance upon new kitchen technology, and stereotyping of everyday household tasks were often at odds with the more pragmatic fashion in which most homes, particularly on the frontier, were actually managed.

Concern over inadequate schooling culminated in the Putman-Weir Commission of 1924–5, set up by Premier Oliver in response to growing public pressure. Much dissatisfaction focused on Vancou-ver's crowded facilities, a consequence of massive pre-war immigra-tion. There was also criticism of the rote-learning method of teaching still used in many schools at a time when scholars such as John Dewey and James L. Hughes were urging more attention to the individual child. By naming as commissioners two recognized school reformers, Ottawa school inspector J.H. Putman and George Weir of UBC's new department of education, the government largely deter-mined the outcome. Over two hundred public hearings were held around the province and every special interest and reform group was given ample opportunity to put its case. The Vancouver Trades and Labour Council's brief echoed popular sentiment in its demand that there 'be equal opportunities for education' across the society.[39] Among other recommendations, the Putman-Weir report urged curriculum diversity, thereby encouraging more children to remain in school a year or two longer than the half-dozen elementary grades which were then the rule.

By responding to the combined thrust of middle-class and working-class reformers' demands, the Putman-Weir recommenda-tions had the somewhat paradoxical effect of maintaining – even furthering – another set of biases that were never far from the surface in the west coast province. A clear dichotomy existed between urban and rural areas in quality of everyday life. Using rhetoric common to the reform movement, educationalists promoted 'efficiency,' itself based on urban assumptions. The needs of rapidly expanding city schools had already prompted occupational training, curriculum standardization, and differentiation by grades.

Schools' oversight favoured urban areas. Vancouver and Victoria, each enrolling thousands of pupils, formed single school districts, but so did over six hundred rural areas with as few as ten or twenty pupils, often in a one-room school. Rural trustees not only lacked the experience to deal with an impersonal provincial bureaucracy but were reluctant to tax cash-strapped neighbours any more than absolutely essential to maintain basic services. In 1930 Anglican missionary Monica Storrs discovered the teacher in one Peace River school district 'lodging in a one-room shack with a man and his wife and two boys, under a roof which was leaking almost everywhere, and every time it rained, soaked all their clothes and furniture.'[40] In sharp contrast some urban boards spent thousands of dollars on even more imposing edifices than the brick buildings already the rule. While the majority of children did stay in school a year or two longer by the end of the 1920s, the gap widened across the province. This was not because frontier families were uncaring but rather because their urban counterparts, with the provincial government's blessing, worked equally hard to improve already superior levels of schooling.

The limits to reform became increasingly evident during the 1920s. Even the social legislation enacted went only so far. Individual benefits, often based on a means test, were only available to British subjects, and even then long residence in Canada was a common requirement. Indian people were excluded almost as a matter of course. Attempts to secure legislation mandating health insurance underlined the extent to which reform was still piecemeal. The unexpected nature of illness and high cost of medical care worried many British Columbians. A survey taken in 1923 indicated that less than 5 per cent of Vancouver's industrial workers had insurance of any kind, much less medical coverage. For a time it seemed as if the Liberals might act, making British Columbia the first Canadian province to legislate health coverage. Despite the efforts of women's groups, labour, and a wide spectrum of interests, nothing was done. The province's doctors were the key, and they opposed any plan that might affect existing relationships with patients able to afford their services even though at the same time they were quite willing to be reimbursed for the free treatment they provided to individuals unable to afford their fees. In the final analysis, the medical profession's opposition prevented government action.[41]

Volunteer, even illicit, social reform was all that still existed in some areas of everyday life. A case in point was birth control. The 1921 federal census revealed that, while the fertility rate was falling generally across Canada, it had plummeted in British Columbia.

From one of the highest in Canada at just over two hundred births per thousand women aged fifteen to forty-nine years of age it became the lowest at eighty-four births by 1921, the Canadian mean standing at 120 (see Table 13). The early figure is hardly surprising, considering there were so few women in the population, and almost all of them were married. The sex ratio began to even out after the First World War (see Table 11). While high marriage rates continued, they were counteracted by other factors, including some access to birth control information despite its prohibition in the federal criminal code. Such information was apparently more generally available on an unofficial, volunteer basis in British Columbia than elsewhere in Canada.[42]

Other social reformers turned their attention to responsible citizenship in exercising the franchise. The New Era League was formed to use women's new right to vote to obtain better legislation in such areas as child welfare, education, and recreation. Suffrage made it possible for women to move directly into the political arena through election to the provincial legislature. The first to do so was Mary Ellen Smith, who won a 1918 Vancouver by-election to succeed her late husband on a platform espousing women's and children's rights. Smith became the province's first female MLA and first cabinet minister not so much because she was any more qualified than were hundreds of other British Columbian women equally active in social reform but because she was 'in the right place at the right time.'[43] Smith, a Liberal, lost her seat in the Conservative victory of 1928. Three women followed Smith into the provincial legislature during the inter-war years. In 1933 Helen Douglas Smith, niece of former premier John Robson and long-time activist in the Vancouver women's movement, won election from Vancouver, again as a Liberal. Like her namesake, she was principally concerned to promote social welfare legislation, including social security and old age pensions. The next year, Dorothy Steeves won in a North Vancouver by-election under the banner of the newly formed Co-operative Commonwealth Federation. In 1939 they were joined by Laura Jamieson, winning for the CCF in a Vancouver by-election.

The four women's success to some extent obscured the limits of women's suffrage. Of some nine hundred candidacies in 225 contested consitutencies during the inter-war years, just 4 per cent – or forty – were female. Most women ran in Vancouver or Victoria and as fringe candidates. Women had more success getting onto school boards. During the 1920s women running for the Vancouver school board, who usually based their candidacies on previous experience with parent-teacher or child welfare groups, polled on average higher proportions of the vote than did their male counterparts. Society, not just in British Columbia but across the western world, continued to hold strong views about women's place.

Women who entered the paid labour force, most often the young and unmarried, continued to face both direct and indirect male opposition. They were still a minority – in the case of Vancouver about one in five at paid work at the end of the 1920s. Suitable occupations remained circumscribed. By the beginning of the twentieth century many offices were being modernized by 'replacing letter-copying presses and scribbling clerks with "writing machines" and "girl typewriters."' Pioneer settler Susan Allison sent her daughter to Victoria to learn secretarial skills: 'I think it is so nice for girls to be able to get their own living if need be and a good stenographer is sure of good pay.' A second daughter trained as a nurse, a third became a school teacher. For a women coming of age in the Nicola Valley in the mid 1920s: 'I was neither teacher nor secretarial material so was pushed into nursing.' Even then, just a year after the young University of British Columbia established the first nursing degree program in the British empire in 1919, the provincial College of Physicians and Surgeons countered that two years of training were quite sufficient: 'The overtraining of nurses is not desirable and results largely in the losing of their usefulness.'[44] Women's destiny lay in marriage. Popular magazines like *Canadian Home Journal* and *Maclean's* emphasized through their short stories and articles that, once married, women's lives were to be devoted to home and family.

The course of organized labour during the 1920s equally testified to the limits of reform in British Columbia. The movement across Canada entered the decade not only demoralized but fragmented by a major ideological split between east and west. Throughout North America, unions formed so optimistically before, during, or in the immediate aftermath of the war were broken up or pressured to disband. A recession in the early 1920s encouraged companies to move against unions, often with the tacit consent of government. Individual workers had to choose between continued employment at reduced wages without union representation or being fired to maintain a principle that seemed in any case impossible to obtain. Some companies introduced industrial councils or company unions, where workers and employers negotiated directly rather than through a bargaining agent. Many simply banned unions altogether.

Paternalism became more visible, be it in large enterprises or single-resource communities. Having successfully defeated workers' attempt to form a union, B.T. Rogers instituted annual summer picnics for BC Sugar workers and their families. Management in the company town of Powell River no sooner broke up pulp and paper unions formed during the war than they constructed a luxurious community hall. In Trail, Consolidated Mining and Smelting's generous social programs were consciously intended to keep workers and their families contented both in and out of the workplace. Benefits such as medical care were provided as early as 1905. Workers were encouraged to establish a 'co-operative committee' to bargain with management. While a handful of critics condemned 'the patronizing attitude of a big company like CM&S that gave Christmas bonuses and turkey instead of living wages,' benevolent paternalism kept Trail and other companies towns across British Columbia relatively immune from union activity through most of the inter-war years.[45]

During the 1920s the growing power of international capitalism combined with internal bickering within the labour movement prevented any major new offensive. The conservative Trades and Labour Congress was unwilling to adapt to a changing economy in which technological change and mechanization were breaking down traditional distinctions between crafts. A few political successes occurred at provincial and municipal levels, the uneven course of pro-labour parties reflecting the ideological tensions between those who were the proponents of direct confrontation and those who espoused gradual reform. Political scientist Martin Robin has argued that 'the Liberal ascendency [which marked the 1920s] was built on labour fragmentation. As a centre party, the Liberals counted upon a sizeable labour vote in urban and interior industrial constituencies.'[46] The Liberals did attract away from the political left sizeable proportions of working men and women concerned with getting ahead. By enacting social reform, the Liberal party – perhaps more aptly termed a coalition – both responded to and ensured a broad base of support maintaining it in power in British Columbia through much of the decade.

Of all the limitations inherent in the reform impetus – be its supporters middle-class or working-class – the most fundamental was a continued inability to face up to racism. The two seemingly paradoxical urges – the one to do good, the other to exclude – cheerfully coexisted in most minds. The otherness attached to native and Asian people extended with few exceptions to all men and women not formed in a Canadian, British, or northern European image.

In 1923 the federal government prohibited Chinese immigration. Over the next two dozen years, forty-four Chinese entered Canada. The falling numbers to some extent muted the dominant society's fears. By 1931 just twenty-seven thousand British Columbians, totalling under 4 per cent of the population, were Chinese by ethnic origin. Many were aging males. Chinatowns, once a part of virtually every British Columbian community, withered away. Cumberland's Chinatown, in 1921 home to nearly nine hundred, two decades later counted ten elderly male residents. Only Vancouver and Victoria Chinatowns retained their character with 1941 populations of about seven thousand and three thousand respectively.

Attitudes nonetheless remained ambivalent. Some of Vancouver's two hundred Chinese families operated small neighbourhood stores, whose lower prices, longer hours, and fresh produce repeatedly made them suspect. When W.H. Malkin, a leading wholesale grocer, ran for mayor, one of his campaign planks was that 'Oriental shops should be confined to fixed Oriental areas.' While Malkin was unsuccessful in his goal, Vancouver's White Lunch restaurants lived up to their name, it being common knowledge that they 'didn't allow orientals to eat there.'[47] Other Asian groups fared similarly. Least attention was given to East Indians simply because their numbers declined through migration southward to California and the population's aging. Just over one thousand lived in British Columbia at the beginning of the Second World War.

Racism was increasingly concentrated on the Japanese: not only were their numbers growing – from fifteen thousand in 1921 to twenty-two thousand a decade later – but they were becoming economically competitive. The numbers of fishing licences issued to Japanese for the Fraser River were cut back in the 1920s because of pressure by European fishermen. Japanese were forced to turn elsewhere. Clusters lived on Mayne and Galiano islands where they fished and farmed; others grew berries or other commodities in the Fraser and Okanagan valleys. While Asians were legally prohibited from buying government land, they could purchase private property. As early as 1920 a local newspaper was querying, 'Is Summerland to continue to be the home of British peoples, or is it to become a settlement for Orientals?'[48]

Many Japanese males brought over picture brides — women courted by correspondence and married by proxy. Looking towards a better future, many a wife took in sewing or worked seasonally in a nearby cannery, 'with the smallest one standing by her skirt in grubby dress, & the blood streams down the wooden cutting board as the "iron chink" (that is what they call it) beheads each fish.' All the while she was, as evoked by Daphne Marlatt, 'dreaming, of fabric she saw at Walker's Emporium, & the ribbon.'[49] The Japanese children's success in school and in university raised new fears of competition in the minds of the dominant society, not from cheap labour as with the Chinese but on the basis of equality. The second generation, the Nisei, saw no reason to accept others' assumption of their inferiority.

Japanese initiative was turned on its head to become a further rationale for discrimination. 'His superior education, his training, and his more plastic nature fit him to compete in a far greater variety of occupations [than the Chinese] and to mould himself to the conditions of the country ... unless restrictions are placed upon his entry every class of the community and every avocation in the province will find this enterprising yellow man slowly, but surely, elbowing his way in and taking possession.'[50] Bruce Hutchison revealed the underlying assumptions held by many Canadians in a description penned as late as 1942. 'Every year their farms spread further into the Fraser Valley, their shops appear in the better retail sections, their homes in the residential districts, their young men and women in new automobiles. There is no hope either of their absorption or their decline. Forever a white race and a yellow race are fated to live beside each other on the Pacific Coast.'[51]

Reformers' achievements during the late nineteenth and early twentieth centuries were considerable. The goals with which labour leaders and social reformers identified became much more broadly accepted across the society. Primarily through trade unions but also by electoral successes, working people established themselves as a distinct and formidable presence in the province. Social reformers' efforts were equally rewarded. Yet reform had its limits, due in part to a popular perception that goals had been achieved or, alternatively, gone too far. Much was achieved, but much still needed to be done.

11

The Best and Worst of Times 1918–1945

The three decades between the end of the First and the end of the Second World War brought the best and the worst of times to British Columbia. The province's economy continued to rely on staples and the uncertainties of the international marketplace, which inhibited long-term planning. Yet expectations rose unrealistically during periods of prosperity, as were the mid and late 1920s. Much like the boom years of the early century, men and women wanted to believe that the good times would go on forever. In consequence the effects of the Great Depression were compounded.

The First World War had spurred industrialization but at the cost of tremendous inflation. A severe recession hung over the western world in its aftermath. Once it lifted in 1923, British Columbia surged ahead. Capitalism appeared triumphant, its hegemony strengthened by organized labour's retreat. Government provided an unobtrusive backdrop against which companies pursued profit and individual men and women could enjoy their new-found prosperity.

John Oliver served as premier from March 1918 until his death in August 1927. In dress and manner this self-made Fraser Valley farmer put forth the image of the rustic sage, a proponent of simpler values in an increasingly complex age. His 1924 campaign for re-election made the point: 'This fearless farmer-premier of ours ploughs a deep, straight furrow.'[1] Although Oliver thereafter headed a minority government viewed by some as lacking direction, he used the good times to consolidate social reform, construct roads, and reduce the provincial debt.

In actuality, Oliver's long tenure rested as much on internal dissension among the opposition Conservatives as it did on his own policies or on those of the Liberal party. In 1922 a right-wing splinter group led by Vancouver businessmen joined forces with dissatisfied farmers to attempt a return to coalition, as opposed to party, government. The Provincial party's name made clear its unhappiness with existing parties, which it viewed as a federal imposition. Oliver exploited the division by excluding Vancouver members from his cabinet. He thus made clear that, however influential might be the city's entrepreneurs, Vancouver could not run roughshod over its hinterland.

The circumstances by which the Conservatives returned to power in 1928 suggest that many British Columbians still identified with individual leaders as opposed to parties. On Oliver's death in 1927, his dedicated but uninspired lieutenant John Duncan MacLean assumed the office. The Provincial party's collapse meant that MacLean's hold on the office was not assisted, as earlier in the decade, by the opposition vote being split. A year later MacLean went down to defeat before a more attractive personality.

The man who reinvigorated the Conservative party was Simon Fraser Tolmie. Son of a Hudson's Bay trader who had married the mixed-blood daughter of fellow trader John Work and then farmed on the Saanich peninsula near Victoria, young Tolmie combined the appeal of the fur trade tradition with a personal image as a working veterinarian and farmer. He had already served as federal minister of agriculture in three post-war cabinets. Prevailed upon by a badly fractured party to assume its leadership, Tolmie led the Conservatives to victory in 1928 in part on the force of his personality, in part because of the strong support given him by Vancouver business leaders angered over their city's long exclusion from representation in cabinet. The Conservatives promised 'the application of business principles to the business of government.'[2] To many voters this suggested that they, as shareholders in the province's prosperity, would now receive even greater profits.

British Columbia's economic growth during the 1920s built on existing strands in the province's development. Vancouver extended its hinterland into the prairies. The impetus for this development was the Panama Canal, opened in 1914. While the canal proved a boon during the war in dispatching the province's products to Canada's European allies, its full potential was only realized in the 1920s. Not just traditional staples such as lumber but new exports like Okanagan apples were sent through the canal to Britain, continental Europe, and the east coast; the province's lead and zinc went to American auto plants. At the beginning of the decade some thirty ocean-going ships a month entered the port of Vancouver; by 1929 the number surpassed one hundred. But the Panama Canal took on its greatest importance with the export of prairie grain. Formerly wheat and other grains had been sent east by the Canadian Pacific Railway through Winnipeg. Just before the war Vancouver MP H.H. Stevens cajoled the federal government into improving harbour facilities and constructing a large elevator in his riding, whence grain could be shipped to Europe and elsewhere. The elevator stood empty during the war, becoming known as Stevens's Folly. At its end Vancouver commercial interests began a deliberate campaign to take the grain market away from Winnipeg. Provincial officials successfully lobbied for reductions in the Crow's Nest freight rates on grain moving west, originally set much higher than on grain sent east.

From then on, shipping became one of Vancouver's biggest industries. In 1921 just over one million bushels of grain were dispatched from the west coast; almost one hundred million passed through the city in the bumper crop year of 1928. By the end of the decade fully 40 per cent of Canada's grain exports were going through British Columbia, almost all of it via Vancouver. Prince Rupert acquired its own terminal elevator in 1926, but the northern city's greater distance from the prairies continued to make Vancouver preferable. As a consequence of partial reductions secured in differential freight rates on goods moving east, box cars returning from the coast were increasingly filled with lumber for construction and with wholesale commodities. The developing trade relationship was confirmed in 1928 when Woodwards department stores, head-quartered in Vancouver, established an Edmonton branch. Whereas previously Vancouver dominated the province, now it challenged Winnipeg as metropolis to a vast prairie hinterland.

Vancouver did not alter much physically. The city put in place before the war was enhanced rather than reshaped. Time for reflection led to interest in town planning, now becoming fashionable across North America and Britain. In 1926 Vancouver and Point Grey joined forces to hire one of America's foremost city planners, Harland Bartholomew, to prepare a comprehensive development plan for Greater Vancouver. While immediate implementation was aborted by the Depression, many of its recommendations, including greater public ownership of the waterfront and creation of public amenities, were eventually adopted.

New construction included two luxury hotels, the Devonshire in 1925 and the Georgia in 1927. Work started on the third, and present, Hotel Vancouver in 1928 but, uncompleted by the beginning of the Depression, it stood unfinished for a decade. Home ownership remained strong, averaging almost 60 per cent of occupancy by the late 1920s compared with about 45 per cent in the typical North American city. Growing numbers of Vancouver families also acquired a holiday cottage. Locations seemed endless. Some went south to Boundary Bay, others across Burrard Inlet to Horseshoe Bay or Deep Cove. Remoter locations included Roberts Creek on the Sechelt peninsula, Buccaneer Bay a bit farther north, and the Gulf Islands. Families of modest income might take a Union steamship excursion to nearby Bowen Island, boasting an elegant resort hotel, holiday bungalows, and a circular dance floor able to accommodate eight hundred couples.

Home and holiday were made possible by a climb in real wages for Vancouver residents of 12 per cent between 1922 and 1928, twice that in Canada as a whole.[3] Yet only in 1929, the last year before the Depression hit, did Vancouver building permits reach their earlier high of 1912 at just over $20 million, and even then only because South Vancouver and Point Grey had been amalgamated with Vancouver at the beginning of that year. On the whole, Vancouver remained the entity put in place during the years before the First World War.

The character of British Columbia's second city altered. Over the decade Victoria witnessed a steady exodus of working people, its isolated location continuing to make manufacturing and other industries unprofitable. They were replaced by government employees and what were often termed the 'better classes.' Some were retirees from the prairies and elsewhere in Canada, other Britons were attracted by the capital city's much-promoted British image. Tourism was encouraged by the Crystal Gardens with its swimming pool and dance floor, by car ferries linking Vancouver Island with Washington State and Vancouver, and by a very modern 'auto camp' at Saanich. At decade's end the proportion of Victorians over sixty-five surpassed every other Canadian city, a demographic characteristic that would continue through subsequent decades.

Vancouver led British Columbia in economic growth, and it may be that British Columbia led Canada as a whole. The net value of production increased by over half from $206 million in the last year of recession, 1922, to $331 million in 1929. The province's proportion of all goods produced in Canada grew from 6.2 per cent at the beginning of the decade to 8.4 per cent in 1929. International demand for the province's staples set the pace. During the 1920s the British Columbian economy became even more dependent on foreign markets. In 1922 Canadian products worth $71 million were exported from British Columbia; in 1929 the total peaked at almost $240 million, including of course prairie grain. Before the First World War only about one-fifth of the province's lumber had been sent abroad; by 1929 the figure was over a half, and added to that was a large part of its fruit crop, most canned salmon, and nearly all its minerals. A growing tendency to do some processing of raw materials within British Columbia was evident in the tremendous growth in net value of manufacturing from $28 million in 1922 to $134 million in 1928, most of it derivative of staples.[4] This expansion was offset by the continued import from central Canada of almost all manufactured products consumed within British Columbia. The pre-war shift towards a continental orientation reversed itself, as British Columbians again looked outward for their well-being rather than eastward to the nation to which they belonged.

Two resources, lumber and minerals, set the pace. Net value of production in forestry rose from $52 million in 1922 to $87 million in 1929, in mining from $37 to $68 million. Forestry benefited most from the Panama Canal. Previously lumber was marketed internationally through agencies in San Francisco; now it was sold directly. The shift was orchestrated by H.R. MacMillan, a young Ontarian who had come west in 1912 as British Columbia's first chief forester and gone on to develop an export marketing firm in Vancouver.[5]

Hardrock mining suffered in the post-war decline but then moved ahead. By the mid 1920s the combined value of silver, copper, lead, and zinc production surpassed $40 million. Although another $12 million came from coal, demand was slackening (see Table 20). With oil powering more and more locomotives and heating more homes, Vancouver Island mines began to be phased out. Mining as an industry consolidated: by 1930 just five mines accounted for 90 per cent of the province's production, whereas the remaining 10 per cent came from 125 enterprises. Net value of production in the fisheries, primarily salmon canning, grew moderately from $19 million in 1922 to $27 million in 1928. While virtually every major coastal inlet near a salmon stream had its own cannery, numbers on the Fraser halved as a consequence of the Hell's Gate rock slide.[6] Occurring during the Canadian Northern's construction through the Fraser Canyon in 1913, the slide prevented salmon from returning to spawn. Between sixty-five and seventy-five canneries operated in a year, of which just ten were along the Fraser.

Agriculture remained a special case. While numbers were declining generally across Canada, at least one in three employed males everywere except British Columbia was still engaged in agriculture. There the proportion stood at one in six. Farming remained overwhelmingly a small-scale, family enterprise. Over half the farms were fifty acres or less, just over 10 per cent larger than two hundred acres. Net value of production rose from $36 million in 1922 to $45 million in 1928 before falling back to $39 million a year later.

The provincial government, to some extent still ignorant of the great extent to which most of the province was unsuitable for farming, continued to encourage men and women onto the land. Even the practical failure of such widely touted enclaves as Walhachin did not dim the optimism. A faculty of agriculture held pride of place at the young University of British Columbia. Farmers' institutes disseminating the latest findings were liberally supported by public funds.

With the intent of opening new areas to farming, several land settlement schemes were initiated under provincial auspices. Strongly supported by Premier Oliver, their purpose was to counteract potential unemployment by assisting returned soldiers onto the land. In the years between 1920 and 1927 the Sumas reclamation project drained thirty thousand marshy acres of the fertile Lower Fraser Valley for mixed and dairy farming. The southern Okanagan land project developed a large semi-desert area centring on Oliver – named after the premier – and Osoyoos; eventually some five thousand acres would be irrigated and planted with fruit trees.

Other projects promoted by the provincial government were less successful. Much land was simply unsuitable for farming. A farmer's wife in the central interior recollected the many 'abandoned little places' on which prospective farmers so optimistically settled. 'Nobody could ever make a living on them, but in their ignorance they thought they could.'[7] Veterans also left for other reasons, including insufficient capital, lack of knowledge about agriculture, and preference for an urban life style.

Agriculture also expanded onto the prairie lands along the Peace River extending east into Alberta. The British Columbian portion had been surveyed and thrown open to settlement before the war. In 1924 it was linked to the outside world by a rail extension from Alberta. Communities began. Fort St John, named for the old Hudson's Bay post, was described in 1929 as comprising 'about a dozen wooden shanties, vaguely springing up on each side of a straight mud road which crosses a high plateau with a fine view of distant hills.'[8] By the end of the decade the Peace's population surpassed seven thousand.

The development of new areas only exacerbated the problem of finding markets for farm produce. As local markets became sated after the war, it was necessary to look farther afield. Overproduction affected mixed farming on Vancouver Island, in the Fraser Valley, and elsewhere, but it was most acute in the fruit-growing area of the Okanagan Valley. Of the major agricultural enterprises, the cultivation of apples and other fruit had expanded most during the period of pre-war immigration. Costs of production included high freight rates on all British Columbian products moving east by rail, and irrigation expenses. Another problem was competition from nearby American growers whose fruit ripened three to four weeks earlier with less susceptibility to frost. From 1917 Washington State led the United States in apple production. The fruit farmers of British Columbia sought various remedies from both levels of government. As early as 1912 the province set up a royal commission, whose recommendations emphasized better methods of cultivation, establishment of a system of agricultural credit, and more co-operation between producers.

Orderly marketing became a favoured solution, not only among fruit growers but in British Columbia generally. In 1913 Okanagan growers established, with provincial funding, a co-operative sales and distribution agency. Milk producers in the Fraser Valley organized the same year. The problems that emerged after the war centred on the inherent nature of co-operation. Success depended on the support of all the growers, but in the Okanagan a significant number did not join, selling fruit for less than the price agreed upon by the majority. Some of the largest milk producers in the Fraser Valley similarly defected.

In 1927 the provincial government stepped in by passing a contentious marketing act to regulate the sale of agricultural produce. Political pressure delayed for two years a similar measure assisting dairy farmers. While some improvement followed, the province's fruit growers continued to be undersold by American producers, who had also turned to co-operative marketing in the face of overproduction. Freya Stark, visiting her fruit-farming father in the Kootenays in 1928, discovered 'none of the buoyancy of prosperity ... Everyone is hard up and a little wistful.'[9] Agriculture remained precarious in Canada's west coast province.

Efforts continued to open up the province. The first airports were constructed, additional miles of road built and paved. In 1922 the province's drivers changed to driving on the right side of the road, not in rejection of English practice but rather in the expectation that British Columbia would be linked by road to the United States and neighbouring Alberta. Five years later a dirt road opened through the Fraser Canyon, the first non-rail link from the coast to the interior and east to Alberta since railway construction had destroyed parts of the Cariboo Wagon Road almost half a century earlier. It was also possible to drive south from Vancouver, Osoyoos, or the West Kootenays and link up with a paved road going east and west across Washington State. British Columbia's natural north-south orientation reasserted itself. More and more British Columbians, even in outlying regions, became proud owners of a Model T Ford or possibly a truck: the total number of vehicles registered in the province rose from about fifteen thousand at the end of the war to almost one hundred thousand by 1930.

During the 1920s British Columbians became caught up in the mass culture spreading across the western world. Indeed, one reason the growing power of employers was not matched by new militancy from their employees lay in the willingness of many workers to enjoy their increased prosperity. By the middle of the decade the labour movement was reduced to a core centred on Greater Vancouver with pockets of support elsewhere across the province. The appeal of consumerism was seductive. Increasingly British Columbians purchased items ranging from foodstuffs to clothing to toys previously made at home. Vancouver acquired its first drive-in restaurant with the opening of the White Spot on South Granville in 1928. Electrical appliances appeared before the First World War in the form of toasters and 'smoothing irons,' and others soon followed. By 1930 seven out of ten Canadian homes were electrified.

In a growing number of British Columbian communities, the radio, popular magazines, and the movie theatre replaced the distinctive working-class culture associated with early unions.[10] Magazines such as *Maclean's* came into their own and, with features dealing with Canada coast to coast, helped develop a popular culture transcending class and geography. When a contest was announced to name a new women's magazine over seventy thousand entries came from all across Canada, the winner being a Mrs Hilda Paine from British Columbia who received a cheque for $1,000 for her suggestion of 'The Chatelaine' as 'having about it a feminine grace.'[11]

In reality much of this popular culture was American. Even in Victoria with its self-conscious British heritage, over two-thirds of the periodicals purchased and 80 per cent of the films shown originated in the United States.[12] Such was hardly surprising given that as early as 1923 the American company Famous Players acquired control over film distribution in Canada, thereby dooming a nascent film industry.

It was not only popular but 'high' culture that grew during the 1920s. With the backing of Bella Rogers, the wife of BC Sugar's founder, and other Vancouver social leaders, a symphony orchestra was founded in 1919. Its long-term survival depended on their repeated injections of financial assistance. Live theatre, earlier limited to touring professionals and local amateur groups performing a mainly British repertory, diversified. Among innovative enterprises was a theatre specially constructed in 1920 in a Naramata peach orchard on the top of a packing shed. Intended to give talented young people from across Canada an opportunity to act in the evenings while holding down fruit-picking jobs during the day, the Okanagan venture was the brainchild of Carroll Aikins, a sometimes poet well connected with the Canadian establishment. Prime Minister Arthur Meighen graced the opening of the venture, which survived three seasons before falling victim to debt. A few years earlier Professor Frederic Wood had founded the Players Club at the University of British Columbia. Performing at the university during the year, the Players Club visited some two dozen coastal and interior communities as soon as examinations were over each spring. Through the inter-war years its appearance was a much anticipated annual event across British Columbia.[13]

Among intellectual pursuits during the 1920s was the ongoing search for a perfect lifestyle. As occurred with Scandinavian idealists, Doukhobors, Mennonites, and others, the province seemed to exercise special appeal to individuals and groups wanting to separate themselves off from the world. Among inter-war exploits was a utopian cult founded in 1927 by the enigmatic The Brother, xii. Located south of Nanaimo and then on the Gulf Islands, the Aquarian Foundation attracted numerous followers, some with considerable wealth and social repute. The Brother, xii, in reality an Englishman named Edward Wilson, hastily departed when charges surfaced of black magic and financial misappropriation.

The visual arts received a boost with the opening in 1925 of the Vancouver School of Decorative and Applied Arts, followed six years later by the Vancouver Art Gallery. Artists such as Emily Carr, Thomas Fripp, and Sophie Pemberton had trained and worked largely in isolation. Some whose art was identified with the province lived in British Columbia only briefly: Frederick Whymper as a surveyor with the abortive Collins Telegraph, Ontario artist Paul Kane out for adventure, and William G.R. Hind as an Overlander soon dissatisfied with the west coast province. A Scottish landscape painter, Charles Scott, was named principal of the new art school. Among early teachers was Frederick Varley, a member of the Group of Seven landscape painters concerned to develop a Canadian art style.

Despite the sense of community created by the school's appearance, most artists continued to view British Columbia through a preconceived, externally based lens. Painter W.P. Weston later recalled how slowly artists learned 'to rely absolutely on ourselves for what we felt like doing.'[14] Public recognition came from having exhibited in Europe or central Canada; even Emily Carr, one of the least influenced by her training elsewhere, had to receive the approval of Ontario galleries and of the Group of Seven before being recognized in British Columbia.

The opening of the Vancouver Art Gallery in 1931, also underwritten by Bella Rogers and friends, only accentuated the situation. It ignored not only British Columbian artists' work but that of almost all Canadian painters. Rogers made the point in her assessment of an Emily Carr picture presented to the gallery. 'I thought it was dreadful.' Garnett Sedgewick, an English professor at UBC, found it difficult to credit that 'so much debris from nineteenth century

England had washed up on the walls' of the gallery.[15] For culture to be truly high in British Columbia during the 1920s, almost by definition it had to originate elsewhere.

The beginnings of an artistic tradition embodied another paradox: although almost all art pupils were female, the art school's teachers were almost all male. Men were also more likely to achieve prominence as artists, as did Paul Rand, Edward J. Hughes, B.C. Binning, and Jack Shadbolt. Binning joined the staff in 1934, Shadbolt four years later. Women who persisted did so in a male shadow, despite growing recognition of Carr's powerful evocations of Indian and forest motifs. Part of the explanation lay in the generally accepted definition of a professional or 'true' artist as one able to make a living from painting, something extremely hard to do except through employment as an art teacher. As W.P. Weston put it, 'teaching was keeping me so I could paint as I pleased.' The accepted mores determined that, despite female suffrage and other reforms, women would not be accorded such positions. Women who painted were thus almost inevitably dubbed amateurs, dabbling as part of their cultural preparation for contracting a suitable marriage. Patriarchal assumptions of inherent female inferiority played a role, as when a male critic informed Carr that 'women *can't* paint; that faculty is the property of men only.'[16] Unequal treatment remained commonplace in the arts as elsewhere in inter-war British Columbia.

The University of British Columbia, despite being co-educational, did little to change existing biases. English and mathematics classes were segregated; the male sections were instructed by two top professors, Garnet Sedgewick and Walter Gage, whereas female sections were relegated to 'lesser luminaries.'[17] While not deliberately restrictive in admissions except for academic reasons, enrolment was skewed in several ways. Only a small handful of students were Chinese or members of other ethnic or racial minorities. The overwhelming majority were the offspring of lower mainland families of relatively high socio-economic status. In 1928–9, the last year before the Depression, just one in twenty-five in the province's mature male work force was a professional, yet over one-quarter of the parents of UBC students came from that category.

As the 1920s drew to a close, the expansion of popular and high culture, together with the quiescence of working people, seemed to confirm the triumph of capitalism. The business community became more confident and, with Tolmie's ascension to power in 1928, even aggressive in imposing its conservative political philosophy onto the mainstream of provincial life. The poor were seemingly less visible, in part owing to the social reforms put in place by government and private groups, in part because of the general prosperity. The economic system was patently working to the benefit of an increasing proportion of British Columbians.

Then came the stock market crash of October 1929, which ushered in the Depression. At first it appeared to be no more than a recession in the pattern of 1873, the early 1890s, late 1912, and the post-war years. For men and women accustomed to the good times, it seemed impossible that anything more then another downturn was occurring. Only as conditions worsened during 1930 and 1931 did British Columbians, like their counterparts across the western world, realize that this was no ordinary slump. As a consequence groups that might have been expected to rally to deal with adversity, ranging from social reformers to trade unionists, did little. As hope evaporated that economic difficulties would somehow right themselves, the provincial government argued that it lacked the necessary funds to ameliorate what was a federal responsibility. Anxiety became desperation, particularly since the federal level appeared to be ineffective and even indifferent in finding remedies.

The economic disaster besetting British Columbia was part of a much larger phenomenon with world-wide causes and consequences. While New York's Wall Street was a long way from British Columbia, both were caught up in the same spiral of capitalist growth. Credit had become over-extended on the assumption of an endlessly elastic capacity for growth. Canada's prosperity depended on external demand for its products. The price of wheat began to fall after 1927; soon that for newsprint also slipped. Excessive production continued even as demand reached its limits. The value of exports from Canada went from a high of $1.3 billion in 1928 to a low of $0.5 billion in 1932. One in four Canadians in the work-force were unemployed by early 1932 and almost one in three by the next March, for a total of one and a half million men and women.

Exports of Canadian products from British Columbia, an important component of which was prairie grain, fell from a high of $238 million in 1929 to just over $100 million by 1934. The decline was intensified by internal dissension in one of the province's marketplaces, the Far East, an area increasingly dominated by war, revolution, and political uncertainty. Net value of production in British Columbia went from its high of $331 million in 1929 to a low of $149 million in 1932. Every component of the economy moved down. The city of Vancouver was particularly hard hit; by 1935 property there was almost worthless – a lot that sold for $1,500 before 1929 could be had for $50 or less. Residents of modest means were particularly hard hit: a 1938 analysis revealed that almost three times as many men and women were unemployed in working-class Collingwood as in middle-class Dunbar.[18] Of the various age groups, the elderly were perhaps the most fortunate by virtue of having access to a small means-based pension.

While some individuals suffered more than others, the Depression affected everyone. Almost all wages were cut. Even companies that managed to survive relatively intact were forced to retrench, at the least to forgo profits. One of the most obvious consequences was in the average age of marriage for women, which moved up to twenty-five by 1931, that for men remaining high at twenty-nine. The fertility rate plummeted from eighty-four births per thousand women aged fifteen to forty-nine in 1921 to sixty-two a decade later, by far the lowest in Canada. Part of the reason lay in the increased use of birth control, the movement acquiring respectability in the face of fears of working-class unrest. An illegal abortion was another alternative. In the words of a Vancouver woman who had four abortions in the 'seedy side of town' during the Depression: 'There was simply no way we could afford to have a baby. There was no form of welfare, no such things as daycare. We were both working and desperately afraid of losing our jobs.'[19]

While numbers make the point in a general way, the human misery wrought by the Depression is most acutely captured in the lives of individuals. In *Waste Heritage*, the classic novel of the Great Depression in British Columbia, a father lamented, 'I got three boys starin' ahead at nothing.' A Vancouver Island resident wrote to the Canadian prime minister:

Please Pardon me for Writing you, but I am in Such a Circumstances That I Really dont Know What to do. When Will This Distress & Mental Agitation Amongst the People come to an End. & how Long Will This Starvation Last. I am on The Relief & only Git 4 days Work on the Public Road ... That are not Sufficient For both of us to Live on ... Next came My Land Taxes ... If I dont Pay it This year. Then the Government of B.C. Will Have My 40 acres Cancelled. & I & My Wife Will be on The bear Ground. is That Way The Government Will Help the Poor Men.[20]

Conditions in British Columbia were intensified by men coming into the province, lured by the generally milder climate. Early wanderers were mostly unskilled, seasonal labourers, often young and single. As time passed they were joined by older, married men whose assets were exhausted. On the prairies the collapse in agricultural prices was accompanied by prolonged drought and grasshopper plagues which turned much of the land into a barren dust bowl. Some family breadwinners left home to find work elsewhere, others simply to escape the shame of an intolerable situation.

Particularly affected were towns along the tracks, as men 'riding the rods' dropped off to try their luck at finding even temporary employment. By the summer of 1931 the unemployed were every-where across the country. 'Anyone who lived in a home or ran a business was sure to be asked for a handout every day of the week.' Jungles, as the improvised stopping places were known, sprang up in most British Columbian towns and cities. In his Depression memoir Sydney Hutcheson explained jungling up: 'In every town there was a "jungle" where no one bothered you, and this is where I cooked my meals over a jungle fire and had a short nap while waiting for the next freight out.' Hutcheson stayed in Kamloops in the summer of 1932. 'We found the "jungles" across the CNR Bridge, above the bridge on the Indian Reserve. There was a continuous flow of men going through the jungles every day. While we were there, at least a thousand men and women were living in the Kamloops jungles ... Six or more men together could get by with a little rustling but one man alone would starve to death ... I remember one time there were twenty-four of us jungled together – we ate good meals.'[21]

Everyday alternatives were sparse, so one unemployed man recalled. 'At this period and for many long years afterward, there was no unemployment insurance in Canada, no health or hospitalization insurance, nothing to ameliorate the stark fact of unemployment. It was private enterprise at its most brutal period.' Hutcheson, typical of thousands of young Canadians, passed through a seemingly endless array of temporary jobs at very low wages: fire fighting, snowploughing, splitting and squaring posts, unloading boxcars, saw milling, surveying, killing animals in a meat plant, blasting, running a construction grader, logging, backpacking in supplies, illicit deer hunting, gold mining.[22]

The hardship was intensified by the breakdown of traditional support systems. Many groups who might have been expected to help at first did not realize the dimensions of the disaster and then looked primarily to their own survival. Labour unions, which were rapidly declining in numbers, concentrated their efforts on maintaining existing standards for remaining members rather than assisting the cause of the unemployed. Direct confrontation was particularly evident among coal miners, working in mines still operating in the East Kootenays and on Vancouver Island. Most men and women fortunate enough to have a job were simply grateful for the opportunity. 'Looking back on working conditions, they were far from good, but they were all we knew at the time ... If you did not like the working conditions or the way the boss treated you, you either put up with it or quit.' Between 1931 and 1935 real wages for employed workers actually increased by 18 per cent because, quite simply, prices fell faster than wages. The consequence was that, in the words of journalist Bruce Hutchison, 'the employed and the unemployed, the comfortable and the destitute [were] divided as by an international boundary. This, in retrospect, was the truly horrifying fact of the Depression, the gulf not merely of money but of mind or, more accurately, feeling between nations, each frozen, remote, and almost incomprehensible to the other.'[23]

For all the Depression's horrendous consequences for unemployed men, it may have been even crueller to women, not considered by society to be part of the workforce and therefore not 'unemployed.' Unable to participate in the 'wide intimacy' that united men riding the rails and jungling up, they were left to fend for themselves as individuals.[24] One unemployed male evoked their situation. 'The plight of the single homeless girls was probably the worst of any section of the unemployed in Vancouver. It was difficult to get relief for single unemployed girls who were always told to go into domestic service ... Girls were actually told by relief officers that with their figures they shouldn't have to seek relief.' Writer and social activist Dorothy Livesay was appalled by 'the economic plight of women, of women caught in the trap of having illegitimate children, begging on the streets, prostituting themselves, of women who had no training for anything but hard jobs cleaning offices, going out to do housework ... There was no employment of women as equals.'[25]

For those British Columbians already pushed to the margins, as were Chinese and men and women on the frontier, the Depression only worsened already harsh conditions. Jobless Chinese, often middle-aged or elderly, discovered that, while excused from relief camps on the grounds that no separate accommodation existed, they were expected to survive on one-third the assistance doled out to unemployed white males.

The Depression took time to reach the hinterland. 'In the beginning the depression meant little to the people on our reserve. Hard times in Stoney Creek were as natural and normal as the changing of the seasons ... We were always poor ... Our hard life became harder – that was all.' Or, 'when the news of the stockmarket crash of 1929 filtered in via the few battery operated radios scattered through the area, it meant nothing tangible – such events belonged to a world they had left behind.'[26] Seasonal labour dried up for Indians and Europeans alike: the number of ties bought by the railway in an area of the central interior fell from a high of 850,000 in 1929 to a low of 75,000 in 1932. Some turned to trapping or fishing, others to the bush as a gyppo logger, using older and cheaper methods to get out smaller timber earlier passed over.

Everyone improvised. Automobiles purchased so proudly just a few years previous were turned into Bennett buggies – named after the prime minister – by being stripped down and fitted with wagon poles. Coffee was made from roasted rye, and soap from a mixture of bear oil and moose fat. Bannock, mixed from flour, baking powder, salt, and water and then fried or baked, had long been a staple for Indian and white alike, and it continued to sustain many lives. Visiting a farm family in the Peace River area, Monica Storrs was 'immensely impressed at the way the eldest daughter was making underclothes and even quite pretty cotton frocks out of *old flour sacks*!' During the Depression years BC Sugar decided against putting granulated sugar into new paper packaging on the grounds that its traditional cloth sacks 'appear to be valued quite highly by the consumers of sugar.'[27]

Families survived somehow. On Mayne Island, with its long tradition of mutual self-help among long-established Japanese and half-breed populations, 'people generally found that they could live on a little less and still get by, because property taxes remained low and most families preserved garden produce, fish and venison to tide them over the winter.' Central interior pioneer Arthur Shelford underlined the point: 'Overall we came through the Depression very well. The times were indeed tough, but we were tough too, and we had been accustomed in our pioneer life not to expect too many of the luxuries of life, so we did not miss them. Our best asset in these trying times was our spirit of camaraderie, which never faltered.'[28]

It was during these years that the young English aristocrat Lord

Martin Cecil and American cowboy adventurer Richmond Hobson separately made their way to what the latter termed 'the last great cattle frontier on the North American continent.'[29] Come to manage a ranch purchased by his father before the war, Lord Cecil would be a major booster of the Cariboo, and more particularly the area around 100 Mile House, until his death in 1988. The cattle empire Hobson established lay farther west, towards Bella Coola. What the two men's experiences underline is the extent to which self-reliance remained critical to survival on the frontier. While success was in part owing to good luck, financial connections, and ongoing demand for beef and for paid employment as ranch hands, it also derived from the willingness of Hobson, Lord Martin, and other pioneers to endure incredibly austere living conditions. In cabins of hand-hewn logs heated by stoves made out of coal-oil tins they somehow withstood winter temperatures dipping to minus 45° Celsius.

At first the provincial government did nothing to combat the hardships caused by the Depression. But by 1931, when unemployment had reached 28 per cent, the highest in Canada, Premier Tolmie was finally forced to act. Conservative thought still held that poverty and unemployment resulted from personal failings. The larger society was not to blame and, therefore, the destitute should work for their support as opposed to receiving a handout. So relief camps were established for single unemployed males who were bona fide BC residents. Men built roads and other facilities in return for room, board, and a cash payment of just over $1 a day, soon reduced to $7.50 a month and then to 20 cents a day.[30] Other men, many heads of families, did local road work as relief or in lieu of paying taxes. While the form relief took varied over time in British Columbia, it was most often in kind, such as vouchers, which publicly identified individuals on relief and only intensified already invidious situations.[31]

Once the government acted, hopes ran high that the unemployment problem was resolved. Relief camps were generally located in remote locations supposedly protecting men from radical agitators but also protecting the larger society from agitators in the men's numbers. 'By taking the men out ... of the cities we were removing the active elements on which the "red" agitators could play.'[32] In reality the camps, together with the jungles, became fertile breeding grounds for unrest. Men protested the necessity to go to the camps in order to receive relief, and hunger marches involved thousands of men in 1932. Slightly higher levels of relief payments resulted, but so did a ban on parades in Vancouver. In 1932 the federal government took over relief camps. Eventually eight thousand men were at work across British Columbia in over two hundred camps, some by choice but others given no option if they wanted to receive public assistance.

Falling government revenues were at the heart of the province's dilemma. In 1931 the financial situation became so desperate that Premier Tolmie, who had come to power three years before on a platform espousing the application of business principles to government, acceded to the request of a deputation of businessmen, most of them from Vancouver, that they be allowed to investigate the whole field of government finance and propose solutions. In effect, the provincial government turned its problems over to private enterprise. Tolmie appointed a committee of five prominent businessmen, chaired by the recently retired president of the BC Electric Company, George Kidd.

The Kidd Report issued in 1932 argued that, further taxation being impossible, the only alternative lay in sharply reducing provincial expenditures. Social services must be cut back drastically. Their expansion by government had never been much favoured by the province's business community, even during the buoyant 1920s. Provincial funding to the sole provincial university, already cut back, should be curtailed. Years of free public schooling should be restricted to children aged from six to thirteen. If not sold in nine months, service should be discontinued on the provincially owned Pacific Great Eastern Railway, even though it provided the only transportation link for some people north of Vancouver.

As well as being an élitist document, the Kidd Report revealed a fundamental dichotomy within British Columbian society. By this date many British Columbians assumed that the role of government extended beyond its traditional functions of maintaining law and order, providing physical infrastructure, and encouraging private enterprise. The wide-ranging reforms already implemented had transferred to the state an obligation to maintain some basic social services. For the Kidd committee, social services remained a privilege to be withdrawn in times of economic difficulty if they threatened the capitalist edifice.

Mainstream public opinion was outraged. Indeed, the Kidd proposals were so conservative, even reactionary, that they genuinely shocked a provincial government willing to grasp at any straws that might keep it in power. Soon after a provincial election was called, which was won by the opposition Liberals. In the final analysis, Tolmie and the Conservatives were defeated not so much by the Kidd Report itself as by more fundamental considerations. The report was only the visible manifestation of the Conservatives' alignment with a business ideology perceived as unable to prevent the Depression or cope with its consequences.

It was also the force of personality that once again altered the political landscape. The individual around whom opposition rallied was the new Liberal leader, Duff Pattullo, who had been busy building up a party organization across British Columbia. Pattullo had arrived from Ontario during the Klondike gold rush. Following a career in the Yukon, he established a strong hinterland base as a Prince Rupert businessman and mayor. He came across as immensely self-confident, dapper, even a bit flamboyant. And he was not afraid to put forth new policies. The Liberal party's long-standing identification with social reform provided a useful backdrop. In Pattullo's view, the state should take a more activist role in dealing with the social inequalities and economic limitations created by unbridled capitalism. Using as a campaign catch-phrase the concept of 'socialized capitalism,' Pattullo linked himself with the New Deal policies of American president Franklin Roosevelt.

The 1933 provincial election offered British Columbians more than a choice between Tolmie's Conservatives and Pattullo's Liberals. Among the most significant responses to the Depression was the formation in 1932 of a new federal political party, the Co-operative Commonwealth Federation. The CCF reflected on a national, institutional level the informal response being played out on the provincial level to the Kidd Report. Bringing together reformist strands in Canadian society, ranging from the remaining proponents of the social gospel to female activists to radical socialists, the CCF proposed no more and no less than the establishment of a socialist government by democratic means. While many working people participated as individuals or groups, the trade union movement was not in the lead in the CCF's formation, being still splintered among separate and divergent groups. The inspiring leader of the movement was the social activist James Woodsworth who, with very strong working-class support, had since 1921 led a small reformist band in the House of Commons.

British Columbia soon felt the CCF's effect on both the provincial and municipal levels. By the time of the 1933 provincial election the new party was sufficiently organized to nominate candidates in all but one of the forty-seven ridings. It claimed that the two mainline parties were played out, unable to carry through promised adjustments in the social and economic order since they could be realized only at the expense of their principal political supporters. The CCF's visionary socialism was unable to meet the challenge offered by Pattullo's more practical promise to expand government services, but the new party did manage to elect seven members. By so doing, it became the official opposition against the thirty-four seats won by the triumphant Liberals. Never before had the left attained such a level of success in British Columbia.

Vancouver was also shaken by the CCF's formation. In 1935 wards, the long-standing basis of voting for civic aldermen, were abolished. A plebiscite on the issue received broad support from all political groups on the grounds that wards only furthered local, entrenched interests to the detriment of the city as a whole. In the first at-large election, held in December 1936, the CCF captured three out of eight aldermanic positions. Entrenched interests were aghast. Previously the Liberals and Conservatives had not been active on the municipal scene; now they came together into what was termed a Non-Partisan Association. Its founders included former mayors W.H. Malkin and Gerry McGeer, and a Woodward and a Spencer of department store fame. The importance of name recognition in garnering support was underlined in future entrepreneur Jack Diamond's observation concerning inter-war Vancouver as it appeared to him as a young Polish immigrant. 'The tallest building was the Woodward's beacon on Hastings Street. At that time, Woodward's was so majestic. Woodward's and God were about the same.'[33] Common opposition to a perceived socialist threat overrode traditional political divisions. The consequence was that, after 1937, the CCF were shut out. Through mid century city hall would be dominated by the NPA, in effect by 'propertied, business-oriented, conservative' aldermen giving primacy to the maintenance of a comfortable status quo.[34]

The CCF's shadow may have spurred Pattullo on in his efforts to initiate public undertakings 'where private endeavour is not able to take up the slack of employment.'[35] The legislature passed a spate of bills reforming taxation, providing some economic assistance to various components of the economy, and restoring social programs.

A major public works program included a bridge over the Fraser River at New Westminster to improve access across the densely populated lower mainland.

Yet depressed conditions persisted. British Columbia was made up of a number of separate economies, each based on a different raw material. Some staples recovered while others remained moribund. Forestry began to turn around in mid decade. So did pulp and paper production, which had only fallen by one-third. The fisheries rebounded by 1935 to two-thirds their pre-Depression high. Prices paid for silver, lead, and zinc slowly moved back upward, but copper and coal remained stagnant. Coal mines on Vancouver Island were phased out. Anyox, a copper-based company town of about four thousand founded early in the century in the northwest region near the Alaska Panhandle, was simply shut down in 1935. The mining company that owned the town had three years' stock of unsold copper and decided it could not continue production. Distraught residents swelled the ranks of the unemployed in Prince Rupert, Prince George, Vancouver, and Victoria.

The price of gold moved up dramatically. The value of gold mined in the province expanded several times over from a low of just over $3 million in 1929 to $14 million by 1935 and $24 million by 1940. Abandoned mines were reopened, resulting in a boom reminiscent of earlier gold rushes. The wife of one hopeful miner recollected that 'once they were out in the bush they lived on almost nothing. Bannock, tea and whatever game and fish they caught.' Travelling from Vancouver to Lillooet in June 1933, Emily Carr shared the train with 'vast quantities of prospectors going to the mines with their packs on their backs ... building airy castles for themselves, and wives, children, aged parents, and who-not, generous in their imagined affluence.'[36]

By 1933 the Bridge River area near Lillooet led the province in the production of gold. Some thirty mining ventures were hoping to emulate the success of the large Pioneer and Bralorne mines being exploited by leading Vancouver businessmen. Carr described working conditions in the Pioneer, which in her view left much to be desired. 'I wondered how they had the grit to go down into the blackness, to sink down, down that awful shaft on a lift – only a platform, no cage, no sides. If anything went wrong with the lift there were ladders perpendicular up the sides of the shaft ... and that awful, awful black hole if one slipped or got dizzy. The telling [about the conditions] sickened me. If a man's light went out he must stand perfectly still and shout ... It [blasting] must be done with exact precision and remembering acutely which [blasting location] was which, then the lighting and the mad rush to get away, far, far as possible. The succession of concussions that split your ears and knocked you down. Oh, is there any gold in all the world worth all that?'[37]

In British Columbia's relatively small agricultural sector, which some came to see as particularly critical given the extreme fluctuations in staples demand, co-operative marketing continued to be pursued as central to long-term stability. In 1931 the provincial marketing act passed four years earlier was declared unconstitutional on the grounds that it acted to restrain trade, whose regulation lay in federal jurisdiction. Many fruit-growers found themselves in the position of West Kootenay farmer and future federal politician, Bert Herridge. Having picked, packed, and shipped 250 boxes of apples he ended up with a $17.50 bill for the boxes.[38] 'A Cent a Pound or on the Ground!' became the rallying cry. Debate was renewed not only in fruit-growing but also in dairying between advocates of open competition and those of co-operative marketing. Efforts at unified action were again thwarted by a minority willing to undersell for immediate advantage.

In 1934 the federal government passed a National Products Marketing Act, which regulated natural products through the establishment, under provincial supervision, of local boards to deal with particular commodities. A Tree Fruit Board was no sooner established in the Okanagan with support of nearly 90 per cent of growers than the federal act was declared unconstitutional. The province did enact legislation permitting producer boards which was constitutionally acceptable as it regulated only intra-provincial trade. The act initiated long-term co-operative marketing not only of fruit but of an increasing number of commodities. During these years groups across the province as diverse as coastal fishermen and Mayne Island tomato-growers began to market their products co-operatively.

Premier Pattullo soon came to believe, as had his predecessor, that the province could only do so much. Most of the economic changes that occurred, such as lumber broker H.R. MacMillan forming his own company when existing supplies of timber dried up, resulted from private enterprise. Apart from attempts in 1937–8 to regulate prices in the key monopolies of coal and public utilities, the province did little to redirect the economy. The responsibility, Pattullo believed, lay with the federal government. Yet Ottawa moved slowly and reluctantly. Jurisdictional legalities were used to avoid action, even over the still serious problem of male unemployment. Pattullo increasingly spoke out for 'better terms' in the federal-provincial relationship.

In mid decade the unemployment situation came to a head. The communist-led Workers' Unity League, active in British Columbia from 1931 until its disbanding on orders from Moscow in 1935, had organized a relief camp workers' union. In December 1934 over a thousand men marched on Vancouver to protest camp conditions. Following a federal promise to investigate, they dispersed. Lack of action prompted the union to declare a 'strike.' A mass migration of well-organized men descended on the city the next April demanding 'work and wages.' Conditions deteriorated and Mayor Gerald McGeer became convinced that the union's goal was a revolution to bring about a communist government in Canada. He cabled the prime minister: 'Am afraid you do not grasp seriousness of situation in Vancouver ... Communist organizers and agitators ... have been able to organize substantial numbers who are openly flaunting constituted authority. With no relief available, force will have to be resorted to to maintain order.'[39]

After two months went by without a federal response, tactics changed. Organized in quasi-military fashion, the men began a mass trek to Ottawa, buoyed by growing public sentiment for abolishing the camps and providing direct relief. About a thousand men boarded freight trains in Vancouver on 3 June 1935. Public reaction was mixed. The On-to-Ottawa Trek picked up additional supporters at each stop along the way. In British Columbian communities such as Kamloops local residents provided food for trekkers. On the other hand, Alberta's relief officer cabled the federal minister of labour following the men's passage through Calgary: 'Regarding British Columbia single men. A dangerous revolutionary army intimidating and defying provincial and municipal governments ... single men relief is a racket.'[40]

The trek, twenty-five-hundred strong, was halted in Regina. Protracted negotiations ensued both there and in Ottawa between its leaders and federal officials, including the prime minister. Negotiations broke down. The Royal Canadian Mounted Police thereupon moved in to stop the protesters before they could leave for Winnipeg, still a centre of labour radicalism. The Regina Riot, as it became known, left one policeman dead, many trekkers injured, and about a hundred protestors in jail. Prime Minister Bennett justifed his actions on the grounds that many of the men's actions were illegal, and that, using a perennial anti-labour theme, all but one of the leaders were not true Canadians anyway. Born elsewhere, they had imported radical ideas into the country.

Despite a bloody finale, the trek was not without its consequences, particularly at the federal level. Facing re-election, Prime Minister Bennett had already realized that something must be done. In early 1935 Parliament passed several measures, including unemployment insurance. Bennett's last-minute actions were undone by events in Regina. In an October federal election his government went down to defeat before the Liberals headed by Mackenzie King. Public opinion, in the view of a contemporary, 'crystallized in the belief that unemployment had become a National responsibility.'[41] In late 1935 relief camps were replaced by temporary winter work camps and other means of assistance.

More and more of the men who were still unemployed drifted to Vancouver; by May 1938 the number had reached six thousand, many from the prairies. In desperation the provincial government stopped relief for all but BC residents. Confrontation broke out after a thousand jobless men occupied the city's main post office, art gallery, and the Hotel Georgia. While the last group was persuaded to leave after ten days, the others held out. Six weeks later, on 19 June, Bloody Sunday, police moved in to evacuate the post office following negotiated withdrawal from the art gallery. Eviction came through use of tear gas, the police using clubs as the men came out into the street. The mêlée moved down Hastings and Granville streets, breaking windows in established businesses such as Birks and Woodwards. Over a hundred were wounded and twenty-two arrested.

While tempers were slowly defused over the next months, a more permanent solution to the problem of unemployment came only with the outbreak of the Second World War. Federal acknowledgment of regional disparities in a nation whose economy was based on a combination of primary and secondary industries came in the 1937 appointment of the Rowell-Sirois Commission on Dominion-Provincial Relations. Backing up British Columbia's long-standing demand for better terms, Pattullo informed the commission that in 1938 'approximately 80 per cent of the manufactured commodities imported into the Province of British Columbia is imported from Eastern Canada, while approximately 75 per cent of our main primary products, apart from agriculture is sold in open competition in the world's markets.' Having long termed himself a 'British Columbia Canadian,' the premier made clear that the province in no way considered itself a supplicant. As early as 1933, he had informed the prime minister that 'we are an empire in ourselves and our hills and valleys are stored with potential wealth which makes us one of the greatest assets of our Dominion.'[42] Reporting in 1940, the commission concluded that regional disparities did indeed exist. Their amelioration was possible only through the federal government exercising greater authority in relationship to the provinces than presently the case. British Columbia, together with some other provinces, was opposed to the federal government acquiring more power, but by then the war had intervened to put the issue on hold.

The economic hardship of the 1930s obscured important changes occurring in everyday life. Physical recreation as a popular pastime was encouraged with the inauguration in 1934 of the British Columbia Provincial Recreation Programme, known popularly as Pro-Rec.[43] The first scheme of its kind in the British empire, Pro-Rec was intended to counteract the demoralizing influence of unemployment among young men. Free regular sessions of calisthenics, gymnastics, and team sports were organized in churches, community halls, schools, and armouries around the province. Pro-Rec became so popular that it was soon broadened to include all interested men and women.

The isolation of the frontier lessened. Bush pilot Grant McConachie began the first scheduled if irregular service between such points as Prince George and Fort St James. When a serious injury occurred in 1935 on Hobson's remote ranch, it was possible to get through to the nearest settlement using a 'telephone-telegraph line' stretched over almost five hundred kilometres of the interior. A doctor flew in by float plane using huge bonfires as signalling beacons. It was 'the second plane ever to wing into the country.'[44] Two years later the Colliers, fur trapping in a remote corner of the Chilcotin, made an important investment. 'From the fall of 1937 on we could when weather said stay home, move a couple of knobs, and at the twitch of a squawfish's fins be in San Francisco, or Seattle, or … move a knob an inch to the right or left and land on our feet on the prairies, maybe at Regina, Saskatchewan, or Calgary, Alberta, or some other place boasting those mysterious somethings called transmitters. The radio, an R.C.A. Victor, cost us four mink and a coyote pelt … it was often our only tie for months on end with the outside world.'[45] Radio communication was especially critical in the northwest, northeast, and central interior regions, where it rapidly become – and remains – the best means to get emergency messages to individuals and families living beyond the telephone.

The declaration of war in September 1939 put British Columbians' lives on hold. Almost overnight attention was redirected outward. The inter-war years had been a time for introspection, first in self-satisfaction at the good times and then in self-pity before the harshness of the Depression. Even Canadian foreign policy had been essentially self-serving, giving primary attention to the assertion of national autonomy against interference by the former mother country of Britain. Immigration became so restricted that by 1931 only farmers of British or American background with capital could secure entry. International events which during the 1930s might be thought to have garnered attention, such as growing Jewish persecution in Europe, were largely ignored. As Carr penned in her journal in April 1936, 'nobody mentions the war clouds hanging so low and heavy over everything.'[46]

Only the outbreak of war in Europe startled British Columbians out of their introspection. Illusions of neutrality were finally shattered when Nazi Germany invaded Poland in defiance of British and French warnings. Carr wrote on 3 September: 'It is war, after days in which the whole earth has hung in an unnatural, horrible suspense, while the radio has hummed first with hope and then with despair, when it has seemed impossible to do anything to settle one's thought or actions, when rumours flew and thoughts sat heavily and one just waited, and went to bed afraid to wake, afraid to turn the radio knob in the morning.' Four days later she observed how 'war halts everything, suspends all ordinary activities.'[47]

With the declaration of war the problem of unemployment was quickly reduced, in part through the tremendous increase in the size of the armed forces. The earlier world conflict had provided the final stimulus to turn Canada from an agricultural into an industrial nation;

industrialization was now confirmed, consolidated, and enhanced. While federal unity was again challenged by the knotty issue of conscription, open conflict between French and English Canada was averted. The Canada that emerged in 1945 was a very different nation from the one that entered the war, stronger and more united than it had been in 1919.

Events in British Columbia reflected shifts at the national level. At the onset of hostilities the province was still depressed, the value of production 12 per cent below that of 1929. Over the war years the value of production doubled. Manufacturing grew, owing in particular to ship and aircraft construction. Workers from the prairies flocked to the coast, and at one time over thirty thousand men and women were employed in shipyards in Greater Vancouver and Victoria alone. Both cities suffered severe housing shortages. According to Victoria's health officer, by 1942 'practically every available space that is roofed over is being used.'[48] Labour became virtually unobtainable, be it ranch hands or mill workers. Women's contributions to the work force increased immensely. Industries traditionally closed to women, from plywood to pulp and paper mills, welcomed their labour. Victory gardens, war saving stamps, rationing cards, and soldier's parcels became the motifs of everyday life. Many men's desire to marry before heading off to war was reflected in lower mean marriage ages of twenty-seven for men, twenty-three for women by 1941.

The province achieved a measure of political stability, not so much from the demands of war as from a desire not to rock the boat in the face of the growth of socialism. The CCF had won a plurality of votes in the 1941 provincial election, even though that had only translated into fourteen members in the legislature. Its support came from the lower mainland and the resource communities, where unions aided the cause. The opposition in Pattullo's own cabinet grew, with the majority now in favour of some form of coalition government with the Conservatives. The premier's strident stance in favour of provincial rights contrasted with a sharp shift in public opinion once war broke out towards a strengthened federal government.

Pattullo's unwillingness to participate in a governing coalition led to his replacement as Liberal leader by John Hart. In the interests of joining together to 'win the war,' the CCF was invited into the coalition, but refused on the grounds that its ideological differences were too fundamental for the three parties to work together effectively. The political left continued to be an independent advocate of causes shared by many British Columbians, ranging from official acknowledgment of unions' legitimacy to rural electrification. The jolt occasioned by the CCF's capture of power in Saskatchewan in 1944 helped maintain the governing coalition at the next provincial election in 1945. The two parties agreed that they would not run opposing candidates in the same riding, and as a result the CCF was reduced to just ten members. The CCF did chalk up one notable victory, however – its candidate defeated Pattullo in his own riding.

The war particularly affected northern British Columbia, so far largely ignored by provincial governments. The exploits of pioneer bush pilots McConachie and Russell Baker had begun to draw attention to the area. Pattullo had called in the late 1930s for the annexation of the adjacent Yukon Territory; and the United States was considering building a highway to Alaska. Pattullo was determined that it should pass through his province. The bombing of Pearl Harbor in December 1941 made the highway a necessary defence project if the Americans were to protect Alaska. The British Columbian portion, constructed in 1942, ran from Dawson Creek near the Alberta border through the Peace country to Watson Lake in the Yukon Territory (see Map 10). The highway opened up the northeast region. Other aspects of American defence policy intended to protect Alaska benefited northern and central British Columbia equally. An airstrip was built at Fort Nelson as a stop for military planes heading north; and Prince Rupert became a supply centre and staging post for American bases as well as a centre for highway construction. By the end of the war the north had in a psychological sense become part of British Columbia.

Working people benefited through trade unions' acceptance by the population at large. It was during the war that the labour movement finally came of age. As explained by labour historian Paul Phillips, 'unionism was no longer just tolerated but rather became an integral part of public policy.'[49] The antagonisms and suspicions that marked the First World War were replaced by an attitude of co-operation, summed up in the optimism of the popular song:

> Hold the Fort for we are coming
> Union men be strong!
> Side by side we battle onward
> Victory will come.

Events in the United States played a role. A National Labor Relations Act passed in 1935 guaranteed workers the right to organize and bargain collectively. The Wagner Act, as it was known, was followed by the spectacular success of the Congress of Industrial Organizations. The CIO rapidly organized mass production industries on a factory or industry-wide basis. While Canadian legislation remained restrictive, in 1940 the Canadian Congress of Labour was formed in direct opposition to the Trades and Labour Congress. If not increasing as rapidly as in the United States, union membership in Canada grew modestly.

Despite wartime restrictions on the right to strike, full employment from late 1941 boosted the unions' bargaining ability. It also accelerated the move towards unionization. Labour did not oppose conscription as in the First World War, abhorrence of fascism overcoming possible objections. Labour's contribution to the war effort prompted an important federal order-in-council in early 1944. It established, much like the Wagner Act, compulsory collective bargaining and the right of employees to form and join unions and the right to strike. The statute was only possible because the war had granted to the federal government emergency powers in areas of provincial jurisdiction. It signified a turning point in Canadian labour relations.

Union membership among British Columbia's non-agricultural labour force, which by 1939 had doubled from a low of 7 per cent five years before, approached 30 per cent by 1943. The CCL gained at the expense of the TLC, being particularly strong among ship-builders, longshoremen, and mine workers. The TLC's strength lay in the building trades, fisheries, and transportation. Employers' hold in single-industry and company towns finally loosened. Among groups unionized were Consolidated Mining employees at Trail by the CCL and pulp and paper workers at Powell River under the TLC. The unions that resurfaced in Powell River in the late 1930s did so with the blessing of the company, concerned to prevent more radical alternatives. Fruit and vegetable workers in the Okanagan formed the first agriculture-based union in the province's history. Office workers and the service sector generally began to organize for the first time. By 1945 the CCL and TLC were of approximately equal strength in the province.

Success was particularly evident in the forest industry. By the end of the war the International Woodworkers of America was probably the strongest union in the province. Many decades of organizing efforts had finally borne fruit. The breakthrough came at mills on Vancouver Island in early 1942, and Scandinavian loggers on the Queen Charlottes soon followed suit. A campaign to organize mainland workers began at Fraser Mills, still a company town dominated by a single large employer. By war's end the labour movement was no longer the underdog, nor was it so viewed by British Columbians.

If working people reaped the benefits of war, Canada's Japanese population, virtually all of whom lived in British Columbia, was its victim. While Germans and Italians experienced considerable discrimination, the Japanese suffered far more. During the inter-war years the Japanese had increasingly set themselves apart from other Asians. They had attempted to integrate more into British Columbian society by pursuing similar career paths, living as families, and converting to Christianity. Prejudice against them was heightened by the unemployment of the Depression years – a mood caught by one of the young transients in *Waste Heritage*, who declares his intention 'to snitch a job some Douk. or Jap had overlooked.'[50]

The birthrate among British Columbians of Japanese descent was double the provincial average. In sharp contrast to the Chinese and East Indians, whose numbers declined over this period, British Columbians of Japanese descent rose to over twenty-two thousand. One in three Mayne Islanders was Japanese, which of itself then became cause for suspicion. To quote the local MLA in 1938: 'In 1920 the population of Mayne Island was almost entirely white ... Then the Japanese invasion started ... there are more Japanese than white children in the Mayne Island school ... They all work, even women with babies strapped to their backs ... They live mostly on rice.'[51] Over half the Japanese in British Columbia at the beginning of the war were Nisei. Born in Canada, speaking English, educated together with other British Columbians, possibly holding a university degree, they considered themselves part of the mainstream society. Yet little difference existed in the popular mind between generations, particularly as the aggressiveness of Japan's foreign policy during the 1930s heightened fears that the Japanese in British Columbia gave primary loyalty to the emperor and thereby posed a military threat.

Japan's invasion of China in 1937 set off a new round of discrimination. Public charges that Japanese military officers were living in disguise as coastal fishermen initiated a parliamentary debate, and as a result intelligence officers and the Royal Canadian Mounted Police put a watch on residents of Japanese background. Tensions within the province and in Ottawa heightened in 1940 with Japan's support for Hitler and Mussolini. Then came Japan's assault on Pearl Harbor in December 1941. Canada's almost immediate declaration of war against Japan brought federal action: some twelve hundred fishing boats owned by British Columbians of Japanese background were seized. On RCMP advice the three Japanese-language newspapers and fifty-nine Japanese-language schools voluntarily shut down. Such measures did little to satisfy public opinion. By January 1942 patriotic societies, service clubs, and town councils were organizing protests. The virtually unanimous demand, backed by politicians at every level, was that all Japanese, regardless of place of birth or citizenship, be immediately evacuated from the coastal areas. Rumours of fifth-column activity were rife, as were reports of Japanese submarine activity off the Pacific coast. Fears of invasion grew, this at a time when Britain seemed unable to stop the Japanese military advance across southeast Asia.

In retrospect, it is clear that Japan never planned an invasion, but contemporaries had no way of knowing its ultimate war strategy. At the time only a handful of individuals stood up for the Japanese. Three UBC scholars objected to 'disqualifications, imposed in terms of *race*,' which meant that they applied 'equally to the second generation, born in Canada, educated in Canadian schools, and in many cases thoroughly Canadian in outlook.'[52]

Initially, evacuation from sensitive areas was partial and limited to male enemy aliens, Germans and Italians as well as Japanese. The federal initiative was announced on 14 January, thus preceding by two weeks a comparable American plan. Within little more than a month the first group of seventeen hundred Japanese men reached road construction camps in Alberta. The action did not stem the outcry for a complete evacuation. The decision lay with the federal government, and British Columbians made sure that public officials heard the message loud and clear. Less than a week after President Roosevelt signed a complete evacuation order, the Canadian government capitulated. On 24 February it approved an enabling measure to remove all persons of Japanese ancestry from a 160-kilometre coastal strip and from the Trail area, whose smelter was critical to the war effort. One of the greatest forced migrations in Canadian history, second only to the Acadians' expulsion from Nova Scotia, received official sanction.

The process of evacuation proceeded smoothly. This was in good part because, according to Ken Adachi, Japanese cultural norms emphasized duty and obligation, conformity and obedience.[53] While a supervisory commission was being formed, all Japanese were placed under curfew. Motor vehicles, radios, and cameras were impounded as a 'protective measure.' A UBC student recalled the traumatic effect confiscation had on a fellow student, one of seventy-six of Japanese descent enrolled during the 1941–2 academic year. 'The lad was in shock. He was not truly capable of understanding what was happening to him. Like most Japanese Canadians, he considered himself no more a Japanese national than I considered myself a British national; we both considered ourselves as Canadians.'[54]

The students at UBC were given deferments allowing them to complete the academic year and in some cases were assisted in transferring to universities elsewhere in Canada, but other British Columbians of Japanese background fared less well. On 14 March the first group of some twenty-five hundred – mainly coastal fishing families – were brought for processing to Vancouver's Hastings Park Exhibition Grounds, where the stables and cattle stalls had been hastily converted for human habitation. Residents living in remote areas were often given only a few hours to leave their homes, the RCMP knocking on doors at all hours of night. A handful of families departed east on their own volition, but most were caught up in forced evacuation during spring, summer, and early autumn of 1942.

Destinations varied. Many single males built roads on the prairies or in Ontario. About a thousand families worked on sugar beet farms in southern Alberta and Manitoba, but many more went to camps in the BC interior. In April an advance group of Japanese males was dispatched to repair vacant houses in several largely abandoned West Kootenay mining towns. Their sparse European populations mostly welcomed the newcomers, in particular the boost that they gave to local economies. The other site selected was Tashme near Hope. In the summer of 1942, after Nisei protested separation from their families, the government allowed married men in road camps to transfer to the Kootenays or to Tashme. The camps' spartan living conditions were compounded by a particularly severe winter in 1942–3. Families used to the mild coastal climate were forced to

huddle together in uninsulated huts. While the barbed wire com-
pounds and watch-towers that marked the camps in the United
States were absent, each site was guarded by an RCMP detachment
that controlled access.

Schooling proved to be a particularly contentious issue. When
children not yet evacuated headed off to school in September 1942,
they found themselves excluded on the grounds that it cost too much
to hire extra teachers for the short period before they were moved. In
the camps the Hart government disclaimed responsibility. Although
education was a provincial matter under the British North America
Act, the Department of Education argued that, because the camps
were under federal jurisdiction, so should be the schooling of their
five thousand or so children. In the end the federal government
assumed limited responsibility; as a result schools were restricted to
the elementary grades and depended on volunteer teachers from
among the evacuees themselves. The churches eventually started some
high school classes, but in the end most children missed a year or more
of schooling. The community as a whole passed largely useless years.

Long-term policy towards the Japanese evolved slowly. The
federal Department of Labour urged evacuees' relocation to Ontario
and Quebec where jobs were available. The few who went east
experienced open discrimination and a prohibition against buying or
leasing farm land, businesses, or residential premises except by
special permission. In August 1944 Prime Minister Mackenzie King
announced a policy to repatriate. Those who opted to stay were
expected to prove their loyalty to Canada by moving east of the
Rockies. Initially the majority in the interior camps requested
repatriation. With the war's conclusion in September 1945 many had
a change of heart. In the end forced deportations were abandoned.
About four thousand evacuees, over half Canadian-born, left Canada
voluntarily with federal assistance.

A major issue became the federal government's policy of disposing
of Japanese property. Fishing boats seized in December 1941 were
sold almost immediately for a song so as to be put back into
operation. Evacuees were permitted to take few possessions with
them, and this had to include household effects and food provisions
for three to four days. No advice was given concerning property left
behind; some families hastily sold off possessions, others put them in
the care of friends, or simply left everything in empty houses often to
be ransacked.

Federal authorities soon began systematically disposing of Japanese property. In June 1942, 542 Fraser Valley farms assessed at over $1 million were sold at two-thirds their value for a soldier settlement scheme. The next January all property except stocks and bonds was ordered liquidated, again without owners' consent. Despite many Japanese letters of protest, notices of public auctions began to appear in Vancouver newspapers from April 1943. Not only was much of the property sold below its fair value, but owners faced deductions for taxes and sale expenses before any remaining funds reached them. In the United States, by comparison, no compulsory sale occurred, and evacuees were even assisted in reoccupying property. Post-war complaints and lawsuits led to a federal royal commission being established in 1947. It concluded that some under-evaluation had occurred in the Fraser Valley and that federal sales commissions had been excessive.

Dissatisfaction over the disposition of property long continued, heightened in the short term by a ban on return to coastal areas. Only in 1949 were people of Japanese ancestry allowed back to the west coast. At the same time Canadians of Japanese descent were given the vote federally and provincially. By that date many of the evacuees had settled elsewhere, including over a thousand at Greenwood in the Boundary region. In any case, the loss of property made it impossible to recreate former livelihoods. Not until 1988 did the federal government offer an official apology and monetary compensation. The war did not end for Canada's Japanese in 1945.

Japanese evacuation was in many ways only the tip of a much larger iceberg. Across British Columbia inequalities abounded during the inter-war years and through the Second World War. Class, race and ethnicity, and gender circumscribed opportunities. The urban-rural dichotomy probably widened, as Vancouver became the metropolis to a vast hinterland extending into the prairies. The jolt provided by the Depression caused serious reflection in some quarters, as evidenced by the CCF's formation. But it took another war to waken British Columbians to the anomalies so long accepted as the way things were, and therefore ought to be.

12

The Good Life
1945–1972

As the Second World War drew to a close, many British Columbians feared a recession similar to that which followed victory in 1918. But their concerns proved groundless; Canada entered a period of economic stability which, with a brief recessionary break from 1958 to 1962, extended into the 1970s. British Columbia was transformed. Badly needed physical infrastructure as well as major hydroelectric projects were built across the province. As never before, economic expansion was directed towards ameliorating regional disparities. While earlier booms had benefited different parts of the province, no comparable attempt had been made previously to link profit-making from resource exploitation to development of the interior and the north.

The west coast province's capacity to capitalize on opportune conditions was enhanced by political realignment. A new party gained power in 1952 headed by a leader committed to change. A single individual – W.A.C. Bennett as premier and as head of the new Social Credit party – came to symbolize the era. Not until 1972 would provincial politics again be redefined in British Columbia.

The boom that gripped Canada during the post-war years had several causes. Individual earnings forcibly saved during the war were just waiting to be spent. Primary resource production benefited from the need to rebuild Europe and from industrial expansion taking place across North America and the world. Agricultural commodities were in short supply in Europe through the mid 1960s. Demand grew both for traditional staples such as coal and for newer metals like molybdenum used to temper steel. The federal government adopted a more activist stance by encouraging industrial expansion and foreign investment. The good times received a boost with the outbreak of the Korean War in 1950, which created new demand for Canada's exports. By the end of the 1960s Canada ranked sixth among the world's trading nations.

British Columbia at the end of the war was sorely in need of economic encouragement. Parts of the province, even where long settled, existed in near frontier conditions. When Richmond Hobson had first contemplated exploring British Columbia's ranching potential before the war, he contacted the provincial government for information only to be informed that the Chilcotin beyond Tatla Lake was uncharted. 'They don't know what's over the other side. Maps don't show.' In the mid 1940s it took two days to get from Vancouver to Lillooet. Part of the distance 'it looked like you were hanging out over the side of a cliff. Actually, in some places you were.'[1]

Living conditions were often rudimentary: in 1944 Vanderhoof reputedly contained just fourteen indoor toilets. Returning to the central interior from fighting the war, Cyril Shelford was appalled. 'The roads in our area were impassable in the spring and fall; there was no electric power and little running water. I just couldn't believe what I'd come back to ... no one seemed to give a damn.' Men and women were in effect penalized for daring to reside outside of the province's southwestern tip, gasoline prices being 'a third higher than for those living in urban areas in the lower mainland.'[2]

Contact with the ouside world was often limited. 'The little towns where I grew up were tiny communities, self-contained universes all of their own.'[7] When game hunting in the 1950s in the area settled by Hobson, lumberman Gordon Gibson was guided by a young man, the son of early pioneers, who 'certainly knew the country we would be travelling through but the largest city he had ever heard of was Williams Lake about 150 miles away.'[3] For many British Columbians of mid century not only were conditions of everyday life spartan but the province as a geographic entity simply did not exist. Little if any sense existed of British Columbia as a unified whole.

The creation of British Columbia as a cohesive unit took precedence during the post-war years. The coalition formed at the beginning of the 1940s held together through a provincial election in October 1945 and the resignation of John Hart as premier two years later. His replacement was fellow Liberal Byron Johnson, known popularly as Boss after his childhood nickname. Confirmed in power in a 1949 election, Boss Johnson looked toward 'the greatest development this province has ever seen.'[4] Of a projected $90 million development program, the government earmarked fully one-third for road construction. The long dormant Pacific Great Eastern Railway was revived, reaching Prince George in 1952. The same year Prince, as it is known locally, was linked by road with the Alaska Highway's BC terminus at Dawson Creek. Rural electrification was promoted. The privately run BC Electric Company had ignored the hinterland in favour of urban areas where profits were easier to reap, so in 1947 the BC Power Commission was established as a public body to provide electricity to outlying areas.

Other major projects were initiated. In 1951 a long-mooted agreement was signed with the Aluminum Company of Canada (Alcan) to build a large smelter about 110 kilometres southeast of Prince Rupert at what would become the town of Kitimat. Almost immediately there were 'camps all over the place, thousands of men and very high wages.'[5] About the same time Consolidated Mining and Smelting, later renamed Cominco, started a major expansion at Trail. Pipeline construction began between Alberta oilfields, discovered and brought into production after the war, and the Pacific coast. In the far northwest 'a whole mountain of asbestos' began to be mined in 1952, a process evoked by journalist Gwen Cash. 'An open-pit operation, it was reached by a spectacularly steep, and dangerously curved seven-mile-long road down which trucks rolled to deliver the miracle known as asbestos to the plant at Cassiar.'[6]

Despite the spurt of activity, all was not well in the popular mind. It was within this context that a major new political force emerged in British Columbia. Social Credit originated in the Depression years on the prairies. An Alberta radio evangelist, William Aberhart, took up a theory first propounded in Britain in the 1920s that capitalism's problem lay in purchasing power being insufficient to equal potential production. The proposed solution, that the state issue a cash payment – a social credit – to all citizens, struck a responsive chord among impoverished farmers who in 1935 voted Aberhart into office. Once premier, he was gratefully relieved of responsibility for implementing 'social credit' by the reality of federal control of banking, credit, and finance. Aberhart's dynamic personality assisted Social Credit's transformation into a populist, highly moralistic, and even religious movement whose rallies were characterized by hymns and such prayers as

> O Lord, do Thou grant us a foretaste of Thy millenial reign.
> Organization is not enough, Lord.
> Our help must come from above.
> Amen.

Social Credit's extension into British Columbia built on two principal factors: the province's changing socio-demographic character, and the personality of W.A.C. Bennett. The Depression's cruel treatment of the prairies drove many men and women west in the hope of getting a second start in farming or working in war industries. Others came to retire, attracted by a more spectacular landscape, or a kinder climate. For some the move represented the culmination of a long-held dream, a mood caught by Emily Carr in her journal in 1933. 'Their ideal was to finish life out at the coast after they had grubbed out a fortune on their prairie farms, toiling through heat, cold, blights and blizzards, with the thought of the mild coast climate, the sea, the trees and gardens always before them.'[7]

The extension of the infrastructure, such as a rail link from Alberta which reached Dawson Creek in 1931, encouraged migration. The number of British Columbia residents who had been born on the prairies doubled during the 1930s; by 1950 it had reached 250,000, or more than one in five British Columbians (see Table 8). The growing proportion of prairie-born residents was evident in the province's changing ethnic structure. Many parents or grandparents had come to Canada in the great immigration campaign early in the century. By 1951 one in three British Columbians were of continental European descent even though the percentage actually born in continental Europe remained under 10 per cent (see tables 5 and 7).

Many prairie arrivals brought with them as part of their cultural baggage a disposition towards – or at the least some familiarity with – the political party in power in their old province. In Saskatchewan this was since 1944 the Co-operative Commonwealth Federation and in neighbouring Alberta the Social Credit. In some cases Social Credit's distinctive tenents and religious orientation set newcomers apart from longer established British Columbians and may have strengthened their willingness to support the party.

British Columbia's religious make-up also changed in ways consistent with the rise of Social Credit. Conservative Protestant denominations – Baptist, Mennonite, Reformed, Pentecostal and various evangelical and fundamentalist groups – grew in numbers to over eighty thousand by mid century (see Table 10). When nursing pioneer Ethel Johns retired to Vancouver in 1949, she almost immediately observed that 'the correspondence columns are given over to debates between Seven Day Adventists and Bible Fundamentalists rather too often.' Evangelist Bernice Gerard, converted as a child to Conservative Protestantism, emphasized in her autobiography written in the mid 1950s how negatively members of established churches viewed fundamentalism. A middle-class Vancouver family with which she lived while attending high school 'were certain that Pentecostal pulpits were filled by racketeers and that the pews were filled with people who had failed in business or in love or had lost their health.' In university Gerard was repeatedly encouraged to 'follow after a faith that would be more in keeping with intelligence and culture.' A survey of fundamentalist ministers in British Columbia in the early 1950s revealed that over 70 per cent supported Social Credit, whereas over 60 per cent of United church ministers preferred the CCF.[8]

Among early adherents to Social Credit in British Columbia was William Andrew Cecil Bennett. His commitment, like that of many others, grew out of frustration with the existing political order in the west coast province. Born in the maritimes, Bennett acquired from his mother strict moral values. An after-school job in a hardware store led to a permanent occupation which young Bennett took with him westward, first to Alberta and eventually to the Okanagan Valley. Like many prairie migrants, his identification with British Columbia was instantaneous. According to Bennett's daughter, when her father first saw the Okanagan's 'blue skies, sparkling lake and cherry-laden orchards ... he thought he had reached the promised land!'[9] Settling in Kelowna, Bennett became increasingly anti-establishment and anti-Vancouver. In 1937 he lost out in his first attempt to stand as a provincial Conservative candidate to a Vancouver lawyer parachuted into the riding. Elected four years later, Bennett was unable to garner support for his idea of a more permanent coalition between the two mainstream parties. He then lost two bids to become provincial Conservative leader to establishment forces centred on the coast. To quote Martin Robin, 'Bennett was the frustrated small businessman writ large, the prototype of the chafing political outsider.'[10] In the spring of 1951 he crossed the floor of the provincial legislature to sit as an independent MLA.

In December 1951 Bennett joined the Social Credit League, betting that the coalition which had held power for a decade would not survive into the next election. Social Credit had existed as a fringe group in British Columbia since the 1930s. In the post-war years the party in Alberta provided some financial support and sent out organizers, but without a popular leader its appeal remained limited to small town and interior merchants, farmers, and loggers attracted to its ethical simplicity. Bennett's move vitalized Social Credit, whose membership across the province rose from about five hundred in 1950 to over eight thousand two years later.

A provincial election set for June 1952 saw the Liberals and Conservatives, as Bennett foresaw, campaigning separately. The coalition had broken up amidst mutual suspicions that the other party was receiving the principal benefits. Suggestions of corruption played a role. So did policy differences in such areas as health insurance, the Conservatives being less favourable to social reform than the Liberals. A transferable ballot was put in place to keep out the CCF, viewed as the common enemy. Instead of voting for a single candidate, voters were asked to rank all candidates in order of preference. After first choices were counted, any candidate receiving an absolute majority would be declared elected. The lowest-ranked candidate in each riding was dropped, and the second choices of those voters added to the remaining candidates, a process repeated until a candidate had a majority. In crafting such a complex process, the two mainline parties did not take Social Credit into account; it was not viewed as a major factor in the election.

Part of the complacency arose because Social Credit concentrated its efforts not on urban British Columbia, where the Conservative and Liberal parties were centred, but in the hinterland. A typical Social Credit candidate was young Cyril Shelford, fed up with his region's long neglect by a power structure centred in the province's southwestern tip. Shelford recollected his first encounter with Social Credit and Bennett. 'I liked Bennet's speech on the need to develop roads and rail to open up the province. Given that we couldn't move on even the main roads in our area for weeks at a time, this sounded very good to me. After the speeches were over ... Bennett reached for six membership books and gave them to me, saying, "Go sell these in Burns Lake and Vanderhoof and run for the nomination."' Much campaign literature came from Alberta, whose prosperity from its post-war oil boom was trumpeted as the model for British Columbia. The party's strong religious and populist overtones made it come across as a true people's movement. As Shelford found out, 'it was easy to sign people up,' since 'feelings around the province were running high against the government.'[11]

After first-choice ballots were counted on 13 June, only five incumbent individuals were declared elected. Three were Social Credit supporters, including Bennett himself, the other two CCF candidates. Even more astonishing was the news that the CCF led in more ridings than any other party. It also had the highest popular vote with 31 per cent compared to 27 per cent for Social Credit, 23 per cent for the Liberals, and 17 per cent for the Conservatives. Without the transferable ballot the CCF would have stood a chance of forming a minority government. It took another month to calculate second and, where necessary, third choice ballots. The final result was nineteen Social Credit members, eighteen CCF, six Liberal, four Conservative, and one independent. Social Credit MLAs came mainly from the south and central interior, Lower Fraser Valley, and parts of Greater Vancouver. The CCF was strongest in the Kootenays, other parts of Greater Vancouver, and Vancouver Island excepting Greater Victoria, where the Liberals held on. More generally, Social Credit and the CCF came out ahead because they were so often mutual second choices. Protest against the status quo won the day.

The question became who was to govern British Columbia. At the time of the election Social Credit did not even have an official leader. An Alberta-based group supported a federal MP from that province. But the actual choice lay with the new Social Credit MLAs, and they elected Bennett on the first ballot. Other problems loomed large. The party had only two experienced members of the legislature: Bennett and Tilly Rolston, who had also crossed the floor from the Conservatives. Nobody – no party member, much less an MLA – possessed the legal training considered essential to become attorney general or the financial background deemed necessary to hold the finance portfolio. Bennett took the offensive and recruited a young lawyer who had earlier supported his campaign to head the Conservatives, Robert Bonner, who was willing to serve as attorney general. As minister of finance he turned to a respected Vancouver accountant who handled the affairs of Bennett Hardware in Kelowna. Bennett would later gamble and secure them legislative seats by pressuring sitting Social Credit members to resign.

Lieutenant-Governor Clarence Wallace equivocated through July. He even travelled to Ottawa to seek advice from the prime minister as to whom he should call on to form a government, only to be told that he was on his own. The lieutenant-governor then consulted British Columbia's chief justice who recommended not calling on Bennett since, in his view, once Social Credit was in power the situation would become like Alberta and they would never be out again. The CCF leader Harold Winch visited Wallace and asked for the opportunity to form a government on the grounds that his party had more experienced legislators, a bigger percentage of the popular vote, and the support of the single pro-labour independent member.[12] On 1 August, fully six weeks after the election, Wallace met with Bennett, telling him that he was considering calling on the CCF. Bennett produced a letter from the independent member indicating his support for Social Credit and then a list of proposed ministers. Forty-five minutes after the meeting the lieutenant-governor phoned Bennett to tell him he would swear in his cabinet that evening. The chief justice, who epitomized Vancouver's long-standing hegemony over provincial life, at first refused to attend but then reconsidered.[13]

Bennett's first cabinet reflected the province's changing socio-demographic character. It included the first woman to hold a portfolio in British Columbia – Tilly Rolston as minister of education – a trade unionist, and men of German, Norwegian, and Italian descent. For the first time evangelical Christians participated in provincial political life in significant numbers: at least half a dozen of the new Social Credit MLAs adhered to such faiths.[14] Indeed Philip Gaglardi, a Pentacostal minister from Kamloops who became minister of public works, declared in his maiden speech in the legislature that he was 'not only a minister of the Crown, of the Queen but also a minister of the King of Kings.'[15] Three of Bennett's ten ministers as well as Bennett himself had lived in Alberta.

Once in office, Bennett's first task was to consolidate power. In a new election, called for June 1953, the Social Credit Party benefited from CCF disarray. Party leader Harold Winch had resigned over a second unsuccessful attempt to persuade the lieutenant-governor to name him premier following a legislative vote that went against Bennett and Social Credit. An embittered Winch was convinced that Bennett had deliberately engineered the vote to bring about the House's dissolution and so an election. The two mainstream parties unsuccessfully sought to discredit Social Credit, which garnered twenty-eight seats compared to the CCF's fourteen, the Liberals' four, and the Conservatives' one. The shifts to Social Credit came in Greater Vancouver and Victoria. Among defeated candidates was the finance minister, and Bennett soon took the porfolio himself, holding it throughout his tenure as premier. In 1954 Bennett abolished the transferable ballot and in the next election Social Credit became entrenched, winning three-quarters of the seats. While dominant on the provincial level, Social Credit was unable to sustain itself as a national party. In British Columbia its proportion of the vote peaked at a quarter in the 1953 federal election.

With the Liberals and Conservatives unable to make a comeback, Social Credit's principal oppostion became the CCF. The secret of Bennett's electoral success and that of the oppostion CCF was that they, in political scientist Ed Black's view, 'truly represented the feelings of protest and the demands for action that many British Columbians were voicing.' Social Credit worked hard to isolate the political left. What the provincial Liberal leader labelled 'a phony class war' was to some extent countered when the CCF reorganized itself federally with a broader political base.[16] In 1961 it joined with the newly formed Canadian Labour Congress, the major national body representing organized labour, to form the New Democratic Party. Unlike the CCF, the NDP was consciously intended to appeal to organized labour as well as to farmers and an educated middle class. Its vision of the future was more moderate, concerned to strengthen social policies, lessen foreign ownership, and exercise state control over public utilities and the exploitation of natural resources. Nonetheless, the political left remained unable to gain the support of more than one-third of the British Columbia electorate.

Bennett also effectively isolated critics from within and in this his hand was strengthened by his retention of the finance portfolio. His treatment of Cyril Shelford was a good example. Shelford remained for over a decade and a half an outsider within Social Credit. His public concern for the problems of his central interior constituents – 'coming from the North, a land of independent loggers and small sawmills ... there were times when I disagreed with some of his policies, as I thought they favoured the larger interests too much' – became a political liability. 'Because of my actions against major companies, both in the forest and the oil and gas industry, they did everything possible to keep me out of cabinet.' Only in the late 1960s, when Social Credit was finally threatened with defeat, did Bennett turn to Shelford as minister of agriculture. Shelford accepted.

Whatever his leader's faults, 'no fair-minded person could ever question his dedication and honesty, which is the best you can expect of any politician.' Shelford later reflected: 'The lesson I learned from all this was that democracy and the party system are stacked heavily against those who refuse to go along with the party on issues of principle.'[17]

Social Credit government was also male government. As the party took hold, so the proportion of female candidacies in provincial elections fell from a high of 10 per cent at mid century. Through the 1960s it stagnated at about 6 per cent, and only maintained that level because other parties nominated women from time to time. Just one in five of the tiny number of women who ran for the provincial legislature did so under the Social Credit banner. Rolston came to the party as a convert. Only four other women were elected during Social Credit's two decades of rule: Lydia Arsens in 1953 followed by Isabel Dawson, Pat Jordan, Grace McCarthy, and Agnes Kripps.

Social Credit was not without its scandals. Charges of patronage in awarding highway and other contracts were almost commonplace. Suspicions were heightened by Social Credit's determination to maintain its political base among the 'grass roots': government must be perceived as accessible to ordinary people across the province. The best-known scandal was the Robert Sommers affair, named for the MLA made minister of lands, forests, and mines in 1952 despite a reputation for heavy drinking and gambling. Sommers soon got into personal difficulties, overspending and then borrowing unwisely in possible exchange for dispensing special favours to forestry companies. An official investigation in 1955 cleared Sommers, but suspicions lingered and Bennett requested his resignation early the next year. By the end of 1957 criminal charges of bribery and conspiracy were laid and the consensus was that Attorney General Bonner had been negligent. While Sommers was eventually sentenced to five years in jail, Bennett to some extent mitigated the damage by holding himself aloof from the affair.

The thrust of the Bennett era lay not in its internal pettiness or intermittent scandals but in the fundamental change in economic policy put in place across British Columbia. Once in power Bennett and the Social Credit party were able to build on a whole range of activities already under way. They equally benefited from a great North American wave of good times characterized by generally rising wages, material prosperity, and growing self-confidence. Provincial revenues rose as British Columbia led the nation in population growth. On the very day Social Credit took power, bank transactions in Vancouver reached an all-time high. The *Sun* later editorialized that 'no other incoming government ever had it so good.' Journalist Bruce Hutchison soon became convinced that he was witnessing 'a total revolution of the British Columbia spirit' with 'the curious figure of Premier W.A.C. Bennett, the gaudy symbol of the whole process, the high priest of the new British Columbia.' 'The fixed neon smile, the bustling salesman's assurance, the ceaseless torrent of speech, the undoubted talents of a small-town hardware merchant writ large and a certain naive, boyish charm are ... the emblem and hallmark of a new province.'[18]

Bennett promised British Columbians what he liked to term 'the good life.'[19] He had come to power by appealing to groups not traditionally within mainstream society, including ethnic minorities swelled by prairie migration and hinterland British Columbians long existing in an urban shadow. This Bennett largely continued to do by putting forward policies held together more by their innovative character than by their ideological consistency. A strong verbal commitment to free enterprise cheerfully coexisted with a willingness to use the power of the state to set capitalism's direction. In the view of Bennett's biographer, David Mitchell, he 'cultivated an activist approach to government.'[20]

Political opposition was often turned on its head. As Shelford recollected, 'when any criticism was directed at us ... our critics were mainly throwing us a challenge to get on with the job.' Hugh Keenleyside, who headed a major government commission under Bennett, was far blunter in his memoirs. 'When he saw particular luscious peaches beginning to ripen on an NDP tree, he was not above a little surreptitious thievery ... He was uniquely successful in being able to gain advantage from taking either side (or even both sides) of any contentious issue.' The advice of experts was generally shunned as representing vested interest groups seeking to usurp control. Bennett, to quote Black, 'seemed to delight in radical policy innovations, which exemplify his party's anti-establishment biases.'[21]

The direction of growth was conservative, building on the province's traditional strength in natural resources. The key to expansion was the attraction of large amounts of extra-provincial investment capital. American money in particular arrived at unprecedented rates; by the mid 1950s over half of the investment in forestry came from the United States. Ties were strengthened by a redirection in exports: at the beginning of the Depression just under half of British Columbia's lumber exports went to Britain and one-quarter to the United States; as early as 1950 the proportions had reversed at 8 and 84 per cent. The value of Canadian products exported from British Columbia shot up five-fold from $675 million in 1952 to $3.3 billion two decades later.[22] Secondary manufacturing was not emphasized, partly owing to such long-standing limitations as federal tariffs, distance from central Canada, and a relatively small population base.

According to Shelford, a day after being elected Social Credit leader Bennett gathered his caucus, heard their views, and then devised a three-stage program centred on transportation, power, and industrial growth as a base for much-needed social programs.[23] Infrastructure creation provided the motif of the 1950s, making possible the big development projects, especially in hydroelectric power, that marked the 1960s. The results extended beyond the projects themselves to the new communities they generated. Bennett's faith in material progress through rapid and concentrated resource development became almost a secular faith within the party and to a considerable extent across the province. Carefully choreographed celebrations accompanied each project's progress. Relations with the federal government were never cordial. Provincial dissatisfaction over federal tax-sharing policies and equalization payments to less wealthy provinces combined with Bennett's independence from the principal federal parties to maintain a degree of detachment.

Social Credit policies were geared towards ameliorating regional disparities. Backed by a cabinet for the first time reflecting British Columbia's diversity, Bennett sought to open up the central interior, northwest, and northeast regions in what was a 'northern vision.' During the first six years of Bennett's tenure more money was spent building highways than in the entire history of the province. Many of the projects had begun earlier, but Social Credit willingly accepted the kudos for seemingly endless expansion. New bridges spanned Okanagan Lake at Kelowna and the Kootenay River at Nelson. A tunnel crossed the Fraser south of Vancouver as part of a freeway linking the mainland metropolis to the American border. The Pacific Great Eastern, finally completed all the way to North Vancouver in 1956, was pushed north to Fort St John in the Peace by 1958 and then to Dawson Creek. Federal policies sometimes assisted, as in the completion in 1962 of a new Trans-Canada Highway. Even then Bennett took the credit. On the grounds that most of the highway's finance, as well as its maintenance, came out of provincial coffers, Bennett rushed in before the official opening to rename the road 'B.C. No. 1.' The character of federal-provincial relations was underlined in Prime Minister John Diefenbaker's later observation that, although 'I did not regard this as abnormal, [it] was one of the most peculiar, self-centred actions that I've ever known.'[24]

Air and water transport were similarly transformed. Scheduled air service grew dramatically from its inter-war origins. In 1939 Vancouver had been linked with central Canada by Trans-Canada Airlines, which became Air Canada in 1965. Major communities began to acquire airport facilities, smaller ones at least a landing strip. In 1945 bush pilot Russ Baker incorporated as Central BC Airways, later becoming Pacific Western. Some early independents were overtaken by large companies. In 1941 the Canadian Pacific Railway purchased Grant McConachie's pioneer line, among others, to form Canadian Pacific Airlines. Six years later Vancouver became its national headquarters. Under McConachie's presidency Canadian Pacific soon flew to Australia, Japan, and Hong Kong, in effect becoming the new Empress liners of the skies.

The role played by water transportation was affected by the growth of scheduled air service, by highway construction, and by the retrenchment of the salmon canning industry. Long-distance passenger service by boat lost its appeal. The last sternwheeler, the venerable *Moyie* on Kootenay Lake, quit running in 1957. Union Steamships gradually abandoned established ports of call along the coast before finally closing down in 1959. When bodies of water had to be crossed, growing automobile ownership put the emphasis on short runs by vessels carrying cars as well as passengers and freight. The CPR line began slowly to convert its boats. More aggressive was an American rival for Puget Sound shipping, which in 1951 established Black Ball Lines as a separate BC subsidiary.

The character of water transportation was dramatically altered in 1958 after labour disputes on the two shipping lines threatened to cut Vancouver Island off from the rest of British Columbia. For some time the provincial government had sought expansion of ferry services. Both companies resisted, the smaller Black Ball for lack of capital, the CPR because greater profits were to be made in the air. While the province possessed only limited powers to coerce the CPR, which operated under federal jurisdiction, it could act against Black Ball –

and act it did. On the pretext of maintaining service to Vancouver Island, Black Ball Line was taken over by Bennett. It was then quickly expanded into a modernized BC Ferry Corporation. For its part, the CPR gradually withdrew from passenger ferry service.

The emphasis on big development projects that reached a crescendo during the 1960s was in tune with a similar expansion across Canada. The St Lawrence Seaway was built in co-operation with the United States and Newfoundland's Churchill Falls hydroelectric project eventually got under way. During these years it was the unquestioned assumption all over North America that a correspondence existed between high levels of energy consumption and a high standard of living. Geologists in British Columbia long believed that the northeast, geographically an extension of Alberta where major oil and natural gas finds had occurred after the war, also contained these valuable resources. Commercial quantities of natural gas were found near the border at Pouce Coupe in 1948 and the first productive wells sunk three years later. Demand for cheap energy in the rapidly industrializing cities of the American Pacific coast led to the construction, later in the decade, of a natural gas pipeline from the northeast to the coast to complement the earlier oil pipeline from Alberta to Vancouver. The main gas pipeline was completed in 1957, an oil pipeline four years later. By 1960 sixty-eight oil wells and two hundred gas wells were in production in British Columbia, a subsequent slump being reversed by the world energy crisis of the early 1970s.

Hydroelectric power provided the focus for much of the activity in energy development in British Columbia. In practice demand held the key. Construction could be justified only if large industries were interested in buying the product. Potential users included smelters, pulp and paper mills, and cement works. Previously development had been undertaken by the companies themselves, as in the case of the plants servicing the Trail smelter, and mills at Powell River and Ocean Falls. Early post-war initiatives were based on the view that British Columbia was, in Bennett's own words, 'the last economic frontier of North America.'[25] Alcan chose British Columbia only after considering alternative sites as widespread as Ghana, Borneo, Venezuela, and Labrador. The water for Alcan's large aluminum smelter came from damming the Nechako River south of Fraser Lake, eighty kilometres to the west at its planned community of Kitimat.

The Nechako's potential for providing hydroelectric power paled beside rivers moving out of the Rocky Mountains, particularly the Columbia River in the south complemented by the Peace in the north. The Columbia, the fourth-largest river in North America in length and water flow, drops nearly one kilometre as it travels through British Columbia into Washington State before emptying into the Pacific Ocean at present-day Astoria, named after the nineteenth-century fort. Joint studies between Canada and the United States began as early as 1944 on harnessing the Canadian portion of the Columbia to control flooding and service industry in the United States. America was far more eager than Canada to see the river's energy developed, and by the 1960s ten hydroelectric plants had been built on the United States' portion of the Columbia.

It was not just Canada and the United States that viewed the Columbia's potential differently. The federal and provincial governments were also at odds. Canada sought to set the terms for development on the grounds that international relations were at stake, while British Columbia believed that, since resource development was a provincial prerogative, it was in charge. In 1954 Bennett made an agreement with a private American company to construct a large storage dam on the Columbia to facilitate power generation downstream in the United States. The federal government countered by enacting legislation requiring a federal licence to make any improvements on an international river. The deal was quashed, to Bennett's dismay.

Ongoing federal negotiations with the United States culminated in the Columbia River Treaty signed in 1961. The treaty called for construction of three storage dams in southern British Columbia and a lump-sum payment by the United States for downstream benefits which would result. Half of the power generated in the United States as a consequence of the dams would be returned to British Columbia. Provincial-federal disagreement over control of downstream water rights delayed the treaty's ratification for three years. British Columbia wanted to sell off the rights to the Americans as opposed to the power being returned, a position to which federal authorities eventually acceded. Dams were constructed over the next decade at the upper end of Kootenay Lake, at the lower end of the Arrow Lakes, and at Mica Creek north of Revelstoke. But the dams' environmental disruption through flooding large areas remained a controversial issue, as did their perceived benefit, through the sale of water rights for the next thirty years, principally to the United States.

The development of the Peace River was initiated in the mid 1950s by Axel Wenner-Gren, a controversial international financier interested in the north's potential mineral wealth. After various studies, it was still not clear as to whether markets existed for the river's tremendous potential. Very soon the provincial government took over what Bennett, using his favourite adjective, termed 'the greatest hydro-electric project in the world.'[26] Bennett first 'provincialized' long-established BC Electric Company. In effect he expropriated the company with compensation, an act generating considerable public support given its long record of favouring urban over hinterland British Columbia in electrification. A year later, in 1962, he amalgamated the former BC Electric with the BC Power Corporation to create the BC Hydro and Power Authority with a mandate to develop the power of the Peace River. The irony of a government committed to private enterprise taking over one of the province's major private businesses was not lost on British Columbians. The Bennett Dam was completed in 1967, thereby increasing the supply of low-cost electricity available to major companies investing in the province. Almost two centuries after Alexander Mackenzie laid eyes on the Peace, its power was harnessed. Electrical generating capacity in British Columbia grew from 950 to 2,600 kilowatts per thousand population between 1951 and 1971.

Of the established components of the provincial economy, forestry underwent the greatest expansion. New processes and products proliferated. Trucks were increasingly used to transport cut timber along makeshift roads, making earlier logging railroads obsolete. The power saw triumphed. As one early user observed, 'I thought it was the best thing ever invented, even though it was only a half horse power.'[27] Plywood became a staple of post-war construction. New sources of wood supply included hemlock, previously unharvested in British Columbia, unlike Europe. It was left to the Koerner brothers, members of a central European lumbering family immigrating to British Columbia just before the war, to grasp hemlock's possibilities, renaming it Alaska pine to enhance its appeal.

The power of government was used to alter the industry's direction. British Columbia's timber supply continued to be almost completely provincially owned, crown lands being leased in exchange for rent and royalty. Despite corporate concentration, many small enterprises were still engaged in logging and sawmilling, often on a seasonal basis in between farming or fishing. The post-war years

saw increasing numbers of small entrepreneurs take advantage of
new road and rail links. 'The financial returns from sawmill work
were so much higher than those from farming that a large proportion
of the younger generation deserted farming, while even those still
working their farms spent most of the winter working in the
woods.'[28]

By 1955 British Columbia possessed nearly twenty-five hundred
operating sawmills. Unlike the inter-war years when the vast
majority were on the coast, now most were in the interior or the
north, some of them diesel-driven portable operations that could be
moved through the bush as timber was depleted.[29] In the Prince
George forestry area extending across the central interior through the
northeast, the number of mills in operation grew from under fifty at
the outbreak of the Second World War to a high of 730 in 1955.[30] Then
a decline set in. While sophisticated technology forced some companies out of business, provincial policy caused the demise of many
more. The government came to view a few large long-term lease-
holders of crown lands as having greater prospects for the future of
the industry than did many small operations. Large enterprises were
perceived as remitting more monies through rent and taxes, being
less likely to go out of business in a recession, and best supporting the
new notion of sustained yield. The concept of forests as a renewable
resource was argued in a provincial royal commission of 1943–5,
chaired by Justice Gordon Sloan. It was re-emphasized in the second
Sloan Commission of 1956. The quantity of timber cut annually
should be determined by government at levels that would ensure
that the process continued indefinitely.

In 1947 provincial legislation implemented the Sloan recommendations by establishing a system of forest management licences.
Essentially long-term leases, their goal was more efficient utilization
and management of the resource. A company given a licence was
expected to operate the designated area as a tree farm, harvesting to
be followed by reseeding either by nature or by replanting. Altera-
tions in the rules for bidding on timber-cutting rights and the raising
of technical standards also helped drive out small entrepreneurs. By
the mid 1960s the number of sawmills in operation in the Prince
George district had fallen by over one-third to 450; by 1971 it was
down to 135. Those that remained were in general much larger than
their predecessors a decade or two earlier. Small portable bush mills
were for the most part a thing of the past. The total number of

sawmills in operation across the province fell to just over three hundred by the mid 1970s.

Much of the post-war expansion of forestry centred on pulp, and this too favoured consolidation. The potential in wood pulp, made out of wood waste left over from sawmilling, expanded dramatically from just paper-making to thousands of uses in manufacturing. The first pulp mill in western Canada to use sawmill and plywood waste was established in 1948 at Port Alberni on Vancouver Island. Over the three decades 1951 to 1971 pulp production in British Columbia quadrupled to over four million tons annually. A wholly new company town was created in the northeast corner of the central interior at a point where Alexander Mackenzie had camped and named in his honour. Companies demonstrating their facility to use wood waste in making pulp were given licensing advantages. Pulp mills' growing demand for wood then encouraged their purchase of small mills, which further forced out independent operators.

Large integrated multinationals became the norm not just in pulp and paper but in the forest industry generally. One of the few Canadian-owned giants was MacMillan Bloedel, formed by a 1951 merger between the long-established company headed by H.R. MacMillan and a smaller competitor. Further expansion came in 1960 through merger with the company that had founded and long owned the pulp and paper town of Powell River. By the end of the 1960s, to quote MacMillan Bloedel's official history, 'few companies produced more pulp and newsprint and none could compete in production of lumber.'[31]

Of British Columbia's other traditional industries, mining was particularly affected by fluctuating world markets. Among new customers was Japan, whose demand for copper concentrates and coking coal helped renew interest in mining. Although the last Vancouver Island coal mine closed in 1966, the Crow's Nest Pass area of the East Kootenays enjoyed renewed prosperity. A special port was constructed at Roberts Bank south of Vancouver to take coal, once it had arrived by rail, directly abroad in large bulk carriers. Gold remained in demand, but even more so were lead, zinc, and other minerals used in automotive and electrical industries. Hardrock mining had earlier been underground; now open-pit operations proliferated as technological improvements and higher prices encouraged large-scale production of lower grade ores. Reliance on strip mining saw relatively large areas being systematically exploited and then abandoned on depletion. In 1973 a new townsite was laid out at Logan Lake southwest of Kamloops. The nearby Highland Valley enterprise was capable of converting over fifty thousand tons of ore a day to concentrate, from which copper and molybdenum were extracted. Moved by truck to nearby Ashcroft and then by rail to Vancouver, the concentrate ended up primarily in Japan. With the notable exceptions of the long-time smelter at Trail and its new counterpart for aluminum at Kitimat, minerals were still exported in raw or semi-processed form through long-term contracts with overseas buyers. The average gross value of mineral production, including petroleum and natural gas, rose from $140 million at mid century to almost $500 million two decades later (see Table 20).

The fishing industry still centred on salmon, which made up from two-thirds to three-quarters of the catch in value. The remainder was principally halibut and herring, the latter's roe a delicacy in Japan. Construction of a fish ladder up Hell's Gate in the Fraser Canyon at the end of the Second World War enabled more salmon to spawn and thereby increased Fraser River harvests: 1989 would finally see a sockeye salmon run reputedly comparable to those predating the slide three-quarters of a century before. Like forestry, fishing was characterized by corporate concentration. Coastal canneries retrenched to Vancouver and Prince Rupert, with just twenty canneries still in operation by the 1950s. In 1968 the last cannery between the lower mainland and Prince Rupert, at Namu near Bella Coola, closed. The next year Anglo-British Columbia Packers folded and sold off its assets; less than a decade later BC Packers emerged triumphant on top of the industry. The use of refrigeration on larger and faster boats encouraged consolidation, as did quick freezing technology.

The fishing industry came under increasing federal regulation to ensure that stocks sustained themselves. Fish conservation and enhancement were promoted through construction of spawning channels and hatcheries. Federal authorities set times and locations for fish to be caught. In 1968 a vessel-licensing system was introduced to control the size of the salmon fishing fleet. A program intended to reduce the number of boats by buying out excess vessels engendered considerable controversy. In 1977 Canada declared a two-hundred-mile economic zone within which it asserted exclusive rights to fish and manage fish stocks. While such actions excluded foreign fishing for halibut and other species in such locations as Hecate Strait between the Queen Charlottes and the mainland, it did little to prevent overfishing of salmon which, after spawning in British Columbia rivers, range over large areas of the Pacific Ocean.

Other traditional industries were less affected by boom conditions. Agriculture expanded marginally, primarily in the Peace. Manufacturing continued to be linked to resource development. Most items were made of wood or paper compared with central Canada with its array of products from steel goods to clothing. Over two-thirds of employees in manufacturing were in primary as opposed to secondary industries. This proportion was almost exactly reversed for Canada as a whole.

Population patterns altered somewhat during the Bennett years. The three northern regions surpassed 225,000 or 10 per cent of the provincial total by 1971. Assisting growth was the extension of the Pacific Great Eastern from Prince George to Fort St James and then towards Dease Lake. The line reached Fort Nelson in 1971, shortly thereafter being renamed BC Rail. Also critical to growth was a new generation of resource-based communities around the province. The government and multinational enterprises co-operated to provide housing distinct from the old-style company town where government, much less residents, had no role to play. An Instant Towns Act was passed in 1965 to encourage self-government, preplanning, and local ownership in new communities. Into the early 1970s eight towns were created ranging from Fraser Lake in the central interior based on molybdenum to coal-based Elkford and Sparwood in the East Kootenays. Benefits were mutual, workers gaining control over their everyday conditions of life and companies being relieved of responsibility for running the town.

Despite efforts to the contrary, post-war economic development was essentially an urbanizing phenomenon. Canada as a whole became more urban. During the five peak boom years of 1951–6 the proportion of urban dwellers rose by 10 per cent to two-thirds of all Canadians. In sharp contrast the previous 10 per cent increase had taken forty years to achieve. In British Columbia the scarcity of agricultural land meant that, even in the hinterland, growth was essentially community-oriented. Government policy, by creating the infrastructure and promoting resource exploitation, had the effect of opening up the central interior, northwest, and northeast as a string of urban entities. Some communitites at the cross roads expanded, in effect becoming mini-metropolises to their own increasingly accessible hinterlands. By so doing, they then buttressed the overall hegemony of Vancouver and the province's southwestern corner. As had long been the case – and would remain so – urban size was to some extent relative, a point made well by Ethel Wilson in a description from about 1960. 'Captain Crabbe's family lived in Alberni proper which to the dweller in a city seems like a fairly raw small town ... and to the dweller up the coast or in the Queen Charlottes seems like a small city with every comfort, every luxury.'[32]

The central interior community of Prince George was typical of this regional urbanization. At war's end a 'settlement of untidy shacks with mud roads,' it soon sported 'long-wide street of shops and stores, restaurants and hotels,' 'paved roads and concrete sideworks ... new public buildings and clinics and cinemas.'[33] The population increased from two thousand in 1941 to thirty-three thousand three decades later. Its hinterland extended west to Vanderhoof and Fort St James, north towards Mackenzie, Fort St John, and Dawson Creek.

The southern interior community of Kamloops was described by Hobson in the 1930s as 'a sunny healthful town of some five thousand people who mixed trout fishing with cattle ranching.' Two decades later it had, in the view of one observer, 'begun to look dangerously like a city.'[34] Kamloop's numbers more than quadrupled to twenty-six thousand by 1971. Kelowna in the Okanagan-Boundary region and Port Alberni on south central Vancouver Island experienced similar boom-time growth. Nanaimo to the east on the Island achieved what few single-industry communities in British Columbia have managed: recovery from a staple's demise. Following coal mining's collapse in the 1920s, Nanaimo struggled through the Depression but then revived as a distribution centre with an economic base in forestry. During the three decades from 1941 to 1971 the total number of urban centres of five thousand or more residents located outside of the province's southwestern tip tripled from seven to twenty-three.

Population became more concentrated. At the end of the First World War British Columbia had contained upwards of a thousand post offices and over seven hundred school districts. Innumerable outlying enclaves, where families scratched a living from the land or the sea, were long defined by a school, a post office, general store, and possibly a sawmill, cannery, or other source of seasonal work.

First the one-room school closed, then the sawmill shut down. Very likely the post office soon followed. In some cases it was the end of steamer service that rang the death knell. No longer was the wait at the local landing for the Union Steamship to arrive 'sometime' a centre for social and economic life. Television played a role. As one northwest resident remarked: 'The coming of TV had a great impact on these communities. People stopped visiting one another and a lot of active clubs became less active.'[35] Over the post-war years about a hundred post offices a decade disappeared across British Columbia (see Table 15).

Contemporaries lamented the passing of an era. A country postmistress put her thoughts to verse:

> I would rather remember Shandilla in the days of its prime
> Than to be disillusioned by the ravages of time.[36]

Writing in 1968, geographer Alfred Siemens described the sagging general stores. 'These structures once served a vital function as the centres of their respective communities, but have now generally fallen into disuse in favour of facilities in the larger town and particularly in Vancouver.' The editor of *Raincoast Chronicles*, a celebration of the thousands of men and women who once lived along the British Columbia coast, vividly recalled his childhood departure from a logging camp on Nelson Island located northwest of the Sechelt peninsula: 'We left in 1954 – victims of the Social Credit government's policy of closing the woods to small free enterprise and delivering it over to the big monopolies ... By the late fifties, Green Bay had won its sunless, rockbound solitude back to itself once again, and buried another generation of settlers' dreams.'[37]

Expanding transportation facilities made it possible for families to get to the nearby service centre whatever the weather, first perhaps as a commuter to a job and then permanently so that children could be closer to the school to which they were likely already being bussed. The next generation was sometimes the first to leave the area altogether. Back to *Raincoast Chronicles'* editor Howard White: 'I had grown up in the last days of the old coast when every bay had a gyppo booming logs and life followed the cycle of the weekly steamer call ... It had seemed a half-existence outside the real march of the twentieth century, a backwater my whole growing-up was aimed at escaping.'[38] To a considerable extent long-standing metropolis-hinterland disparities were ameliorated in British Columbia during the post-war years not so much due to positive government policy as to the disappearance of much of hinterland life.

As urban concentration increased in post-war British Columbia, so suburbs also grew in number and size. One measurement of this is the growth of sub-post offices, which doubled on Vancouver Island between the 1930s and 1950s, and increased even more on the lower mainland (see Table 16). And it was not only Vancouver and Victoria that spread out but regional urban centres as well. Housing estates and shopping malls were increasingly located at a distance from the traditional downtown area. At the beginning of the Second World War about one-fifth as many people lived in the adjacent Saanich peninsula as in Greater Victoria; by 1971 that proportion had more than doubled (see Table 17).Victoria politicians repeatedly pressed for amalgamation, but outlying muncipalities opted to retain their separate identities and establish their own social services.

The same pattern of population growth occurred on the lower mainland. In 1941 Vancouver city still contained three-quarters of Greater Vancouver's population; three decades later its proportion stood at just over half. The outer limits for commuting pushed inland as roads improved and the automobile became the norm. Streetcars disappeared from the city's streets, as they did in Victoria and elsewhere. In 1938 the Lions Gate Bridge was built to span Burrard Inlet. British investors, headed by the Guinness family of brewing fame, then profited by promoting their British Properties in West Vancouver as an exclusive residential district. The flight to the north shore of Burrard Inlet was spurred by the construction in 1958 of a second bridge across the inlet. By 1971 the north shore and Burnaby, which bordered Vancouver on the east, each housed over 125,000 residents. Much of the Lower Fraser Valley also became a residential suburb of Vancouver, its population approaching 400,000 by 1971.

Victoria and Vancouver escaped the inner-city decay and intrusive freeway systems characterizing some post-war American cities. Victoria's inner harbour near the Parliament Buildings and Empress Hotel was redeveloped to remove the last vestiges of industrial activity. Granville Street in downtown Vancouver underwent a similar process. Such developments did not go unopposed. Following civic approval of a major freeway route through Vancouver's Chinatown in late 1967, a wide range of groups – the Chinese community, professionals, UBC faculty – formed The Electoral Action

Movement, or TEAM, a civic reform movement that for a time successfully challenged the long-standing control of municipal politics of the Non-Partisan Association. TEAM's pinnacle of power came in the early 1970s. Their influence on city council killed the freeway proposals and redirected Vancouver's growth, encouraged neighbourhood involvement in policy-making, and began the transformation of the south side of False Creek from an industrial to a residential area. During these same years the city's skyline was transformed. The West End's mansions, many of which had been turned into flats during the inter-war years, were replaced by high-rise apartments. Symbolic of post-war Vancouver was BC Electric's architecturally innovative headquarters on Burrard Street, which soon housed the newly provincialized BC Hydro.

Despite economic transformation in metropolis and hinterland alike, over time the coalition put together by W.A.C. Bennett began to unravel. Repeated victories at the polls had been assisted by the distribution of seats in the provincial legislature, which still favoured hinterland voters. A member still needed fewer votes to get elected in a rural constituency, for as Bennett once put the case, 'it's more awkward to represent it, more difficult.'[39] Of fifteen ridings that consistently elected Social Credit members, thirteen were located north or east of the province's densely populated southwestern tip. At the same time vastly improved communications weakened the old argument for differential population bases. As early as 1952 the Vancouver *Province* asserted: 'The geographic problems which were the basis of boundaries many years ago no longer exist.' 'How can there be fair representation when more than 40,000 voters in Burnaby have no more voice in public affairs than 1,700 people of Atlin?'[40] Bennett was well aware of where his strength lay, and redistributions of seats in 1955 and 1966 maintained the principle of inequity on the grounds that the thrust of growth lay in the interior and the north and the 'historical and regional claims for representation' needed to be recognized.[41]

Bennett's perspective was supported by hinterland voters, who feared 'dominance of the province by the Lower Mainland, and especially by Vancouver.' Many British Columbians firmly believed, as a royal commission on redistribution concluded in 1966, that 'the people of the lower mainland were economic parasites, producing little wealth themselves, and intent on exploiting the people of the "underdeveloped areas." '[42] So buttressed, Bennett was able to limit concessions in the subsequent redistribution of seats to the worst of the inequities. 'Reform' focused on ridings traditionally held by the opposition NDP. Dual-member ridings were created in some urban and suburban areas. Even this was not sufficient to maintain the Social Credit regime in power indefinitely.

Some political opposition had always existed, ranging from critics on the left to their counterparts on the right who in their extreme still believed the government's sole role was to assist its supporters to maximize their private profit. In the four provincial elections of the 1960s, Social Credit obtained between 40 and 46 per cent of the popular vote (see Table 4). Its base of support was described as 'a conglomeration drawn from the unorganized ranks of lower class and low middle-class groups all over the province.' To these were added, 'chiefly outside the big cities, important segments of the true middle class comprising small to medium-sized businessmen, ranchers, orchardists, retail merchants, and struggling private enterprisers of all types,' many of them harbouring resentments against the economic dominance of the lower mainland and Vancouver.[43] The remaining vote was split between the Liberals, which polled a consistent 20 per cent, and the CCF and its successor the NDP, which garnered about one-third.

The two principal forces in provincial politics, the right and the left, had come to share a common commitment to the philosophy that the state should play a greater role in the economy. Where they differed fundamentally was on the reasons why it should do so. Social Credit's goal was the stimulation of private enterprise, in particular small as opposed to big business. The CCF/NDP, on the contrary, supported increased government intervention in order to promote greater economic parity between individual men and women.

Social Credit's success lay largely with the personality of W.A.C. Bennett who by the beginning of the 1970s had been in power longer than any government leader then in office in North America. Dissatisfaction was almost inevitable given such a long tenure, yet no other individual had emerged as a rallying point to sustain the power of Social Credit as a party and as a popular movement. As many of the large projects with which Social Credit identified itself came to fruitation, discontent grew among the grass roots over inflation, unemployment, and necessary curtailment of expectations. British Columbians had, once again, been led to believe that the good times would go on for ever. As it became obvious that this might not be the case, many had great difficulty reconciling themselves to a harsher reality. As Robert Bonner put the case the day after he resigned as attorney general in 1968: 'We may have oversold it. Now there is a feeling there is no limit to what can be done at once ... there is a failure to relate our expectations with our capacities. We have deluded ourselves into believing there is some sort of magic in government financing.'[44] The unemployment rate, generally one of the highest in Canada, passed 9 per cent in early 1971.

The good life seemed to be slipping away. Vancouver, which had benefited enormously from a booming economy but whose interests had been deliberately subordinated to those of the grass roots, became more open in its opposition. Professionals, whose numbers had mushroomed through post-war expansion of social services, could be less easily dismissed than traditional trade unionists as wild-eyed radicals. Special interest groups were coming to the fore on such issues as reforestation, strip mining, and the environment generally. Bennett himself may simply have grown tired. The legislative sessions of 1970 and 1971 were uncharacteristically barren of new initiatives to inspire the voters. A consequence was the revival of the Conservative party. Both it and the Liberals targeted their appeal to the 'neglected majority.'

Then came the provincial election of autumn 1972. Asserting that 'the socialist hordes are at the gates in British Columbia,' Bennett once again fought the political left.[45] The result was not so much a victory by the oppostion New Democratic Party as it was the break-up of Social Credit. The NDP leader, Dave Barrett, was a social worker who had grown up in working-class East Vancouver and was committed to wide-ranging reform. In many ways the election only pitted a tired populist of the right against a more energetic populist of the left. Each based his appeal on being an anti-establishment outsider, essentially a loner. The NDP received just under 40 per cent of the vote compared with 31 per cent for Social Credit, 16 per cent for the Liberals, and 13 per cent for the Conservatives. The key to victory by the political left lay in the unexpected strength of the provincial Conservative party which had polled only 0.1 to 0.2 per cent in the two previous elections.

So the Bennett era came to an end. In Mitchell's view, 'in the best sense, Bennett was a "confidence man": he understood the psychological basis of economic development and saw his role as building up confidence in his province, since its material progress depended on people's faith in the future and on opportunity.' British Columbia was opened up as an integrated economic unit. So far as possible, given demographic and geographic constraints, Bennett channelled change to the benefit of the province as a whole. 'W.A.C. was a one-man government,' which for a man with a mission encouraged action. The post-war economy facilitated growth and made change inevitable; Bennett choreographed the transformation. In the view of Hugh Keenleyside, a university professor specializing in Canadian history before becoming a diplomat and government administrator, 'Bennett was undoubtedly the most effective political leader in British Columbia history.'[46]

The first streetcar running along Fourth Avenue
in Vancouver's Kitsilano district, 1909

By the early 1900s
Vancouver was the metropole for a growing hinterland:
left, the CPR station by the docks;
right, grain elevators overshadowing East Vancouver homes

C. JACOBSEN, QUATSINO SOUND, V. I.

The struggle to make a living from the land:
left, a wilderness enclave at Quatsino Sound,
Vancouver Island, 1901;
right, a ranch near Soda Creek, 1919

Diverse forms of transportation
across British Columbia's difficult terrain:
left, a sternwheeler approaching Prince George, 1910;
right, a pack train leaving Hazelton, 1910

Mule Train
Hazelton B.C.

VRIGHT 1909 BY G. H.   KELOWNA, B. C.

OPPOSITE

Summertime in Kelowna, *c.* 1908

Camping at Horseshoe Bay, *c.* 1900

The enforced evacuation of Japanese Canadians from the coast
during the Second World War:
farewells by Japanese men at the Vancouver railway station

W.A.C. Bennett,
British Columbia's premier from 1952 to 1972,
on the campaign trail

OPPOSITE

British Columbia's native peoples
protesting cutbacks in education funding, April 1989

At the end of the twentieth century
Vancouver has become a major city
on the Pacific Rim.

13

Equality Revolution
1945–1980

The changes occurring in British Columbia during the post-war years and into the 1970s went far beyond economic growth and regional expansion. A fundamental shift in attitudes occurred. The Depression had made clear the necessity for the state to take a more active role in ensuring minimum standards of life for all Canadians. The war challenged many long-standing prejudices. The consequence was an equality revolution that transformed British Columbia just as it did much of the western world. Equality of treatment, of opportunity, of access, of experience, of acceptance – all acquired credibility as the way things ought to be.

Despite reform's long roots in Canada, it took the Depression and then the war to reveal how partial and piecemeal were measures so far enacted by the state. Parliament passed unemployment insurance in 1935, but the courts ruled the legislation outside of federal jurisdiction. Constitutionally valid insurance was enacted only in 1940. The most significant of earlier achievements – the old age pension – was two-thirds that required for an adequate living standard.[1] The Co-operative Commonwealth Federation and many other groups repeatedly spoke out. Their recommendations took a variety of forms, including an influential 1943 report prepared for the federal government by social activist Leonard Marsh. Though rejected, it reflected growing public opinion that the state must provide for those unable to provide for themselves. More and more Canadians came to believe that capitalism must be harnessed in such a way that its profits would provide all people, not just a few individuals, with a minimum standard of living.

The actual process by which basic social services were established after the war was somewhat haphazard and complicated by the division of responsibilites for health and welfare between federal and provincial governments. Federal programs often provided a framework within which provinces were given the option of participation. In the case of protection against the high cost of illness, it was British Columbia that took the lead. Legislation was enacted in 1936 which, if promulgated, would have made British Columbia the first jurisdiction in North America with state health insurance. While supported by the union movement, the act encountered strong opposition from the medical profession. In a referendum held in June 1937 the proposed act received 59 per cent approval, but the government took fright and the legislation was shelved.

It was only in 1948, after Saskatchewan's CCF government had acted, that a provincial scheme was again brought forward in British Columbia. The BC Hospital Insurance Service, implemented in 1949, experienced early difficulties. Collection of the individual contributions on which the plan was based became an administrative nightmare, given a provincial labour force still highly transient and seasonally employed. Universality seemed impossible to achieve. About 7 per cent of hospital accounts were incurred by uninsured persons. Public dissatisfaction made the plan a major election issue in 1952, contributing to Social Credit's initial victory at the polls. Shortly afterwards premiums were replaced by a tax hike, ensuring universal coverage. In 1957 the federal government enacted a program wherein it agreed to pay half of specified hospital costs. British Columbia was one of five participating provinces on its implementation the next year.

In 1965 the provincial government put in place a medical care plan to insure all British Columbians, subsidizing those whose incomes fell below a certain level. A year later the federal government passed a comparable program in which it agreed to contribute half the cost of provincial programs. British Columbia was one of two provinces to qualify for the new scheme when it came into effect in 1968. Thereafter, as the medical profession introduced better methods of diagnosis and treatment, and more attention was given to preventative care, the proportion of provincial budgets devoted to medical care and hospitalization grew. Had individual men and women been forced to bear the costs, differentials in levels of health care between British Columbians would almost certainly have become acute.

The two groups that received special attention in provision of social services were the very old and the very young. Greater visiblity played a role. Canadians were living longer, average life expectancy rising from sixty-one years in 1931 to sixty-eight in 1951 and then seventy-three by 1971. British Columbia presented a special case, its relatively mild climate making it increasingly attractive as a retirement haven for men and women who had spent their working lives on the prairies, in central Canada, in Britain, or elsewhere. Since 1931 Victoria had led Canada in the proportion of residents over sixty-five: by 1981 they represented one-quarter of its population. Other areas with a moderate climate and attractive environment also appealed, notably Vernon, Kelowna, and Penticton in the Okanagan Valley and the Gulf Islands and adjacent coastal areas from the Sechelt peninsula south to the American border. The existing old age pension plan, based on a means test, was superseded in 1952 by a universal federal pension for all those seventy and over. By 1970 the qualifying age was down to sixty-five. Unlike the earlier plan, native peoples were included in this and other post-war social services. In 1966 a Canada Pension Plan was established as a contributory program.

A baby boom erupted after the war. Just as Canadians postponed consumer purchases during the war, so they delayed parenthood, something many had also been forced to do during the Depression. Children's well-being now acquired importance. In 1945 the federal government began paying a family allowance for every child under the age of sixteen, the age limit extended to eighteen for young people still in school in 1964. Not only was additional purchasing power placed in the hands of workers but, by being paid to women, the monthly allowance permitted them some economic independence on leaving wartime jobs for the home.

Concern for children and young people was also expressed in changing attitudes towards schooling. Equality of access to education still did not exist across British Columbia. Urban-rural disparities remained daunting. Dissatisfaction increased, particularly as secondary education became viewed as a prerequisite for getting a decent job. The Depression had merely underlined the precarious economic conditions in most outlying districts. Many simply could not raise the money necessary to keep a school in operation, much less compete with urban counterparts. Locally elected trustees were often unable to cope, and scores of hinterland districts ended up under the official trusteeship of the provincial government.

The key to equalization was increasingly perceived to lie in amalgamation into larger administrative units, a concept becoming fashionable across North America. As the war drew to a close, the provincial government appointed a one-man commission – Maxwell Cameron, a professor of education at the University of British Columbia – which in 1945 recommended consolidation of the province's 650 school districts into under one hundred. Each was to be large enough to permit adequate facilities through grade twelve. Where poor roads prevented children from travelling to a central high school, subsidized boarding facilities would be provided. In the 1945 provincial election the ruling coalition made the Cameron report part of its platform. Re-elected, it implemented the recommendations in early 1946. A gap in social services long dividing urban and hinterland British Columbia was ameliorated. New, larger schools were soon being constructed, bussing becoming the rule.

As in all major shifts, trade-offs were inevitable. In some senses school consolidation only represented a triumph of the urban model; rural schooling was finally corresponding to what city bureaucrats long considered it should become. The consequences were felt by innumerable outlying enclaves whose sense of cohesion had been forged around a school and post office. Many small school buildings were still used for Saturday night dances, fall fairs, and other community activities, including religious services. As the one- and two-room school disappeared from the landscape, many tiny settlements lost another base of existence.

Consolidation gave new impetus to secondary education. More children had stayed in school to grade twelve during the Depression, in part because many jobs traditionally taken by school leavers became attractive to unemployed adults. After consolidation the numbers climbed again. As well as better physical facilities, curricula were made more appealing by offering a greater variety of academic and career-oriented programs.

Yet concern remained widespread, not just in British Columbia but across North America, over the quality of schooling. It coalesced in the late 1950s over supposed Russian scientific supremacy following the first space flight of Sputnik. The consequence was another provincial commission, established in 1958 under S.N.F. Chant, dean of arts and science at UBC. The question was, once again, how to ensure that British Columbian children were on a par with their counterparts elsewhere. The Chant report of 1960 emphasized the need for all young people to remain in school through the secondary level. Its recommendations probably assisted the gradual rise in the proportion of young people remaining in school to grade twelve to about 70 per cent.

The Chant report also turned attention to post-secondary education, as did a study two years later by the president of UBC, John B. MacDonald. The Chant report recommended that an 'institute of advanced technology' be established to provide practical training in a wide variety of areas, from electronics to hotel management. The MacDonald report argued that one-fifth of high school students would benefit from some post-secondary education. This meant in practical terms thirty thousand students or three times the number currently enrolled.

A variety of factors made expansion of higher education inevitable. British Columbia had traditionally relied on other parts of Canada and elsewhere for professional training and for professionals in such fields as dentistry, medicine, veterinary medicine, law, and architecture. World-wide expansion of demand made this no longer possible. The limitations of existing facilities – University of British Columbia, Victoria College, and teacher training institutions in Vancouver and Victoria – became manifest during the post-war years as veterans took advantage of federal funding to secure a post-secondary education. The economic boom and accompanying growth of broadly based affluence turned more families towards some advanced schooling for their offspring. Many women were beginning to consider higher education.

Federal policy was conducive to post-secondary expansion. In 1949 the federal government established a Royal Commission on Arts, Letters, and Sciences chaired by Vincent Massey. The wide-ranging Massey Report of 1951 stressed that the demand for higher education was outpacing provincial resources and recommended federal support. By 1960 federal funds were absorbing one-fifth of operating costs of post-secondary education in Canada as well as some capital costs. The priority W.A.C. Bennett gave to opening up British Columbia also encouraged action. By the early 1960s the province possessed the necessary financial resources to fund futher expansion. On the other hand, even as provincial dollars for education grew, critics pointed out that much of the impetus and funding was in fact federal. British Columbians fared less well than did their counterparts in many other parts of Canada.

Post-secondary education expanded in three directions. Technical training was instituted shortly after the Chant report's release. A Burnaby site was selected for what became the British Columbia Institute of Technology. Secondly, two provincial universities were added in 1963. The University of British Columbia, which since the war had slowly been adding some professional training, remained at the heart of the system. Victoria College acquired independence as the University of Victoria and a new campus was created for it just outside the capital. A completely new university was 'to be established somewhere in the Fraser Valley.' The individual put in charge, the retired academic and administrator, Gordon Shrum, was, in his own words, 'taken by the opportunity for an old man to do something spectacular.' So he opted instead to create Simon Fraser University on 'top of a mountain' located in Burnaby just east of Vancouver.[2] Designed by Arthur Erickson, SFU opened in 1965. Intended to be innovative in programs and personnel, SFU soon became a centre for student protest as the activism spreading across much of the western world during these years took hold in British Columbia during the late 1960s.

Two church-affiliated post-secondary institutions also existed in British Columbia. Notre Dame at Nelson, begun by the local Catholic bishop in 1950, was in 1961 permitted to grant degrees and, later, to receive some government funding. Financial difficulties closed Notre Dame in 1983. Trinity Western College, founded by a Conservative Protestant group in the Fraser Valley in 1962, obtained the right to grant bachelors' degrees in 1979. Six years later it acquired status as a university.

The third, and probably most important, initiative in higher education was the introduction of community colleges. The concept of local two-year institutions offering both transfer and technical programs became popular in the United States before the war, and the interest spread to Canada. Community colleges were viewed in British Columbia as an extension of secondary education and so placed under the jurisdiction of local school districts. The first opened in Vancouver in 1965, followed in the next few years by colleges in Castlegar in the West Kootenays, Kelowna, North Vancouver, Prince

George, Nanaimo, Kamloops, and New Westminster. Subsequently colleges were established in Victoria, Chilliwack, Cranbrook in the East Kootenays, Dawson Creek, Comox, Terrace in the northwest, and Surrey. Many operated subsidiary campuses in nearby communities, further extending access.

Critical to the equality revolution were changing attitudes toward groups traditionally not a part of the dominant society: women, the union movement, and racial and ethnic minorities. At war's end women had for the most part returned willingly to the home. The preference given to veterans for jobs encouraged the move, as did amended federal tax regulations reducing by two-thirds the income a woman could earn and still be claimed on her husband's return. Traditional prejudices sometimes operated, as in the 1947 decision by a boy's private school to force its last three female teachers to resign. The minority of women who dared resist the trend chanced moral censorship. Ethel Wilson, herself childless, likely reflected the views of many British Columbians. 'Sometimes the mother is the main support of the family. How can she not "work"? ... But if the mother "works," to the neglect of the children, in order to have a car, a t.v., a fine house, a fur coat – is the car worth that? The price of the car is too high.'[3]

Demographic data suggest that British Columbian women were in the forefront in moving back out of the home, if not into the work-force at least to pursue further education. Not only did their fertility rate remain the lowest in Canada, but average age of marriage, while falling, was still the highest in English Canada. In 1966 the province, together with Ontario, possessed the lowest average number of children per family at 1.7 compared with a high of 2.6 in Newfoundland. New organizations encouraged female activism in both the workplace and everyday life. The various groups used a range of tactics from direct lobbying to demonstrations to publishing ventures, such as Press Gang in Vancouver.

In reality women's move towards equality remained modest. Despite more and more women at paid work, most also continued to bear the main burden in the home. A 1970s study conducted in Vancouver determined that, in the case of childless couples, a wife's entry into the labour force meant that her husband contributed an average of six additional minutes a week to household work. Where families had children, it totalled an extra hour a week.[4] Gains at the political level were slight. While the proportion of female MLA candidates rose to about one in eight by the end of the 1970s and then to almost one in five in the 1986 provincial election, very few ran under the Social Credit banner. Just as had been the case earlier, the ruling party usually nominated no more than three or four female candidates for a provincial house whose membership rose from fifty-two to sixty-nine.

Labour unions became recognized as an integral part of employer-employee relations. While strikes did not cease, their character changed from bitter confrontations with employer and government over union recognition to mostly peaceful demonstrations for higher wages and improved conditions of work. The wartime statute legitimizing union activity was superseded by other federal and provincial legislation, viewed by some as more pro-employer. At war's end almost 30 per cent of British Columbia's non-agricultural labour force was organized, a proportion that slowly moved upwards to a high of 55 per cent in 1958. While British Columbia remained the most unionized province in Canada, it was no longer at the forefront in strike activity; the province was home to just sixteen of the eighty largest disputes occurring in the 1950s and 1960s. Labour unrest in British Columbia was distinguished by the large numbers of workers involved and the duration of work stoppages, both attributable to the uncertainties of the province's economy and to a centralized bargaining structure controlled out of Vancouver.

Unions that emerged during the war years, notably the International Woodworkers of America, were consolidated. In 1946, following a strike involving over thirty thousand workers across British Columbia, the IWA became the largest union in the province and one of the four largest in Canada. A long internal struggle that wracked the IWA across Canada culminated four years later in the defeat of its communist leadership. Other established unions as well as the Canadian Congress of Labour sought the ouster of the communists in their midst. So did the CCF, deprecated by radicals as advocating 'watered-down class-collaborationist socialism.'[5] Internal factionalism played a role. The communist presence in the BC labour movement, very evident at the end of the war, was isolated. Business unionism, to use one scholar's term, triumphed.[6]

The ongoing tension between craft and industrial unions dissipated with the merger in the United States in 1955 of the AFL and CIO. A year later the Trades and Labour Congress and the Canadian Congress of Labour became the Canadian Labour Congress, representing 80 per cent of union members across the country. In British Columbia the provincial arm of the united body took the name of an earlier organization and became the BC Federation of Labour. While some union leaders still used strong rhetoric to make their case, most members probably echoed the sentiments of the sawmill worker who opined, 'What you need is a responsible union that management will respect, instead of making the bosses worry about revolution. Don't get sidetracked trying to change the world when you really just want to change working conditions.'[7]

The changing character of work affected union membership.[8] Job opportunities, not just in British Columbia but across North America, were increasingly linked to the provision of services rather than goods. Both the federal and provincial governments supported burgeoning bureaucracies. The number of teachers and university professors needed in the west coast province grew so rapidly, particularly during the 1960s, that many had to be recruited from outside of the province and outside of the country. School teachers came from as far away as Australia and New Zealand, many academics from Britain and the United States. Jobs opened up in such areas of the private sector as tourism, which experienced world-wide expansion. A decade after the establishment of a campsite system in British Columbia's provincial parks at mid-century, 650,000 overnight visits were recorded annually. The total then more than doubled to 1.5 million by 1970. In Victoria in 1971 and again in 1981 more men and women worked in tourist-related activities than in any other kind of occupation, including government service.

Two-thirds and then almost three-quarters of the gross provincial product came from the provision of services (see Table 19). Service and other jobs rose from one-quarter of the work force in 1911 to two-thirds of all jobs in the province by 1981. A majority were held by women, many of them being poorly paid. Unions again expanded as service workers organized. The BC Teachers' Federation, BC Government Employees' Union, and Hospital Employees' Union became extremely active in pressing their demands for higher wages and better working conditions.

British Columbia's racial and ethnic minorities strove for equal treatment, being less than ever willing to accept the discriminatory practices meted out to them. Legal restrictions disappeared; Chinese and East Indians received the franchise provincially in 1947, Japanese and native people in 1949. The vote made a difference, not the least to individual self-respect. As one elderly Japanese first resident in British Columbia in 1910 put it, 'when I voted I felt like I could finally join the human race.'[9] Acquisition of the vote meant that individuals could work in the civil service, obtain licences as pharmacists or lawyers, serve on juries, and qualify for public office.

The broadening social mainstream also drew in ethnic groups earlier apart by choice. While many Norwegians still lived in Bella Coola, most newcomers found the community little different from its coastal counterparts. Among Doukhobors and Mennonites, the passage of time lessened isolation. Most members of the two groups had been disenfranchised provincially in 1931 by virtue of their exemption from military service. In 1948 the right to vote was restored to the Mennonites, four years later to the Doukhobors. Within the two communities some members of the second generation broke away from traditional ways of life. English came to replace German and Russian as the principal means of communication.

Economics played a role. Good times during the war gave Fraser Valley Mennonites a higher living standard. Some sons and daughters went off to university where they came into everyday contact with new ideas and other young British Columbians. Growing numbers also made for a more disparate Mennonite community. Newcomers arrived from the prairies, Europe, and Paraguay, to where some Canadian Mennonites had migrated during the interwar years. The total number of Mennonites in British Columbia quadrupled to twenty thousand between 1941 and 1961. English increasingly replaced German as the language of church and community.

The Doukhobors had suffered leadership difficulties following Peter Verigin's death in 1924 in a train bombing. The Depression heightened economic difficulties. Mismanagement and some disaffection in favour of individual landholding contributed to the Doukhobors' huge mortgage being foreclosed in 1939. The provincial government stepped in to take control of Doukhobor property in order to prevent complete disruption. Some individuals purchased land back, others became government tenants paying nominal rent. By the time of the Second World War the Doukhobor people were visibly divided between a main group largely co-existing with mainstream society and a smaller sect, the Sons of Freedom, unwilling to compromise with outside authority. The latter's willingness to flout civic authority through arson and other illegal acts escalated after the war. Over four hundred zealots were imprisoned in 1950. Three years later about 170 Doukhobor children were made wards of the state on their parents' repeated refusal to permit school attendance. Many children spent half a dozen years in a government boarding school in the West Kootenays before Freedomite families acquiesced.

Of the various racial minorities in British Columbia, the native peoples were the most caught up by events. Numbers were rising, moving up by half from their nadir to almost thirty thousand by mid century. Residential schooling, for all its destructive aspects, brought students together and forced on them a realization of their dependence and subordination. They became aware, as did one Kwakiutl, that 'one of the biggest problems for the Indians was that they weren't equal to the other citizens of Canada.'[10] Conditions of everyday life were often appalling. At Fort St James, for example, Europeans and natives had co-existed for a century and a half; yet 'there appears to be complete disregard of the fact of the Indian presence.' No reserve home in Fort St James had running water, and in some communities public places refused to serve Indian people. 'Even if our pockets had been full of dollar bills, we weren't allowed to enter any of the cafes in Vanderhoof. Natives knew that if they walked into a restaurant, they would be asked to leave, and if they refused, the police would be called.'[11]

But attitudes were changing. Veterans and others realized that, despite war service, Indian people were not even citizens. Hubert Evans's *Mist on the River* made the point: 'Lo, the poor Indian. Normandy, Holland, all the way. Good comrades, good soldiers. Fine body of men. Best in the world. The tumult and the shouting dies. What happens? ... Does a grateful nation stop treating their sorrowing mothers and fathers like second-class citizens? It does not.'[12] In 1946 a Select Joint Committee of the Senate and House of Commons was established to examine the Indian Act, the collection of federal laws dealing with native people. British Columbian Indians called for control over their own affairs without being expected to adopt the ways of the dominant society. The committee's report urged repeal of the most coercive aspects of the Indian Act and Indians' integration into the mainstream.

Native children were encouraged to attend provincial schools rather than the segregated institutions to which they had been relegated for almost a century in British Columbia. However, the shift did not necessarily bring with it equality of opportunity or of treatment. For a young Indian woman growing up in Merritt in the late 1950s, 'it was difficult going to [public] school, a lot of ideas and attitudes haven't changed much. Segregation is happening, not visibly but in the classes.' There, at Hazelton, and elsewhere, native children were seated separately in the classroom, and it remained very much a 'white man's school.'[13] The few children who managed to make it to high school were almost always directed towards vocational programs. Overall, the number of Indian pupils doubled during the 1950s, and by 1970 three-quarters of the thirteen thousand young Indians in school in British Columbia were attending integrated institutions.

Other changes to the Indian Act in 1951 removed prohibitions on the potlatch, political fund raising, and consumption of alcohol in public places. Potlatching resumed, often in modified forms more suited to the times. A Haida woman 'spent about a thousand dollars on little presents' – 'lots of towels, all kinds of cups, mugs, aprons, and nylons.'[14] Following repeated demands, some of the six hundred ceremonial pieces that had been confiscated from the Kwakiutl at the beginning of the 1920s were returned, to form the basis for two local museums.[15]

Canadians became more aware of the plight of native peoples following two federally commissioned surveys under the direction of UBC anthropologist Harry Hawthorn. The first, in the mid 1950s, was the most comprehensive study undertaken of Indians in British Columbia. It provided a powerful indictment of the existing situation. The post-war boom was transforming the province, but Indians were standing still. 'The position of Indians in the provincial economy is marginal and in some respects potentially precarious. Their employment is confined almost entirely to a few primary industries, particularly fishing, logging, trapping, farming and farm labour, in which they are usually highly dependent upon local resources within easy access of their band villages.' Some of the jobs long held by Indian men and women were being taken by prairie migrants or newly arrived continental Europeans. Others were disappearing. Technological change played a role. Unionization put the emphasis on job seniority. Some industries, notably salmon canning, were being consolidated in urban centres distant from the isolated reserves where many natives lived. To some Indians, 'the whole system often seems unintelligible and pointless.' In their society, going away from family and village to earn high wages did not confer prestige and status and was not worth the sacrifice. 'The reserve still means security, social contacts, a known environment.'[16]

The first Hawthorn report, perhaps unintentionally, made a fundamental point. Many natives were becoming trapped – even imprisoned – by the reserve system. Individuals opting to move away in search of employment or for other reasons were in effect penalized for their initiative. Unlike other British Columbians, Indians did not possess security of tenure over the property they may have worked for generations to improve. They could not easily sell out, take the profits from their earlier efforts, and relocate. 'Indians, because of their special legal status, do not have clear and unimpeded legal title to their individual land holdings and they cannot sell their land or improvements to other than band members.'[17] In many cases individual holdings had never been allocated or marked out. If native people wanted to move to regional urban centres in search of a better life, the enormous personal cost inevitably affected their prospects of making a successful transition.

The second Hawthorn report, appearing in 1966, was a national study. It determined that Indian per capita income of a little over $300 a year was just one-fifth that of non-Indians. Life expectancy was lower; infant mortality and suicide rates were higher. So were accidental deaths, the overwhelming majority being alcohol-related. As traditional economic activities and opportunities for paid work declined, social assistance programs had come to play a major role in native lives. Of Indians across Canada, those in British Columbia were judged 'the most prosperous' with 'the most favourable prospects.' Specific recommendations aimed at 'increasing the educational attainments of the Indian people, increasing their real income, and adding to their life expectancy.' Departing from past precedent, the Department of Indian Affairs 'should act as a national conscience to see that social and economic equality is achieved between Indians and Whites.'[18]

Awareness grew among native people themselves. Political leaders such as Frank Calder, Len Marchand, and George Manuel came to prominence. Calder, a Nishga running as a CCF candidate in the Atlin riding in the northwest containing a majority of native voters, became in 1949 the first Indian to serve in a provincial legislature in Canada. In 1968 Marchand, an Okanagan, was elected from the Kamloops riding to the federal Parliament, subsequently being named by Prime Minister Pierre Trudeau the first native federal cabinet minister. Manuel, a long time Shuswap political activist, became in 1970 president of the National Indian Brotherhood, formed two years earlier to resolve Indians' problems within the context of Indian culture. As well as mobilizing political activity within Canada, Manuel was instrumental in raising the consciousness of indigenous peoples around the world. Manuel argued that, as internal colonies located within the nations of the first, second, and third world, aboriginal peoples constituted a potentially significant fourth world.[19]

Activism grew in the 1960s. Christian churches, having traditionally worked in tandem with the federal government, now began to reassess their policies and became more sympathetic to native aspirations. The Department of Indian Affairs encouraged certain community development programs. The artistry of the Kwakiutl carver, Mungo Martin, his Haida counterpart, Bill Reid, and others symbolized the new vitality. Their work also emphasized a continuity with past traditions; Martin had learnt his art from his stepfather, Reid from his maternal grandfather in a line of descent going back to the great Haida carvers of the nineteenth century.

During the 1960s racial and ethnic equality became the object of government fiat. In an attempt to appease an increasingly dissatisfied Quebec, Prime Minister Lester Pearson established a Royal Commission on Bilingualism and Biculturalism in 1963. The commission was still under way when a federal election of spring 1968 swept into power the charismatic Quebec intellectual Pierre Trudeau on the slogan of a 'just society.' Trudeau, who was personally caught up in the fervour of the day and enjoyed enormous popularity in British Columbia, as elsewhere in Canada, was strongly opposed to growing Quebec nationalism. He proceeded to implement the royal commission's recommendations in two contradictory directions – the first to accommodate Quebec, the second to appease the rest of Canada. The Official Languages Act of 1969 put French on a par with English. Two years later a policy of multiculturalism was adopted to encourage ethnic groups to maintain their heritages. By suggesting that no single culture or even a biculture existed in Canada, Trudeau managed to offend not only many in Quebec but the dominant society in English Canada. In British Columbia multiculturalism never aquired much appeal, just as French did not become an official language.

Prime Minister Trudeau also took the initiative with native people. A white paper was issued in 1969 proposing native integration into his just society. Federal agencies maintaining formal separation would be abolished, being replaced by the provincial organizations. Indian peoples would become another tile in his multicultural mosaic. In Trudeau's words, 'we must all be equal under the laws and we must not sign treaties ... We can't recognize aboriginal rights because no society can be built on historical "might-have-beens."'[20] The native response was uniformly negative, which was only to be expected following the decade and more of awakening pride in heritage and culture. Indian leaders saw the white paper as an abrogation of their treaty rights, a betrayal of their historical relationship with the British crown. In 1970 Trudeau was forced to withdraw the proposal in favour of Indian control over their own affairs. While the Department of Indian Affairs retained ultimate responsibility, Indian agents were withdrawn from reserves. Their replacement was self-government in the form of band councils. Emphasis was given to resolution of land claims and to band-operated schools emphasizing pride in native languages and cultures alongside necessary skills to participate in the Canadian economy.

The movement towards a more racially fair society was also evident in immigration policy. After the population explosion of the early twentieth century, growth had come principally through natural increase. This was particularly so after 1931 when the federal government effectively barred new arrivals. During the war realization grew that a larger population made good sense, and the post-war economic expansion created demand for both skilled and unskilled labour. In 1947 the Canadian government repealed its 1923 Chinese exclusion legislation, permitting men holding Canadian citizenship to bring in wives and unmarried children under eighteen years of age. Over the next decade restrictions on entry by Chinese gradually loosened. Other legislation in 1947, still aimed at maintaining Canada's existing ethnic and racial balance, sought to increase immigration from European and Commonwealth countries.

Men and women from countries devastated by the war were among those who came to British Columbia. Residents born in Italy tripled to over eighteen thousand by 1961, those from Germany grew five-fold to over twenty-five thousand. British Columbia's rapid economic growth made the province especially appealing. Journalist Gwen Cash recalled her amazement during the mid 1950s. 'All over British Columbia, I had watched workmen leave planes to disappear into waiting buses. Mostly, they were new Canadians – Portuguese, Italians, Czechs, Ukrainians – speaking a few words of English, puzzled but hopeful, as they made history working on vast projects in a strange new land.'[21] Arrivals included refugees from Eastern Europe: the entire student body and faculty of a Hungarian school of forestry, Sopron, escaping the country in the 1956 uprising, came to UBC.

Among distinctive groups entering British Columbia during the post-war years were several thousand Dutch Calvinists whose preference for social separation echoed Mennonite and Doukhobor predecessors. Many were young couples, pushed to emigrate by wartime devastation and lack of opportunity in their homeland. The Dutch settled primarily in the Fraser Valley, already the centre of a dairying industry. Often buying farms that had deteriorated during the Depression, they were soon recognized as 'shrewd and hard-working.'[22] Some four hundred farms, or one-fifth of the total, became Dutch-owned. The Dutch Calvinists created new social and religious structures. Their cultural baggage extended from a preference for dairying to an everyday life divided along religious lines. They quickly transplanted familiar institutions from churches to labour unions to private 'Christian' schools. The first complete Christian elementary school in Canada opened in the Fraser Valley in 1955. While Christian-based unions never acquired much influence, schools founded by this new generation of immigrants grew in significance. Like their earlier counterparts on the British model, Christian schools soon became popular with some of mainstream society's parents who similarly sought religious and social distinctiveness.

In 1966 the newly formed federal Department of Immigration and Manpower released a white paper linking immigration to the expanding Canadian economy. The next year a point system was adopted, whereby potential immigrants were assessed in terms of their supposed ability to adapt to and benefit Canada. Criteria included educational level, occupational skills and their demand, prearranged employment, facility in English and French, presence of relatives in Canada, and personal qualities. A revised policy was introduced in 1978 based on family reunification, humanitarian concern for refugees, and promotion of national goals, including entrepreneurship. The latter qualification made it possible to acquire landed immigrant status by investing a specified sum in Canada. The consequence of immigration plus natural increase was to double Canada's population during the four decades from 1941 to 1981 to twenty-four million.

While Canada as a whole was demographically transformed, growth was concentrated in the industrial heartland of Ontario and in British Columbia. Immigration, migration from elsewhere in Canada, and natural increase combined to put the west coast province at the forefront of population growth, tripling to 2.7 million by 1981. The province's racial and ethnic character was also altered (see tables 5 and 7). The proportion of British Columbians of British descent fell from its inter-war high of almost three-quarters to under 60 per cent by 1961, 55 per cent by 1981. Sustained by prairie migration, the proportion of continental Europeans held at one-third. But after 1960 the area of most rapid population growth lay with men and women of Asian descent, whose proportion of the population tripled to 7.5 per cent between 1961 and 1981.

British Columbians of Chinese descent quadrupled to almost one hundred thousand. Arrivals tended to concentrate in the Greater Vancouver area to such an extent that by 1981 it contained almost 90 per cent of British Columbian residents whose mother tongue was a Chinese language. While Vancouver's Chinatown thrived as a commercial and tourist area, it did not return to its earlier role as a place of residence. Most Canadian-born Chinese had already moved elsewhere and new arrivals also preferred other locations.[23]

Conflict sometimes broke out between old and new British Columbians of Chinese background. The Communist victory in mainland China in 1949 also created dissension. Young people born and educated in the province were moving into the professions and, more generally, into the dominant society: in 1957 Douglas Jung was elected MP for the riding of Vancouver Centre. Many long-time residents resented being lumped in with the new arrivals. A Vancouver high school student of these years explained the situation. 'The newcomers were seen the same way as the whites had once looked upon us as kids. Finally acceptance had arrived for us and we felt confident. Then there was this influx of people who were the same race as us, but who behaved in ways that we didn't want them to behave; they didn't speak the language, they didn't dress the same way, and we said, "These people are an embarrassment to us!"'[24] The newcomers soon adapted, the poorest working double and triple time to get ahead. Asian women lacking facility with English spent long hours for low wages in fish-processing or clothing manufacture to give their children the opportunities that they themselves would never experience.

British Columbians of East Indian background also grew dramatically in numbers from forty-five hundred in 1961 to over fifty-six thousand two decades later. Unlike the Chinese who congregated in the Vancouver area, numerous East Indians were attracted elsewhere, as to the central interior where forestry was rapidly expanding. But they were not always well received. At Fort St James, for example, men arriving directly from India to work in a new sawmill and veneer plant created resentment both among Europeans and native people, whose reserve lay within Fort St James itself. The newcomers' lack of English, their desire for familiar foodstuffs, tendency to barter and wear traditional clothing, and difficulties in adjusting to the bitter winter cold all set them apart. So did local entrepreneurs' willingness to exploit them by constructing 'slapdash' living accommodations which grouped them together in the centre of the town. Native Indians, East Indians, and 'rough neck ignorant whites,' to quote an observer, were soon in open conflict in local beer parlours and on the street.[25] Only slowly, as East Indian men were able to bring over wives and families, did tensions moderate and the immigrants become accepted in the community.

Another group of migrants to British Columbia during the 1960s and 1970s equally put their stamp on the west coast province. Across the western world restlessness gripped an entire generation of young men and women. Expressed as student protest at Simon Fraser University and elsewhere, it was manifest more generally in a desire for new experiences. British Columbia became a favoured destination for many dissatisfied individuals. Asked why he settled on British Columbia, one Nova Scotian responded: 'I was a coward. This was the farthest away I could get and still stay in Canada. I grew up with a postcard image of the last frontier.'[26] The Vietnam War attracted thousands of young Americans to British Columbia, many unofficial arrivals avoiding the military draft.

Vancouver's Kitsilano neighbourhood became the centre of a

growing counter-culture enveloping young British Columbians together with newcomers. 'Fourth Avenue was Vancouver's Haight-
Ashbury, crowded with multicoloured dropouts and draft dodgers
selling hash pipes and love beads.' 'You could experiment. It was just
that point in the sixties when being weird was no longer an isolated
and lonely activity.' The controversial weekly the *Georgia Straight*
made its appearance in 1967. One of its founders recalled: 'No one
here seems to know (or admit to knowing) any particular reason for
the founding beyond a general pervasive desire to annoy establishment institutions in general and established newspapers in particular. Also, if one wishes to be flowery, to provide a local voice for
whatever counter-culture exists in Vancouver.'[27] Greenpeace started
in Kitsilano in 1970 in opposition to nuclear testing in the Pacific. It
eventually became a world-wide non-violent environmental force no
longer based in British Columbia or even in Canada.

The search for alternative, generally simpler lifestyles took many
arrivals across the province to diverse locations ranging from Slocan
Lake and the northern arms of Kootenay and Shuswap lakes to the
Gulf Islands and adjacent coast. One young American later explained
his decision to live as a vegetarian in a one-room log cabin on a remote
corner of Saltspring: 'I didn't grow up a vegetarian; I grew up as the
only son of the founder of Baskin-Robbins. I grew up in a sense, as a
prince in a kingdom. But I was aware that outside this kingdom there
was profound suffering, an environment just going down the drain,
profound social injustice, famine and war.'[28] The most popularized of
the ventures was undoubtedly that portrayed by Mark Vonnegut in
his bestseller, *The Eden Express*. Recounting his experiences on an
isolated farm north of Powell River, Vonnegut explored the motives
impelling young men and women to settle so far from their
middle-class American homes:

We hadn't taken to the woods just for a change of scenery and a different
way of life. The physical and psychical aspects of our adventure were
inextricably intertwined, but the head changes were what we were really
after. We expected to get closer to nature, to each other and our feelings ...
We wanted to go beyond that and develop entirely new ways of being and
experiencing the world. We had only vague ideas about the shape of these
changes or when they would happen, but we looked forward to them
eagerly. Since they would result from being free of the cities, of capitalism,
of racism, industrialism, they had to be for the better.[29]

Most of the hoped-for utopias never came to fruition. A few endured relatively intact, particularly in more remote locations, into the late twentieth century, but many of the enthusiasts gradually moved closer to the provincial mainstream. A number from this generation of discontent would make significant contributions to the quality of life in British Columbia in areas ranging from the environment to literary and artistic expression.

The equality revolution extended into popular and high culture. It became less necessary to move elsewhere to achieve recognition as an artist, writer, or performer. Nor was it so important to come from elsewhere in order to be recognized in British Columbia. Federal initiatives were important; it was growing concern over what many viewed as American cultural imperialism that helped initiate the Massey Commission. Among its recommendations was greater use of tax dollars to foster a distinctively Canadian culture. Such inter-war creations as a publicly owned Canadian Broadcasting Corporation and National Film Board were strengthened. The arts, letters, humanities, and social sciences began to be subsidized. In reality most British Columbians, like Vancouver's long-time society leader Bella Rogers, had no difficulty watching on television first Queen Elizabeth's coronation, made possible a day after the event by the film being especially 'flown across the Atlantic in a Royal Air Force jet,' and then 'The $64,000 Question' originating in the United States.[30]

A self-confident literary tradition finally took hold in British Columbia.[31] Some earlier works had a BC setting. Among the most enduring were Martin Allerdale Grainger's *Woodsmen of the West* depicting loggers' everyday lives, Bertrand Sinclair's *The Inverted Pyramid* probing the morality of early twentieth-century capitalism, and Irene Baird's *Waste Heritage* recreating the world of the unemployed during the Depression. These semi-documentary novels each acquired their primary force as social critiques. So did the essays, short stories, and juvenile novels turned out by Roderick Haig-Brown and Hubert Evans, using nature as a strong underlying motif. Haig-Brown became best known as a conservationist, Evans for *Mist on the River*. Published in 1954, it was lauded for its sensitive portrayal of the conflicting pressures facing native young people.

The first two individuals achieving widespread recognition as British Columbian writers were Emily Carr and Ethel Wilson. The two women shared a characteristic that may have contributed to their success. Each turned to writing later in life, drawing on a rich accumulation of experiences. Every phrase and paragraph was carefully crafted before appearing in print. Carr became an author when failing health forced her to curtail painting. Her first book, *Klee Wyck*, drew its inspiration from the native people she had come to know through sketching trips. An instant success on publication in 1941, it won the Governor General's non-fiction award that year. British Columbia's first literary journal, *Contemporary Verse*, was founded that same year; it became a medium for the publication of the poems of Dorothy Livesay and Earle Birney among others. Wilson began writing in the late 1930s, drawing on her decades as a well-travelled Vancouver matron. *Hetty Dorval* was published to critical and popular acclaim in 1947, *The Innocent Traveller* two years later. By the time *Contemporary Verse* folded in 1952, the province's literary landscape was broadening. Birney, who in 1946 began teaching creative writing at his alma mater of UBC, had already twice won the Governor General's Award for poetry, in 1942 and 1945. Livesay did so in 1944 and again in 1947. Before her death in 1945, Carr successfully completed three more autobiographical gems: *The Book of Small*, *The House of All Sorts*, and *Growing Pains*.

Ethel Wilson's initial concern not to be recognized solely for her powerful settings suggests the tentative nature of British Columbian and Canadian literature during these years. 'It seems to me that what Canadians have to aim at is not to write something *Canadian* (they'll do that anyway) but to write *well*.'[32] Soon lauded as 'one of the most charming and accomplished writers of English fiction now living,' Wilson became less defensive concerning the role British Columbian settings played in her writing.[33] 'I feel very strongly that the writing of Canadians should and must be Canadian in aspect, but not deliberately so, ... that is second-rate!' 'But *region* – that's a different matter. I'm all against conscious nationality in a novel (for a novel is about people and is universal), and *for* regionalism, *if* region means a lot to the writer.'[34]

Wilson's strong sense of place made her critical of what she perceived as the ready acceptance of writers who happened to live in the west coast province as Canadian merely in order to strengthen the claim to a literary identity. 'A good *Canadian* noveliest/writer [ought] to be a product of Canada.' She was opposed to someone like 'Malcolm Lowry, for example, referred to as "a Canadian novelist" just because he sometimes lived in Dollarton, a sort of place up the north arm of Burrard Inlet.'[35] Lowry, who made British Columbia his home from 1940 to 1954, used the province as a setting in *October Ferry to Gabriola*. In reality the energy of newcomers encouraged the emergence of a literary tradition. Writer and critic George Woodcock, who arrived in 1949, was at first scathing concerning 'the effete and secondhand influences which ... seem to hover always over the culture of a colonial country.' A decade later he moved to help remedy the situation by founding *Canadian Literature* as 'the first review devoted only to the study of Canadian writers and writing.'[36] *Prism*, concerned with 'imaginative writing' as opposed to criticism, began about the same time.

Two years later, in 1961, the innovative poetry newsletter, *Tish*, appeared. Subsequent events, described by one participant as 'the Poetry Wars,' saw different groups of poets refusing to read or even acknowledge each others' work.[37] Somewhat ironically, only the growth in literary consciousness made the conflicts possible. *Tish's* success, together with that of *Canadian Literature*, *Prism*, and *The Malahat Review*, founded in 1967 by poet Robin Skelton at the University of Victoria, underlined that 'significant literary change did not have to originate in the now traditional centres of Eastern Canada.'[38]

More and more men and women began to write creatively in the west coast province. Novelists Jane Rule and Audrey Thomas arrived in the late 1950s. Poet bill bissett, writers D.M. Fraser and W.P. Kinsella, playwright John Gray, and others came over the next decade. Among authors with their roots deep in the province were Phyllis Webb from Victoria, Sheila Watson from New Westminster, Robert Harlow from Prince George, George Bowering and Patrick Lane from the Okanagan, and Jack Hodgins from Vancouver Island's Comox Valley. Webb's powerful poetry first appeared in the mid 1950s. Watson's *The Double Hook*, published in 1959, was considered by some as the beginning of contemporary writing in Canada. It was set in an isolated BC community, as was Harlow's trilogy, the best known being *Scann*. In 1969 Bowering won the Governor General's Award for poetry, again eleven years later in the fiction category for *Burning Water*, a novel about Captain George Vancouver. In 1979 Lane captured the award for poetry, Hodgins its fiction counterpart for a fantasy set on Vancouver Island, *The Resurrection of Joseph Bourne*. Growing diversity of subject matter was exemplified in two novels of the early 1980s. Anne Cameron's *Daughters of Copper Woman* was based on coastal Indian legends, Joy Kogawa's *Obasan* on the experience of Japanese evacuation as seen through a child's eyes.

Critical to the growth of literary consciousness was the development of regional publishing. Just a few decades before, when Carr and Wilson sought publishers, they turned to Toronto and London. As Wilson later recollected, 'I knew of no outlet for "my kind of thing" nor for any individual in Vancouver who was so looney as to think of writing, then.'[39] Between the mid 1960s and early 1970s the number of small presses based in the province grew from a handful to some two dozen.[40] Deliberately intended to encourage aspiring poets, novelists, dramatists, and other creative artists, they survived in part through federal support but also owing to British Columbians' growing commitment to a vital indigenous culture. Among publishers were Talonbooks, Pulp Press, Douglas and McIntyre, Harbour, Oolichan, Sono Nis, and New Star emerging out of the *Georgia Straight*. Authors taking advantage of the opportunity to publish as well as write in British Columbia included Brian Fawcett and D.M. Fraser, whose short stories drew respectively on a central interior childhood and long residence in East Side Vancouver. While Ethel Wilson's earlier hesitations as to the role of place in the literary process was still being expressed from time to time, little question existed but that a distinctive tradition had emerged.

The performing and visual arts developed apace. An early attempt to keep young actors at home was Everyman Theatre, a professional repertory company founded in 1946 by a long-time Players Club promoter, Sydney Risk. Continually beset by financial woes and the lack of a permanent home, Everyman survived seven seasons. As well as performing regularly in Vancouver, the company toured British Columbia and even neighbouring provinces before collapsing in 1953. Six years later Vancouver acquired the Queen Elizabeth Theatre as a home for professional performances. The same year an opera company was formed, to complement the city's symphony orchestra. Increasingly, other communities and areas of the province acquired theatres and orchestras, as in the Okanagan Valley.

The premier locale for the display of painting and sculpture remained the Vancouver Art Gallery. It still identified not with artists working in the province but with becoming, as it probably did do, 'a major contemporary art gallery in Canada.' Individuals already internationally recognized were promoted. Canadian artists' acceptablility depended, to quote an art historian, on their 'breaking old conventional figurative painting barriers,' most often in the direction of abstractionism, then the fashion across the western world.[41] Among painters at work in British Columbia were Jack Shadbolt, B.C. Binning, Group of Seven member Lawren Harris who had moved to Vancouver in 1941, Gordon Smith, and Toni Onley. Only slowly were native artists recognized as possibly of comparable stature. The comparatively few from the province led some critics, including Edith Iglauer, to observe concerning the Vancouver Art Gallery and, more generally, art in British Columbia: 'When you get through with Emily Carr and Jack Shadbolt, what have you got? Not too much.'[42]

This growing diversity of opportunity extended to popular culture. Although Pro-Rec was discontinued by the provincial government in 1953, a practical replacement was emerging in the form of community centres. Their activities ranged from pottery to swimming lessons to language instructions. Soon almost every settlement, big or small, possessed its own centre. By the early 1970s even such remote enclaves as McBride, huddled up against the Rockies, were receiving television signals. Among musical successes to be enjoyed on radio and television were British Columbia's Juliette, Terry and Susan Jacks, best known for their hit song 'Seasons in the Sun,' and the rock group Bachman-Turner Overdrive.

Sports was another BC pastime; the host of early teams have ranged from lacrosse to hockey, from the New Westminster Salmonbellies to the Trail Smoke Eaters. The post-war years saw greater emphasis on professional teams competing in national or international arenas. Vancouver's Empire Stadium was built to host the 1954 British Empire games. The stadium then became home to the BC Lions football club, whose appeal grew when they won the Grey Cup championship in 1964. Seven years later the Lions acquired a competitor for spectators in the Vancouver Canucks, who took the name of an earlier hockey team. The presence of recent British and continental European immigrants encouraged the appearance of professional soccer. In 1979 the Whitecaps captured the North American Championship. Provincial construction of the large BC Place Stadium in Vancouver during the early 1980s provided yet another venue for sports and other elements of popular culture.

By the end of the 1970s the equality revolution of the post-war years had largely run its course across the western world. The next decade would be a time for consolidation and to some extent retreat as men and women once again looked inward to their personal well-being rather than outward to the society as a whole. The shifts that had occurred were fundamental, moving Canadians and British Columbians away from the racist and patriarchal assumptions of an earlier age. Hugh Keenleyside aptly summed up these years, writing in 1982 that 'it would be false, of course, to claim that all remnants of social prejudice have even yet been eliminated, but what now exists is for the most part confined to the personal or private organizational level.' Cyril Shelford echoed Keenleyside in his observation that 'today nearly everyone accepts at least the theory of equality.'[43] For the most part the old clichés no longer held.

14

A New Dynamic
1972–1995

The defeat of W.A.C. Bennett as premier in the autumn of 1972 marked a watershed in British Columbia.[1] Bennett and the Social Credit party had overseen the province's transformation into a cohesive social and economic entity, and now British Columbians were ready to move on. The political direction that they would take remained uncertain for the next two decades. The left-oriented New Democratic Party's accession to power turned out to be a brief interlude seemingly only preparing the way for Social Credit's return. Unable to get beyond a committed support base of 40 to 45 per cent of the electorate, the NDP's principal function as an opposition party became to hold together a centre-right coalition that lost its way. Social Credit hung on to power to 1991 when the Liberal party's revival facilitated the NDP's election under Mike Harcourt.

During these years a new dynamic took hold in British Columbia. In 1972 the province was a Canadian backwater; by 1995 the world rather than Canada had become British Columbia's stage. As North America turned towards the Pacific Rim, the province's location on the edge of a continent turned from being a liability to an asset. The economy remained as dependent as ever on the export of staples, but the products British Columbia had to offer gained in appeal, especially in Asia. The growing emphasis on environmentalism made the province's striking natural beauty and opportunities for outdoor recreation valuable commodities, attracting growing numbers of visitors as well as new British Columbians. Expo 86, an international exposition held to mark Vancouver's centenary, both exemplified and heralded the city's coming of age on the world stage. Back in charge, the NDP tackled two of the principal problems constraining the new dynamic, both with deep roots in the province's history: the absence of treaties with British Columbia's native peoples, and the multinational companies' hold over the economy at the cost of environmental sustainability.

The NDP's 1972 victory under David Barrett was a political anomaly made possible by dissension within Social Credit's traditional constituency, but that in no way prevented the party's supporters from viewing it as a major triumph. The province's left had been waiting in the wings for over two-thirds of a century; now Barrett and the NDP attempted to do everything at once. Under W.A.C. Bennett about forty bills were passed in a legislative session, of which half a dozen had major importance. In its first year in power the NDP enacted ten times that number, three-quarters of substance. Social services were reorganized, a new taxation and royalty structure was imposed on mining, the sale of agricultural land for development was frozen, discrimination was prohibited in employment and housing, provincial employees were given full collective bargaining rights, a new labour code was drafted, and rent controls were introduced. In a pattern established by Bennett with his expropriation of BC Electric and Black Ball ferries, new provincial corporations took control of such diverse activities as automobile insurance, the production and marketing of natural gas, the company town of Ocean Falls, and a Fraser Valley poultry operation.

The consequence of this flurry of activity soon rebounded on the NDP. Land developers, the mining and forestry industries, and a wide range of vested interests were adversely affected and became extremely critical. Even such a strong support group as teachers was alienated by erratic educational policies. Unions were upset when the government legislated an end to several major strikes on the grounds that the interest of all the people took precedence over that of the labour movement. In part because power was concentrated in the hands of Barrett and one or two ministers, the government's strength did not lie in public relations. Political realism was not a strong suit, neither was overall planning or co-ordination. Barrett's middling ability as an administrator and his penchant for verbal mishaps enabled the opposition to exploit the NDP's weaknesses.

The NDP soon found itself a victim of the larger world economy, which entered a period of severe recession with which the provincial government was inevitably identified. Yet Barrett continued to spend. The provincial budget moved from $1.2 billion in 1972 to $3.2 billion three years later. For growing numbers of British Columbians the NDP's largesse seemed designed to destroy the province's economic base in resource exploitation.

The NDP's inability to gauge public reaction was most evident in the 1975 decision to call an election with almost two years left in the government's mandate. While Barrett, still largely running a one-man show, clearly thought that he would emerge victorious, he had not taken into account Social Credit's recovery. At the time of the 1972 defeat no heir to W.A.C. Bennett, then seventy-two years of age, was on the scene. About the same time that the leader of the provincial Conservatives approached Bennett to lead a new coalition to defeat the NDP, his son expressed interest in entering politics. In mid 1973 William Bennett captured the Okanagan seat vacated on his father's retirement, and at a leadership convention later in the year he took over the party. What followed over the next two years was the emergence of a new anti-socialist coalition, spurred on by the defection of Liberal and Conservative MLAs to Social Credit.

In the election campaign Bill Bennett's political inexperience was evident. In spite of this, he had public opinion on his side and received almost half the popular vote. The NDP retained virtually the same proportion as in 1972: 39.2 per cent as opposed to 39.6 per cent three years earlier. But this time it was not enough (see Table 4). Bill Bennett took over the province, his father remaining behind the scenes until his death in 1979. In the provincial election of that year the NDP actually increased its proportion of the vote to 46 per cent. Although the highest ever received by the political left in British Columbia, it fell short of Social Credit's 48 per cent. The interregnum of the early 1970s only confirmed for many their belief that socialism, even in its parliamentary and democratic variant, was, if not dangerous, then barren in its contribution to provincial well-being.

Social Credit as led by the young Bennett was not the same party as that of his father. Cyril Shelford, still an MLA, early became critical of Bill Bennett's reliance on 'the Liberal contingent from the lower mainland' and on the concomitant disregard of 'the whole area from McBride to Prince Rupert,' which was not given representation in the cabinet. 'I soon got to realize that government today was a totally new ball game.' For the first time Social Credit possessed, mainly through the mass support carried into the party by defecting Liberal MLAS, a solid political base in establishment Vancouver. Both of the leading parties' principal bases of support were shifting; whereas Social Credit was making inroads into the Vancouver establishment, the NDP acquired growing hinterland support among workers in large-scale resource industries brought into existence under the elder Bennett. As Shelford recollected, some of Social Credit's staunchest supporters early warned hinterland MLAS that 'our efforts to bring development and industry would be our eventual downfall ... With development would come unionized workers, many of whom would vote NDP.'[2]

Bill Bennett headed a more austere administration than had his father. In the view of some he lacked any overall plan for the future. 'Slick advertising types and many non-elected people from outside the province have more say than MLAS and many ministers ... The party machinery lost its grassroots approach.' David Mitchell argued in 1983 that 'W.A.C. Bennett was the last B.C. government to have a clear idea of where it was going and how to get there.'[3] The younger Bennett did emulate his father in road-building, overseeing during his decade in office the construction of the Coquihalla highway linking the southern interior to the coast. He also privatized the catch-all organization formed under the NDP to run the enterprises they had taken over. Every British Columbian was given five shares in the new BC Resources Investment Corporation, largesse that turned sour when the shares plummeted in value.

The British Columbia that entered the 1980s was at one and the same time more prosperous and more vulnerable than any other provincial or regional economy in Canada.[4] Corporate concentration continued unabated. The four largest fish companies accounted for over four-fifths of all canned salmon. Ten large integrated forestry companies controlled between 80 and 93 per cent of the resource in each of the province's seven forestry districts. Together they also owned 90 per cent of pulp enterprises and three-quarters of plywood and veneer plants. Seven of these ten companies were owned outside of British Columbia, half outside of Canada. The province supported one of the highest per capita incomes in Canada, but the resources on which that income depended were themselves dependent on world demand. A minor fluctuation in the pace of house construction in the United States became a major event, as did the smallest change in the value of the Canadian dollar compared with its American counterpart. Seasonable fluctuations characterized many personal incomes.

The promise in new planned resource communities so heralded in the 1960s was not realized, and the problems raised were reminiscent of those in earlier company towns. The cost of living was high compared to longer settled and less remote areas; informal company dominance transferred the hierarchy of the mill or mine into social structure; and there were limited jobs for the wives and daughters of workers. Despite tremendous development, British Columbia's resource-based hinterland retained many of its earlier limitations.

By 1981 four regional metropolises ruled supreme: Prince George with sixty-eight thousand residents, Victoria and Kamloops with sixty-four thousand each, and Kelowna with almost sixty thousand (see Table 18). The number of communities of five thousand or more residents outside of the province's southwestern corner climbed to thirty-one. Greater Vancouver, and more particularly the city itself, held undisputed sway over the province as a whole. During the 1970s the reform coalition of TEAM gradually gave way to the long-standing Non-Partisan Association, a shift that only reflected Vancouver's prosperous and self-satisfied character. Replete with actual and would-be home owners, the metropolis seemed primarily concerned with maintaining a comfortable status quo as service centre to a very large hinterland.

The hinterland economy on which Vancouver depended for its affluence continued to be based on two principal staples: minerals and timber. World prices set the rhythm and pace of mineral exploitation, assisted in some cases by improved extraction techniques. Open-pit strip mining continued to be favoured, ventures being shut down as ore was depleted. Coal and copper expanded in the 1970s, because of rising prices and new technology. At the beginning of the twentieth century ore had to contain 2 per cent copper to be commercially exploited; now the necessary proportion stood at 0.4 per cent. The gross value of mineral production surpassed $3 billion by 1980 (see Table 20). Almost one-quarter of it came from copper, another quarter from petroleum and natural gas. Also contributing to the total was growing Japanese demand for coking coal. Northeast coal, centred on the new resource community of Tumbler Ridge, came into production in 1984. A deep-water terminal was constructed on Ridley Island near Prince Rupert to take northeast coal brought there by rail to Japan.

Forestry still marched at the forefront of the economy, accounting for more than half of exports originating in the province. Over 40 per cent of employees in forestry were in sawmilling, about 25 per cent in logging, almost 20 per cent in the pulp and paper industry. By the mid 1970s the province contained two dozen pulp mills, ten of them constructed in the past decade. Almost all were a response to growing worldwide demand for a much greater variety of paper products, not just the newsprint previously associated with most mills' operation but strong kraft paper used in corrugated cartons, supermarket bags, and packaging in general. British Columbia produced over a quarter of the Canadian supply of pulp, almost 5 per cent of the world supply.

Events in the early 1980s, as another worldwide recession played itself out in the west coast province, again jarred British Columbians into realizing that the economic advantages accruing from resource dependency had their limits. Of all the provinces in Canada, British Columbia was the hardest hit. Re-elected in 1983 with almost half the popular vote, Bennett soon announced a policy of restraint intended to counter the sharp economic downturn. Reductions were proposed in social services and education, which were brought under tighter government control. A direct attack was launched on the labour movement, perceived as excessive in its wage demands.

Massive popular opposition erupted. A Solidarity coalition brought together British Columbians from across the province, joined by deep concern over proposed cutbacks. Its emergence pointed up the long-term implications of the post-war shift towards non-manual work. Wage labourers in resource industries could be – and were – let go whenever the economy turned down. By 1983 the proportion of the paid workforce belonging to a union had slipped from a post-war high of just above 50 per cent to 45 per cent, including agriculture. Four out of the five largest unions in British Columbia represented public employees, teachers, or other service and non-manual workers. Such men and women were far less expendable than wage labourers in resource industries. Frequently possessing special skills, they were often protected by some form of job security and were unwilling to lower their earning expectation at times of falling provincial revenues. They refused to accept that the resource economy upon which their well-being depended should work to their disadvantage during a recession as well as to their benefit during halcyon years.

In November 1983, amidst work stoppages by government employees and teachers, Solidarity leaders worked out a compromise with Bill Bennett. Most members of the movement viewed the agreement as far more favourable to the government than to Solidarity. While some of the proposed legislation was modified, much of it passed intact.[5]

Three years later the provincial government again changed. Rule by the Bennetts, in power for more than thirty years except for a brief three-year hiatus, finally drew to a close. William Vander Zalm's accession to power, still under the Social Credit banner, appeared to herald an end to the confrontation and bitterness emanating from the battles with Solidarity. Possessed of very devoted supporters and, in the view of some, charismatic qualities, Vander Zalm was a true populist. He was a Dutch immigrant, as were four other Social Credit MLAS, two of whom were soon named ministers. Of the five, four came out of the Calvinist religious tradition, although Vander Zalm himself was a Catholic. The strong moral views of these men, as well as fellow Conservative Protestants in the caucus, repeatedly intruded into public policy on issues ranging from abortion to private education.

Vander Zalm's goal was to reduce the role of the state in British Columbians' lives. Social and other services undertaken by government, from highway maintenance to tree nurseries to government publishing, were privatized. Bill Bennett's restraint program of the early 1980s had eliminated thousands of positions in the provincial civil service; Vander Zalm continued the process through cutting back and contracting out. The government also undertook electoral reform, following on a commitment made during the 1986 election campaign. Long-standing urban-hinterland inequities still held: in that election it took up to twenty thousand votes to win in the province's southwestern tip but six thousand or fewer in most of the north. A commissioner appointed to investigate the situation recommended that boundaries be redrawn on the basis of population, and legislation followed.

The labour movement once again became a target. Legislation passed in 1987 to curb the power of unions had limited success, but it did serve to heighten tensions between organized labour and the provincial government. Social Credit's conservative stance, penchant for scandal, and fractious hold on power assisted the opposition NDP to reach out towards the political mainstream. Led by Vancouver's popular former mayor, Mike Harcourt, the party won every by-election.

Even as the NDP was gathering strength, Social Credit collapsed. Forced to resign in the spring of 1991 over dubious business dealings, Vander Zalm was succeeded by his lacklustre deputy premier and protégé, the Surrey MLA Rita Johnston. Johnston then won a bitter leadership race over longtime Vancouver MLA Grace McCarthy. The contest had a certain irony, given that for the past two decades just one in ten MLAS was a woman, mostly representing NDP ridings. The victory of suburban and hinterland populism over the metropolis was in any case a pyrrhic one. Johnston became the first female premier in Canada, but also one of the shortest serving.

Disorganized and without vision, the province's ruling coalition imploded. A fall 1991 election campaign saw disenchanted establishment forces abandon Social Credit for a revived provincial Liberal party headed by the feisty Gordon Wilson. The centre-right vote split. Social Credit retained 24 per cent, good for just seven seats; 33 per cent went to the Liberals, who garnered seventeen seats (see Table 4). The Liberals returned to the legislature for the first time since 1975; not since 1941 had they claimed such a larger proportion of MLAS. The NDP retained its traditional share of the popular vote. Only this time their bare 40 per cent was sufficient to take fifty-one of the seventy-five seats in the redistributed legislature. Mike Harcourt became the province's second New Democratic premier.

It was not only in provincial politics that British Columbian women scored a bittersweet first. Following Prime Minister Brian Mulroney's resignation as Progressive Conservative party leader in the face of growing public disaffection, Vancouver MP Kim Campbell won out as his successor at a June 1993 leadership convention. Canada's first female prime minister was a relative political rookie. A lawyer born in Port Alberni, Campbell had briefly sat as a Social Credit MLA and run for the party leadership against Vander Zalm in 1986 before moving into the federal arena. Like her provincial counterpart, Campbell found herself unable to restore sagging party fortunes before the next election and took the party down to defeat with her. In an October 1993 drubbing, Campbell and all but two other Tories were defeated. British Columbia may have acquired its first home-grown prime minister, but it also had the distinction of having one of the briefest in power. In the view of some, British Columbia's distance from Ottawa contributed to Campbell's fall, along with her inexperience and gender.

Other events at the federal level also intruded upon British Columbia. In 1982 Canada acquired a new constitution replacing the British North America Act of 1867. The Constitution Act, 1982 included a Charter of Rights and Freedoms. The changes did nothing to dissipate long-lived separatist sentiment in Quebec, and in 1992 premiers proposed to rewrite the constitution to give the French-speaking province greater autonomy. In the overall defeat of the referendum on the Charlottetown Accord, 67 per cent of British Columbia voters said no, the largest percentage anywhere in Canada. The province's strong populist tradition gave ordinary British Columbians the confidence that their opinion mattered and that their voice deserved to be heard.

The vote was as much, if not more, of a rebuff of the federal government as it was of Quebec. For most British Columbians Quebec was unfamiliar terrain. The proportion of the province's population born there had never risen above one in fifty (see Table 8), and some of these were anglophone Montrealers who had migrated west precisely because of the separatist movement. Fewer than one in every two hundred British Columbians spoke French as their first language, and only one in sixteen was bilingual in English and French. Yet, while most British Columbians had little sympathy towards Quebec's aspirations for special status in Canada, the notion of greater provincial autonomy exercised considerable appeal. Discontent over the status quo was fuelled by such federal actions as the 1989 curtailment of transcontinental rail service, intended by the Fathers of Confederation to link the west coast province 'forever' with the rest of Canada. British Columbia's population now approached half that of Quebec, yet it received far less federal attention. The sense of alienation that many Quebeckers felt towards federal Canada resonated in British Columbia, and had similarly deep historical roots.

Like its predecessor of two decades earlier, the NDP strode self-confidently onto the provincial scene in 1991 and acted in power as if it had widespread popular support. It did so with some justification. Apart from the Liberal advance across parts of the lower mainland and Social Credit's hinterland pockets, the new government's political base was reasonably dispersed across the province. Almost a third of its fifty-one MLAs were female; overall the proportion of women in the legislature had doubled. The election of four Indo-Canadians reflected the coming of age of that increasingly politicized segment of the British Columbia population. The NDP's policy initiatives, though equally ambitious, were far more moderate than under Barrett. The party in 1991 was socialist by legacy alone. Its move towards the political centre reflected the generally conservative tenor of the 1990s, the collapse of planned economies elsewhere, and Harcourt's populist, conciliatory personality.

Nonetheless, political sniping became the order of the day, as new actors jockeyed for position. The Social Credit party proved unable to regroup, but the Liberal revival and a new provincial Reform party more than compensated. Despite singlehandedly catapulting the Liberals back into the legislature, party leader Gordon Wilson proved unequal to the task. Business and other entrenched interests, including disenchanted Social Creditors, saw power in their grasp, and they eagerly used Wilson's romantic involvement with a fellow MLA to bring him down. Wilson's replacement in 1993 was Harcourt's successor as Vancouver mayor, Gordon Campbell. The dapper Campbell personified the province's urban face. In contrast, the Reform party, founded in emulation of its federal counterpart, appealed to hinterland interests earlier aligned to Social Credit. The selection of Peace River MLA Jack Weisgerber, formerly of Social Credit, as Reform party leader completed the refashioning of provincial politics. By 1995 all but one of the Social Credit MLAs had defected.

However moderate in its ideology, the new government embodied a strong moral imperative. Its goal was the reconciliation of long-time protagonists in key areas of provincial life – big business with the NDP's allies in organized labour, multinationals with conservationists, mainstream society with native peoples. Owing in part to inexperience, many of the government's efforts were frustrated by gaffes or tarnished by scandal. The BC 21 spending fund launched in 1993 to renew infrastructure and construct local amenities by borrowings outside of the provincial debt never lost the stigma of being a partisan boondoggle to curry local favour and assist re-election. The government seemed to be spending and spending with no end in sight. Yet, despite provincial budgets approaching the $20 billion range, British Columbia was able to maintain the leanest bureaucracy in Canada. In 1994 the cost of public services including provincial and local governments, education, and hospitals was 12 per cent below the national average. The province's credit rating remained the best in Canada.

Harcourt was assisted by a strong provincial economy and the lowest per capita provincial debt in Canada. The standard of living, which fell dramatically during the early 1980s, again approached the national average by the early 1990s. In 1993 per capita personal income in British Columbia was just over $23,000, a thousand dollars more than the average across Canada.

The province's well-being continued to be dependent on its natural resources. In 1988 the Canadian government agreed to a large measure of free trade with the United States, to be phased in over the next decade. British Columbia became even more closely drawn into the world economy: between 1990 and 1994 the value of goods and services it sold outside Canada grew by 43 per cent, to other provinces by just 16 per cent. Over 80 per cent of forest products were exported, primarily to the United States to be used in construction; so was almost all coal, principally to Japan. In 1994 the value of exports reached $23 billion, of which 54 per cent went to the United States, 35 per cent to Asia, mostly to Japan, and 8 per cent to Europe. Strong international demand for British Columbian products was largely responsible for the economy's growth rate of 4.3 per cent in 1994, just below the national rate of 4.5 per cent. Imports were also increasing owing to the free trade agreement with the United States, and then its expansion to include Mexico. Fewer goods were being purchased from other provinces than had traditionally been the case; by 1994 55 per cent of goods coming into the province were imported.

As a consequence, while business never embraced Harcourt, animosities were less than under his NDP predecessor. As the labour force contracted in the increasingly mechanized resource sector, union membership fell to 38 per cent of paid workers. Although the government acted from time to time to buttress trade unions, it remained more sensitive to business interests than might have been expected. The activity of successor companies to the CPR exemplified the continued ability of big business to benefit financially. Even as passenger service came to an end, the CPR's real estate arm began to develop the last of the Vancouver property it had acquired in exchange for the line's construction over a century earlier. CPR interests built opulent new hotels at the prestigious ski resort of Whistler, about 125 kilometres north of Vancouver, and on the Vancouver waterfront, in addition to renovating two established landmarks, the Hotel Vancouver and the Empress Hotel in Victoria.

The government's attempt to reconcile the interests of the companies exploiting the province's resources, and of British Columbians dependent on them for their livelihood, with conservationists proved to be extraordinarily contentious. In entering the fray, the NDP responded both to its supporters in the rapidly growing environmental movement and to the more general realization that the staples driving the economy were not endlessly renewable. While the provincial government could do relatively little with the fisheries, which were in federal jurisdiction, and only so much with mining, they could take the lead with forestry. This key resource now accounted for 35 per cent of world softwood lumber exports, and 20 per cent of its newsprint. The mechanisms for greater control over forest land, which covers almost half of British Columbia, lay with the provincial government, for just 6 per cent is privately owned and another 1 per cent is federal land. The remaining 93 per cent is crown land, made available to private entrepreneurs through tenure and licence arrangements.

From the province's early years, when crown lands were readily alienated through long leases to friends of the government, the assumption had held that the forests were endless. Ordinary British Columbians were slow to assert their rights as a 'landlord' over this public resource or even to realize that trees were being cut down at a much faster rate than new timber was becoming available. Only a handful of social critics, such as novelist Bertrand Sinclair, had dared to speak out: 'Outside of two or three concerns, logging in B.C. to-day is an orgy of waste. They're skimming the cream off the forest, spilling half of it.' Naturalist and writer Roderick Haig-Brown was equally scathing. 'A civilization built on foul air and polluted water, on destroyed timber lands, overgrazed ranges, exhausted farm lands, on water sucked from one river system to make cheap electricity on another, is too costly and too insecurely based to last.' The common response of the industry was to heap indignant scorn on what a lumber publication in 1928 had termed an 'active little band of hard-boiled pessimists.' 'In spite of all that can be pointed out to them regarding natural reproduction ... they will continue to write to the papers and address community organizations on the importance of preserving virgin timber for aesthetic contemplation by posterity.'[6]

Little changed, even after the Second World War. Despite the rhetoric that the notion of sustained yield engendered under the two Bennetts, it still came nowhere near to realization. As late as 1980 the annual report of the provincial ministry of forests revealed that only one-third of logged land was being reforested, referring hopefully to natural restocking to excuse a patent lack of concern.[7] The deep recession of the early 1980s, when several large companies collapsed, finally brought realization that the limits for lumbering had been reached in British Columbia.

In the meantime the environmental movement came into its own. During the 1980s sensitivity grew around the world to the need to maintain ecosystems, ensure biodiversity, and protect wilderness areas. Practices long considered the norm, such as clear-cut logging, came under severe criticism; groups as diverse as kayakers on the west coast of Vancouver Island and Alaska cruise ship operators based in Vancouver protested the practice. When first-growth stands of trees were threatened in such locations as the Stein and Carmanah valleys, public indignation was thoroughly aroused.

The NDP's tactic was to use British Columbia's strong populist tradition to seek input from ordinary citizens as to which areas should be protected and which should be logged. The strategy was soon sidelined. In 1993 the government gave multinational MacMillan Bloedel permission to clear-cut up to 70 per cent of the 350,000-hectare Clayoquot Sound on the west coast of Vancouver Island, one of the world's last intact temperate rain forests. Anger among environmentalists was unprecedented. That summer direct action by British Columbians and outsiders of all ages and backgrounds led to over eight hundred arrests at Clayoquot Sound and some prison terms. The province was repeatedly castigated in the press worldwide, and its forest products were boycotted. As a Greenpeace organizer quipped, Clayoquot Sound became the 'poster child' of the international environmental movement.[8] The counter-offensive saw the government set up a scientific panel on Clayoquot. In July 1995 it accepted all of the panel's recommendations, including an end to conventional clearcuts and priority to the sound's ecology over immediate economic advantage.

It was in the shadow of Clayoquot that the government's land-use strategy got under way. The CORE process, intended to produce a coherent vision of British Columbia's future, lay at its heart. The Commission on Resources and Environment was established in 1992 to work with local interest groups to develop and implement sustainable land-use plans defining areas for protection, resource development, and commercial use. Amidst considerable dissension, plans were approved for Vancouver Island, the Cariboo-Chilcotin region, and the Kootenays. By 1995 the NDP was halfway towards its publicly declared goal of doubling protected wilderness areas from 6 to 12 per cent of the province's land base.

Other measures also targeted forestry. Harcourt announced a forest renewal plan in 1994. Increased fees for logging crown lands would be used to create new jobs in tree planting and watershed restoration. Allowable annual cuts on crown lands were to be regularly updated, and reduced as necessary, also in the interests of sustainability. A new forestry practices code became law later in 1994, reducing the maximum size of clearcuts, mandating replanting of harvested areas, and tightening regulations and enforcement. Reflecting European practice, greater emphasis was put on value-added wood products such as specialty sizes and furniture, doors, and windows. By 1994 raw log exports fell below 1 per cent of the annual harvest. Shifts at the University of British Columbia's flagship Faculty of Forestry both reflected and promised to reinforce the trend: it had in the late 1980s launched a new program in natural resources conservation, and in 1995 it did the same thing in wood products processing. The NDP's wide-ranging strategy, buttressed by a strong worldwide environmental movement, effectively manoeuvred the forestry industry into accepting restrictions on output and, more generally, engaging in an entirely new way of doing business in British Columbia.

Although the fisheries were a federal responsibility, those in charge were equally slow to acknowledge a dwindling resource.[9] Too many boats with too much capacity were chasing too few fish, and they had been doing so since the 1960s. The salmon's migratory path well beyond British Columbian waters and the industry's federal oversight added to the complexities. International agreements to regulate excessive fishing remained tentative and unsatisfactory. Plans for conservation through constructing hatcheries and encouraging fish farming were unable to rectify a deteriorating situation with its roots in overexploitation, an unworkable federal bureaucracy and enforcement policy, and jurisdictional disputes with other nations.

The province's career fishers increasingly came into conflict with new competitors for a declining resource. The sport fishery was expanding as part of a burgeoning tourist industry. In 1990 the Supreme Court of Canada unanimously ruled that Indians had a constitutional right to fish for food and ceremonial purposes that took priority over commercial or sports fishers. Two years later the federal government gave Indians along the Fraser River permission also to fish for sale. In the years 1990 to 1993 a yearly average of about 4,300 commercial gillnetters, trollers, and seiners caught 94 per cent of salmon, 350,000 licensed anglers 3 per cent, and Indians about 3 per cent. Native fishers also held about 20 per cent of commercial licences.

The situation came to a head in 1994 when over a million salmon expected to ascend the Fraser River to spawn simply did not arrive, for reasons that even the best of experts could not fathom. Conditions worsened in 1995 as various species of salmon again refused to return. The search for solutions continued to be hampered by uncertain scientific knowledge and by disagreement, both internationally and within Canada, on how best to sustain fish populations over the long term and who should have priority to fish. British Columbia's fishing industry – be it aboriginal, sport, or commercial – appeared in grave danger.

Initiatives in other areas of the economy were less contentious, in part because there was less room to manoeuvre. The Columbia River Treaty came up for renewal, and it was anticipated that the negotiations with the United States would bring new income into the provincial economy and into the Kootenays. Responding to concerns over the depletion of salmon stocks, the province pulled out of an agreement permitting the aluminum giant Alcan to drain the Nechako River to about 10 per cent of its flow to generate hydroelectric power. The gross value of mineral production reached $3.8 billion in 1990 (see Table 20) with some declines thereafter due to falling world prices.

In sharp contrast to staples, tourism boomed as a component of the provincial economy. Expo 86 recorded twenty-two million visits, many from outside of the province and the nation. Six and a half million Americans came to British Columbia in 1986. Canada Place, built as the federal site at Expo 86, helped to sustain the momentum; it now became a combined trade and convention centre, hotel, and cruise ship facility. The attributes of natural beauty and opportunities for outdoor recreation that exist in abundance across the province became increasingly valued around the world, heightening British Columbia's visibility as a holiday destination. Entrepreneurs responded by providing facilities, be it for sport fishing, skiing, golfing, camping, or water sliding. Whistler Mountain and nearby Blackcomb Mountain were developed into internationally known ski resorts and summer recreation areas. A number of smaller ski resorts appeared across the interior and the north. The lead column in a special 1992 *Maclean's* issue on British Columbia began: 'British Columbia's most visible asset is not its coal, timber or mineral potential. Its riches are mostly rooted in the fact that it is postcard pretty.'[10] In 1994 the province recorded twenty-five million overnight trips, about two-thirds of them by British Columbians visiting other parts of their home province. Almost four million Americans came, as did over a million visitors from overseas countries.

The limitations and contradictions inherent in resource dependency extended into attitudes towards British Columbia's first peoples. Aboriginal policy became a particularly troubled arena for the provincial government, and for British Columbians more generally, in the last decade of the twentieth century. Ongoing aboriginal demands to resolve land claims challenged, in many minds, the very base upon which the province's settler economy was constructed.

The 1980s were a crucial decade for native peoples. By 1981 they reached seventy-five thousand (see Table 5), a figure which brought them back to their estimated numbers at the time of the first contacts with Europeans. The goal of Indian self-government acquired new legitimacy through the reorganization of the National Indian Brotherhood into the Assembly of First Nations in 1982. The change of name emphasized, among other things, Canadian Indians' right to negotiate as equals with other governments or nations. In a long Canadian tradition of compromise, the new federal constitution of 1982 recognized and affirmed 'existing' aboriginal and treaty rights. Although disagreement existed on what these rights might be, they were nonetheless placed beyond the reach of the federal Parliament and of provincial legislatures. The question of status, of who qualified to be an Indian for the purposes of land claims, took on new meaning in 1985 when Indian women won a victory by getting overturned the century-old equation of status with male descent. Revision to the Indian Act, known popularly as Bill c-31, made it possible for women and some of their offspring to recover status lost when they married a non-Indian. By 1991 the number of aboriginal British Columbians reached one hundred thousand.[11]

More than any other issue, land claims rallied British Columbia's native peoples. As explained by a respected elderly Kwakiutl: 'I think the biggest problem to be solved and the most important is the land question ... When the Europeans came here and settled, they just took all our minerals and timber and salmon and everything that we rightfully owned and they have never settled it with us. We have been pounding and pounding on the doors of the government because we

would like to settle it so we can satisfy the minds of the Indians.'[12]
Stalemate continued through the 1980s owing to the provincial government's unwillingness to take an active role in resolving matters or
even to recognize that it had any role to play. The province argued
that aboriginal title to the lands never existed. If perchance the courts
were to rule otherwise, then the federal government rather than the
province was obliged to pay the bill since Indians had become a federal responsibility under the terms of union between British Columbia and Canada.

Provincial indifference was possible because most indigenous people still hovered at the edges of society or, as Hugh Brody aptly
phrased it, 'even to pockets at the edges, of the territory that had
always been theirs.' Restricted through the reserve system, they were
caught in a vicious circle. During a lifetime in close contact, Cyril
Shelford witnessed time and again how, as a consequence of discrimination and lack of economic opportunities, 'many just gave up and
let Indian Affairs look after them.' Yet reliance on federal largesse
was not a solution, for 'Indian Affairs gives handouts which really
only help to maintain the present poverty level of the Indians.' Men
and women wanted to support themselves, but it was only rarely that
the non-natives who controlled industries located near reserves
encouraged their participation, most often as cowboys, sawmill
workers, or fishers. In 1991 one in every three Indians living on
reserve who were seeking employment was out of work, as compared with under one in ten in the overall British Columbia work
force.[13]

The consequence was a standard of life substantially inferior to
that enjoyed by other British Columbians. In 1990 44 per cent of Indians in British Columbia lived below the poverty line, compared with
15 per cent in the general population. Infant mortality was almost
twice the provincial rate, deaths of infants between twenty-seven
days and a year three times higher. A Carrier reserve in the central
interior had a tuberculosis rate twenty times the national average,
and 'sometimes twelve and sixteen people living in two-room
shacks,' no sewers, and high unemployment. Another reserve, just
over one hundred kilometres out of Fort St John, comprised 'houses
crowded together by planners in order to achieve economies of
administration and service.' The typical 'prefabricated, three-bed-
room standard-issue government house' lacked garbage collection,
'running water, drains, or electricity.' In 1991 a quarter of reserve

households in British Columbia reported the water unsafe for drinking, 9 per cent lacked electricity, and 8 per cent had no indoor bathroom facilities. As Brody noted cynically in his book *Maps and Dreams*, 'they pay the price for modernity, yet receive few of its benefits.'[14]

Heavy alcohol and drug use was among the most detrimental consequences, leading all too often to serious injury or death from fighting, automobile accidents, suicide, and other forms of self-destruction. Such deaths were three to five times greater than for the general British Columbia population. Suicide rates in the fifteen to twenty-four age group were six times higher. Status Indian men had a life expectancy ten years less and women seven years less than the average British Columbian. Through the 1980s nearly one-quarter of family-related slayings in Canada involved native people. While the majority were alcohol- or drug-related, many resulted from a combination of poverty and hopelessness. Natives, status and non-status, comprised under 5 per cent of British Columbians, yet made up 18 per cent of the prison population. Mutual distrust and hostility characterized encounters with a non-native justice system. During the 1980s some Indians, such as those at Alkali Lake in the southern interior, became increasingly worried over excessive alcohol consumption. Bands and other organizations began to work together to heighten awareness.

Provincial policy moderated in 1990. Shortly before the Social Credit party lost power, the government declared its willingness to negotiate land claims in partnership with the federal government, and joined in long-standing talks with the Nishga people of northwestern British Columbia. The incoming NDP government made resolution of land claims through negotiation of treaties on a government-to-government basis a central pillar of its larger agenda of reconciliation between peoples.

In doing so, the provincial government was influenced by the Delgamuukw court case. Following on the Nishga lead, in 1987 hereditary chiefs of the neighbouring Gitskan and Wet'suwet'en peoples asked the BC Supreme Court to recognize their claim to traditional lands. In 1991 Justice Allan MacEachern ruled that aboriginal rights had been extinguished at the time of Confederation but that the province was obliged to permit sustenance activities on unoccupied crown land. The controversial decision was appealed to the BC Court of Appeal. In 1993 it dismissed the claim for ownership, but stated that aboriginal rights had not been extinguished in respect to activities maintaining a traditional lifestyle. The court recommended that these rights be negotiated rather than litigated.

In 1993 the federal and provincial governments signed a cost-sharing agreement for land claims; federal authorities accepted primary responsibility for the cash portion of any future treaty settlements, the province for providing crown land and natural resources. The British Columbia Treaty Commission was set up as an independent body to facilitate settlements, including self-government, between native peoples and the two levels of government. The First Nations Summit was established at about the same time to be an umbrella aboriginal organization to oversee treaty resolution. The summit's protagonist became the long-established Union of British Columbia Indian Chiefs, whose supporters insisted that no negotiations take place until governments recognized that aboriginal title to land had never been extinguished.

It soon became evident that the treaty-making process would be lengthy.[15] As a consequence, interim measures were put in place to protect asserted traditional use areas until treaties could be negotiated. The first step towards an actual treaty was for a First Nation – possibly one of the province's 198 bands, otherwise some combination of bands – to file a statement of intent to negotiate. Once mandates were established by all parties, a framework agreement would be negotiated to set up a timetable and identify the substance and objectives of specific claims. Further negotiation would lead to an agreement in principle on the major components of a treaty and, when all details had been settled, to a final agreement in the form of a treaty. Then would come implementation, including legislation if required. By the end of 1995 forty-seven First Nations representing 65 per cent of the province's status Indians had filed statements of intent to negotiate, and the federal government had laid a self-government proposal on the table. A century and a half after non-natives arrived in substantial numbers on the land that is British Columbia, serious treaty making was under way.

At the same time, the assumption that more territory or monetary compensation would equate with economic self-sufficiency and satisfactory conditions of everyday life was largely untested. The treaty-making process presaged growing dissension between the approximately fifty thousand Indians living on reserve and generally controlling the land claims process, and the equivalent number of status persons living off reserve as to who should participate in the anticipated largesse. Another seventy thousand non-status persons, also claiming native descent, were completely outside the treaty process. Interim agreements encouraged an erroneous perception that jurisdiction and authority had already been obtained over claimed territories. Expectations grew: a map released by the BC Treaty Commission in late 1994 revealed that overlapping land claims set out in the forty-two statements of intent filed to date totalled 111 per cent of the province.[16] Rising expectations were unlikely to be satisfied to anyone's satisfaction, given that status Indians represented just 3 per cent of a very diverse provincial population. And no one quite knew what was being negotiated; what, for instance, would be the legal status of land handed over as part of treaty settlements? Dissident aboriginal groups, mostly allied with the Union of British Columbia Indian Chiefs, turned to blockades and other forms of direct action. Protection of burial grounds, sacred sites, or other archaeologically sensitive areas escalated into questions of principle over aboriginal title. The relative youth of native people, half being under twenty-five, and their high rates of unemployment, encouraged militancy. In the eyes of some, the gulf was widening between native and non-native British Columbians, such as happened at Gustafson Lake in the southern interior in the summer of 1995. Nevertheless, aboriginal people had for the first time in over a century become a force to be reckoned with, not only politically but also economically in the fisheries.

British Columbia's other major racial minority, its sizeable Asian population, also came of age in the late twentieth century. The growing tolerance since the Second World War moved towards equality in all aspects of provincial life. The hegemony exercised by individuals of British descent was finally broken. Indicative was the removal in 1985 of the long-standing privilege of British citizens to vote in provincial elections. Individuals of Chinese and East Indian descent, as well as blacks, were elected at all levels of government, and in 1988 a Chinese immigrant, David Lam, was named the province's lieutenant-governor. Many young British Columbians no longer distinguished as to which of their friends might be Asian and which European or of some other background. Intermarriage became more common.

Growing numbers of arrivals from Hong Kong and elsewhere, many bringing with them considerable wealth and sophistication, erased forever the image of the Chinese as contract labourers or coolies. Britain's return of its colony of Hong Kong to China in 1997 encouraged some individuals to leave, and others to invest capital in British Columbia, in case they might eventually want to take up residence in Canada. In 1970 one out of five immigrants to British Columbia arrived from Asia; by 1994 four out of five did so. Half of all new arrivals to the province in 1994 spoke no English. In 1981 62 per cent of the province's immigrant population still came from Europe, but by 1991 it had dropped below half; in contrast, the proportion born in Asia rose from 21 to 34 per cent.

While the province's economy benefited, the phenomenon generated antipathies. Some British Columbians became perturbed by the unusual situation of an immigrant group being better off than many members of the host society. Generational tensions developed. A letter to the editor written in late 1989 expressed concern 'about the resurgence of anti-Asian sentiments caused by the recent influx of Hong Kong immigrants [who] for the most part do not attempt to fit into Canadian society ... The situation is distressing for Chinese-Canadians like me. We are victimized by the same generalizations.' Lieutenant-Governor Lam stressed that it was up to newcomers to adapt and British Columbians to show patience and understanding of the fundamental change taking place in their province. 'The old British Columbia has passed, the new era is upon us.' On leaving office in 1995, Lam considered his greatest success to have 'encouraged greater understanding between the races.'[17]

Vancouver and the lower mainland were the areas most transformed. Newcomers' preference for an urban lifestyle meant that by 1991 over 92 per cent of ethnic Chinese in British Columbia lived in the Greater Vancouver area. One in every five Vancouverites was Chinese by descent. Suburban Richmond, once 'plain Jane' without Vancouver's big-city gloss, was transformed into a Eurasian metropolis reminiscent of Honolulu or even Hong Kong itself. Chinese and Japanese investment became a significant motor of expansion, bringing a sharper edge to business. At first concentrated in real estate, money began to diversify into such areas as garment manufacture, pharmaceuticals, and electronics. Many newcomers, to quote Lam, 'came with capital, with a lot of skills, a lot of know-how.'[18] They also came with families: in 1994–5 one in three Vancouver school children spoke primarily a Chinese language at home, one in six another Asian language; 55 per cent of all children in public school spoke some language other than English at home. The intermingling went both ways: in the fall of 1995 a Vancouver elementary school began Mandarin immersion for English-speaking children. By 1995 there were three Richmond shopping centres catering to Chinese tastes, as well as three Chinese newspapers, two television stations, and two radio stations serving the lower mainland. The Vancouver Public Library's collection of Chinese-language books surpassed seventy thousand volumes.

Asians' visibility masked the more general population growth taking place in British Columbia. As the economy revived from the recession of the early 1980s, the province became increasingly perceived as an attractive place to live and work. Into the mid 1990s men and women continued to arrive from elsewhere in Canada and from abroad in far greater numbers than British Columbians moved away: net migrants from other provinces grew from just over twenty-five thousand in 1988 to almost forty thousand persons in 1994, mostly from Alberta and Ontario. Net immigrants expanded from about 17,500 to over forty thousand a year. In comparison, natural increase accounted for about twenty thousand new British Columbians annually, or between one-third and one-fifth of overall population growth. By itself, natural increase was about 20 per cent below the level necessary for the British Columbian population to maintain itself; every woman of child-bearing age needed to have 2.1 children, whereas the mean was only 1.7.[19] Newcomers were generally younger and better educated than the average British Columbian. Nonetheless, the median age crept upward, to thirty-five years by 1993, reflecting the post-war baby boom and subsequent drop in fertility rates (see Table 13). Longer life expectancies and the province's appeal to retirees, as well as to young people, contributed to the proportion aged sixty-five and over rising from 9 per cent in 1971 to 13 per cent by 1993.

British Columbia continued to be a province unlike any other in Canada. In 1991, as in every previous decade since Confederation, less than half of the non-native population, or 48 per cent, was born in British Columbia (see Table 8). This compared with 57 per cent of Albertans, 65 per cent of Ontarians, 73 per cent of Manitobans, and 80 per cent or more elsewhere. British Columbia remained a land of newcomers who in adapting also refashioned the status quo.

Population growth exacerbated regional disparities. Between 1981 and 1991 the population grew by 21 per cent to 3,282,061, even though only the three most densely populated and populous of the province's ten regions actually gained substantial numbers (see Tables 5 and 14). Reliance on staples and the vicissitudes of the economy worked against the hinterland. The closure of the huge pulp and paper mill at Ocean Falls in 1980 and the subsequent demise of the town itself epitomized the ongoing shift in British Columbia's demography. Urban centres outside of the southwestern tip were often unable to compete on an equal basis: tonnage going through the province's second major port of Prince Rupert fell by the late 1980s to less than 20 per cent of that passing through Vancouver. The number of communities beyond the populous southwestern tip with a population of five thousand or more remained constant at thirty-one.

In 1991 the average per capita income in British Columbia was below the provincial mean in every region except the lower mainland and greater Victoria; it was the lowest in the Cariboo, parts of the Kootenays, and the central coast. The number of separate post offices – an indication of autonomous market towns, resource communities, or other settlements – continued to decline. British Columbia possessed one hundred and sixty fewer post offices during the 1970s than it had in the previous decade (see Tables 15 and 16). While two dozen of them were turned into sub-post offices, the overwhelming majority simply closed. The pattern continued through the 1980s, accelerated by Canada Post's policy of transferring postal services into convenience stores or other commercial settings.

Rural British Columbia, to the extent that it had ever existed, was slipping away. In 1981 the province contained just 6 per cent of Canada's farms. In the Peace region family homesteads gave way to more profitable large-scale operations sometimes employing tenant farmers, as was also occurring in adjacent Alberta and through the prairies. Ginseng for export to Asia began to be commercially grown in the dry interior. In the Okanagan the wine industry successfully restructured with new grape varieties. Agriculture became big business, creating growing awareness that dreams of individual self-fulfilment on the land would never be realized.

By comparison, three of British Columbia's ten regions boomed (see Table 14). During the 1980s forty-five thousand more people settled in Okanagan-Boundary, just under a hundred thousand more on Vancouver Island, and almost four hundred thousand more in the lower mainland. Kelowna surpassed its regional competitors of Prince George and Kamloops with a 1991 population of over seventy-five thousand (see Table 18). The appeal of the Okanagan Valley for retirement or escape was matched by Vancouver Island, from Campbell River south through Nanaimo to the Saanich peninsula. Victoria was particularly attractive to migrants from elsewhere in Canada, which helps explain why almost 35 per cent of its residents claimed British ethnicity in 1991 compared to just 25 per cent in British Columbia as a whole. The increasingly suburbanized Fraser Valley led the lower mainland's growth (see Table 17).

The new dynamic was also visible in education and culture. Private schools on the British model of class exclusivity and the Conservative Protestant model of religious separation had long existed, together with their Catholic private and parochial counterparts. Until 1978 they did so without any public funding or other official support. In that year legislation came into effect, whereby non-public schools that met basic guidelines were accorded provincial funding at 30 per cent of the cost of educating each of their enrolled pupils in the local public school. Alternative schools catering to religious, ethnic, class-based, and other interests proliferated. The phenomenon was particularly striking in the Fraser Valley, where Mennonites, Dutch Calvinists, prairie migrants, and others contributed to a strong Conservative Protestant ethos. According to one estimate, up to half of all residents attended church regularly compared with about one-fifth elsewhere in the province.[20] Legislation passed in 1989 raised the maximum support level for private schools to 50 per cent and, for the first time, gave official encouragement to home schooling. The NDP government, historically opposed to funding non-public alternatives, did nothing to reverse the trend, confirming that private schools had become an integral component of the British Columbia fabric. In 1994–5 about 7 per cent of the province's 628,000 school children were being educated privately. Of these, 44 per cent were attending a Catholic school, just under 20 per cent a Christian school, 13 per cent a school in the elite British tradition, and the reminder any one of a wide variety of private schools.

Educational alternatives also expanded at the post-secondary level. In 1978 the provincial government instituted 'open learning.' It was already possible for students to take correspondence courses with individual universities; now that opportunity was standardized and expanded through a single provincial agency. British Columbians could complete high school, enrol in technical and vocational programs, or acquire a bachelor's degree without ever stepping into a classroom. In the early 1990s about fourteen thousand students a year were taking courses through the Open Learning Agency.

Post-secondary education received a major boost in 1989 when the provincial government gave community colleges in the regional centres of Kamloops, Kelowna, Nanaimo, and subsequently the Fraser Valley permission to add upper-level courses in conjunction with one of the existing universities, which would then grant a bachelor's degree. About the same time Prince George successfully lobbied for an autonomous University of Northern British Columbia that would respond to the central interior's distinctive needs. The UNBC opened in September 1994 with about thirteen hundred students. The same year the provincial government granted independent degree-granting status to the four colleges that had been awarding joint degrees and to the British Columbia Institute of Technology created in the early 1960s, Emily Carr Institute of Art and Design which had originated in 1925 as the Vancouver School of Decorative and Applied Arts, and Kwantlen University College in Surrey. As part of an emphasis on skills training in advanced technologies, the government also committed itself to a new technical university to be located in rapidly growing Surrey just outside of Vancouver.

These initiatives did not signal the retreat of the established universities but rather the general expansion of higher education. Simon Fraser created a second, downtown Vancouver campus to complement its original Burnaby hilltop location. In 1993 the University of British Columbia's president, David Strangway, completed a successful funding campaign, raising over $260 million to revitalize the campus through new buildings, endowed chairs, and scholarships. The university's identity as a distinct community was ensured when the forest separating it from the city of Vancouver, long mooted for housing, became the Pacific Spirit regional park. By the early 1990s just over a quarter of young British Columbians were studying full-time at the post-secondary level, up from one in six a decade earlier.

The extension of comparable educational opportunities across British Columbia was paralleled by the growth of a common culture. During the 1980s cable television became available to over 80 per cent of homes. Proliferation of video cassette recorders and then electronic communication via e-mail and the Internet accelerated culture's internationalization.

British Columbians did not just absorb the common culture that enveloped the province; they helped to influence it. International successes as diverse as rock star Bryan Adams and *Generation X* novelist Douglas Coupland continued to call the province home. In 1991–2 three hundred and fifty new book titles were produced by several dozen large and small regional publishers. Total book sales in British Columbia approached $25 million a year. Film-making became integral to the economy. In the mid 1990s over eighty film and television productions were being completed annually in British Columbia. While most were by American companies simply using the province as a location, there were notable exceptions such as Sandy Wilson's 1985 evocation of the post-war Okanagan Valley in *My American Cousin*, and Mina Shum's 1994 characterization of a contemporary Chinese-Canadian household in *Double Happiness*. Annual awards for the best work by British Columbians in literature, journalism, theatre, music, and other aspects of culture testified to the diversity of talent at work in the province.

Professional sports surged. In 1994 the Vancouver Canucks hockey club came within one goal of taking home the Stanley Cup, and the BC Lions again won the Grey Cup. A professional basketball team, the Vancouver Grizzlies, began playing in the autumn of 1995 in a new sports stadium shared with the Canucks. Located adjacent to BC Place, General Motors Place competed for name recognition with the new Ford Centre for the Performing Arts just a few blocks away. Conceived by the Canadian entrepreneur Garth Drabinsky, it was intended to bring international theatrical productions to the west coast, and opened with the musical *Show Boat*.

If culture and sports thrived, organized religion was on the decline. Perhaps it was the emphasis on lifestyle, or perhaps environmentalism had become a secular faith. For whatever reason, in 1991 about one in every three, or almost a million British Columbians had no religious affiliation. This was up from just over one-fifth a decade earlier and one in eight in 1971 (see Table 10). Nationally, the proportion was about one in eight in 1991.

British Columbians who professed religious faith were less likely to belong to one of the traditional Christian denominations. In the decade between 1981 and 1991 the proportions adhering to the Anglican, United, or Presbyterian faiths each fell between a quarter and almost 40 per cent. Altogether they captured the attention of just one in four British Columbians, unlike one in three a decade earlier and

half to two-thirds over the previous century. The Conservative Protestant denominations, Catholicism, and Judaism each held their own
during the 1980s, and Eastern non-Christian faiths grew in appeal,
together attracting one in twenty British Columbians.

Economists Craig Davis and Thomas Hutton have argued that
'increasingly, the economy of British Columbia is becoming divided
between two distinct segments: the service-oriented urban economy
of metropolitan Vancouver and the resource-based hinterland economy of the remainder of the province, particularly the interior.'
Escaping the worst of the cyclical and seasonal fluctuations inherent
in staple dependence, Vancouver not only led the recovery from the
recession of the early 1980s but thereafter thrived as Canada's gateway to Asia. The city became a centre for trans-Pacific commerce,
banking, and trade. Between 1990 and 1995 almost twenty countries
either opened new consulates or upgraded offices to full-time operations; by 1995 there were sixty-four consulates in Vancouver
compared to eighty-two in Toronto. With characteristic British
understatement, *The Economist* summed up the shift: 'Vancouver
used to be dismissed as "a beautiful city on the wrong side of
Canada." No longer.'[21]

The metropolis put on a new face. During the last decades of the
twentieth century traditional architecture gave way to some daring
new designs alongside the many replications of dominant styles in
other North American cities.[22] Arthur Erickson created Vancouver's
new law courts largely in glass in order to open up and demystify the
legal process. The low angular building complemented the far less
attractive CBC headquarters, also constructed during the 1970s. Erickson also put his stamp on Vancouver in an imposing Sikh temple in
the city's southeast and a striking Museum of Anthropology on the
UBC campus showcasing native art. Two decades later it was a new
Vancouver public library designed by Canadian architect Moshe
Safdie which set the agenda. Mocked by some as a postmodern
Roman coliseum, the new library located adjacent to the Ford Centre
caught the popular imagination and promised to bring new energy to
the city.

Part of Vancouver's vibrancy lay in its growing appeal as a tourist
destination. Visitors coming to British Columbia by plane almost certainly touched down there. The open skies agreement implemented
in 1995 under free trade meant that flights could arrive much more

freely from across the United States. That year more scheduled international flights landed in Vancouver than in either of its two nearest west coast competitors, Seattle and San Francisco. An international terminal and second runway opening in 1996 both recognized and promised to accelerate the city's hub location between North America and Asia. Expo 86 opened up Vancouver to the cruise ship industry. By 1993 twenty ships from nine international lines were using the city as a southern base to carry over half a million passengers a year to and from Alaska. With an average age of fifty-five, almost all their passengers were Americans, and an increasing number spent time in Vancouver, or elsewhere in the province, before or after their cruise.

One consequence was the renewed appeal of the historic Gastown area just to the east of Canada Place, where most ships docked. Revitalized in the late 1960s, Gastown's return to popularity pushed farther east the disenfranchised who lived in its vicinity. Late in 1989 the Woodward family severed its final link with the western Canadian department stores bearing their name, and the defunct flagship store seemed destined to be recycled as largely middle-class housing, as were growing numbers of Gastown's old brick structures.

So, too, was much of the city centre. The south side of False Creek had been developed in the 1970s for housing, with adjacent Granville Island rehabilitated around a very popular public market; two decades later it was the north side's turn. The residential appeal of the longtime wholesaling area known as Yaletown rested in part on its proximity to Concord Pacific's massive new condominium project on the Expo 86 lands. Canadian Pacific's land holdings at Coal Harbour, stretching along Burrard Inlet from Canada Place to Stanley Park, were also being developed. In 1991 about forty-six thousand people lived in the city centre extending from Main Street west to Stanley Park; the new developments anticipated another forty thousand, many of them newcomers to the province.

In the view of some Vancouver was trying too hard to become a world-class city. Growth highlighted the poverty of the lower mainland's infrastructure. It was not that existing facilities atrophied, but they did not expand apace. The highest house prices in Canada sent increasing numbers of young families out to the rapidly suburbanizing Fraser Valley to live. The lack of freeways within the city and inadequate feeder roads to its boundaries made commuting increasingly time-consuming. New initiatives in public transit such as the sea bus across Burrard Inlet to North Vancouver, the sky train into

Surrey to the southeast, commuter rail service to Mission on the north shore of the Fraser River, and designated bus lanes on some commuter routes did little to assuage discontent.

The emergence of Vancouver as an international city encouraged British Columbians' historic tendency to conceive Canada in their own terms. As the 1992 referendum revealed, priorities put in place elsewhere in the national interest did not necessarily resonate in 'the west beyond the west' that was British Columbia. Political scientist Norman Ruff reflected during the referendum campaign: 'I think there's a sense that British Columbia is a sovereign entity behind the mountains.' 'You push a British Columbian and ultimately you find a Canadian. But in day-to-day life they're British Columbians and the rest of the country is essentially irrelevant.' A bit earlier fellow political scientist Terry Morley queried whether 'British Columbia would be better off out of Canada.' 'In this province there are lots of circumspect folk to believe that B.C. always grabs the skinny end of the Confederation stick.' As put by a columnist in the province's most influential newspaper, the *Vancouver Sun*, in 1995: 'B.C. remains a political outsider in Ottawa. This province is three time zones and a world away from the central Canadian hub we call the federal government.'[23] In late 1995, following the narrow defeat of a Quebec referendum on sovereignty, British Columbians indignantly demanded their own regional veto over changes to the Canadian Constitution similar to that being proposed for Quebec, Ontario, Atlantic Canada, and 'the west.' Then, when the province was designated a fifth distinct region within Canada, British Columbians only used the sequence of events to buttress their long-held conviction that the national government little understood, or cared, about them. Shifts in the economy, the province's changing social demography, and the internationalization of culture encouraged such thinking.

Not only did some British Columbians feel strongly about personal and provincial autonomy, but regional loyalties competed. 'Cascadia' took its impetus from 'ecotopia,' one of the 'nine nations' of North America popularized by Joel Garreau in the early 1980s.[24] Conceived as a cultural, economic, and perhaps even political union across the Pacific Northwest built on a shared landscape and environmental sensitivity, the dream of Cascadia bubbled up from time to time during the first half of the 1990s. Free trade, the open skies agreement, and revival of rail service between Vancouver and Seattle encouraged its proponents. Shortly before the 1992 vote Ruff explained that

British Columbians felt able to reject the pro-nation rhetoric because they 'have the sense that this is really the Promised Land.' If Canada did not work out, there were always other 'other options' such as Cascadia.[25]

British Columbians anticipated the twenty-first century with a combination of self-confidence and trepidation. Despite a new vitality, serious issues agitated many minds. Long-time residents fretted that the province they knew as children was disappearing. New British Columbians might fuel the economy through consumer spending and job creation, but they also put their stamp on a place that they too called home. Migration and immigration depended on forces beyond the province's control, just as did the economy as a whole. Boom and bust were still the order of the day. Economic and environmental sustainability remained elusive. So did resolution of aboriginal land claims and, more generally, respect for British Columbia's first peoples. The NDP in power had set a new direction, but the survival of their initiatives was uncertain beyond the next provincial election, slated for 1996. And that election would be fought by a new premier and party leader, Harcourt having resigned in late 1995 amid criticism of his leadership style. Greater Vancouver's growing identification with Eurasian sophistication, wealth, and privilege seemed destined to widen the gap between the city and the bush. The more British Columbians looked towards the Pacific Rim, the more the rest of Canada receded into irrelevance. As a new century approached, British Columbia promised to continue to be an exciting, if at times troubling, place in which to live and work.

15

The British Columbia Identity

The province of British Columbia has been home to indigenous peoples for countless generations, to Europeans and other non-natives for almost two centuries. Out of their experiences a British Columbia identity emerges. British Columbians are not bound together by geographic coherence. Nor can they be so, given the province's difficult topography and the differing character of its ten regions. But a cohesive physical entity need not exist for there to be a distinct identity. Shared attitudes also draw people together. So do strong visual images that strike residents and visitors alike. British Columbia is not so much a place as a state of mind. Whether members of the dominant society or of a slighted minority, residents of Canada's west coast province are joined by what Emily Carr aptly termed 'British Columbia seeing.'[1]

British Columbia hovers on the edge of a continent. Mountains cut off most of the province on the east, an inhospitable environment on the north, an ocean to the west, and another nation on the south. Compared to most of the western world, non-native settlement is very recent. Even a hundred and fifty years ago British Columbia contained only a handful of fur traders together with first peoples possessed of distinctive cultures. It took extraordinary events – the lure of gold, a transcontinental railway, a federal immigration campaign, the Depression – to bring large numbers of Europeans and Canadians to the Pacific Northwest.

But British Columbia also attracted a sizeable portion of its population not so much because of its remoteness but because of its proximity. The first human inhabitants crossed over a land bridge from Siberia. Kanakas travelled from Hawaii to work for the Hudson's Bay Company. The most persevering of the gold miners came from China, as did the labour for British Columbia's rail link with the rest of Canada. Resource exploitation long depended on Asian workers; so did many European households. Most recently, men, women, and finance from Hong Kong and elsewhere in Asia are making British Columbia their home. By 1991 the proportion of British Columbians who were Asian by descent had risen to one in eight, surpassing the earlier high of one in nine at the beginning of the twentieth century (see Table 5).

Many of those finding their way to the Pacific Northwest came as adventurers. Some soon departed, but others remained. In 1850 John Sebastian Helmcken was offered an appointment as Hudson's Bay surgeon after spending time in Bombay, Hong Kong, Canton, and Singapore. 'I had become a wanderer and wanted to see things.' On inquiring 'Where on earth is Vancouver Island?' Helmcken was informed that it was in the Pacific with 'a climate like that of England.' He accepted primarily for the excitement. 'Have I always been a frivolous butterfly? Always flying from sweet to sweet.'[2] Helmcken became a leading politician in colonial British Columbia and one of the principal negotiators of its entry into Confederation.

For some, the west coast province represented the end of the line, figuratively as well as literally. The land stopped. Not without reason, a gold miner entitled his memoir 'Very Far West Indeed.' Emily Carr recalled a couple from central Canada who began to move west. 'They travelled right across Canada, on, on, till they came to Vancouver and the end of the rail.' Then the wife asked, '"Now there is no further to go, can we get our house?" "There is still Vancouver Island," he said.' In the 1950s Alvin Balkind and Abraham Rogatnick 'resolved to get as far as their money would take them from McCarthyite America.' They made it all the way to Vancouver, where they established successful careers as, respectively, art critic and professor of architecture. For the protagonist in Margaret Atwood's *Cat's Eye*, British Columbia was 'as far away from Toronto as I could get without drowning.' Or, as the writer Peter C. Newman put it, it is 'as far as you can escape to, and still have medicare.'[3]

British Columbia's vast emptiness, what forester-novelist Allerdale Grainger termed 'the great charm of life in uncivilized parts,' has sometimes been its attraction. A Skeena pioneer 'delighted in a freedom that comes only in an untouched land.' British Columbia promised escape from the world, be it for religious reasons as with Doukhobors and Mennonites, adventure as with Richmond Hobson and Arthur Shelford, the moral regeneration sought by Scandinavian idealists and many of the 1960s enthusiasts, or simply for the pleasure, as with genteel Britons. Bruce Hutchison once observed that 'from the beginning it was the land of men who wanted to get away from everything, to start afresh, to be on their own.' In the words of *Raincoast Chronicles* creator Howard White, 'What you have here is a pattern of settlement which tended to attract people who were unhappy where they were before and wanted something different. They moved on and eventually ended up on the West Coast, each with their own different little program for solving the universe's problems.'[4]

British Columbians have for the most part been content to be set apart. Shortly after moving to the west coast province in 1892, Charles Mair complained to a close friend in Ontario how 'the feeling is "British Columbia," – first, last & always ... It is a Province *sui generis*, each valley with its little secluded community, shut off until yesterday from the outer world.'[5] Until the Second World War many who had never left the province of their birth spoke with a modified English accent. Their second tongue was very possibly Chinook, long used as an everyday means of communication between natives and non-natives. A sense of autonomy early on became part of the British Columbia identity.

The same physical features that have restricted outside contact determined that natural resources would be the basis of British Columbia's economy. The province's rich endowment proved to be both a blessing and a curse. Providing a decent living for generations of British Columbians, the plenitude of natural resources also ensured dependence on external markets and capital. The structure of the economy has remained relatively unchanged from the arrival of the first Europeans. All that alters are the names of the particular staples being exploited, the ownership of the means of production, and the countries to which they go. Even a rapidly developing tourist industry is premised on external demand and on the province's setting, hence the slogans 'Beautiful British Columbia' and 'Super Natural British Columbia.' The entire province except for southern Vancouver Island and the lower mainland remains for the most part a resource frontier.

The priorities of international capitalism set the pace and direction of development. From the earliest years of European penetration, the finance necessary for exploitation of the land and sea came almost wholly from outside of British Columbia. Ships taking away sea otter skins were registered in London and Boston, the companies trading in pelts headquartered in Montreal and London. As gold mining became more complex during the early 1860s, so enthusiasts such as Donald Fraser of *The Times* of London set about selling the Pacific Northwest as 'a fit subject for the capitalists of England.'[6] The young province was no different. Britons invested in coal mining, salmon canning, and streetcar lines; central Canadians underwrote railways; Americans dominated lumbering. Local entrepreneurs such as the Dunsmuirs, B.T. Rogers, and the Woodwards were notable for their paucity.[7] It is from this combination of circumstances that a common perception forming part of the British Columbia identity – its supposed plunder by uncaring outside interests – derives.

In reality British Columbians have participated just as enthusiastically as have outsiders in the rape of their natural heritage. The mentality of the gold rush did not disappear with British Columbia's entry into Confederation. As teacher Jessie McQueen noted in 1891, 'everybody is on the lookout for a chance to make something.' The young province was early carved up by speculators with the strong encouragement of the provincial government. The sentiment extended across the society, from establishment Victoria and Vancouver to the small-time logger in *Woodsmen of the West* who 'was going to butcher the woods as he pleased. It paid!'[8] The later twentieth century has been little different; it is epitomized by the appeal of the Vancouver Stock Exchange, whose specialization in venture capital only institutionalizes and legitimizes a get-rich-quick mentality.

To a considerable extent, the British Columbian economy influenced the contours of political and social life. Elections were most often fought, as Bruce Hutchison noted, on an assurance of 'unlimited resources, boundless future, no need to conserve or think about tomorrow.' Governments repeatedly overspent during any boom, be it the gold rush overseen by James Douglas, Richard McBride's prosperity of early this century, or the post-war surge under W.A.C. Bennett. They each wanted to believe that, by creating easier access to resources and otherwise encouraging their utilization, the good times could be made to go on forever. The next downturn became all the more severe, not just for government but for thousands of individual

British Columbians. Grainger's protagonist in *Woodsmen of the West*, the wandering Carter, had no sooner set himself up on the British Columbian coast than his small logging company was 'tottering through no fault of theirs, shaken by some tremor in the New York money-quake.'[9] Again and again, British Columbians have faced Carter's dilemma. Prosperity and vulnerability go hand in hand.

Little incentive has existed for governments to initiate structural change. The consequence would only be greater financial burdens on entrepreneurs forced to compete in an uncertain world economy. Thus the province lacked a university or even a teachers' training college after virtually every comparable jurisdiction in North America had them. Social reform was initiated not by politicians but by middle-class female reformers, social gospellers, and working people. It took the Depression and then the Second World War to jolt the state into decisive action.

Similarly, the perception that resource exploitation would provide an inexhaustible source of wealth only slowly lost its power. While a few individuals had long been concerned over depleted mines, fished-out rivers, and devastated forests, it was not until the 1970s that diverse groups within British Columbia became seriously worried about reforestation, fish enhancement, and conservation generally. It was then that Greenpeace, one of the most fervent environmental movements anywhere, emerged in British Columbia. From its foundation to the fight to preserve old-growth forest in Clayoquot Sound, men and women from the province have led the way in moving the balance away from exploitation for immediate gain to long-term economic and environmental sustainability.

Historically, provincial governments have been little concerned with a broader vision of what British Columbia might become, were they to venture beyond the immediate demands of a resource-based economy. To look to the long term was to risk political suicide. Competing interests were simply too entrenched, too far apart, and too convinced of their own points of view. A strong populist strain in provincial politics legitimized sniping at the government, whatever the party in power, as the New Democratic Party discovered to its chagrin when it attempted significant change in the early 1990s. This, too, is part of the British Columbia identity.

In the populist tradition, strong leaders rather than ideas have dominated political life. James Douglas single-handedly shaped the two British colonies whence the future province emerged. Richard

McBride, Duff Pattullo, and the elder Bennett each governed in good part through their capacity to bring together a loyal following. Political parties entered provincial life only as population growth made impossible earlier personal alliances. The two parties were identified with different approaches to power. The Conservatives favoured unrestricted capitalism, the Liberals embodied a reform tradition. Yet the three changes occurring between the two parties prior to the formation of a governing coalition at the beginning of the Second World War each resulted primarily from non-ideological factors: the Conservatives were defeated in 1916 over persistent charges of corruption rising out of prewar prosperity, the Liberals remained in power until 1928 largely owing to Conservative dissension, in 1933 the Conservatives fell victim to the Depression as well as to internal disagreement.

The years following the formation in 1932 of the left-oriented Co-operative Commonwealth Federation underlined the extent to which the differences separating the two mainline parties possessed a superficial quality. Before the common enemy – a socialist menace perceived as disrupting a capitalist, free-enterprise status quo – Liberals and Conservatives joined forces, both on the provincial level and in British Columbia's principal city of Vancouver. Polarization may have been the inevitable consequence of an economy based on staples, without an autonomous middle sector. 'You can't grow up in British Columbia without becoming political. Either you get on the bandwagon and try to milk the land, or become a socialist – there seems to be no easy middle ground out here.'[10] The victory of the Social Credit party in 1952, which soon effectively absorbed both the provincial Liberals and Conservatives, only institutionalized the existing tendency. Except for a three-year hiatus, the Social Credit coalition maintained control into the last decade of the twentieth century. The CCF's successor, the NDP, gained power in 1972 and again in 1991 not because it captured the majority of the popular vote but because the governing centre-right coalition splintered. And perhaps the time had come for another flurry of reform to interrupt a comfortable status quo. With those two exceptions, each with a lasting legacy of change, the ideological left's very strength has served to maintain in power populist, coalitionist attitudes and policies a century and more old.

Equally critical to the British Columbia identity are the province's linkages with the larger world. Access has been easiest to the self-confident and determined nation to the south. From the first Boston traders, the American presence helped forge the identity of its northern neighbour. The international boundary was so determined, first through the Treaty of Washington and then by the Pig War. American proximity likely forced Britain's hand in the gold rush and encouraged British Columbia's entry into the young Canadian dominion. Ironically, had the United States presence been less daunting, the entire Pacific Northwest might have drifted into American hands.

While the National Policy determined that direct trade with the United States would be minimal, the American presence within the economy could not be restrained. Physical infrastructure, first the Cariboo Wagon Road and Dewdney Trail and then the Canadian Pacific Railway, were carefully routed to curtail American influence. In the words of historical geographer Cole Harris, 'politics overrode topography.'[11] It was shortly after the CPR contained American expansion into the Kootenays that the invasion from the south began in earnest. A massive influx of capital and entrepreneurship into forestry, mining, and other industries transformed the west coast province.

Over time, British Columbians learned to live with American proximity and found its consequences fairly prosaic. A young woman visiting Seattle from the Okanagan in 1911 noted in her diary: 'My first trip under the "Stars and Stripes." It is not so very different from our own country except that one sees the American flag flying every where and the ladies wear hats to the theatre and one can buy shoes for half the price and one uses gold and huge silver dollars instead of bills.' What developed was, in the view of three leading British Columbia scholars writing at the beginning of the Second World War, 'good-natured tolerance.' Fears of cultural and economic contamination that took centre stage in the rest of Canada after the war were as a consequence muted in the west coast province. Economist Anthony Scott offered an intriguing explanation in 1972. 'The nationalistic exercise is salutary for thinkers in central Canada, as a sort of psychoanalysis, renewed in every generation. The present "political disintegration" which they deplore, and blame on foreign political and economic control, would lead to more concern on the west coast if the integration they claim to seek had once been a transcontinental reality.'[12]

Historical circumstances determined that the other principal direction in which British Columbians would look was to Britain. While such identification only reflected the norm across English Canada, the relationship stood apart in being direct rather than filtered through a Canadian lens. British ways were not transplanted into British Columbia because they existed elsewhere in Canada. The link was with Britain itself. British Columbia began its political life as two British colonies. Early immigration came in good measure from Britain, be it Nanaimo coal miners or Okanagan apple growers. British Columbians quit driving on the left in 1922 not because emotional ties lessened but simply because of the expansion of roads leading south and east. Through the inter-war years the only source of news for the Shelford family in the central interior was the London *Times*, sent out by relatives in England. Like numerous counterparts across the province, young Cyril recollected that by the age of fourteen he 'knew the name of every prime minister, foreign minister or dictator in Europe,' but nothing about British Columbia.[13] It was not so much that British Columbians consciously thought of themselves as British but simply that certain assumptions persisted, together with the quiet knowledge that the province was, after all, *British* Columbia. As the province's demography altered from mid century, an explicit British ethos largely disappeared, elements of it being subsumed within the British Columbia identity.

In contrast, British Columbians long remained ambivalent towards the nation of which they had been a part since 1871. British Columbia was pushed into Confederation, in the end submitting voluntarily on being offered economic plums its leaders could not afford to refuse. Helmcken summed up common knowledge in his observation that 'this Colony had no love for Canada; the bargain for love could not be; it can only be the advancement of material interest which will lead to union.' Confederation's most ardent proponent, Amor de Cosmos, publicly declared himself 'a British Columbian first and a Canadian second.'[14]

Historian Keith Ralston has viewed the first decade and a half in Confederation as critical in forming attitudes towards Canada as a whole. 'A settled community grew up on the Pacific coast and in the valleys and plateaus of the Western Cordillera which owed next to nothing to any link with the Canadas, and practically everything to its oceanic ties to the rest of the world ... It is the existence of this self-conscious community which dictated the nature of the initial struggles within the new federation and which called forth and hardened attitudes in British Columbia to the central government of the federation, attitudes basically unchanged to this day.'[15]

For a time following the CPR's arrival and with it settlers from Ontario and elsewhere, it seemed as if John A. Macdonald's prediction that 'the railway will at once Canadianize the Province' was being borne out. Considerable capital came from within Canada. Yet, with some exceptions, such as lumber dispatched to the prairies, the world rather than Canada was the destination for most of British Columbia's staple products. To the extent that the province was linked eastward, the chain grew weak once it extended beyond Manitoba. W.A.C. Bennett used British Columbians' ambivalence to political advantage. In almost the same breath his speeches juxtaposed such lines as 'we believe in the Canadian dream, Ocean to Ocean' and 'we're the only part of Canada that really could go it alone [as] the Dominion of British Columbia.'[16]

British Columbian governments repeatedly sought to rewrite the terms of union, the first time short years after 1871 on news of the promised railway's delay. The quest for better terms became a recurrent theme of political life, having as convenient bases the National Policy and discriminatory freight rates. While a rich abundance of staples encouraged resource dependency, the National Policy, together with British Columbia's location on the periphery, ensured that such would be the case. The Depression heightened British Columbians' belief that Canada as a whole did not understand – or even attempt to understand – its particular circumstances. Politicians and populace alike were convinced that the thousands of unemployed who flocked west to British Columbia were a federal responsibility. The post-war controversy over Columbia River water rights again pitted the two levels of government against each other. Back to Ralston: 'The cumulative effect of economic and political trends was to increase the isolation and self-preoccupation of British Columbia within the Canadian federation.' The attitude of many British Columbians was summed up in the popular aphorism variously attributed to Vancouver's mayor of the mid 1930s, Gerry McGeer, and to W.A.C. Bennett. 'It's 2,500 miles from Vancouver to Ottawa, but 25,000 from Ottawa to Vancouver.'[17]

Historian Walter Sage mused in 1945 that 'British Columbians do not seem to have played any large part at Ottawa.' Provincial political leaders did not as a rule seek a federal arena. Richard McBride was a case in point; he twice refused invitations, first to assume leadership of the national Conservative party and then to enter the federal cabinet. Ottawa held little attraction for him; he 'preferred to devote his entire energies to British Columbia and to look to London as his spiritual home.'[18] The argument has two sides: in late 1989 former premier David Barrett was defeated for the national leadership of the New Democratic Party in part because he was perceived as possessing only regional appeal.

Sage's observation was echoed by Hutchison in his assertion that British Columbia has 'never produced a national idea or statesman of importance.'[19] The three partial exceptions testify to Hutchison's acuity. The first two prime ministers holding federal seats in British Columbia – John A. Macdonald who sat for Victoria in 1878–82 after being defeated in his Ontario constituency and John Turner who won in Vancouver in 1984 as part of an unsuccessful national campaign to retain the office of prime minister – did so only out of political expediency, not as a logical consequence of an earlier career in provincial politics or even in national politics as a representative of British Columbia. In 1991 Vancouver MP Kim Campbell assumed the post of prime minister on winning the leadership of a Progressive Conservative party which was in a state of disarray. Just a few months later Campbell and the party went down to inglorious defeat. British Columbia still hovers on the edge of a nation. And so too is the British Columbian's identity formed.

However far British Columbians might sometimes feel themselves to be from the centres of power in Canada, the province shared in the new Canadian vitality and self-confidence given its impetus by the Second World War. A national flag, Canada's centennial, and the patriation of the constitution encouraged a sense of unity. Today British Columbians listen to and watch the CBC, appreciate the productions of the National Film Board, and take pride in Canada's generally humane approach to international relations. Along with travel writer Jan Morris, British Columbians value Canada's 'goodness,' which 'shows itself in courtesies of everyday life, in social services, in the relative safety of the streets, in the general feeling that people care about one another and about their neighbourhoods.' As summed up by Roderick Haig-Brown, 'Canadian law is over all of us, a Canadian way of thought is ours. We shall hold them and build on them because we believe they have meaning and worth.'[20]

British Columbians are no less Canadian because they sometimes view Canada through a distant prism and do not necessarily agree, as revealed in the 1992 referendum, with decisions made elsewhere on their behalf. As Reform party leader Preston Manning remarked about British Columbia in 1995, 'It's a place for new ideas, where if you don't like something you do something to change it.' Former prime minister Kim Campbell observed that British Columbia brings 'an adventurous entrepreneurial spirit' to the rest of Canada.[21]

Ambivalence towards Canada as a whole is facilitated, perhaps made possible, by the existence of an alternative hub around which most lives willingly or unwillingly revolve. Even in the late twentieth century much of the west coast province lies uninhabited or thinly peopled with villages, towns, and a handful of regional urban centres strung out along transportation routes 'like occasional beads on long necklaces.'[22] One small area, British Columbia's southwestern tip, exercises tremendous, overwhelming influence.

Vancouver's succession to Victoria as metropolis to a vast hinterland was inevitable from the day the CPR made its decision on a western terminus. By the end of the nineteenth century the mainland city had taken charge. The Panama Canal only lengthened the spokes of a hub centred in Vancouver. So did the economic reality that most other British Columbia communities were linked only to a single staple, and thereby liable to its particular booms and busts. With the two notable exceptions of the Peace River area and the Kootenays, Vancouver became the service centre to the entire province and beyond. The economic transformation wrought under W.A.C. Bennett, while intended to open up the interior and the north, benefited British Columbia's southwestern tip even more. In forestry the government deliberately phased out small companies and with them local entrepreneurship in the interests of making multinational corporations more efficient. Innumerable small enclaves lost first their school, then their sawmill or cannery, likely their post office, and finally their separate identity.

The handful of regional urban centres that came to prominence after the Second World War did not challenge Vancouver's status as metropolis par excellence. Newspapers and television news programs around the province most often originate there. The city is the almost inevitable transit point to fly from one hinterland locale to the other or even to Victoria. Prince Rupert and Prince George are both located at about 54° just over five hundred air kilometres apart, yet flights linking the two go via Vancouver at 49° for a total of almost thirteen hundred kilometres.

Economists Craig Davis and Thomas Hutton have theorized that Vancouver's dominance only builds on itself, the differential with the rest of the province ever widening. 'The service-orientation of the Greater Vancouver economy results in a greater measure of economic stability as well as a significantly greater growth potential.' Such dominance generates substantial 'leakages to the core, especially with respect to financial and business services.' Every working day experts and service personnel by the hundreds wing their way in commuter fashion from Vancouver to the rest of the province. 'This is partially attributable to the lack of a major, second-order business centre within the hinterland which can provide specialized commercial services: there is instead a number of third- and fourth-order centres (Prince George, Kamloops, Kelowna).'[23] Even though Victoria is the provincial capital, it might be added to that number. For very many British Columbians it has often seemed that, while it is 'x' distance from their home town to Vancouver, it is ten times that far in the other direction.

For hinterland British Columbians, the imperatives of everyday life differ in substantial ways from those animating the metropolis. More people in the north travel by bush plane than by jet. In remote areas of the province some time each day is still given over to free radio messages to persons beyond direct communication, beyond even the telephone. 'To Joe at the Dew's Ranch, the pickup rear axle is broken. Please borrow Sam's car.' 'To Mary: your mum is in hospital. She says, please go visit her.' 'To the chiefs and managers of all the Fort St John Indian bands: there will be a meeting at the Friendship Centre on Tuesday afternoon.' Urban pretensions fall by the wayside. Writing in the early 1930s about the newly settled Peace, Monica Storrs was amazed that 'appearances really *do* seem to be nothing. The men can look like tramps or cowboys or mechanics or bank-managers, nobody notices. The women can go out in fur coats or silk dresses and fleshy stockings or breeches and heavy boots – nobody notices.' A Prince George resident made much the same point half a century later in her observation that, unlike the lower mainland, it is possible 'to shop in work clothes and have respect ... People are still in touch. You move into a new house and the neighbours are over the first night, their children the second day, and you are socializing by the weekend.'[24]

The British Columbia identity is also shaped on the level of individual lives by the critical triad of gender, class, and race. The inequitable relationship long existing between males and females across the western world was refined in the case of the west coast province by their sharply differing numbers. For every non-native adult female, there were three times as many males up to the end of the nineteenth century, over twice as many through the end of the First World War. Only since have women acquired rough parity. What existed was in many ways a truly male culture. The character of such occupations as fur trading, gold mining, ranching, logging, and fishing encouraged an adventurous frontier spirit. So did unlimited opportunities for sport and other forms of outdoor recreation. Prohibition's short duration testified to British Columbia being a man's province.

Yet, in the larger scale of things, women may not have fared that badly. The social reform movement achieved notable successes. As biographer Irene Howard demonstrated, change came because women like Helena Gutteridge went about their business quietly but also confidently and persistently.[25] Plummeting birth rates testify to women's independent will, as does growing sensitivity to inequities based in gender. Even if both were only briefly in office, the first female premier in Canada and the first female Canadian prime minister came from British Columbia. They succeeded male leaders whose high levels of voter disaffection they were meant to overcome, in part by virtue of their gender; they then suffered in the subsequent election for the very same reason, as well as other factors. Gender remains a double-edged sword in British Columbia and in Canada.

Class and class antagonisms have been fundamental in shaping the British Columbia identity. The scarcity of arable land deprived the province of a middle sector in the form of farmers and small-town entrepreneurs acting as a buffer between capital and labour. As early as 1867 a visitor observed that 'adventurers in political science will find in Nanaimo an excellent field for the study of the first principles of political economy,' because of 'the absence of the usual intermediate social elements betwixt the employer and the employed.' A Vancouver Island coal miner offered promotion at work recalled: 'When I accepted the job of superintendent I knew that a thin line would separate me from my underground workmates and miner friends. I was now on the other side of the fence, and one basic tenet of labour, embedded by hundreds of years of class warfare, was that workers do not fraternize with the bosses.'[26]

For a time Karl Marx's prediction of inevitable conflict between the owners of capital and those with only their labour to sell appeared to be borne out in British Columbia. Open confrontation in the work place was perceived by many as the sole means by which to force employers to make concessions. During the first two decades of the twentieth century, the province was in the forefront of the struggle for recognition of the right of workers to join together into unions. Strikes, buttressed by the ballot box, seemed for a time to be the order of the day.

Moreover, class consciousness did not develop in British Columbia only from the bottom up. The presence of middle-class Britons, from Hudson's Bay officers to gentlemen emigrants, ensured that notions of class, so much a part of the older society, would also be transplanted from the top down. The private schools and other institutions of social exclusivity that these men and women recreated in British Columbia were soon co-opted by their counterparts of Canadian background, extending notions of class-based superiority across the dominant society.

Whatever the ways in which antagonisms between employer and employee emerged and were exacerbated, over time they also moderated. In British Columbia, as elsewhere in Canada, many wage labourers were recent immigrants. They came, not to retain existing status, but in search of upward mobility. Painter Jack Shadbolt attributed his parent's emigration to British Columbia to their determination to escape a lower working-class life. 'No matter how hard the going, my sister and I were to grow up to be a lady and gentleman – the bourgeois dream.' Such aspirations sometimes muted willingness to identify over the long term with a separate working class. As immigrants garnered the resources necessary to find a spouse and start a family, they developed a stake in the society as it existed rather than as radical reformers would have it become. Many men and women took pride in their work. Jobs in resource industries, even those based in hard manual labour, demanded considerable skill and expertise. To handle a seiner or steam donkey was no easy task. A coal miner observed that his contemporaries generally sought no other work. 'Despite sometimes trying conditions, most of them – particularly the middle-aged and older men – were quite content with their lot.'[27] Employers sometimes took the initiative. In company towns and other resource communities they recognized workers' desire for family stability and built upon that longing – in effect made material concessions – in order to co-opt employees rather than have to confront them in trade unions.

Following the Second World War the union movement entered the mainstream, consolidating its position as a strong voice for working people. That voice became less shrill owing, some would argue, to the growth of business unions, of bureaucracies in effect sharing power with employees to dominate the lives of working people. According to political scientist Donald Blake, 'the terms "left" and "right" have lost their traditional meanings both in terms of policy positions they are intended to describe and the class interests to which they once appealed.' Shortly after taking power under the Social Credit banner in 1975, the younger Bennett acknowledged, 'we are a populist party slightly to the right of centre. The NDP is a populist party slightly to the left.'[28] Both parties represented coalitions of voters believing that their voice had a right to be heard. The collapse across the western world of planned economies, and of their left-oriented political underpinnings, virtually ensured that the NDP in power in the 1990s would act more moderately than had its predecessor two decades earlier. In British Columbia populism cuts across the political spectrum, and classes as Marx defined them and as they have most often been conceived recede in significance.

The importance of class in shaping British Columbia's identity has been paralleled or surpassed by that of race and ethnicity. British Columbia was long the most overtly racist province in Canada simply by virtue of possessing the overwhelming majority of individuals against whom almost all Canadians of the dominant society would just as eagerly have discriminated. Any individuals, not just Asians, who did not conform to a stereotype formed in Canadians' own image were unacceptable. But the force of race in shaping the British Columbia identity went beyond the particular groups doing the discriminating or being discriminated against. To a significant extent it was race that helped create and maintain the province as a place apart. British Columbians of the dominant society were long convinced that they possessed a unique problem not understood by the federal government or by other Canadians. The most racist of the actions taken in the west coast province – the head tax on Chinese arrivals, rejection of the *Komagata Maru*, Japanese evacuation – each contributed to a sense of autonomy. Only after mid century did attitudes moderate in the dominant society. The tendency for new arrivals to be better educated and more sophisticated than the host society has played a role, but so have changing attitudes more generally across Canada and the world.

The dominant society's ambivalence towards racial minorities has been especially visible with British Columbia's first peoples. Coming to terms with the province's indigenous population has been extra-ordinarily difficult. Reduced in numbers and pushed to the margins, Indian peoples nonetheless survived. 'More than anywhere else, we have maintained our culture here, and our native bonds with each other.'[29] From mid century an aboriginal presence reasserted itself. The major goal has become economic and cultural self-sufficiency through settlement of land claims. Resolution at some point in time is inevitable, and so too will the British Columbia identity be forged.

Even as the dominant society struggles to come to terms with the province's first peoples, such decisions are being taken out of both their hands. No longer is it a case of 'we' and 'they' but rather of 'us' altogether in this place called British Columbia. As put by a Vancouver community newspaper, 'There is no going back in time for any of us, no matter how just the cause or how much we might yearn for it.' The province remains the only one in Canada where newcomers outnumber locally-born residents, and it will almost certainly continue to be so. Groups once considered outside of the province's social and cultural mainstream, those who have in historian Hugh Johnston's phrase 'lived between two cultures,' increasingly shape and reshape the British Columbia identity from within.[30] One measure is participation in public life, exemplified by David Lam's successful tenure as lieutenant-governor and by the electibility of MLAS and MPs of diverse cultural and racial backgrounds.

Another measure is the willingness with which British Columbians have shared life experiences once considered exceptional, made them ordinary, and have thereby made them part of a common identity. In the film *My American Cousin* Sandy Wilson evoked growing up at mid century in the highly anglophile Okanagan Valley; in *Double Happiness* Vancouver's Mina Shum used humour to reveal generational tensions in a contemporary Chinese-Canadian household. Sarjeet Singh Jagpal interviewed his parents' generation to retrieve the everyday lives of Sikh immigrants intent on 'becoming Canadian.'[31] Denise Chong wrote unsparingly about her grandmother and mother in *The Concubine's Children*, Tara Singh Bains opened up his own life in *The Four Quarters of the Night*.[32] Okanagan and Bella Coola storytellers Harry Robinson and Clayton Mack, Carrier and Haida elders Mary John and Florence Edenshaw Davidson, and Kwakiutl and Squamish chiefs Harry Assu and Simon Baker are among the many native people who have shared their lives in print.[33] British Columbia's diversity of peoples has become integral to the province's identity.

So too has British Columbia's diversity of landscape. The longtime licence plate tag, 'Beautiful British Columbia,' resonates whatever the locale. Be the view out of a Vancouver highrise or a north coast kitchen, the natural world intrudes. The raw physical features long isolating British Columbians from each other and from the larger world have become a precious commodity. On a rainy British Columbia Day 1995, talk show host and former provincial politician Rafe Mair summed up many British Columbians' perspective: 'I love its beauty, I have a feeling for its isolation, I like its culture, ... I love its weather except for today, I just love British Columbia.'[34]

In the final analysis, the British Columbia identity goes beyond economics or politics or human and spatial diversity. A certain irrationality intrudes. Emily Carr repeatedly agonized over the character of her native province. It was only in middle age that 'I stopped grieving about the isolation of the West. I believe now I was glad we were cut off.' Carr struggled to make sense of British Columbia. 'There is something bigger than fact: the underlying spirit, all it stands for, the mood, the vastness, the wildness, the Western breath of go-to-the-devil-if-you-don't-like-it, the eternal big spaceness of it. Oh the West! I'm of it and I love it.' Returning home by train, she penned in her journal: 'All night the demon monster has been rushing us into the West ... It is all West now, no trace of East left – low sky, dense growth, bursting, cruel rivers, power and intensity everywhere.'[35]

Carr has not been alone in searching for British Columbia. Bruce Hutchison once observed: 'Crossing the Rockies, you are in a new country, as if you had crossed a national frontier. Everyone feels it, even the stranger, feels the change of outlook, tempo, and attitude ... We cannot go back to our old homes east of the mountains. In our hearts we never recross that barrier.' Ethel Wilson reminisced in old age: 'I have a life-long love for this province of ours which I share with many people, this British Columbia, as if it were a person, as it is and a person of infinite variety and inference.' 'There are other places in the world that I know and love, but none that I know, and feel, and love in the same way. But I did not choose it. It chose. It is very strong.' For native leader Leonard George, 'if there is still an Eden in the world, it would be British Columbia.'[36]

The British Columbia identity builds on a rich and diverse history. Over time British Columbians have come to share attributes encouraging a distinctive outlook. No one perspective, be it geographic, economic, political, or social, is sufficient to interpret this west beyond the west. Yet each contributes to an understanding of the whole, to why British Columbia is and remains a place unto itself. The passage of time continues to exercise its force in shaping British Columbia. As today's issues enter the history books of tomorrow, so the British Columbia identity is constructed, deconstructed, and reconstructed.

Tables

TABLE 1
Colonial Governors of Vancouver Island and British Columbia

	Appointed	Sworn in	Last year in office
Vancouver Island			
Blanshard, Richard	1849	1850	1851
Douglas, James	1851	1851	1864
Kennedy, Arthur	1863	1864	1866
British Columbia			
Douglas, James	1858	1858	1864
Seymour, Frederick	1864	1864	1866
United Colony of British Columbia			
Seymour, Frederick	1866	1866	1869
Musgrave, Anthony	1869	1870	1871

TABLE 2
Premiers of British Columbia, 1871–1903

	Sworn in	Left office	Reason
McCreight, John Foster	1871	1872	No-confidence vote
de Cosmos, Amor	1872	1874	To run federally
Walkem, George Anthony	1874	1876	No-confidence vote
Elliott, Andrew Charles	1876	1878	Electoral defeat
Walkem, George Anthony	1878	1882	Judicial appointment
Beaven, Robert	1882	1883	No-confidence vote
Smithe, William	1883	1887	Died
Davie, Alexander Edmund Batson	1887	1889	Died
Robson, John	1889	1892	Died
Davie, Theodore	1892	1895	Judicial appointment
Turner, John Herbert	1895	1898	Electoral defeat
Semlin, Charles Augustus	1898	1900	Lack of support
Martin, Joseph	1900	1900	Lack of support
Dunsmuir, James	1900	1902	Resigned
Prior, Edward Gawler	1902	1903	Conflict of interest

SOURCE: *Electoral History of British Columbia 1871–1986* (Victoria: Elections British Columbia 1988), 545–6

TABLE 3
Premiers of British Columbia, 1903–1996

	Sworn in	Left office	Reason	Party affiliation
McBride, Richard	1903	1915	Other appointment	Conservative
Bowser, William John	1915	1916	Party electoral defeat	Conservative
Brewster, Harlan Carey	1916	1918	Died	Liberal
Oliver, John	1918	1927	Died	Liberal
MacLean, John Duncan	1927	1928	Party and personal electoral defeat	Liberal
Tolmie, Simon Fraser	1928	1933	Party and personal electoral defeat	Conservative
Pattullo, Thomas Dufferin	1933	1941	Resigned as party leader	Liberal
Hart, John	1941	1947	Resigned as party leader	Coalition (Liberal)
Johnson, Byron Ingemar	1947	1952	Party and personal electoral defeat	Coalition (Liberal)
Bennett, William Andrew Cecil	1952	1972	Party electoral defeat	Social Credit
Barrett, David	1972	1975	Party and personal electoral defeat	New Democratic
Bennett, William Richard	1975	1986	Resigned as party leader	Social Credit
Vander Zalm, William Nick	1986	1991	Resigned as premier	Social Credit
Johnston, Rita Margaret	1991	1991	Party electoral defeat	Social Credit
Harcourt, Michael Franklin	1991	1996	Resigned as party leader	New Democratic

SOURCES: *Electoral History of British Columbia 1871–1986* (Victoria: Elections British Columbia 1988), 546–7; and *Canadian Who's Who 1993*, vol. 28 (Toronto: University of Toronto Press).

TABLE 4
Summary of Vote in Provincial Elections in British Columbia, 1903–1995

	Votes	%	Members
1903			
Conservative Party	27,913	46.4	22
Liberal Party	22,715	37.8	17
Socialist Party of BC	4,787	8.0	2
Labour Party	4,421	7.4	1
Other left-oriented parties	284	0.5	0
Totals	60,120		42
1907			
Conservative Party	30,781	48.7	26
Liberal Party	23,481	37.2	13
Socialist Party of Canada	5,603	8.9	3
Other left-oriented groups	3,193	5.1	0
Independent	147	0.2	0
Totals	63,205		42
1909			
Conservative Party	53,074	52.3	38
Liberal Party	33,675	33.2	2
Socialist Party of Canada	11,665	11.5	2
Other left-oriented groups	222	0.2	0
Other groups	154	0.2	0
Independent	2,625	2.6	0
Totals	101,415		42
1912			
Conservative Party	50,423	59.7	39
Liberal Party	21,443	25.4	1
Socialist Party of Canada	9,366	11.1	1
Independent and others	3,297	3.9	1
Totals	84,529		42
1916			
Conservative Party	72,842	40.5	9
Liberal Party	89,892	50.0	36
Socialist Party of Canada	2,106	1.2	0
Other left-oriented parties	5,318	3.0	1
Other parties	4,690	2.6	0
Independent	4,296	2.7	1
Totals	179,774		47

TABLE 4 (continued)

	Votes	%	Members
1920			
Conservative Party	110,475	31.2	15
Liberal Party	134,167	37.9	25
Soldier-Farmer/Labour	10,780	3.0	0
Federated Labour Party	32,230	9.1	3
Socialist Party of Canada	12,386	3.5	0
Other left-oriented parties	1,803	0.5	1
Other parties	15,511	4.4	0
Independent	36,736	10.4	3
Totals	354,088		47
1924			
Conservative Party	101,765	29.5	17
Liberal Party	108,323	31.3	23
Provincial Party	83,517	24.2	3
Canadian Labour Party	39,044	11.3	3
Socialist Party of Canada	4,364	1.3	0
Other left-oriented parties	478	0.1	0
Other parties	5,595	1.6	2
Independent	2,520	0.7	0
Totals	345,606		48
1928			
Conservative Party	192,867	53.3	35
Liberal Party	144,872	40.0	12
Independent Labour Party	17,908	5.0	1
Other left-oriented parties	316	0.1	0
Other parties	2,193	0.6	0
Independent	3,658	1.0	0
Totals	361,814		48
1933			
Liberal Party	159,131	41.7	34
Non-Partisan Independent Group	38,836	10.2	2
Unionist Party	15,445	4.1	1
Independent Conservative	7,114	1.9	0
Co-operative Commonwealth Federation	120,185	31.5	7
Other left-oriented parties	4,993	1.3	0
Other parties	6,013	1.6	1
Independent	29,506	7.7	2
Totals	381,223		47

TABLE 4 (continued)

	Votes	%	Members
1937			
Conservative Party	119,521	28.6	8
Liberal Party	156,074	37.3	31
Social Credit League of BC	4,812	1.2	0
Co-operative Commonwealth Federation	119,400	28.6	7
Other left-oriented parties	2,641	0.6	1
Other parties	8,140	1.9	0
Independent	7,341	1.8	1
Totals	417,929		48
1941			
Conservative Party	140,282	30.9	12
Liberal Party	149,525	32.9	21
Co-operative Commonwealth Federation	151,440	33.4	14
Other left-oriented parties	7,880	1.7	1
Other parties	3,128	0.7	0
Independent	1,638	0.4	0
Totals	453,893		48
1945			
Coalition (Liberal and Conservative parties)	261,147	55.8	37
Social Credit	6,627	1.4	0
Co-operative Commonwealth Federation	175,960	37.6	10
Labour Progressive Party	16,479	3.5	0
Other left-oriented parties	4,465	1.0	1
Other parties	1,431	0.3	0
Independent	1,532	0.3	0
Totals	467,641		48
1949			
Coalition (Liberal and Conservative parties)	428,773	61.4	39
Social Credit Party	8,464	1.2	0
BC Social Credit League	3,072	0.4	0
Co-operative Commonwealth Federation	245,284	35.1	7
Other left-oriented parties	3,899	0.6	1
Other parties	4,168	0.6	0
Independent	5,163	0.7	1
Totals	698,823		48

TABLE 4 (continued)

	Votes	%	Members
1952			
Social Credit Party	203,932	30.2	19
Progressive Conservative Party	65,285	9.7	4
Liberal Party	170,674	25.3	6
Co-operative Commonwealth Federation	231,756	34.3	18
Other left-oriented parties	2,689	0.4	1
Other parties	1,318	0.2	0
Totals	675,654		48
1953			
Social Credit Party	300,372	45.5	28
Progressive Conservative Party	7,326	1.1	1
Liberal Party	154,090	23.4	4
Co-operative Commonwealth Federation	194,414	29.5	14
Other left-oriented parties	2,609	0.4	1
Other parties	752	0.1	0
Totals	659,563		48
1956			
Social Credit Party	374,711	45.8	39
Progressive Conservative Party	25,373	3.1	0
Liberal Party	177,922	21.8	2
Co-operative Commonwealth Federation	231,511	28.3	10
Other left-oriented parties	4,702	0.6	1
Independent and other	3,178	0.4	0
Totals	817,397		52
1960			
Social Credit Party	386,886	38.8	32
Progressive Conservative Party	66,943	6.7	0
Liberal Party	208,249	20.9	4
Co-operative Commonwealth Federation	326,094	32.7	16
Communist Party	5,675	0.6	0
Independent	2,557	0.3	0
Totals	996,404		52
1963			
Social Credit Party	395,079	40.8	33
Progressive Conservative Party	109,090	11.3	0
Liberal Party	193,363	20.0	5

TABLE 4 (continued)

	Votes	%	Members
New Democratic Party	269,004	27.8	14
Independent and others	1,139	0.1	0
Totals	967,675		52
1966			
Social Credit Party	342,751	45.6	33
Progressive Conservative Party	1,409	0.2	0
Liberal Party	152,155	20.2	6
New Democratic Party	252,753	33.6	16
Independent and others	2,808	0.4	0
Totals	751,876		55
1969			
Social Credit Party	457,777	46.8	38
Progressive Conservative Party	1,087	0.1	0
Liberal Party	186,235	19.0	5
New Democratic Party	331,813	33.9	12
Independent and others	1,444	0.2	0
Totals	978,356		55
1972			
Social Credit Party	352,776	31.2	10
Progressive Conservative Party	143,450	12.7	2
Liberal Party	185,640	16.4	5
New Democratic Party	448,260	39.6	38
Independent and others	2,046	0.2	0
Totals	1,132,172		55
1975			
Social Credit Party	635,482	49.3	35
Progressive Conservative Party	49,796	3.9	1
Liberal Party	93,379	7.2	1
New Democratic Party	505,396	39.2	18
Independent and others	6,398	0.5	0
Totals	1,290,451		55
1979			
Social Credit Party	677,607	48.2	31
Progressive Conservative Party	71,078	5.1	0
Liberal Party	6,662	0.5	0
New Democratic Party	646,188	46.0	26
Independent and others	3,542	0.3	0
Totals	1,405,077		57

TABLE 4 (concluded)

	Votes	%	Members
1983			
Social Credit Party	820,807	49.8	35
Progressive Conservative Party	19,131	1.2	0
Liberal Party	44,442	2.7	0
Western Canada Concept	14,185	0.9	0
New Democratic Party	741,354	44.9	22
Independent and others	9,614	0.6	0
Totals	1,649,533		57
1986			
Social Credit Party	954,516	49.3	47
Progressive Conservative Party	14,074	0.7	0
Liberal Party	130,505	6.7	0
New Democratic Party	824,544	42.6	22
Independent and others	11,814	0.6	0
Totals	1,935,453		69
1991			
Social Credit Party	351,660	24.1	7
Progressive Conservative Party	426	0.0	0
Liberal Party	486,208	33.3	17
New Democratic Party	595,391	40.7	51
Green Party	12,650	0.9	0
Reform Party	2,673	0.2	0
Independent and others	13,459	0.9	0
Totals	1,462,467		75

SOURCES: *Electoral History of British Columbia 1871–1986* (Victoria: Elections British Columbia 1988), 546-7; and Chief Electoral Officer, *Statement of Votes* (Victoria: Elections British Columbia 1992), 13.

TABLE 5
British Columbia Population by Ethnic Origin, 1871–1991

	British	Continental European	Asian	Native Indian	Total
1871	8,576 (23.7%)		1,548 (4.3%)	est 25,661 (70.8%)	36,247
1881	14,660 (29.6%)	2,490 (5.0%)	4,350 (8.8%)	25,661 (51.9%)	49,459
1891	n.a.	n.a.	n.a.	est 27,305 (27.8%)	98,173
1901	106,403 (60.0%)	21,784 (12.2%)	19,524 (10.9%)	28,949 (16.2%)	178,657
1911	266,295 (67.8%)	69,799 (17.8%)	30,864 (7.9%)	20,174 (5.1%)	392,480
1921	387,513 (73.9%)	72,743 (13.9%)	39,739 (7.6%)	22,377 (4.3%)	524,582
1931	489,923 (70.7%)	127,246 (18.3%)	50,951 (7.3%)	24,599 (3.5%)	694,263
1941	571,336 (69.9%)	175,512 (21.5%)	42,472 (5.2%)	24,882 (3.0%)	817,861
1951	766,189 (65.8%)	319,056 (27.4%)	25,644 (2.2%)	28,504 (2.4%)	1,165,210
1961	966,881 (59.4%)	554,712 (34.1%)	40,299 (2.5%)	38,814 (2.4%)	1,629,082
1971	1,265,455 (57.9%)	767,808 (35.2%)	76,695 (3.5%)	52,430 (2.4%)	2,184,625
1981	1,505,467 (55.5%)	874,269 (32.2%)	204,856 (7.5%)	73,670 (2.7%)	2,713,615
1991	1,417,143 (43.2%)	1,287,256 (39.2%)	392,698 (12.0%)	118,731 (3.6%)	3,282,061

SOURCES: *Census of Canada*, 1931, 2: 106; 1941, 1: 691; 1951, 1: Table 32; 1961, catalogue 92-544, Table 35; 1971, 92-737, Table 26; 1981, 92-901, Table 1; and 1991, 93-315, Table 2A.
NOTES: Totals for 1871 were estimated retrospectively by Census Canada using 1870 colonial estimates and 1881 totals for native people; see Dominion Bureau of Statistics, *Population for Electoral Districts by Enumeration Areas; British Columbia 1870, 1881, 1891, 1901* (Ottawa: Dominion Bureau of Statistics, n.d.). Native Indian total for 1891 is estimated as mean between 1881 and 1901. Totals include 'other' and 'not stated' categories. Before 1981 each individual had a single ethnicity, which was paternally determined. Multiple ethnic origins introduced in 1981 have been divided between the various origins.

TABLE 6
Summary of Groups Disenfranchised Provincially
in British Columbia

	Year disenfranchised	Year enfranchised
Women	–	1917
Chinese	1874	1947
Native Indians	1874	1949
Japanese	1895	1949
East Indians	1907	1947
Mennonites	1931	1948
Doukhobors	1931	1952

SOURCE: *Electoral History of British Columbia 1871–1986*
(Victoria: Elections British Columbia 1988), 530

TABLE 7
British Columbia Non-Native Indian Population by Birthplace, 1881–1991

	British Columbia	Other Canada	Britain and empire	Continental Europe	United States	Asia	Other and }unknown	Total
1881	6,514 (27.4%)	3,541 (14.9%)	5,997 (25.2%)	840 (3.5%)	2,295 (9.6%)	c.4,300 (18.1%)	311	23,798
1891	9,396 (13.3%)	20,699 (29.2%)	20,709 (29.2%)	3,140 (4.4%)	6,567 (9.3%)	8,910 (12.6%)	1,447	70,868
1901	30,640 (20.5%)	40,976 (27.4%)	31,982 (21.4%)	9,400 (6.3%)	17,164 (11.5%)	19,176 (12.8%)	370	149,708
1911	64,316 (17.3%)	86,364 (23.2%)	116,529 (31.3%)	40,131 (10.8%)	37,548 (10.1%)	26,988 (7.2%)	430	372,306
1921	134,666 (26.8%)	108,876 (21.7%)	158,879 (31.6%)	31,658 (6.3%)	34,926 (7.0%)	32,649 (6.5%)	551	502,205
1931	208,596 (31.2%)	143,420 (21.4%)	187,843 (28.1%)	58,809 (8.8%)	34,706 (5.2%)	35,746 (5.3%)	544	669,664
1941	290,783 (36.7%)	199,213 (25.1%)	180,515 (22.8%)	61,716 (7.8%)	35,903 (4.5%)	24,252 (3.1%)	597	792,979
1951	438,209 (38.6%)	359,300 (31.6%)	192,911 (17.0%)	88,734 (7.8%)	41,845 (3.7%)	14,795 (1.3%)	912	1,136,706
1961	722,025 (45.4%)	445,111 (28.0%)	197,112 (12.4%)	162,375 (10.2%)	43,273 (2.7%)	18,279 (1.1%)	2,093	1,590,268
1971	1,003,735 (47.1%)	631,795 (29.6%)	187,380 (8.8%)	183,395 (8.6%)	57,720 (2.7%)	42,130 (2.0%)	26,040	2,132,195
1981	1,181,245 (44.8%)	827,085 (31.3%)	187,730 (7.1%)	201,360 (7.6%)	63,115 (2.4%)	133,810 (5.1%)	45,600	2,639,945
1991	1,454,199 (44.3%)	911,010 (27.8%)	177,800 (5.4%)	195,485 (6.0%)	54,310 (1.7%)	256,215 (7.8%)	233,042	3,282,061

SOURCES: *Census of Canada*, 1941, 4: 662; 1951, 1: Table 45; 1961, catalogue 92-547, Table 49; 1971, 92-727, Table 36; 1981, 92-913, Tables 1A and 1B; and 1991, 93-316, Tables 1 and 2.
NOTE: Geographical areas alter somewhat over time because of shifts in political units and in census definitions.

TABLE 8

British Columbia Non-Native Indian Population Born Elsewhere in Canada, 1881–1991
(as percentages of the total British Columbia non-native population)

	Maritimes	Quebec	Ontario	Prairies	'Canada' only	Total born elsewhere in Canada
1881	784 (3.3%)	396 (1.7%)	1,572 (6.6%)	38 (neg)	751	3,541 (14.9%)
1891	5,395 (7.6%)	2,567 (3.6%)	11,658 (16.5%)	967 (1.4%)	112	20,699 (29.2%)
1901	9,575 (6.4%)	4,329 (2.9%)	23,642 (15.8%)	3,194 (2.1%)	236	40,976 (27.4%)
1911	18,569 (5.0%)	7,496 (2.0%)	45,518 (12.2%)	13,097 (3.5%)	1,684	86,364 (23.2%)
1921	19,235 (3.8%)	8,240 (1.6%)	50,361 (10.0%)	30,117 (6.0%)	923	108,876 (21.7%)
1931	20,853 (3.1%)	9,226 (1.4%)	54,486 (8.1%)	57,970 (8.7%)	885	143,420 (21.4%)
1941	19,639 (2.5%)	9,627 (1.2%)	54,160 (6.8%)	115,627 (14.6%)	160	199,213 (25.1%)
1951	24,906 (2.2%)	14,968 (1.3%)	69,818 (6.1%)	249,608 (22.0%)	n.a.	359,300 (31.6%)
1961	28,366 (1.8%)	17,704 (1.1%)	76,016 (4.8%)	323,025 (20.3%)	n.a.	445,111 (28.0%)
1971	41,275 (1.9%)	31,465 (1.5%)	107,295 (5.0%)	451,760 (21.2%)	n.a.	631,795 (29.6%)
1981	58,160 (2.2%)	52,640 (2.0%)	173,345 (6.6%)	542,940 (20.6%)	n.a.	827,085 (31.3%)
1991	65,000 (2.0%)	61,905 (1.9%)	200,660 (6.1%)	582,360 (17.7%)	1,085	911,010 (27.8%)

SOURCES: *Census of Canada*, 1941, 4: 662; 1951, 1: Table 45; 1961, catalogue 92-547, Table 51; 1971, 92-727, Table 34; 1981, 92-913, Table 1A; and 1991, 93-316, Tables 1 and 2.
NOTE: Newfoundland is included within the Maritimes. Prairies includes Yukon and Northwest Territories, whose proportions are minute.

TABLE 9
Immigrant Population of Western Canada, 1911 and 1921

	Born in Britain or possessions	Born in Continental Europe	Born in the United States	Born in Asia	Total born outside Canada
Manitoba					
1911	94,874 (49.7%)	78,056 (40.9%)	16,328 (8.6%)	863 (0.5%)	190,840
1921	112,763 (50.7%)	85,902 (38.6%)	21,644 (9.7%)	1,321 (0.6%)	222,372
Saskatchewan					
1911	80,849 (33.2%)	91,104 (37.4%)	68,628 (28.2%)	1,218 (0.5%)	243,681
1921	99,959 (33.4%)	108,352 (36.2%)	87,617 (29.2%)	2,710 (0.9%)	299,677
Alberta					
1911	69,336 (32.6%)	58,771 (27.7%)	81,357 (38.3%)	2,028 (1.0%)	212,426
1921	98,699 (36.1%)	69,765 (25.5%)	99,879 (36.5%)	3,796 (1.4%)	273,364
British Columbia					
1911	116,434 (52.2%)	40,131 (18.0%)	37,548 (16.8%)	26,713 (12.0%)	223,158
1921	158,778 (60.9%)	31,658 (12.5%)	34,926 (13.4%)	32,457 (12.5%)	260,536

SOURCE: *Census of Canada*, 1921, 2: 240–1

NOTE: Britain or possessions excludes Newfoundland. Asia includes only China and Japan.

TABLE 10
British Columbia Population by Religious Affiliation, 1881–1991

	Anglican	United	Presbyterian	Lutheran	Conservative Protestant	Roman Catholic	Jewish	Confucian Buddhist	Other and none	Total
1881	10,913 (22.1%)	5,042 (10.2%)	5,753 (11.6%)	632 (1.3%)	621 (1.3%)	14,141 (28.6%)	104 (0.2%)	n.a.	12,252	49,459
1891	24,196 (24.7%)	15,440 (15.7%)	15,655 (16.0%)	2,129 (2.2%)	3,648 (3.7%)	21,350 (21.8%)	277 (0.3%)	n.a.	15,478	98,173
1901	41,457 (23.2%)	26,541 (14.9%)	34,478 (19.3%)	5,395 (3.0%)	7,555 (4.2%)	34,020 (19.0%)	554 (0.3%)	15,050 (8.4%)	13,607	178,657
1911	101,582 (25.9%)	55,308 (14.1%)	82,735 (21.1%)	19,483 (5.0%)	20,533 (5.2%)	58,760 (15.0%)	1,384 (0.4%)	22,435 (5.7%)	30,260	392,480
1921	161,494 (30.8%)	67,590 (12.9%)	123,419 (23.5%)	17,709 (3.4%)	24,451 (4.7%)	64,180 (12.2%)	1,654 (0.3%)	30,317 (5.8%)	33,768	524,582
1931	206,867 (29.8%)	166,233 (23.9%)	84,941 (12.2%)	36,938 (5.3%)	32,025 (4.6%)	88,106 (12.7%)	2,666 (0.4%)	32,917 (4.7%)	43,570	694,263
1941	246,191 (30.1%)	201,357 (24.6%)	94,554 (11.6%)	41,884 (5.1%)	49,323 (6.0%)	109,929 (13.4%)	3,244 (0.4%)	29,215 (3.6%)	42,167	817,861
1951	315,469 (27.1%)	341,914 (29.3%)	97,151 (8.3%)	60,641 (5.2%)	81,712 (7.0%)	168,016 (14.4%)	5,969 (0.5%)	6,928 (0.6%)	87,410	1,165,210

TABLE 10 (Concluded)

	Anglican	United	Presbyterian	Lutheran	Conservative Protestant	Roman Catholic	Jewish	Confucian Buddhist	Other and none	Total
1961	367,096 (22.5%)	504,317 (31.0%)	90,093 (5.5%)	100,393 (6.2%)	113,141 (7.0%)	285,184 (17.5%)	7,816 (0.5%)	7,893 (0.5%)	153,143	1,629,082
1971	386,670 (17.7%)	537,565 (24.6%)	100,940 (4.6%)	120,335 (5.5%)	172,552 (7.9%)	408,330 (18.7%)	9,715 (0.4%)	7,080 (0.3%)	441,438	2,184,625
1981	374,055 (13.4%)	548,360 (20.2%)	89,810 (3.3%)	122,395 (4.5%)	233,635 (8.5%)	526,355 (19.5%)	14,680 (0.5%)	11,820 (0.4%)	792,499	2,713,615
1991	328,580 (10.0%)	420,755 (12.8%)	63,985 (2.0%)	108,190 (3.3%)	277,900 (8.5%)	595,315 (18.1%)	16,565 (0.5%)	36,555 (1.1%)	1,434,216	3,282,061

SOURCES: Census of Canada, 1951, 10: Table 36; 1961, catalogue 92-546, Table 43; 1971, 92-724, Table 10-2; 1981, 92-912, Table 1; and 1991, 93-319, Table 1.

NOTES: Denominations which in 1926 came together as the United Church were Methodist, Congregationalist, and some Presbyterians. Conservative Protestant is defined, as in Robert Burkinshaw's doctoral thesis ('Strangers and Pilgrims in Lotus Land,' UBC 1988, 308 and 310–11) to include Baptist, Pentecostal, Mennonite, Church of God, Church of Nazarene, Evangelical, Free Methodist, Salvation Army, Christian Reformed, Canadian Reformed, Christian and Missionary Alliance, Evangelical Free, Plymouth Brethren, Church of Christ, Disciples of Christ, and any other comparable bodies. Numbers of British Columbians with no religious affiliation, earlier unspecified in the censuses, stood at 287,115 or 13.1 per cent in 1971, 566,905 or 20.9 per cent in 1981, and 987,985 or 30.4 per cent in 1991. Numbers adhering to Eastern non-Christian faiths, also earlier unspecified apart from Confucists and Buddhists, were 78,640 or 2.9 per cent of the population in 1981 and 159,965 or 4.9 per cent in 1991. The largest groups in 1991 were the Sikhs at 74,550 or 2.3 per cent, Moslems at 24,930 or 0.8 per cent, and Hindus at 18,140 or 0.6 per cent.

TABLE 11
British Columbia Non-Native Indian Adult Population by Sex, 1870–1991

	Males	Females	Total
1870	5,477 (72.9%)	2,035 (27.1%)	7,512
1881	13,431 (74.4%)	4,613 (25.6%)	18,044
1891	41,354 (74.6%)	14,081 (25.4%)	55,435
1901	81,946 (70.9%)	33,687 (29.1%)	115,633
1911	198,783 (70.0%)	89,528 (30.0%)	288,311
1921	211,029 (58.5%)	149,781 (41.5%)	360,800
1931	290,727 (57.3%)	216,614 (42.7%)	507,341
1941	338,492 (54.0%)	288,492 (46.0%)	626,984
1951	432,830 (51.4%)	409,751 (48.6%)	842,581
1961	553,621 (50.7%)	538,478 (49.3%)	1,092,099
1971	773,277 (50.2%)	768,227 (49.8%)	1,541,504
1981	1,040,206 (49.3%)	1,068,811 (50.7%)	2,109,017
1991	1,248,566 (49.1%)	1,295,256 (50.9%)	2,543,822

SOURCES: *Census of Canada*, 1881, 4: 376; 1931, 1: 431 and 431–55; 1941, 3: 330–1; 1951, 2: Table 11; 1961, catalogue 92-555, Table 90; 1971, 92-737, Table 26; 1981, 92-901, Table 1; and 1991, 93-310, Table 1.

NOTES: Adults are considered to be individuals aged fifteen and over: 1870 figures are estimates only. The number of Indians in 1891 is not given in the census but taken to be the mean between the 1881 and 1901 totals. Native sex and age ratios, not available in the census prior to 1931 are estimated. Native sex ratios are considered to be equal, as they approximately were in 1931. The proportion of natives aged fifteen and over is estimated at 64 per cent, the mean between the Canadian average of about 67 per cent (see Warren E. Kalbach and Wayne W. McVey, *The Demographic Bases of Canadian Society*, 2nd ed. [Toronto: McGraw-Hill Ryerson 1979], 162) and the native proportion of 61 per cent in 1931 (*Census of Canada*, 1931, 3: 172).

TABLE 12

Average Age of First Marriage in Selected Canadian Provinces, 1891–1991

	Nova Scotia	Quebec	Ontario	Manitoba	Saskatchewan	British Columbia
Males						
1891	30.1	27.5	29.3	29.8	–	32.7
1911	29.5	27.4	28.8	29.5	30.6	31.5
1921	28.7	27.3	27.7	28.5	29.1	28.5
1931	28.7	28.5	28.0	29.3	29.2	29.1
1941	25.6	26.8	25.8	26.5	26.3	26.8
1951	24.8	25.1	24.4	25.0	25.2	24.9
1961	22.3	24.6	23.8	23.9	23.9	24.2
1971	23.1	24.0	23.5	23.2	22.8	23.5
1981	25.3	25.8	25.8	25.5	25.2	26.2
1991	27.4	27.8	27.7	27.2	27.0	28.2
Females						
1891	26.4	25.3	26.6	23.8	–	22.3
1911	25.7	25.1	25.8	24.2	22.3	23.7
1921	24.8	25.1	24.7	24.0	22.4	23.8
1931	24.9	26.4	24.9	25.2	23.8	24.8
1941	22.4	23.9	22.7	23.0	22.4	23.3
1951	21.6	22.6	21.9	21.9	21.7	22.1
1961	20.6	21.9	21.1	20.9	20.7	21.2
1971	21.1	22.0	21.3	21.0	20.5	21.0
1981	22.3	24.0	23.6	23.1	22.6	23.7
1991	25.5	26.1	25.9	25.1	24.7	26.1

SOURCES: Ellen Gee, 'Fertility and Marriage Patterns in Canada: 1851–1971; PH D thesis, University of British Columbia, 1978, 221; *Vital Statistics: Marriage and Divorce*, 2: 1975, 50, and 2: 1982, 2–3; and Statistics Canada, *Marriages, 1991*, catalogue 84-212, Table 1.
NOTE: Years 1891–1931 compute mean ages; subsequent years median ages.

TABLE 13

Fertility Rates in Selected Canadian Provinces, 1881–1988

	Canada	Nova Scotia	Quebec	Ontario	Manitoba	Saskatchewan	British Columbia
1881	160	148	173	149	366	–	202
1891	144	138	163	121	242	–	204
1901	145	132	160	108	209	550	184
1911	144	128	161	112	167	229	149
1921	108	105	155	98	125	135	84
1931	94	98	116	79	81	100	62
1941	87	98	102	73	77	84	73
1951	109	114	117	100	103	110	99
1961	112	119	109	108	111	119	104
1971	68	79	98	68	78	79	67
1981	52	52	49	50	58	68	53
1988	56	51	48	54	61	68	55

SOURCES: *Vital Statistics: Births*, 1: 1972, 64–74, and 1984, 8–9; and Statistics Canada, *Health Reports, supplement no. 14*, vol. 2, 1 (1990), Table 5. NOTES: Fertility rate equals annual number of births per 1,000 women aged fifteen to forty-nine years. No more recent data were located.

TABLE 14

British Columbia Population Distributed between Regions, 1881–1991

	Vancouver Island	Lower mainland	Southern interior	Okanagan/ Boundary	West Kootenays	East Kootenays	Central coast	Northwest	Central interior	Northeast
1881	17,292 (35.0%)	7,939 (16.1%)	6,753 (13.7%)	817 (1.7%)		863 (1.7%)	2,208 (4.4%)	2,762 (5.6%)	9,825 (20.0%)	1,000 (2.0%)
1891	35,744 (36.4%)	41,507 (42.3%)	8,191 (8.3%)	3,360 (3.4%)	2,185 (2.2%)	1,220 (1.2%)	2,475 (2.5%)	548 (0.6%)	2,003 (2.0%)	940 (1.0%)
1901	50,886 (28.5%)	53,641 (30.0%)	11,563 (6.5%)	12,085 (6.8%)	23,516 (13.2%)	8,446 (4.7%)	3,743 (2.1%)	9,270 (5.2%)	4,523 (2.5%)	984 (0.6%)
1911	81,241 (20.7%)	183,108 (46.7%)	19,031 (4.8%)	28,066 (7.2%)	28,373 (7.2%)	22,466 (5.7%)	3,545 (0.9%)	16,595 (4.2%)	8,411 (2.1%)	1,644 (0.4%)
1921	108,792 (20.7%)	256,579 (48.9%)	24,484 (4.7%)	35,522 (6.8%)	31,075 (5.9%)	19,137 (3.6%)	10,232 (2.0%)	18,986 (3.6%)	17,631 (3.4%)	2,144 (0.4%)
1931	120,933 (17.4%)	379,858 (54.7%)	30,025 (4.3%)	40,523 (5.8%)	40,455 (5.8%)	22,566 (3.3%)	12,658 (1.8%)	18,698 (2.7%)	21,534 (3.1%)	7,013 (1.0%)
1941	150,407 (18.4%)	449,376 (54.9%)	30,710 (3.8%)	51,605 (6.3%)	48,266 (5.9%)	21,345 (2.6%)	14,344 (1.8%)	18,051 (2.2%)	25,276 (3.1%)	8,481 (1.0%)
1951	215,003 (18.5%)	649,238 (55.7%)	41,823 (3.6%)	77,686 (6.7%)	60,060 (5.2%)	27,628 (2.4%)	18,247 (1.6%)	20,854 (1.8%)	40,276 (3.5%)	14,395 (1.2%)
1961	290,835 (17.9%)	907,531 (55.7%)	66,290 (4.1%)	94,646 (5.8%)	70,707 (4.3%)	34,244 (2.1%)	21,325 (1.3%)	38,203 (2.3%)	74,240 (4.6%)	31,061 (1.9%)
1971	381,796 (17.5%)	1,189,864 (54.5%)	102,668 (4.7%)	135,472 (6.2%)	77,442 (3.5%)	46,601 (2.1%)	22,515 (1.0%)	56,242 (2.6%)	128,205 (5.9%)	43,816 (2.0%)
1981	491,333 (17.9%)	1,432,753 (52.2%)	136,059 (5.0%)	207,067 (7.5%)	84,844 (3.1%)	60,135 (2.2%)	26,203 (1.0%)	69,433 (2.5%)	182,320 (6.6%)	54,320 (2.0%)
1991	588,256 (17.9%)	1,828,912 (55.7%)	138,438 (4.2%)	251,182 (7.7%)	82,253 (2.5%)	59,213 (1.8%)	23,398 (0.7%)	67,968 (2.1%)	181,174 (5.5%)	58,267 (1.8%)

SOURCES: *Census of Canada*, 1951, 1: Table 6; 1971, catalogue 92-702, Table 2; 1981, 92-901-912, Tables 1 and 3; and 1991, 93-304, Table 2. NOTES: Regions are differentiated in Map 1. Regions correspond to census areas 1 to 10, as calculated by Statistics Canada, 1881–1971: 1 – East Kootenays, 2 – West Kootenays, 3 – Okanagan-Boundary, 4 – Lower Mainland, 5 – Vancouver Island, 6 – Southern Interior, 7 – Central Coast, 8 – Central Interior, 9 – Northwest, and 10 – Northeast. Totals for 1981 and 1991 are estimated by comparing Statistics Canada maps delineating census areas 1 to 10 with 1981 and 1991 divisions and subdivisions.

TABLE 15

British Columbia Post Offices Distributed between Regions, 1881–1981

	Vancouver Island	Lower mainland	Southern interior	Okanagan/ Boundary	West Kootenays	East Kootenays	Central coast	Northwest	Central interior	Northeast	Total
1871–1881	15	19	17	1	0	2	0	3	12	2	71
1882–1891	44	61	31	7	10	16	2	8	10	0	189
1892–1901	92	92	45	39	52	37	8	14	17	1	397
1902–1911	131	166	89	67	105	70	15	39	41	2	725
1912–1921	180	227	133	80	118	73	30	71	97	12	1,021
1922–1931	169	192	117	64	106	65	32	62	113	34	954
1932–1941	163	162	106	56	101	58	32	48	122	42	890
1942–1951	158	167	100	53	98	55	32	46	124	41	874
1952–1961	144	137	97	49	82	51	31	42	107	40	780
1962–1971	116	107	88	41	71	51	30	35	92	38	669
1972–1981	92	76	73	30	51	37	27	33	55	34	508

SOURCE: William Topping, ed., *British Columbia Post Offices* (Vancouver: privately printed 1983), 9-59

NOTES: Regions are differentiated in Map 1 and Table 14. Total for each decade includes all post offices that opened or were open at some point in time within the decade. Post offices changing their name are counted only once. The changing nature of postal service in Canada, in particular Canada Post's preference for providing service in stores and other private facilities, makes 1991 data non-comparable with earlier years.

TABLE 16

British Columbia Sub-Post Offices Distributed between Regions, 1881–1981

	Vancouver Island	Lower mainland	Southern interior	Okanagan/ Boundary	West Kootenays	East Kootenays	Central coast	Northwest	Central interior	Northeast	Total
1871–1881	0	0	0	0	0	0	0	0	0	0	0
1882–1891	0	0	0	0	0	0	0	0	0	0	0
1892–1901	1	2	0	0	0	0	0	0	0	0	3
1902–1911	7	17	0	0	0	0	0	0	0	0	24
1912–1921	19	49	1	0	0	0	0	0	0	0	69
1922–1931	26	91	0	0	0	0	0	1	0	0	118
1932–1941	31	106	1	0	4	0	0	1	0	0	143
1942–1951	47	191	3	3	8	0	0	4	2	0	258
1952–1961	61	255	8	6	9	0	0	8	5	0	352
1962–1971	79	340	12	12	9	5	0	8	12	1	478
1972–1981	97	308	23	20	15	11	0	4	18	6	502

SOURCE: William Topping, ed., *British Columbia Post Offices* (Vancouver: privately printed 1983), 61–71

NOTES: Regions are differentiated in Map 1 and Table 14. Total for each decade includes all sub-post offices that opened or were open at some point in time within the decade. The changing nature of postal service in Canada, in particular Canada Post's preference for providing service in stores and other private facilities, makes 1991 data non-comparable with earlier years.

TABLE 17

Population in British Columbia's Southwestern Corner 1881–1991

	Victoria City	Other Greater Victoria	Saanich Peninsula	New Westminster	Vancouver City	Other Greater Vancouver	Other Lower Fraser Valley
1881	5,925	c.600	488	1,500	n.a.	n.a.	n.a.
1891	16,841	c.750	610	6,678	13,709	n.a.	n.a.
1901	20,919	c.1,250	n.a.	6,499	27,010	6,069	12,521
1911	31,660	5,919	6,026	13,199	100,401	35,890	29,138
1921	38,727	7,617	10,534	14,495	117,217	76,747	43,616
1931	39,082	9,166	12,968	17,524	246,593	52,405	57,480
1941	44,068	12,977	18,173	21,967	275,353	63,848	79,744
1951	51,331	22,113	30,550	28,639	344,833	123,828	139,157
1961	54,941	28,983	53,386	33,654	384,522	209,379	243,184
1971	61,761	31,348	78,645	42,835	426,256	286,421	385,660
1981	64,379	32,896	103,500	38,550	414,281	377,497	573,453
1991	71,228	34,007	130,687	43,585	471,844	448,585	820,844

SOURCES: *Census of Canada*, 'Population by electoral districts by enumeration areas; British Columbia,' 1901, 1: 22; 1911, 1: 38–9; 1921, 1: 337–9; 1951, 1: Table 6, and 10: Table 4; 1971, catalogue 92-702, Table 2; 1976, 92-800-808, Table 3; 1981, 92-901-912, Table 4; and 1991, 93-304, Table 2.

NOTES: Greater Victoria includes Victoria, Esquimalt, and Oak Bay. Saanich includes South Saanich, Central Saanich, North Saanich, and Sidney. Greater Vancouver includes Burnaby, Hastings Townsite (through 1901), North Vancouver, Point Grey (through 1921), Richmond, South Vancouver (through 1921), West Vancouver, and intervening areas. Lower Fraser Valley includes Abbotsford, Chilliwack, Coquitlam, Delta, Hope, Langley, Maple Ridge, Matsqui, Port Coquitlam, Port Moody, Surrey, White Rock, and intervening areas, as defined in *Census of Canada*, 1951, 1: Table 6. Lower Fraser Valley totals for 1961–81 take in a slightly larger area than earlier; totals for 1941 and 1951 can be recalculated using the larger area as 80,904 and 142,118. Vancouver's population from 1931 includes South Vancouver and Point Grey, previously included in Other Greater Vancouver; sometimes Vancouver's population in 1921 is retrospectively revised upward to include those two municipalities, in which case it totals 163,220. In some cases boundary changes explain growth.

TABLE 18
Population of Regional Urban Centres in British Columbia, 1901–1991

	Nanaimo	Port Alberni	Prince Rupert	Prince George	Kamloops	Vernon	Kelowna	Nelson	Trail
1901	6,130	–	–	–	1,594	802	261	5,273	1,360
1911	8,306	–	4,184	–	3,722	2,671	1,663	4,476	1,460
1921	6,304	1,056	6,393	2,053	4,501	3,685	2,520	5,230	3,020
1931	6,745	2,356	6,350	2,479	6,167	3,937	4,655	5,992	7,573
1941	6,635	4,584	6,714	2,027	5,959	5,209	5,118	5,912	9,392
1951	7,196	7,845	8,546	4,703	8,099	7,822	8,517	6,772	11,430
1961	14,135	11,560	11,967	13,877	10,076	10,250	13,188	7,074	11,580
1971	34,029	20,063	15,747	33,101	26,168	13,283	19,412	9,400	11,149
1981	47,069	19,892	16,197	67,559	64,048	19,987	59,196	9,143	9,599
1991	60,129	18,403	16,620	69,653	67,057	23,514	75,950	8,760	7,919

SOURCES: *Census of Canada*, 1911, 1: 537; 1921, 1: 220–1; 1951, 1: Table 6; 1971, catalogue 92-702, Table 2; 1976, 92-800-808, Table 3; 1981, 92-901-912, Table 1; and 1991, 93-304, Table 2.
NOTE: In some cases boundary expansions explain growth.

TABLE 19
British Columbia Economy Measured by Gross Domestic Product, 1880–1980
(percentages)

	Growth in real GDP over previous decade	Per capita growth in real GDP over previous decade	Primary products	GDP distribution		
				Primary mfg	Secondary mfg	Services
1880			49.7	8.4	8.8	33.1
1890	+285.4	+106.8	30.5	7.0	12.1	50.4
1900	+100.0	+7.7	41.2	8.6	7.0	43.2
1910	+117.7	+1,528.9	28.9	10.6	8.2	52.3
1920	+24.3	−11.8	23.2	9.6	7.5	59.7
1930	+47.1	+10.9	18.4	11.0	6.0	63.7
1940	+24.9	+4.9	22.0	12.4	8.3	57.3
1950	+91.2	+35.4	18.4	14.5	9.6	57.5
1960	+58.0	+12.2	10.6	11.3	10.3	67.8
1970	+73.3	+30.4	8.9	9.1	8.2	73.8
1980	+75.8	+40.4	11.3	10.0	7.6	71.1

SOURCE: Robert C. Allen, *The B.C. Economy: Past, Present, Future* (Vancouver: B.C. Economic Policy Institute 1985), Table 4
NOTE: Gross domestic product (GDP) equals total value of all goods and services produced in British Columbia. Real GDP is in 1971 dollars.

TABLE 20

Gross Value of Products Mined in British Columbia, 1860–1990

($ million)

	Placer gold	Lode gold	Coal/ coke	Silver	Copper	Lead	Zinc	Molyb- denum	Iron	Petroleum/ natural gas	Total
1860	2.2	–	0.1	–	–	–	–	–	–	–	2.3
1865	3.5	–	0.1	–	–	–	–	–	–	–	3.6
1870	1.3	–	0.1	–	–	–	–	–	–	–	1.5
1875	2.5	–	0.3	–	–	–	–	–	–	–	2.8
1880	1.0	–	0.8	–	–	–	–	–	–	–	1.8
1885	0.7	–	1.1	–	–	–	–	–	–	–	1.5
1890	0.5	–	2.0	0.1	–	–	–	–	–	–	2.7
1895	0.5	0.8	2.8	1.0	neg	0.5	–	–	–	–	5.7
1900	1.3	3.5	4.7	2.3	1.6	2.7	–	–	–	–	16.4
1905	1.0	4.9	5.5	2.0	5.9	2.4	0.1	–	–	–	22.5
1910	0.4	5.5	11.1	1.2	4.9	1.4	0.2	–	–	–	26.4
1915	0.8	5.2	7.1	1.6	10.0	1.9	1.5	–	–	–	29.5
1920	0.2	2.5	13.5	3.2	7.8	2.8	3.1	–	–	–	35.6
1925	0.3	4.3	12.2	5.3	10.2	18.7	7.7	–	–	–	61.5
1930	0.2	3.3	9.4	4.3	12.0	12.6	9.0	–	–	–	55.8
1935	0.9	12.9	5.0	6.0	3.1	10.8	7.9	–	–	–	48.8
1940	1.2	22.5	7.1	4.7	7.9	15.7	10.6	–	–	–	75.0
1945	0.4	6.8	6.5	2.9	3.2	16.8	19.0	–	–	–	62.0
1950	0.6	10.8	10.1	7.7	9.9	41.4	43.8	–	–	–	140.0
1955	0.2	8.4	9.0	6.9	16.9	45.2	52.0	–	3.2	neg	173.9
1960	0.1	7.0	5.2	6.6	9.6	38.7	50.7	neg	10.3	9.2	177.4
1965	neg	4.4	6.7	6.9	32.7	43.1	48.7	12.4	21.5	44.1	280.7
1970	neg	3.7	19.6	12.0	124.7	35.1	44.1	52.6	17.4	91.0	488.6
1975	0.2	25.1	317.1	28.4	331.7	24.5	80.6	71.2	15.3	320.7	1,364.1
1980	6.2	163.9	461.5	156.5	670.6	66.1	49.4	288.9	13.7	828.3	3,077.0
1985	5.4	89.1	1,028.1	100.9	579.7	42.3	112.7	63.2	3.8	1,049.5	3,427.2
1990	10.0	231.8	979.9	115.1	985.0	16.0	103.4	88.3	3.7	886.9	3,857.8

SOURCES: *Statistics of Industry in British Columbia 1871 to 1934* (Victoria: Economic Council of British Columbia 1935), Table M2; and *British Columbia Mineral Statistics: Annual Summary Tables, Historical Mineral Production to 1990* (Victoria: Ministry of Energy, Mines and Petroleum Resources 1992), Tables 2-A, 8-A, 9-A, 10-A, and 12-A.

NOTES: Total includes other lesser minerals. Minor discrepancies sometimes exist between the two sources, in which cases the latter has been preferred. This table is *not* comparable with Table 19, where dollars have been adjusted to 1971.

Notes

Fuller details of works cited in short form in the notes are given in the References.

Chapter 1 In Search of British Columbia

1 Atwood, *Cat's Eye*, 420; Woodcock, *Ravens and Prophets*, 9; Hodgins, *Resurrection of Joseph Bourne*, 1; Cash, *Off the Record*, 152
2 Martin and Hall, *Brooke*, 122; Wilson, *Innocent Traveller*, 121; Stephen Leacock, 1937, cited in Geddes, *Skookum Wawa*, 46; Lumsden, *Through Canada*, 280
3 Playfair, 'British Columbia's Fifty-Seven Varieties,' 903
4 Harrison, 'Pioneer Judge's Wife,' March 1952, Prince Rupert Pioneers' Association booklet, 1914, cited in Bowman, *Road, Rail and River!*, 122. I am grateful to Louise Wilson for bringing this memoir to my attention.
5 Cash, *Off the Record*, 152
6 Carr, *Hundreds and Thousands*, 201; Wilson 'Mrs. Golightly and the First Convention,' in *Mrs. Golightly*, 3
7 Wilson, 'Tuesday and Wednesday,' 96–7
8 Collier, *Three against the Wilderness*, 91–2
9 Cail, *Land, Man and the Law*, 19; *The West Shore* 10, no. 9 (September 1884), 292
10 Parkin, *Great Dominion*, 160; *The Times* (London), 17 February 1859
11 Collier, *Three against the Wilderness*, 199
12 Wilson, *Swamp Angel*, 36
13 Susan Musgrave, 'Other Parts of Canada,' in White, *British Columbia*, 103
14 Richard Clement Moody to Arthur Blackwood, Victoria, 1 February 1859, in Ireland, 'First Impressions,' 92–3
15 Wilson, *Swamp Angel*, 58–9. Very similar descriptions are found in Wilson, *Hetty*

Dorval, 7–8 and 110; and Ethel Wilson to Earle Birney, Kamloops, 27 May 1953, in Stouck, *Ethel Wilson*, 178.

16 Quoted in 13 September 1863 entry in Cheadle, *Journal*, 230

17 James Douglas to the Duke of Newcastle 25 October 1860, cited in Ormsby, *Pioneer Gentlewoman*, 91 fn

18 Blanchet, *Curve of Time*

19 Money, *This Was the North*, 3–4

20 Brody, *Maps and Dreams*, 17–18

21 Henry Labouchere in 'The Canadian Dominion Bubble,' *Truth*, 1 September 1881, quoted in Colombo, *Quotations*, 24

Chapter 2 First Encounters, 1741–1825

1 Fladmark, *Prehistory*, 13–19

2 Duff, *Indian History*, 8; and Fladmark, *Prehistory*, 1. Precise knowledge is difficult to disentangle. Moving beyond archaeological research and material culture, it is necessary to draw on early written observations which reflect the writers' Eurocentricity. The names that early explorers and traders gave to peoples living across British Columbia often related to terms actually being used, or perceived to have been used, at the time of contact. These names then continued in common usage until recently when some native peoples began redefining themselves more accurately to reflect their own traditions, the Nootka becoming the Nuu-chah-nulth, the Kwakiutl the Kwakiulth or a variant, the Nishga the Nisga's and so forth. The names used over historical time have for reasons of consistency and clarity been preferred here.

3 Duff, *Indian History*, 38–46. Duff used Department of Indian Affairs population totals, whereas federal census totals make possible direct comparisons between components of the BC population over time. Estimates have ranged as high as one million. See Thornton, *American Indian Holocaust*, 26–32; Dobyns, *Their Number Became Thinned*, 38–9; and interview with Richard Inglis, curator at the Royal British Columbia Museum, in Vancouver *Sun*, 21 November 1987.

4 Harris, *Historical Atlas*, plate 13, also plate 14

5 Assu with Inglis, *Assu of Cape Mudge*, 49

6 Mitchell and Franklin, 'When You Don't Know the Language,' 19. Also insightful is Blackman, *During My Time*.

7 Brody, *Maps and Dreams*, 85

8 Duff, *Indian History*, 8

9 Servin, 'Instructions,' 240

10 Bruno de Hezeta, Diary; Juan Francisco Bodega y Quadra, Diary, both cited in Cook, *Flood Tide*, 78, 80

11 Juan Francisco Bodega y Quadra, Diary, cited in Pethick, *First Approaches*, 51

12 Totals are calculated from Howay, 'List of Trading Vessels.' Vessels changing both their name and national flag are considered to be different ships. Vessels

only coming to pick up furs from an existing trading post are excluded. It should be noted that figures given in Cook, *Flood Tide*, Appendix E, are inflated, counting as separate vessels the second and subsequent seasons that a single ship remained in the Pacific Northwest. Cook also seems to include ships specifically noted by Howay as setting out for the Pacific Northwest but not reaching their destination. Numbers and countries of ships visiting the coast for any reasons, including Russian vessels, are usefully charted by year in Harris, *Historical Atlas*, plate 66.

13 Hill, *Remarkable World*; Hill, 'frightful appendage,' 36
14 Translated in Andrews, 'Russian Plans,' 86
15 This is the fundamental point made in Fisher, *Contact and Conflict*. The description of Indian-European relations presented here is based on Fisher, as supplemented by Archer, 'Spain and the Defence.'
16 William Bayley, Journal, 116, cited in Fisher, 'Cook and the Nootka,' 88; Cleveland, *Voyages*, 94; 6 July 1793 entry in Lamb, *Mackenzie*, 344

Chapter 3 The Trade in Furs, 1789–1849

1 21 and 22 June 1793 entries in Lamb, *Mackenzie*, 314, 319, 320 including fn4, and 322; 26 June 1808 entry referring to Fraser Canyon, in Lamb, *Fraser*, 96
2 12 and 16 June 1808 entries in Lamb, *Fraser*, 79 and 84; also 3 June 1808 entry on 71 (emphasis in original)
3 22 July 1793 entry in Lamb, *Mackenzie*, 378
4 Locations and years of operation are depicted in Harris, *Historical Atlas*, plate 66
5 3 July 1808 entry, in Lamb, *Fraser*, 109
6 Quoted in Akrigg and Akrigg, *Chronicle 1778–1846*, 170
7 13 May 1813 and 20 July 1816 entries in Lamb, *Harmon*, 159 and 186
8 HBC Governor and Committee to George Simpson, London, 24 December 1826, in Merk, *Fur Trade and Empire*, 285–6
9 Ibid., London, 27 February 1822, and J.H. Pelly to the Lords of the Committee of the Privy Council for Trade, London, 7 February 1838, in Merk, *Fur Trade and Empire*, 175 and 343
10 28 October and 17 November 1824 entries in ibid., 48, 65, and 72 (emphasis in original)
11 Rich, *Simpson's 1828 Journey*, 38–9
12 J.H. Pelly to the Lords of the Committee of the Privy Council for Trade, London, 7 February 1838, in Merk, *Fur Trade and Empire*, 343
13 James Douglas to James Hargrave, Fort Vancouver, 5 February 1843, in Glazebrook, *Hargrave Correspondence*, 420–1
14 Simon Fraser to James McDougall, Naugh-al-chun [Stuart Lake], 31 August 1806, in Lamb, *Fraser*, 237; 23 September 1811 entry in Lamb, *Harmon*, 143–4
15 17 April 1821 entry in Fort St James post journal, cited in Bishop, 'Kwah,' 196
16 The point is made in Van Kirk, *'Many Tender Ties,'* and Brown, *Strangers in Blood*.

17 10 October 1805 entry in Lamb, *Harmon*, 98; also 7 August 1800 and 11 August
    1802 entries, 28–9 and 62–3 (emphasis in original)

18 28 February 1819 entry in ibid., 194–5

19 James Douglas to James Hargrave, Fort Vancouver, 24 March 1842, in
    Glazebrook, *Hargrave Correspondence*, 381

20 Rev. Herbert Beaver to the Bishop of Montreal, Colchester, 31 July 1839, cited in
    Slater, 'New Light,' 24

21 Quoted in Marion B. Smith, 'The Lady Nobody Knows,' in Watters, *British
    Columbia*, 472; 28 February 1861 entry in *Lady Franklin*, 23

22 See Rich, *Fur Trade*, 278–81, and Akrigg and Akrigg, *Chronicle 1778–1846*, 270–2

23 For example, Schwantes, *Pacific Northwest*, 61

24 Woodcock, *Ravens and Prophets*, 25

25 Galbraith, *Hudson's Bay Company*, 174

Chapter 4 Impetus to Settlement, 1846–1858

1 'Charter of Grant to Vancouver's Island to the Hudson's Bay Company,' cited in
   Hendrickson, *Journals*, 1: 378

2 James Douglas to Archibald Barclay, Fort Victoria, 3 April 1850, in Bowsfield, *Fort
   Victoria Letters*, 77

3 This section draws on Mackie, 'Colonial Land,' and Ormsby, 'Introduction.'

4 James Douglas to Governor of HBC, Fort Vancouver, 18 October 1838, in Rich,
   McLoughlin, 242

5 Archibald Barclay to James Douglas, 17 December 1849, cited in Ormsby,
   'Introduction,' liii

6 James Douglas to John Henry Pelly, Fort Victoria, 5 December 1848, in
   Bowsfield, *Fort Victoria Letters*, 34

7 James Douglas to James Hargrave, 17 January 1850, cited in Ormsby, 'Introduction,' li; James Douglas to Archibald Barclay, 1 September 1850, in Bowsfield, *Fort
   Victoria Letters*, 116

8 Archibald Barclay to James Douglas, December 1849, cited in Madill, *Indian
   Treaties*, 19

9 Madill, *Indian Treaties*, 67–73; James Douglas to Duke of Newcastle, 25 March
   1861, cited in ibid., 22

10 Smith, *Helmcken*, 76, 116, and 133–4; James Douglas to Archibald Barclay,
    8 October 1851, in Bowsfield, *Fort Victoria Letters*, 222

11 Smith, *Helmcken*, 111

12 Mayne, *Four Years*, 31

13 Smith, *Helmcken*, 288

14 Testimony of Richard Blanshard in *Report of Select Committee on the Hudson's Bay
    Company, 1857*, 290

15 John Fall Allison to his parents, cited in Margaret A. Ormsby, *Pioneer Gentle-
    woman*, xxv

16 Money, *This Was the North*, 61 and 103

17 Benjamin, *Three Years*, 137

18 Queen Charlotte Islands Papers, 1, cited in Howay, *British Columbia*, 1

19 Queen Charlotte Islands Papers, 2, cited in Akrigg and Akrigg, *Chronicle 1847–1871*, 49; Colonial Secretary Sir John Parkington to James Douglas, September 1852, cited in Taylor, *Mining*, 14

20 14 September 1860 entry in James Douglas, Diary, cited in Akrigg and Akrigg, *Chronicle 1847–1871*, 93

21 James Douglas to Colonial Office, 15 July and 27 December 1857, cited in Taylor, *Mining*, 17

22 Gold Discovery Papers, 8, cited in Howay, *British Columbia*, 12–13

23 *Pioneer and Democrat* (Olympia, Washington Territory), 5 March 1858, cited in Howay, *British Columbia*, 15; *Overland Monthly* 3, 524, cited in ibid., 18

24 Names of ships and numbers of passengers are given in Howay, *British Columbia*, 17–18.

25 Waddington, *Fraser Mines* 16–17

26 Johnson, *Very Far West Indeed*, 48–9; 4 March 1861 entry in *Lady Franklin*, 38–9

27 Johnson, *Very Far West Indeed*, 110; Benjamin, *Three Years*, 139

28 Higgins, *Mystic Spring*, 215; *Times*, 25 December 1858. Sections on Fraser and his dispatches are based on Mason, 'To See Ourselves.' I am grateful to Phyllis Mason for permission to draw on her research.

29 *Victoria Gazette*, 18 December 1858, cited in Akrigg and Akrigg, *Chronicle 1847–1871*, 118

30 Richard Clement Moody to Arthur Blackwood, Victoria, 1 February 1859, in Ireland, 'First Impressions,' 97, 103 and 106 (capitals and emphasis in original); John Fall Allison to his parents, cited in Margaret A. Ormsby, *Pioneer Gentlewoman*, xxv

31 *Victoria Gazette*, 25 November 1858, cited in Akrigg and Akrigg, *Chronicle 1847–1871*, 140

32 Sir E.B. Lytton to James Douglas, 2 September 1858, Despatch 8, in *Papers Relative to the Affairs of British Columbia*, Part 1, 56

33 E.B. Lytton to James Douglas, 16 October 1858, cited in Woodward, 'Influence,' 15; Lytton, *Bulwer* 2: 191–3; Richard Clement Moody to Arthur Blackwood, Victoria, 1 February 1859, in Ireland, 'First Impressions,' 92–3

Chapter 5 Distant Oversights, 1858–1871

1 *British Colonist*, 11 September 1860; *Times*, 5 February 1862

2 29 August, 11 September, and 26 October 1863 entries in Cheadle, *Journal*, 222, 228, and 253; *Times*, 5 February 1862

3 *British Colonist*, 10 July 1863

4 *Statistics of Industry*, Table M2

5 James Douglas to E.B. Lytton, 26 October 1858, in *Papers*, Part II, 10; Smith, *Helmcken*, 174

6 Richard Clement Moody to Arthur Blackwood, Victoria, 1 February 1859, in Ireland, 'First Impressions,' 97–103, and 106

7 Brigadier General William Harney to General Winfield Scott, 8 July 1859, cited in Richardson, *Pig War Islands*, 55

8 Richard Clement Moody to Arthur Blackwood, Victoria, 1 February 1859, in Ireland, 'First Impressions,' 100

9 *Times*, 1 November 1859

10 Johnson, *Very Far West Indeed*, 111–12; *Radiator* (Lewiston, Idaho), August 1865, cited in Ramsay, *Ghost Towns*, 148

11 27 November 1863 entry in Cheadle, *Journal*, 266

12 3 October 1863 entry in ibid., 239; quotation cited in Williams, *Begbie*, 99

13 *Times*, 14 May 1860, also 28 December 1859

14 12 September 1863 entry in Cheadle, *Journal*, 229

15 See, for example, Ormsby, 'Douglas,' and Karr, 'Douglas.' Among contemporary critiques are Richard Grant to James Hargrave, Fort Vancouver, 6 April 1842, in Glazebrook, *Hargrave Correspondence*, 390; 29 August 1863 entry in Cheadle, *Journal*, 222 and 236; Smith, *Helmcken*, 81; 11 March 1861 entry in *Lady Franklin*, 64; 6 January 1860 entry in Hills, *Journal*; and Macfie, *Vancouver Island*, 393–4.

16 Ormsby, *Pioneer Gentlewoman*, 6

17 11 March 1861 entry in *Lady Franklin*, 63–4

18 James Douglas to Duke of Newcastle, 13 May 1863, cited in Ormsby, *British Columbia*, 191

19 Howay, Sage, and Angus, *British Columbia*, 180

20 Smith, 'Kennedy Interlude,' 76

21 Johnson, *Very Far West Indeed*, 238

22 Ibid., 76–8

23 McMicking, *Overland from Canada*, 53; 18 October 1863 entry in Cheadle, *Journal*, 247

24 Carr, *Book of Small*, 75–6

25 *Times*, 26 July 1859

26 *New Government Colony*, 65; Canon T. Butler to Samuel Butler, 3 August 1859, in Silver, *Family Letters*, 88–9

27 4 December 1863 entry in Cheadle, *Journal*, 267; also 21 September entry, 236

28 4 and 14 October and 3 November 1863 entries in ibid., 239, 245, and 257; also 10, 11, and 12 October 1863 entries, 243–4

29 *Times*, 14 December 1861 and 10 December 1862; 8 and 26 August 1863

30 10 September 1863 entry in Cheadle, *Journal*, 228. 'Cantabs' refers to graduates of Cambridge University.

31 Cited in Barman, 'Transfer,' 243

32 Robson, *How Methodism Came*, 9

33 Selman, 'Adult Education,' 40; Walkem, *Stories*, 278–9; McMicking, *Overland*, xxvii

34 6 October 1863 entry in Cheadle, *Journal*, 240; *Times*, 19 June 1862 and 13 January 1862, also 21 November 1863

35 *British Colonist*, 27 and 19 September 1862
36 *Times*, 19 March 1863; Whymper, *Travels*, 3; Lugrin, *Pioneer Women*, 150
37 *British Columbian*, 4 July 1866
38 Smith, *Helmcken*, 247–8; George Hills, Bishop of British Columbia, in Anglican Church, Diocese of Columbia, *Annual Report*, 1868, 102; Rattray, *Vancouver Island*, 171
39 Frederick Seymour to the Duke of Buckingham and Chandos, 20 November 1868, cited in Ormsby, 'Frederick Seymour,' 20; *Times*, 18 December 1869
40 Smith, *Helmcken*, 247
41 Ibid.
42 Memorial of Yale Convention, cited in Kendrick, 'Amor de Cosmos,' 84
43 Allen Francis to William Seward, 15 September 1866, cited in Shi, 'Seward's Attempt,' 222
44 George E. Baker, ed., *The Works of William H. Seward* (New York 1972), 3: 409, cited in Gibson, 'Sale of Russian America,' 194 n5; Edouard De Stoeckle, Russian Legation head in Washington, DC, to Russian Minister of Foreign Affairs Alexander Gorchakov, 1867, cited in Gibson, 'Sale of Russian America,' 286, also 292; Smith, *Helmcken*, 243; cited in *British Columbian*, 18 May 1867
45 Smith, *Helmcken*, 251
46 Anthony Musgrave to Earl Granville, 30 October 1869, cited in Ormsby, *British Columbia*, 242
47 Henry P.P. Crease to Alfred R. Roche, 28 May 1868, cited in Elliot, 'Crease,' 68 (capitals in original); 30 April and 13 June 1870 entries in *Lady Franklin*, 116 and 145
48 Legislative debate, 9 and 10 March 1870, in Hendrickson, *Journals*, 5: 450–1 and 467

Chapter 6 The Young Province 1871–1900

1 Demographic data come from *Census Canada*, except for pre-Confederation data which is based on a variety of approximations. British Columbia did not become a province in time to be included in 1871 census; only overall figures were given.
2 Speech by Thomas Wood in the Legislative Debate, 10 March 1870, in Hendrickson, *Journals*, 5: 464
3 Jessie McQueen to her mother, Lower Nicola, 12 June 1890, in McQueen Correspondence, Merritt; Charles Mair to George Denison, Okanagan Mission, 6 October 1892; Kelowna, 22 May 1893; 18 April 1895, Mair Correspondence
4 Howay, *British Columbia*, esp. 412
5 George Walkem to J.A. Macdonald, 12 March 1882, cited in Ormsby, *British Columbia*, 285
6 'An Act to Make Further Provision for the Government of British Columbia (9th August 1870),' reproduced in Howay, *British Columbia*, 696–7
7 Joseph Trutch to John A. Macdonald, 20 April 1875, cited in Ormsby, *British Columbia*, 269
8 W.H. Holmes, writing in 1936, cited in Turner, *West of the Great Divide*, 6

9 Sandford Fleming to John A. Macdonald, North Bend, 7 November 1885, cited in ibid., 22; *British Colonist*, 22 November 1885
10 Jessie McQueen to her mother, Lower Nicola, 6 August 1888, McQueen Correspondence, Merritt
11 Sladen, *On the Cars*, 372 and 378
12 Kluckner, *M.I. Rogers*, 26
13 *Vancouver News*, 29 March 1887
14 Beanlands, *British Columbia*, 8
15 This issue is examined in Lutz, 'Losing Steam.'
16 This section draws on McDonald, 'Victoria.'
17 Freya Stark to Herbert Young, Creston, 30 November 1928, in Stark, *Beyond Euphrates*, 35
18 *Occupational Trends*, 6–9; *Statistics of Industry*, Table A1
19 Bulman, *Kamloops Cattlemen*, 29
20 *Guide to the Province of British Columbia, 1877–1878*, 52; Grainger, *Woodsmen*, 61
21 Edward Stamp, cited in Phillips, 'Confederation,' 55. Sections on salmon canning draw on Lyons, *Salmon*.
22 Carr, *Growing Pains*, 95
23 Yoshida, 'Issei Life,' 3; Gerard, *Converted in the Country*, 12
24 Marlatt, 'Steveston, B.C.,' in her *Steveston*, 85
25 E.K. DeBeck, quoted in Norman W. Lidster, 'Fraser teemed with salmon, the language was Chinook,' *Columbian*, 11 March 1972
26 Wicks, *Memories*, 14
27 Lumsden, *Through Canada*, 241
28 *Record* (Cascade City), 26 August 1899, cited in Ramsay, *Ghost Towns*, 168–9
29 *Statistics of Industry*, introductory tables and tables M2, T1, and T2–T8
30 Charles Mair to George Denison, Kelowna, 22 May 1893, Mair Correspondence
31 Jessie McQueen to her mother, Lower Nicola, 29 August 1889, in McQueen Correspondence, Merritt (emphasis in original)
32 Money, *This Was the North*, 63–4
33 Charles Mair to George Denison, Okanagan Mission, 6 October 1892, Mair Correspondence
34 Cail, *Land, Man and the Law*, 14
35 Ibid., 157–68 and 283

Chapter 7 Population Explosion, 1886–1914

1 Mitchell, 'Jessie (Olding) Hunter,' 1, and McQueen Correspondence, Merritt and Victoria; BC salaries are detailed by teacher in Department of Education, *Annual Report*. The comparison with Nova Scotia come from Annie McQueen to her mother, Nicola, 16 November 1887, and Jessie McQueen to same, Nicola Lake, 24 September 1891, Merritt. Both women taught in Nova Scotia before coming to British Columbia.

2 Jessie McQueen to her mother, Nicola Lake, 10 April 1893, in McQueen Correspondence, Merritt; Charles Mair to George Denison, 4 January 1896, Mair Correspondence

3 Parkin, *Great Dominion*, 157, 159–60 and 190; Bancroft, *History of British Columbia*, ix and 661; Begg, *History of British Columbia*, 434; and Sage, 'British Columbia,' 183

4 McEvoy, *From the Great Lakes*, 184–6; H.P.P. Crease to Hewitt Bostock, 2 April 1898, cited in Johnson-Dean, *Crease Family Archives*, 31

5 Charles Mair to George Denison, Okanagan Mission, 6 October 1892, Mair Correspondence (emphasis in original); Emily Carr, *Book of Small*, 66–7, also 13; *Growing Pains*, 185; *Heart of a Peacock*, 71 and 145

6 British Columbia, *Statutes*, 1894, ch. 27, art. 13; Carr, *Book of Small*, 84

7 Carr, *Book of Small*, 132–3; Elliott, *Mayne Island*, 63; and Jessie McQueen to her mother, Nicola Lake, 9, 19, and 30 May 1892 and 29 May 1893, in McQueen Correspondence, Merritt (emphasis in original)

8 Charles Mair to George Denison, Kelowna, 17 July 1895, Mair Correspondence; Harrison, 'Pioneer Judge's Wife,' December 1952, 18

9 This assessment comes from the author's research in progress utilizing the provincial directories and 1881 and 1891 manuscript census for British Columbia and from observations by Patricia Roy.

10 Matthew Begbie to Royal Commission on Chinese Emigration, 1885, cited in Yee, *Saltwater City*, 12; Von Hesse-Wartegg, 'Visit,' 36

11 Sarah Crease, 1864, cited in Baskerville, *Beyond the Island*, 45; Mrs Clive Phillipps-Wolley to Lena, Victoria, September 1887, cited in Phillipps-Wolley, *Sportsman's Eden*, 181–2; MacGill, *My Mother the Judge*, 99

12 Yee, *Saltwater City*, 10

13 Carr, *Book of Small*, 113

14 Jessie McQueen to her mother, Lower Nicola, 25 June 1888, in McQueen Correspondence, Merritt

15 Carr, *Book of Small*, 105 and 107

16 Constitution cited in Kopas, *Bella Coola*, 246; Rev. Christian Saugstad, Report to Congregation in Neby, Minnesota, cited in ibid., 245

17 17 June and 16 November 1894 and 26 December 1896 entries in Fougner Diary. I am grateful to Milo Fougner for access to his father's diary.

18 Federal budget speech, 16 April 1901, cited in Royal Commission on Dominion-Provincial Relations, *Report*, 1: 73

19 Sladen, *On the Cars*, 395; Lumsden, *Through Canada*, 169

20 Kipling, *Letters of Travel*, 210; *From Sea to Sea*, 56; Kipling press clippings file in City of Vancouver Archives. The property was located on the southeast corner of Scott Street and Eleventh Avenue.

21 Bradley, *Canada*, 391; MacDonald, *Distant Neighbours*, 60, also 87; Lumsden, *Through Canada*, 251. This point underlies McDonald, 'Working-class Vancouver.'

22 Munro, *Short Stories*, 494; also Barman, *Growing Up British*

23 Sykes, *Home-Help*, 140; Stark, *Beyond Euphrates*, 23 and 27; Annie McQueen Gordon to sister Mary, Victoria, 21 February 1925, in McQueen Correspondence, Victoria

24 Stursberg, *Those Were the Days*, 38–9; 21 September 1882 entry in Hills, Diary; Bridie, *Across Canada*, 68 (emphasis in original)

25 Woodsworth, *Strangers*, 135

26 This description, including the quotations, comes from interviews by Imbert Orchard with Fraser delta fishermen transcribed in *Fishing at the Delta*.

27 Isenor, Stephens, and Watson, *One Hundred Spirited Years*, 133

28 Woodcock, *Ravens and Prophets*, 111

29 Statement by Brilliant Doukhobors, 1912, cited in Tarasoff, *Plakun Trava*, 118–19

30 Marlatt, 'Imperial Cannery, 1913,' in her *Steveston*, 16

31 Wilfrid Laurier to Earl Grey, 10 September 1907, cited in Ormsby, *British Columbia*, 351

32 Schreiner, *Refiners*, 17–18; Barman, 'Dynamics'

33 Ward, *White Canada Forever*, 169; Roy, *White Man's Province*, ix, 38, and 267

34 Florence Wilson in Mitchell and Duffy, *Bright Sunshine*, 16

35 1 October 1893 entry in Ivar Fougner, Diary

36 Grainger, *Woodsmen*, 40–8

37 Shelford and Shelford, *We Pioneered*, 53–71

38 Hutchison, *Far Side*, 29

Chapter 8 Disregard of Native Peoples, 1858–1945

1 Cell, 'Imperial Conscience,' 176, 179

2 James Douglas to Archibald Barclay, Fort Victoria, 3 September 1849, in Bowsfield, *Fort Victoria Letters*, 38

3 James Douglas to Archibald Barclay, Fort Victoria, 16 April 1851, in ibid., 176 (emphasis in original)

4 *British Colonist*, 8 March 1861

5 *British Columbian*, 13 May 1864

6 Joseph Trutch, 'Memorandum,' 29 January 1870, cited in Madill, *Indian Treaties*, 34

7 Wilson, *Hetty Dorval*, 1

8 Sproat, *Scenes and Studies*, 8; James Bell to John Thompson, 27 February 1859, cited in Fisher, *Contact and Conflict*, 104–5; *British Columbian*, 1 June 1869; Chittenden, *Travels in British Columbia*, 69

9 Treaty No. 8 is reproduced in Madill, *Indian Treaties*, 86–92.

10 Report of 1933 by G.M. Kerkhoff, Fort St John detachment, BC Game Department, cited in Brody, *Maps and Dreams*, 90

11 Boddam-Wetham, *Western Wanderings*, 287; cited in Wickwire, 'Jimmie Teit,' 5

12 Moran, *Stoney Creek Woman*, 79

13 William Duncan, Notebook, June 1862, cited in Usher [Friesen], *William Duncan*, 92 (emphasis in original)

14 Ibid., 60 and 63. Conflict with the Anglican church persuaded Duncan to relocate his community north to a new Metlakatla in Alaska in 1887.

15 Mulhall, *Will to Power*, x

16 British Columbia, Terms of Union with Canada, cited in Madill, *Indian Treaties*, 36; Fisher, *Contact and Conflict*, 176–7

17 J.A.J. McKenna, Address to chiefs and delegates representing interior tribes of British Columbia, Spence's Bridge, cited in Thomson, 'History of the Okanagan,' 153

18 Moran, *Stoney Creek Woman*, 61

19 W.H. Lomas to I.W. Powell, 27 February 1884, cited in Fisher, *Contact and Conflict*, 206; William Duncan to David Laird, May 1875, cited in ibid., 207

20 Ford, *Smoke from Their Fires*, 224; Assu with Inglis, *Assu of Cape Mudge*, 103–4

21 Speare, *Days of Augusta*, 7; Mitchell and Franklin, 'When You Don't Know the Language,' 24

22 Department of Indian Affairs, *Annual Reports*, with calculations included in Barman, 'Separate and Unequal'

23 *West Shore*, 10, no. 9 (1884), 275; Charles Mair to George Denison, Okanagan Mission, 5 December 1892, Mair Correspondence

24 Tennant, 'Native Indian Political Organization,' 6 and 8; Bolt, 'Conversion,' 39. This point is also made in Patterson, 'Kincolith.'

25 François Timoykin to Royal Commission on Indian Affairs for the Province of British Columbia, cited in Thomson, 'History of the Okanagan,' 155

26 Neispuck, quoted in Patterson, 'A Decade of Change,' 45

27 H.A. Conroy to Superintendent General of Indian Affairs, 29 October 1910, cited in Madill, *Indian Treaties*, 49; Assu with Inglis, *Assu of Cape Mudge*, 18; Allied Tribes of British Columbia, 'A Half Century of Injustice Towards the Indians of British Columbia,' cited in Thomson, 'History of the Okanagan,' 164

28 Moran, *Stoney Creek Woman*, 44; Assu with Inglis, *Assu of Cape Mudge*, 95–6

29 Carr, *Klee Wyck*, 6–7. For a similar description see Carr, *Heart of a Peacock*, 98.

30 This section draws on Hudson, 'Traplines and Timber.'

31 Hobson, *Rancher Takes a Wife*, 231; Shelford and Shelford, *We Pioneered*, 128

32 Collier, *Three against the Wilderness*, 2, 92–3, 96

33 Brody, *Maps and Dreams*, 91 and 96

34 This point is stressed in Knight, *Indians at Work*, which modifies Robin Fisher's assertion that native people were by the late 1880s reduced 'to a peripheral role in British Columbia's economy.' Fisher, *Contact and Conflict*, 210

35 Schreiner, *Refiners*, 24–5 (emphasis in original); Department of Indian Affairs, *Annual Report*, 1910, 327; repeated verbatim in 1911, 372

36 Blackman, *During My Time*, 59; Spradley, *Guests Never Leave Hungry*, 55; Burrows, '"Much-needed Class",' 34

37 Ford, *Smoke from Their Fires*, 192; Spradley, *Guests Never Leave Hungry*, 60; Assu with Inglis, *Assu of Cape Mudge*, 61, also 64–5

38 Assu with Inglis, *Assu of Cape Mudge*, 68; Blanchet, *Curve of Time*, 114

39 Carr, *Book of Small*, 107; Jessie McQueen to her mother Lower Nicola, 29 August

1888, in McQueen Correspondence, Merritt; Carr, *Growing Pains*, 228, referring to the baskets made by Indians living on the north shore of Burrard Inlet

40 Children grown, she became a Coast Salish language teacher in a local band school begun once Indians acquired some control over schooling in the 1970s. Frenchie, 'Self Educated Woman.' I am grateful to Lorraine Frenchie for permission to quote from this paper.

41 Susan Allison, *In-Cow-Mas-Ket* manuscript, cited in Ormsby, *Pioneer Gentlewoman*, xliii; 25 March 1938 entry in Stanwell-Fletcher, *Driftwood Valley*, 170–1

42 Carr, *Heart of a Peacock*, 104; and *Growing Pains*, 237

43 26 February 1861 entry in *Lady Franklin*, 14

44 John Fall Allison to his parents, cited in Ormsby, *Pioneer Gentlewoman*, xxv; Simson, 'Gastown,' 6; Assu with Inglis, *Assu of Cape Mudge*, 69

45 Harrison, 'Pioneer Judge's Wife,' December 1952, 18 (capitals in original); quoted in Cash, *Off the Record*, 16, and in her *I Like British Columbia*, 5. Roughly translated, the cheer's bastardized Chinook gave a greeting, followed by a call to make a lot of noise.

46 This point is made in Brody, *Maps and Dreams*, 27: 'Almost no one in northeast British Columbia refers to himself or herself as a Métis.' At first glance Andrews, *Métis Outpost*, is an exception, but the volume in fact describes a cluster of people who had migrated west from Alberta.

47 Elliott, *Mayne Island*, 7; Lean, 'Commemorating,' 1, 'Garcia Story,' 2–3, 'Coutlee,' 3 and 6

48 Jessie McQueen to her mother, Lower Nicola, 14 April, 28 May, and 27 September 1888, 27 March 1889 and 26 February 1890, in McQueen correspondence, Merritt

49 Wicks, *Memories*, 64; Moran, *Stoney Creek Woman*, 26; Speare, *Days of Augusta*, 8 and 22; Pennier, *Chiefly Indian*, 12, 90, and 125

50 Lean, 'Coutlee,' 3 and 5

51 Carr, *Klee Wyck*, 68; also 74

52 Canada, House of Commons, *Debates*, 1897, col. 4076, 14 June 1897; Department of Indian Affairs, *Annual Report*. 1898, xxvii

53 Department of Indian Affairs, *Annual Report*, 1912, 396; ibid., 1911, 385

54 Ibid., 1909, xxxiv, 1910, 273–5, 1911, 337

55 Tennant, 'Political Organization,' 16

56 Blanchet, *Curve of Time*, 108–9

57 Ford, *Smoke from Their Fires*; Spradley, *Guests Never Leave Hungry*; Assu with Inglis, *Assu of Cape Mudge*; and Blackman, *During My Time*

58 Spradley, *Guests Never Leave Hungry*, 59

59 Ford, *Smoke from Their Fires*, 224 and 227–8

60 Brody, *Maps and Dreams*, 262; Carr, *Klee Wyck*, 105–6. Similar is Speare, *Days of Augusta*, 70. An almost identical description of the process as undertaken each year in the Nicola Valley by local native people was given the author in late 1988.

Chapter 9 Growing Self-Confidence, 1900–1918

1 Ormsby, *British Columbia*, 336
2 A complete list is given in Cail, *Land, Man, and the Law*, 283–93
3 Playfair, 'Fifty-seven Varieties,' 907; Martin, 'Nechaco Valley,' 410
4 Fort Fraser advertisements in *Westminster Hall Magazine* 1, no. 7 (December 1911); 1, no. 8 (January 1912) and 2, no. 1 (July 1912)
5 Sir Harry Britain, *Pilgrims and Pioneers*, 3rd ed. (London, n.d.), 188, cited in Ormsby, *British Columbia*, 359
6 Wicks, *Memories*, 89
7 Grainger, *Woodsmen*, 20 and 34
8 Royal Commission on Timber and Forestry, *Report*, 1910, cited in Bernsohn, *Cutting up the North*, 17
9 Sinclair, *Inverted Pyramid*, 327–8
10 Ibid., 105; Bob Swenson, cited in MacKay, *Lumberjacks*, 185
11 Shelford and Shelford, *We Pioneered*, 66
12 Sinclair, *Inverted Pyramid*, 181; Grainger, *Woodsmen*, 14; Pennier, *Chiefly Indian*, 90 and 110
13 Bulman, *Kamloops Cattlemen*, 51
14 Shelford and Shelford, *We Pioneered*, 86; Hobson, *Grass beyond the Mountains*, 125
15 Mould, *Stump Farms*, 13–14
16 Day, 'Eustace Smith,' 47–8 (emphasis in original)
17 Stone, *Urban Development*, Table 2.2, 29
18 Noel, *Blanket-stiff*, 183
19 MacGill, *My Mother the Judge*, 138
20 Carr, *Book of Small*, 166; Kipling, *Sea to Sea*, 58; *Times*, 10 October 1908
21 Jack Hetherington, 'Ship Shop,' *Times* (North Vancouver), n.d., cited in Rushton, *Echoes of the Whistle*, 50
22 Lowther, 'Mill Town,' 17
23 Ron Round, personnel manager at Fraser Mills, cited in Gould, *Logging*, 43; *British Columbia Federationist*, 1 June 1923
24 Duff Pattullo, 1917, cited in Bradbury, 'New Settlements Policy,' 55
25 Rev. Dr Mackay, cited in MacDonald, *Distant Neighbours*, 102
26 Sharpe, 'Enlistment'
27 Smith, 'McBride: A Study,' 1
28 Roy, 'Progress,' 28

Chapter 10 Reform and Its Limits, 1871–1929

1 Carr, *Growing Pains*, 4
2 Annie McQueen Gordon to her mother and sister Jessie, Phillipps, BC, 26 July 1901, in McQueen Correspondence, Victoria (emphasis in original)
3 Fraser, *Canada As It Is*, 217

4 MacDonald, *Distant Neighbours*, 39

5 Hutcheson, *Depression Stories*, 109

6 Palmer, *Working-Class Experience*, 96–135

7 Shelford, *Snowshoes to Politics*, 11; Janet A. Beets, Port McNeill, cited in *Shopping Guide*, xii, xiii

8 Jessie McQueen to her mother, Lower Nicola, 28 May 1888, 22 October 1888, 13 February 1889, and 26 November 1891, Kamloops, 4 July 1892, and Nicola Lake, 14 November 1892, in McQueen Correspondence, Merritt; 25 June and 22 October 1911 entries in Craig, *But This Is Our War*, 13 and 15

9 Constance MacKay, 'Vancouver's New Novelist,' *Mayfair*, November 1947, 67, cited in Howard, 'Shockable and Unshockable Methodists,' 119; Ethel Wilson to Mazo de la Roche, Toronto, 30 June 1955, in Stouck, *Ethel Wilson*, 198

10 *B.C. Handbook of Women's Institutes* (Victoria: Department of Agriculture 1913), 4, cited in Zacharias, 'Women's Institute,' 59

11 Carr, *Book of Small*, 86; Jessie McQueen to her mother, Lower Nicola, 12 June 1889, and Nicola Lake, 22 February 1892, McQueen Correspondence, Merritt (emphasis in original)

12 Hutchison, *Far Side*, 32; Keenleyside, *Memoirs*, 1: 46

13 16 November 1895 entry, cited in Kluckner, *M.I. Rogers*, 37

14 *British Colonist*, 27 October 1871

15 Schwantes, *Pacific Northwest*, 251; Hutcheson, *Depression Stories*, 110

16 Bowen, *Boss Whistle*, esp. 196–7

17 This section draws on Ralston, '1900 Strike.'

18 *Province*, 4 August 1913, cited in Jamieson, *Times of Trouble*, 128, also 121

19 Edmund S. Kirby to T.C. Blackstock, Rossland, 31 January 1901, cited in Robin, *Radical Politics*, 4, fn 2; Grainger, *Woodsmen*, 43

20 Quoted in Orr, 'Western Federation,' 237

21 MacGill, *My Mother the Judge*, 115 and 119

22 These comments draw on Wade, 'Helena Gutteridge,' and conversations with Irene Howard.

23 *B.C. Federationist*, 22 December 1916

24 Sinclair, *Inverted Pyramid*, 315–16; Blythe Rogers, Diary, cited in Schreiner, *Refiners*, 51

25 This section is derived from Hak, 'British Columbia Loggers.'

26 This point is elaborated in McDonald, 'Working-Class Vancouver,' 345–6.

27 Shelford, *Snowshoes to Politics*, 3

28 Grigg, *One to Seventy*, 65. This attitude underlies what is one of the few completely self-written and published autobiographies of a very ordinary British Columbian. Grigg, born in 1883, maintained a growing family in sometimes makeshift living conditions mostly by intermittent logging jobs, from time to time through fishing attempts at farming.

29 Hutcheson, *Depression Stories*, 111, 114; Knight and Knight, *Very Ordinary Life*, 200

30 This section draws on Campbell, 'Liquor and Liberals.'

31 February 1918 entry, cited in Kluckner, *M.I. Rogers*, 83

32 MacGill, *My Mother the Judge*, 198

33 A.M. Manson, Minister of Labour, March 1927, cited in *British Columbia's Progress*, 75; MacGill, *My Mother the Judge*, 171

34 Cited in Davies, '"Services Rendered",' 257. This section draws on Sutherland, *Children*.

35 Angus McInnis, 'As We See It – Concerning Education,' *B.C. Federationist*, 15 and 19 August 1924

36 Wilson and Stortz, '"May the Lord"'; Wilson, 'Visions'

37 Bateman, 'Stories,' 3

38 Ross, 'Romance,' 19

39 *Labour Statesman* (Vancouver), 22 August 1924

40 29 September 1930 entry in Morton, *God's Galloping Girl*, 168

41 Naylor, *Private Practice*, 40–57

42 Henripin, *Trends and Factors*, 82–5, 101, 172–3, 198–200, and 341; and McLaren and McLaren, *Bedroom and the State*, 11, 59

43 Norcross, 'Mary Ellen Smith,' 357 and 359

44 MacGill, *My Mother the Judge*, 132; Susan Allison to George Allison, 1899, cited in Ormsby, *Pioneer Gentlewoman*, xli; Inga Teit Perkin, quoted in Howes and Lean, 'Interview,' 2; and Street, *Watch-fires*, 115 and 128–9, also 135

45 Frank Frisby, cited in Hodgson, *Squire*, 89. This topic is elaborated in Turnbull, *Trail*.

46 Robin, *Company Province* 2: 213

47 Cited in Yee, *Saltwater City*, 79; Yoshida, 'Issei Life,' 7

48 *Penticton Herald*, 1 January 1920, cited in Ward, *White Canada Forever*, 106

49 Marlatt, 'Imperial Cannery,' in her *Steveston*, 15–16

50 Howay, *British Columbia*, 576

51 Hutchison, *Unknown Country*, 287

Chapter 11 The Best and Worst of Times, 1918–1945

1 *Province*, 16 June 1924

2 *British Columbia's Next Premier* (1928), cited in Robin, *Company Province*, 1: 229

3 This topic is detailed in Bartlett, 'Real Wages.'

4 *Statistics of Industry*, net value table and also tables M2 and T1.

5 For an informal vignette of MacMillan, see Garner, *Never Chop Your Rope*, 39–79

6 Canneries' location in 1928 is given in Farley, *Atlas of British Columbia*, 89; numbers in Lyons, *Salmon*

7 Bourgon, *Rubber Boots*, 72–3

8 19 October 1929 entry in Morton, *God's Galloping Girl*, 11–12

9 Freya Stark to Herbert Young, Creston, 30 November 1928, in Stark, *Beyond Euphrates*, 35

10 This point is emphasized in Palmer, *Working-Class Experience*, esp. 177–8.

11 Marjorie Harris, 'Fifty Years of Chatelaine,' *Chatelaine*, March 1978, 43

12 New, *History*, 143

13 Clough, 'Carroll Aikins,' 116–22; Sydney Risk, 'The Players' Club As I Knew It,' in *Way We Were*, 37

14 W.P. Weston, cited in Rogers, 'W.P. Weston,' 177, also 283

15 16 June 1933 entry, cited in Kluckner, *M.I. Rogers*, 140–1; Garnett Sedgewick, cited in Philip Akrigg, 'Sedgewick: The Man and the Achievement,' in *Way We Were*, 6

16 W.P. Weston, cited in Rogers, 'W.P. Weston,' 17; Carr, *Hundreds and Thousands*, 63 (emphasis in original)

17 Elizabeth Leslie Stubbs, 'Dean Mary Bollert,' in *Way We Were*, 21

18 *Province*, 16 July 1938

19 Mamie Maloney in *Sun*, 29 July 1989

20 Baird, *Waste Heritage*, 80; letter to R.B. Bennett, Sayward, 28 June 1935, cited in Grayson and Bliss, *Wretched*, 160

21 Hutcheson, *Depression Stories*, 34, 45, and 59–60

22 Liversedge, *Recollections*, 5; Hutcheson, *Depression Stories*

23 Sigurd Teit, quoted in Robinson, 'Sigurd Teit,' 11; Hutchison, *Far Side*, 90

24 Liversedge, *Recollections*, 5. Hutcheson implies that a few women resided in jungles, but does not indicate how they got there.

25 Liversedge, *Recollections*, 24; Dorothy Livesay, 'Coming West,' cited in White, *British Columbia*, 46–7

26 Moran, *Stoney Creek Woman*, 27; Mould, *Stump Farms*, 134

27 8 September 1930 entry in Morton, *God's Galloping Girl*, 154 (emphasis in original); Ernest Rogers, cited in Shreiner, *Refiners*, 108

28 Elliott, *Mayne Island*, 63; Shelford and Shelford, *We Pioneered*, 184

29 Hobson, *Grass beyond the Mountains*, 9; also Foster, *One Heart*

30 The process is described in Grigg, *One to Seventy*, 119–27.

31 Programs are differentiated in Guest, *Emergence of Social Security*, 84–6.

32 General Andrew McNaughton, cited in Struthers, *No Fault*, 99

33 Jack Diamond, cited in Sirotnik, *Running Tough*, 41

34 MacDonald, *Distant Neighbours*, 118; also Smith, 'CCF, NPA'

35 *Colonist*, 21 September 1935

36 Knight and Knight, *Very Ordinary Life*, 131; Carr, *Hundreds and Thousands*, 34 and 37

37 Carr, *Hundreds and Thousands*, 38

38 Hodgson, *Squire of Kootenay West*, 83

39 Gerry McGeer to R. B. Bennett, Vancouver, 21 May 1935, cited in Liversedge, *Recollections*, 164

40 A.A. Mackenzie to W.A. Gordon, 11 June 1935, cited in ibid., 177

41 BC Conservative Association to C.A. Stewart, 15 May 1935, cited in Struthers, *No Fault*, 137

42 *British Columbia*, 273; Duff Pattullo to R.B. Bennett, 18 December 1933, cited in Ormsby, *British Columbia*, 458

43 This section relies on Schrodt, 'History of Pro-Rec.'

44 Hobson, *Grass beyond the Mountains*, 223 and 224, also 219–32

45 Collier, *Three against the Wilderness*, 198–9

46 Carr, *Hundreds and Thousands*, 233

47 Ibid., 302 and 304

48 Quoted in Baskerville, *Beyond the Island*, 101

49 Phillips, *No Power Greater*, 121

50 Baird, *Waste Heritage*, 311

51 *Sun* and *Province*, 19 January 1938

52 Howay, Sage, and Angus, *British Columbia*, 404 (emphasis in original)

53 Adachi, *Enemy That Never Was*, esp. 225–7

54 Ken Grieve, 'Civil Rights, 1942,' cited in *Way We Were*, 58

Chapter 12 The Good Life, 1945–1972

1 Hobson, *Grass beyond the Mountains*, 16 and 18; Knight and Knight, *Very Ordinary Life*, 143

2 Hobson, *Rancher Takes a Wife*, 144; Shelford, *Snowshoes to Politics*, 119 and 172

3 Patrick Lane, born in 1939 in Nelson and quoted in Twigg, *Strong Voices*, 156; Gibson, *Bull of the Woods*, 269–70

4 *Sun*, 12 February 1949

5 Knight and Knight, *Very Ordinary Life*, 261

6 Cash, *Off the Record*, 139

7 Carr, *Hundreds and Thousands*, 62

8 Street, *Watch-fires*, 257; Gerard, *Converted in the Country*, 79 and 85; Ellis, 'Some Aspects'

9 Tozer, 'Biographies,' 55

10 Robin, *Company Province*, 2: 127

11 Shelford, *Snowshoes to Politics*, 137 and 143

12 Winch's perspective is detailed in Steeves, *Compassionate Rebel*, 180–3.

13 This sequence of events is recounted from Bennett's perspective in Mitchell, *Bennett*, 170–3.

14 This assessment is based on Ellis, 'Some Aspects,' 170–89.

15 Press report cited in Mitchell, *Bennett*, 194

16 Black, 'British Columbia'; Ray Perrault in *Province*, 6 September 1960, cited in Robin, *Company Province*, 2: 219

17 Shelford, *Snowshoes to Politics*, 149, 174, and 176

18 *Sun*, 4 February 1953; Hutchison, 'Interior,' 23; Hutchison, 'Coast,' 40 and 47

19 Mitchell, *Bennett*, 384

20 Ibid., 207

21 Shelford, *Snowshoes to Politics*, 212; Keenleyside, *Memories*, 2: 494; Black, 'British Columbia,' 27

22 *British Columbia External Trade Report*, 1987, 41
23 Shelford, *Snowshoes to Politics*, 148
24 Quoted in Mitchell, *Bennett*, 350
25 Bennett's first province-wide speech after the 1952 election, cited in ibid., 205
26 *Sun*, 10 October 1957
27 Shelford, *Snowshoes to Politics*, 126. This section draws on Marchak, *Green Gold*.
28 Shelford and Shelford, *We Pioneered*, 200
29 For a visual comparison between the two time periods, see Farley, *Atlas of British Columbia*, 65.
30 Mullins, 'Changes,' 30, also figures 5 and 11
31 MacKay, *Empire of Wood*, 276
32 Wilson, 'From Flores,' in *Mrs. Golightly*, 35–6
33 Woodcock, *Ravens and Prophets*, 181 and 53; Hutchison, 'Interior,' 34
34 Hobson, *Grass beyond the Mountains*, 18; Hutchison, 'Interior,' 38–9
35 Quoted in Bowman, *Road, Rail and River!*, 57
36 Essex, 'Memories of Shandilla (East of Kitwanga),' in Essex, *Rhymes*, 44. I am grateful to Shirley Hobenshield of Kitwanga for alerting me to this publication.
37 Siemens, 'Process of Settlement,' 48, and his 'Introduction,' 6; White, 'Bomb,' 27
38 White, 'Minstrel Island,' 35
39 W.A.C. Bennett, cited in Mitchell, *Bennett*, 369
40 *Province*, 27 September 1952 and 12 June 1953
41 Instructions given to Commission Inquiry into Redefinition of Electoral Districts, as detailed in its *Report* (Victoria 1966)
42 Commission of Inquiry, *Report*, 16
43 Black, 'British Columbia,' 32
44 *Sun*, 28 May 1968
45 Ibid., 22 August 1972
46 Mitchell, *Bennett*, 258; Mitchell, *Succession*, 15; Keenleyside, *Memoirs*, 2: 494

Chapter 13 Equality Revolution, 1945–1980

1 Prentice, *Women in Canada*, 259
2 Shrum, *Autobiography*, 99
3 Ethel Wilson, 'The Life and Death of Mrs. Grant: A Didactive Tale, with Questions,' in Stouck, *Ethel Wilson*, 71. Perhaps significantly, the manuscript was rejected by her London publisher as not enhancing Wilson's stature as a writer (56).
4 Data cited in Prentice, *Canadian Women*, 383–4
5 White, *Hard Man to Beat*, 159–61
6 The importance of factionalism is evident from White, *Hard Man to Beat*, and Palmer, *Communist Life*; Lembecke and Tattam, *One Union in Wood*, viii and 176.

7 Quoted in Bernsohn, *Cutting Up the North*, 52

8 This section draws on Warburton and Coburn, 'Rise of Non-Manual Work.'

9 Knight and Koizumi, *Man of Our Times*, 86

10 Spradley, *Guests Never Leave Hungry*, 198

11 Hawthorn, Belshaw and Jamieson, *Indians of British Columbia*, 65; Moran, *Stoney Creek Woman*, 27

12 Evans, *Mist on the River*, 66

13 Sharon McIvor Grismer, quoted in Niehaus, 'Grismer,' 7

14 Blackman, *During My Time*, 131

15 The process is detailed in Assu with Inglis, *Assu of Cape Mudge*, 104–8.

16 Hawthorn, Belshaw, and Jamieson, *Indians of British Columbia*, 84, 86, and 256

17 Ibid., 154

18 Hawthorn, *Survey*, 1: 13 and 145

19 The concept is developed Manuel and Posluns, *Fourth World*.

20 Pierre Trudeau, cited in Miller, *Skyscrapers Hide the Heavens*, 224

21 Cash, *Off the Record*, 138

22 Siemens, 'Process of Settlement,' 42. On the distribution of Dutch dairy farms, see the map in Ginn, 'Dutch and Dairying,' 120.

23 This point is underlined by Map 7, 'Chinese in Vancouver, 1981,' in Robinson, 'Vancouver,' 76.

24 Ian Lee, cited in Yee, *Saltwater City*, 127

25 Troper and Palmer, *Issues in Cultural Diversity*, 52–60

26 D.M. Fraser, quoted in Twigg, *Strong Voices*, 92

27 John Gray, 'The Vancouver in My Mind,' in White, *British Columbia*, 1–2; Fraser, quoted in Twigg, *Strong Voices*, 92; letter of Dan McLeod to Grace Tratt, 7 November 1973, cited in Tratt, *Check List*, 54

28 John Robbins, quoted in *Sun*, 15 July 1989

29 Vonnegut, *Eden Express*, 48. Among a spate of books appearing in the United States with British Columbia as the focus were Birmingham, *Vancouver Split*; Brower, *The Starship and the Canoe*; and Ziner, *Within This Wilderness*. I am grateful to Peter Seixas for bringing these sources to my attention.

30 2 June and 14 September 1953 entries, cited in Kluckner, *M.I. Rogers*, 150

31 No consensus exists among critics as to what constitutes BC literature. Inclusion here as a BC author is based on a somewhat arbitrary combination of public recognition, residence, sense of identity, and the province's role as a setting.

32 Ethel Wilson to John Gray, Vancouver, 2 November 1947, in Stouck, *Ethel Wilson*, 145 (emphasis in original)

33 Sean O'Faolain, *The Listener*, cited in McAlpine, *Other Side of Silence*, 160

34 Ethel Wilson to Malcom Ross, 8 July 1953, in Stouck, *Ethel Wilson*, 182; Ethel Wilson to Mazo de la Roche, Kelowna, 20 August 1955, in ibid., 200 (emphasis in original)

35 Ethel Wilson to John Gray, Victoria, 14 April 1955, in ibid., 195. For Wilson's

similar comments on Brian Moore, see Ethel Wilson to John Gray, Vancouver, 29 September 1962, in ibid., 226 (emphasis in original).

36 Woodcock, *Ravens and Prophets*, 86; 'Editorial,' *Canadian Literature* 1, no. 1 (Summer 1959), 3

37 Patrick Lane, quoted in Twigg, *Strong Voices*, 158; also Dorothy Livesay, 179–83, Al Purdy, 229, and Peter Trower, 263

38 New, *History*, 224, also 223 and 337; Stouck, *Major Canadian Authors*, 273

39 Wilson, 'Cat Among the Falcons,' 17

40 By comparison the number in the Maritimes averaged ten from the early 1970s. The total refers to Canadian-owned, owner-managed English-language presses publishing up to ten titles a year, primarily non-commercial literary fiction, and at least two over their lifetime. Tratt, *Check List*; Mellanson, *Literary Presses*.

41 Richardson, *First Class*, 19, 22 and 27, fn85; Harper, *Painting in Canada*, 351; Reid, *Concise History*, 287, also 200–1 and 284–9

42 Edith Iglauer, quoted in Twigg, *Strong Voices*, 134

43 Keenleyside, *Memoirs*, 2: 178; Shelford, *Snowshoes to Politics*, 156

Chapter 14 A New Dynamic, 1972–1995

1 Because of the paucity of scholarly resources, parts of this chapter are based on a critical reading of the British Columbian and national press. Most numerical data are taken from provincial or federal publications and, where controversial, have been confirmed with affected groups.

2 Shelford, *Snowshoes to Politics*, 264 and 230

3 Ibid., 267 and 271–2; Mitchell, *Bennett*, 423

4 This concept is developed in Marr and Paterson, *Canada*, 445–8.

5 The fate of each of the twenty-six bills making up the restraint program is given in Magnusson, *New Reality*, 281–5.

6 Sinclair, *Inverted Pyramid*, 97; Haig-Brown, *Measure of the Year*, 217; and *British Columbia Lumberman* 12 (March 1928), 20; W.R. Ross, quoted in Gould, *Logging*, 63

7 Ministry of Forests, *Annual Report*, 1981, cited in Gould, *Logging*, 13

8 Karen Mahon, quoted in Patricia Lush, 'World watches as B.C. releases Clayoquot report,' *Globe and Mail*, 29 May 1995

9 This section draws on Marchak, Guppy, and McMullan, *Uncommon Property*; Scott Simpson, 'The battles over precious stocks of salmon migrate with seasons,' *Vancouver Sun*, 5 August 1995; and Miro Cernetig, 'Scaling back to save salmon,' *Globe and Mail*, 8 July 1995.

10 Diane Francis, 'Visible assets fuel an economy,' *Maclean's*, 24 August 1992, 11

11 Table 5, based on the federal censuses, apportions persons declaring multiple origins in 1981 or 1991 between their various origins, to which were added, in the case of 1991, all 69,060 persons declaring only North American Indian origin and 290 persons declaring only Inuit origin. The 1991 federal Aboriginal Peoples' Survey counted 101,135 people in British Columbia 'reporting Aboriginal identity'

(Statistics Canada, 1991 Aboriginal Peoples' Survey, catalogue 899–533, Table 1.1). The Department of Indian and Northern Affairs (DIAND) estimated British Columbia's population of registered, or status, Indians to be 94,006 in 1993 and 102,829 by 1996 (DIAND: *Basic Departmental Data* 1994, Table 3).

12 Spradley, *Guests Never Leave Hungry*, 261

13 Brody, *Maps and Dreams*, 97; Shelford, *Snowshoes to Politics*, 130, 156, and 208. Numerical data taken from British Columbia, Provincial Health Officer, *Annual Report*, 1994, and British Columbia, Premier's Forum, *Untangling the Social Safety Net for Aboriginal Peoples*, 1995.

14 Moran, *Stoney Creek Woman*, 117; Brody, *Maps and Dreams*, 2, 72, and 194

15 See *Report of the British Columbia Claims Task Force*, 28 June 1991; British Columbia Treaty Commission, *Report*, 1994–95; and Stewart Bell and Gordon Hamilton, 'Treaties in the Making,' *Vancouver Sun*, 15 December 1994

16 BC Treaty Commission, 'Traditional Territories of British Columbia First Nations,' November 1994; Stewart Bell, 'Staking Claim,' *Vancouver Sun*, 1 April 1995

17 Richard Eng, in ibid., 7 December 1989; David Lam in ibid., 17 February 1989; Peter McMartin, 'David Lam: He made a stolid job blossom,' ibid., 31 March 1995

18 David Lam in ibid., 19 March 1989

19 Robert Sarti, '100,000 more people now living in B.C. despite fewer births,' ibid., 28 September 1994

20 Robert Burkinshaw in ibid., 17 February 1989

21 Davis and Hutton, 'Two Economies,' 3; Robert Matas, 'Hard corps Vancouver,' *Globe and Mail*, 27 May 1995; and 'A western welcome for Asia,' *The Economist*, 26 August 1995, 40

22 This section draws on Kalman, Phillips, and Ward, *Exploring Vancouver*.

23 Norman Ruff, quoted in Tom Barrett, 'B.C. will be tough battleground,' *Vancouver Sun*, 19 September 1992; column by Terry Morley in ibid., 8 May 1990; and Barbara Yaffe, 'Who's really getting shafted? (B.C., that's who),' ibid., 26 August 1995

24 Garreau, *Nine Nations of North America*

25 Quoted in Deborah Wilson, 'Fear and loathing in British Columbia,' *Globe and Mail*, 5 October 1992

Chapter 15 The British Columbia Identity

1 Carr, *Growing Pains*, 239. Among attempts to define a British Columbia identity are Elkins, 'State of Mind,' and Cole, 'Intellectual Imaginative Development.'

2 Smith, *Helmcken*, 75 and 110

3 Johnson, *Very Far West Indeed*; Carr, *House of All Sorts*, 64–5; John Bentley Mays, 'To be an art lover like Alvin Balkind,' *Globe and Mail*, 31 December 1992; Atwood, *Cat's Eye*, 14; Peter C. Newman, 'British Columbia,' *Maclean's*, 24 August 1992, 13

4 Grainger, *Woodsmen*, 34–5; Wicks, *Memories*, 38; Hutchison, *Unknown Country*,

315; Howard White, quoted in Robert Matas, 'Coasting through life not the style of every B.C. resident,' *Globe and Mail*, 10 February 1992

5 Charles Mair to George Denison, Okanagan Mission, 6 October 1892, Mair Correspondence

6 *Times* (London), 5 February 1862; also 1 November 1859, 30 January 1860, and 19 March 1863

7 The autobiography of another indigenous entrepreneur, Jimmy Pattison, underlines the difficulties; see Pattison with Grescoe, *Jimmy*.

8 Jessie McQueen to her mother, Lower Nicola, 2 February 1891, in McQueen Correspondence, Merritt; Grainger, *Woodsmen*, 55

9 Hutchison, *Unknown Country*, 314; Grainger, *Woodsmen*, 98

10 Gary Geddes, quoted in Twigg, *Strong Voices*, 109

11 This observation underlies the entirety of Harris, 'Moving Amid the Mountains.'

12 6 October 1911 entry, cited in Craig, *Our War*, 14–15; Howay, Sage, and Angus, *British Columbia*, 408; Scott, 'Notes,' 8

13 Shelford, *Snowshoes to Politics*, 54

14 Legislative debate, 10 and 11 March 1870, in Hendrickson, *Journals*, 5: 467 and 480

15 Ralston, 'Theme and Pattern,' 4

16 Joseph Trutch to J.A. Macdonald, 9 February 1886, cited in Ormsby, *British Columbia*, 291; W.A.C. Bennett, interview with Peter Newman, 1967, cited in Mitchell, *Bennett*, 351–2

17 Ralston, 'Theme and Pattern,' 8; McGeer, *Politics in Paradise*, 155; Mitchell, *Succession*, 45, which uses as the basis for comparison three thousand and three million miles

18 Sage, 'British Columbia Becomes Canadian,' 64; Brian Smith, 'McBride,' 23

19 Hutchison, 'Interior,' 34

20 Jan Morris, 'Canada at 125 – a modest young giant,' *Globe and Mail*, 1 July 1992; Haig-Brown, *Measure of the Year*, 18

21 Manning, quoted in Miro Cernetig, 'B.C.'s a popular place for populist uprisings,' *Globe and Mail*, 28 January 1995; Kim Campbell on the Bill Good show, CKNW radio, Vancouver, 31 July 1995

22 Wood, 'Population,' 309

23 Davis and Hutton, 'Two Economies,' 3 and 13

24 Quoted in Brody, *Maps and Dreams*, 140; 25 October 1929 entry in Morton, *God's Galloping Girl*, 15 (emphasis in original); Rena Kinney in conversation with the author, Prince George, 14 October 1989. I am grateful to Rena Kinney for permission to quote from her observations.

25 Howard, *Struggle for Social Justice*

26 'A Trip to Comox,' *British Colonist*, 20 April 1867; Johnstone, *Coal Dust*, 140; also Ward, 'Class and Race'

27 Jack Shadbolt, 'Setting the Compass,' in White, *British Columbia*, 39; Johnstone, *Coal Dust*, 119

28 Blake, *Two Political Worlds*, 8; Allan Fotheringham, cited in ibid., 61

29 Leonard George, 'Native Spirit Rising,' in White, *British Columbia*, 29
30 Mick Maloney, 'Natives must stop dwelling on the past,' *Vancouver Courier*, 3 September 1995, 6; Bains and Johnston, *Four Quarters*, xiii
31 Jagpal, *Becoming Canadians*
32 Chong, *Concubine's Children*; Bains and Johnston, *Four Quarters*
33 Robinson with Wickwire, *Write it on Your Heart*; Robinson with Wickwire, *Nature Power*; Mack with Thommasen, *Grizzlies & White Guys*; Mack with Thommasen, *Bella Coola Man*; Moran, *Stoney Creek Woman*; Blackman, *During My Time*; Assu with Inglis, *Assu*; Kirkness, ed., *Khot-Law-Cha*
34 Rafe Mair on the Rafe Mair show, CKNW radio, 7 August 1995
35 Carr, *Growing Pains*, 239; Carr, *Hundreds and Thousands*, 5 and 83
36 Hutchison, *Unknown Country*, 315; Wilson, 'Somewhere Near the Truth,' in Stouck, *Ethel Wilson*, 89; Wilson, 'Bridge,' 44; George, 'Native Spirit'

References

Adachi, Ken. *The Enemy That Never Was: A History of the Japanese Canadians*. Toronto: McClelland and Stewart 1976

Akrigg, G.P.V. and Helen B. Akrigg. *British Columbia Chronicle, 1778–1846 and 1847–1871*. 2 vols. Vancouver: Discovery Press 1977

Allen, Robert C. *The B.C. Economy: Past, Present, Future*. Vancouver: BC Economic Policy Institute 1985

Andrews, Clarence L. 'Russian Plans for American Dominion,' *Washington Historical Quarterly* 18 (1927), 83–92

Andrews, Gerry. *Métis Outpost: Memoirs of the First Schoolmaster at the Métis Settlement of Kelly Lake, B.C., 1923–25*. Victoria: G. Andrews 1985

Anglican Church, Diocese of Columbia. *Annual Report*

Archer, Christon I. 'Spain and the Defence of the Pacific Ocean Empire, 1750–1810,' *N/S: Canadian Journal of Latin American and Caribbean Studies* 11 (1986), 15–41

Assu, Harry, with Joy Inglis. *Assu of Cape Mudge: Recollections of a Coastal Indian Chief*. Vancouver: UBC Press 1989

Atwood, Margaret. *Cat's Eye*. Toronto: McClelland and Stewart 1988

Bains, Tara Singh and Hugh Johnston. *The Four Quarters of the Night: The Life-Journey of an Emigrant Sikh*. Montreal: McGill-Queen's University Press 1995

Baird, Irene. *Waste Heritage*. Toronto: Macmillan 1939

Bancroft, Hubert Howe. *History of British Columbia, 1792–1887*. San Francisco: History Company 1887

Barman, Jean. *Growing up British in British Columbia: Boys in Private School*. Vancouver: UBC Press 1984

– 'The Dynamics of Control in a Model Company Town: Powell River, Canada, 1910–1955.' Paper presented to the American Historical Association 1988

– 'Separate and Unequal: Indian and White Girls at All Hallows School,

1884–1920,' in Jean Barman, Yvonne Hébert, and Don McCaskill, eds., *Indian Education in Canada*, 1: 110–31. Vancouver: UBC Press 1986

– 'Transfer, Imposition or Consensus? The Emergence of Educational Structures in Nineteenth-Century British Columbia,' in Nancy M. Sheehan, J. Donald Wilson, and David C. Jones, eds., *Schools in the West: Essays in Canadian Educational History*, 241–64. Calgary: Detselig 1986

Bartlett, Eleanor A. 'Real Wages and the Standard of Living in Vancouver, 1901–1929,' *BC Studies* 51 (Autumn 1981), 3–62

Baskerville, Peter A. *Beyond the Island: An Illustrated History of Victoria*. Burlington: Windsor 1986

Bateman, Lillian. 'Stories from the Horseshoe Valley,' in Howard White, ed., *Raincoast Chronicles: Forgotten Villages of the BC Coast*, 1–9. Madeira Park: Harbour 1987

[Beanlands, A.] *British Columbia as a Field for Emigration and Investment*. Victoria: Queen's Printer 1891

Begg, Alexander. *History of British Columbia*. Toronto: William Briggs 1894

Benjamin, I.J. *Three Years in America, 1859–1862*. Vol. 2. Philadelphia: Jewish Publication Society of America 1956

Bernsohn, Ken. *Cutting up the North: The History of the Forest Industry in the Northern Interior*. North Vancouver: Hancock House n.d.

Birmingham, John. *The Vancouver Split*. New York: Simon and Schuster 1973

Bishop, Charles A. 'Kwah: A Carrier Chief,' in Carol M. Judd and Arthur J. Ray, eds., *Old Trails and New Directions: Papers of the Third North American Fur Trade Conference*, 191–304. Toronto: University of Toronto Press 1980

Black, Edwin R. 'British Columbia: The Politics of Exploitation,' in R.A. Shearer, ed., *Exploiting Our Economic Potential: Public Policy and the British Columbia Economy*, 23–41. Toronto: Holt, Rinehart and Winston 1968

Blackman, Margaret B. *During My Time: Florence Edenshaw Davidson, A Haida Woman*. Seattle: University of Washington Press 1982

Blake, Donald E. *Two Political Worlds: Parties and Voting in British Columbia*. Vancouver: UBC Press 1985

Blanchet, M. Wylie. *The Curve of Time*. Sidney: Gray's 1968, orig. 1961

Boddam-Wetham, J.W. *Western Wanderings: A Record of Travel in the Evening Land*. London: Richard Bentley and Son 1874

Bolt, Clarence R. 'The Conversion of the Port Simpson Tsimshian: Indian Control or Missionary Manipulation?' *BC Studies* 57 (Spring 1983), 38–56

Bourgon, Nan. *Rubber Boots for Dancing and Other Memories of Pioneer Life in the Bulkley Valley*. Smithers: Hetherington 1979

Bowen, Lynn. *Boss Whistle: The Coal Miners of Vancouver Island Remember*. Lantzville: Oolichan 1982

Bowman, Phylis. *Road, Rail and River!* Prince Rupert: Sunrise 1981

Bowsfield, Hartwell, ed. *Fort Victoria Letters 1843–1851*. Winnipeg: Hudson's Bay Record Society 1979

Bradbury, J.H. 'New Settlements Policy in British Columbia,' *Urban History Review* 8, no. 2 (October 1979), 42–76

Bradley, A.G. *Canada in the Twentieth Century*. Westminster: Archibald Constable 1903

Bridie, M.F. *Across Canada with Two Cameras*. Axminster: Bagshawe 1938

British Colonist. Victoria

British Columbia, Department of Education, *Annual Reports*.

British Columbia in the Canadian Confederation: A Submission Presented to the Royal Commission on Dominion-Provincial Relations by the Government of the Province of British Columbia. Victoria: King's Printer 1938

British Columbia. *British Columbia Financial and Economic Review* (formerly *Economic and Statistical Review*)

British Columbia. *Statutes*

British Columbia Federationist. Vancouver

British Columbia Lumberman. Vancouver

British Columbia Magazine. Vancouver

British Columbia Mineral Statistics: Annual Summary Tables, Historical Mineral Production to 1990. Victoria: Ministry of Energy, Mines and Petroleum Resources 1992

British Columbia annual provincial directories

British Columbian. New Westminster

British Columbia's Progress. Victoria: King's Printer 1928

Brody, Hugh. *Maps and Dreams: Indians and the British Columbia Frontier*. Vancouver: Douglas & McIntyre 1981

Brower, Kenneth. *The Starship and the Canoe*. New York: Holt, Rinehart and Winston 1978

Brown, Jennifer S.H. *Strangers in Blood: Fur Trade Company Families in Indian Country*. Vancouver: UBC Press 1980

Bulman, T. Alex. *Kamloops Cattlemen: One Hundred Years of Trail Dust!* Sidney: Gray's 1972

Burkinshaw, Robert Kenneth. 'Strangers and Pilgrims in Lotus Land: Conservative Protestantism in British Columbia, 1971–1981.' PH.D. thesis, University of British Columbia 1988

Burrows, James K. ' "A Much-needed Class of Labour": The Economy and Income of the Southern Interior Plateau Indians, 1897–1910,' *BC Studies* 71 (Autumn 1986), 27–46

Cail, Robert. *Land, Man and the Law: The Disposal of Crown Lands in British Columbia, 1871–1913*. Vancouver: UBC Press 1974

Campbell, Robert A. 'Liquor and Liberals: Patronage and Government Control in British Columbia, 1920–1928,' *BC Studies* 77 (Spring 1988), 30–53

Canada, House of Commons. *Debates*

Carr, Emily. *The Book of Small*. Toronto: Irwin 1942

– *Growing Pains*. Toronto: Clarke, Irwin 1946

– *The Heart of a Peacock*. Toronto: Irwin 1986

– *Hundreds and Thousands: The Journals of Emily Carr*. Toronto: Clarke, Irwin 1966

– *Klee Wyck*. Toronto: Irwin 1941

Cash, Gwen. *I Like British Columbia*. Toronto: Macmillan 1939
– *Off the Record: The Personal Reminiscences of Canada's First Woman Reporter*.
   Langley: Stagecoach 1977
Cell, John. 'The Imperial Conscience,' in Peter Marsh, ed., *The Conscience of the
   Victorian State*, 173–213. Syracuse: Syracuse University Press 1979
Census of Canada. Ottawa: Statistics Canada
Cheadle, Walter B. *Cheadle's Journal of Trip across Canada 1862–1863*. Edmonton:
   Hurtig 1971
Chittenden, Newton H. *Travels in British Columbia*. Vancouver: Gordon Soules 1984,
   orig. 1882
Chong, Denise. *The Concubine's Children*. Toronto: Viking 1994
Cleveland, Richard J. *Voyages and Commercial Enterprises of the Sons of New England*.
   New York: Leavitt and Allen 1855
Clough, Betty. 'Carroll Aikins,' *Okanagan History* 42 (1978), 116–22
Cole, Douglas. 'The Intellectual and Imaginative Development of British Columbia,'
   Journal of Canadian Studies 24, no. 3 (Fall 1989), 70–9
Collier, Eric. *Three against the Wilderness*. London: Hutchinson 1960
Colombo, John Robert. *Colombo's Concise Canadian Quotations*. Edmonton: Hurtig
   1976
Colonist. Victoria
Columbian. New Westminster
Commission of Inquiry into Redefinition of Electoral Districts, *Report*. Victoria:
   Queen's Printer 1966
Cook, Warren L. *Flood Tide of Empire: Spain and the Pacific Northwest, 1543–1819*. New
   Haven: Yale University Press 1973
Craig, Grace Morris. *But This Is Our War*. Toronto: University of Toronto Press 1981
Davies, Megan, J. ' "Services Rendered, Rearing Children for the State": Mothers'
   Pensions in British Columbia, 1919–1931,' in Barbara K. Latham and Roberta J.
   Pazdro, eds., *Not Just Pin Money: Selected Essays of the History of Women's Work in
   British Columbia*, 249–63. Victoria: Camosun College 1984
Davis, H. Craig and Thomas A. Hutton. 'The Two Economies of British Columbia,'
   BC Studies 82 (Summer 1989), 3–15
Day, David. 'Eustace Smith: The Last Authority,' *Raincoast Chronicles* 10 (1984), 46–9
Department of Indian Affairs, *Annual Reports*
Dobyns, Henry F. *Their Number Become Thinned: Native American Population Dynamics
   in Eastern North America*. Knoxville: University of Tennessee Press in co-operation
   with the Newberry Library 1983
Duff, Wilson. *The Indian History of British Columbia*. Vol. 1. Victoria: Provincial
   Museum 1965
Electoral History of British Columbia 1871–1986. Victoria: Elections British Columbia
   1988
Elkins, David J. 'British Columbia as a State of Mind,' in Donald E. Blake, ed., *Two
   Political Worlds: Parties and Voting in British Columbia*, 49–73. Vancouver: UBC Press
   1985

- 'Politics Makes Strange Bedfellows: The B.C. Party System in the 1952 and 1953 Provincial Elections,' *BC Studies* 30 (Summer 1976), 3–26

Elliott, Gordon, R. 'Henry P. Pellew Crease: Confederation or No Confederation,' *BC Studies* 12 (Winter 1971–2), 63–74

Elliott, Marie. *Mayne Island & the Outer Gulf Islands: A History*. Mayne Island: Gulf Islands Press 1984

Ellis, Walter E. 'Some Aspects of Religion in British Columbia Politics.' MA thesis, University of British Columbia 1959

Essex, Edith Mary. *Rhymes of a Country Postmistress*. N.p., n.d.

Evans, Hubert. *Mist on the River*. Toronto: Copp Clark 1954

Farley, A.L. *Atlas of British Columbia: People, Environment, and Resource Use.* Vancouver: UBC Press 1979

Fisher, Robin. *Contact and Conflict: Indian-European Relations in British Columbia, 1774–1890*. Vancouver: UBC Press 1977

- 'Cook and the Nootka,' in Robin Fisher and Hugh Johnston, eds., *Captain James Cook and His Times*, 81–98. Seattle: University of Washington Press 1979

Fishing at the Delta, in *People in Landscape* series, no. 2468–2. Victoria: Provincial Archives n.d.

Fladmark, Knut R. *British Columbia Prehistory*. Ottawa: National Museum of Man 1986

Ford, Clellan S. *Smoke from Their Fires: The Life of a Kwakiutl Chief*. New Haven: Yale University Press 1941

Foster, Chris. *One Heart, One Way: The Life and Legacy of Martin Exeter*. 100 Mile House: Foundation House 1989

Fougner, Ivar. Diary, 30 December 1889 – 30 December 1915, in possession of Milo Fougner, Vancouver

Fraser, John Foster. *Canada as It Is*. London: Cassell 1909

Frenchie, Lorraine. 'Self Educated Woman.' Unpublished essay submitted for Educational Studies 314, University of British Columbia 1989

Galbraith, John S. *The Hudson's Bay Company as an Imperial Factor 1821–1869*. Toronto: University of Toronto Press 1957

Garneau, Joel. *The Nine Nations of North America*. Boston: Houghton Mifflin 1981

Garner, Joe. *Never Chop Your Rope: A Story of British Logging and the People Who Logged*. Nanaimo: Cinnibar 1988

Geddes, Gary, ed. *Skookum Wawa: Writings of the Canadian Northwest*. Toronto: Oxford University Press 1975

Gee, Ellen. 'Fertility and Marriage Patterns in Canada: 1851–1971.' PH.D. thesis, University of British Columbia 1978

Gerard, Bernice. *Converted in the Country: The Life Story of Bernice Gerard as Told by Herself*. Jacksonville: McColl-Gerard Publications 1956

Gibson, Gordon. *Bull of the Woods: The Gordon Gibson Story*. Vancouver: Douglas & McIntyre 1980

Gibson, James R. 'The Sale of Russian America to the United States,' in S. Frederick Starr, ed. *Russia's American Colony*, 271–94. Durham: Duke University Press 1987

Ginn, E. Margaret. 'The Dutch and Dairying,' in Alfred H. Siemens, ed., *Lower Fraser Valley: Evolution of a Cultural Landscape*, 117–37. Vancouver: Tantalus 1968

Glazebrook, G.P. deT. *The Hargrave Correspondence 1821–1843*. Toronto: Champlain Society 1938

Gold, Wilmer. *Logging as It Was: A Pictorial History of Logging on Vancouver Island*. Victoria: Morriss 1985

Gould, Ed. *Logging: British Columbia Logging History*. Saanichton: Hancock House 1975

Grainger, M. Allderdale. *Woodsmen of the West*. Toronto: McClelland and Stewart 1964, orig. 1908

Grayson, L. M. and Michael Bliss, eds. *The Wretched of Canada: Letters to R.B. Bennett 1930–1935*. Toronto: University of Toronto Press 1971

Grigg, D.H. *From One to Seventy*. Vancouver: Mitchell 1953

Guest, Dennis. *The Emergence of Social Security in Canada*. 2nd ed. Vancouver: UBC Press 1985

Guide to the Province of British Columbia for 1877–8. Victoria: T.N. Hibben 1877

Haig-Brown, Roderick. *Measure of the Year*. New York: Morrow 1950

Hak, Gordon. 'British Columbia Loggers and the Lumber Workers Industrial Union, 1919–1922,' *Labour/Le Travail* 23 (Spring 1989), 67–90

Halliday, W.M. *Potlatch and Totem, and the Recollections of an Indian Agent*. London: J.M. Dent 1935

Harper, J. Russell. *Painting in Canada: A History*. 2nd ed. Toronto: University of Toronto Press 1977

Harris, R. Cole, ed. *Historical Atlas of Canada*. Vol. 1. Toronto: University of Toronto Press 1987

– 'Moving amid the Mountains, 1870–1930,' *BC Studies* 58 (Summer 1983), 3–39

Harrison, Eunice M.L. 'Pioneer Judge's Wife,' *Northwest Digest*, November 1951– May 1953

Hawthorn, H.B., ed. *A Survey of the Contemporary Indians of Canada*. 2 vols. Ottawa: Indian Affairs Branch 1966

Hawthorn, H.B., C.S. Belshaw, and S.M. Jamieson. *The Indians of British Columbia*. Toronto: University of Toronto Press 1958

Hendrickson, James E., ed. *Journals of the Colonial Legislatures of the Colonies of Vancouver Island and British Columbia 1851–1871*. 5 vols. Victoria: Provincial Archives 1980

Henripin, Jacques. *Trends and Factors of Fertility in Canada*. Ottawa: Statistics Canada 1972

Higgins, D.W. *The Mystic Spring and Other Tales of Western Life*. New York: Broadway Publishing 1908

Hill, Beth.' — if such a frightful appendage can be called ornamental ...' *Raincoast Chronicles* 8 (1980), 36–8

– *The Remarkable World of Frances Barkley: 1769–1845*. Sidney: Gray's 1978

Hills, Rev. George, Bishop of Columbia. Diary, 1860–95. Anglican Archives, Vancouver School of Theology, University of British Columbia

Hobson Jr., Richmond. *Grass beyond the Mountains*. Toronto: McClelland and Stewart 1951

– *Nothing Too Good for a Cowboy*. Toronto: McClelland and Stewart 1955

– *The Rancher Takes a Wife*. Toronto: McClelland and Stewart 1961

Hodgins, Jack. *The Resurrection of Joseph Bourne*. Toronto: Gage 1979

Hodgson, Maurice. *The Squire of Kootenay West: A Biography of Bert Herridge*. Saanichton: Hancock 1976

Howard, Irene. 'Shockable and Unshockable Methodists in *The Innocent Traveller*,' *Essays on Canadian Writing* 23 (Spring 1982), 107–34

– *The Struggle for Social Justice in British Columbia: Helena Gutteridge, the Unknown Reformer*. Vancouver: UBC Press 1992

Howay, F.W. *British Columbia from the Earliest Times to the Present*. Vancouver: S.J. Clarke 1914

– 'A List of Trading Vessels in Maritime Fur Trade, 1785–1825,' Royal Society of Canada, *Transactions*, Section II: 1930, 111–34; 1931, 117–49; 1932, 43–86; 1933, 119–47; and 1934, 11–49

Howay, F.W., W.N. Sage, and H.F. Angus. *British Columbia and the United States*. Toronto: Ryerson 1942

Howes, Katherine and Pat Lean. 'An Interview with Inga Teit Perkin, Daughter of Noted Ethnologist James A. Teit,' *Nicola Valley Historical Quarterly* 2, no. 2 (April 1979), 1 and 4

Hudson, Douglas. 'Traplines and Timber: Social and Economic Change among the Carrier Indians of Northern British Columbia.' PH.D. thesis, University of Alberta 1983

Hutcheson, Sydney. *Depression Stories*. Vancouver: New Star 1976

Hutchison, Bruce. *The Far Side of the Street*. Toronto: Macmillan 1976

– 'B.C.: The Interior,' *Maclean's*, 26 May 1956, and 'B.C.: The Coast,' 9 June 1956

– *The Unknown Country: Canada and Her People*. Toronto: Longmans, Green 1942

Ireland, Willard E. 'First Impressions: Letter of Colonel Richard Clement Moody, R.E., to Arthur Blackwood, February 1, 1859,' *British Columbia Historical Quarterly* 15 (1951), 85–107

Isenor, D.E., E.G. Stephens, and D.E. Watson. *One Hundred Spirited Years: A History of Cumberland 1888-1988*. Campbell River: Ptarmigan Press 1988

Jagpal, Sarjeet Singh. *Becoming Canadians: Pioneer Sikhs in Their Own Words*. Madeira Park: Harbour 1994

Jamieson, Stuart Marshall. *Times of Trouble: Labour Unrest and Industrial Conflict in Canada, 1900–66*. Ottawa: Task Force on Labour Relations 1968

Johnson, R. Byron. *Very Far West Indeed: A Few Rough Experiences on the North-West Pacific Coast*. London: Sampson Low, Marston, Low, & Searle 1872

Johnson-Dean, Christina B. *The Crease Family Archives: A Record of Settlement and Service in British Columbia*. Victoria: Provincial Archives of British Columbia 1982

Johnstone, Bill. *Coal Dust in My Blood: The Autobiography of a Coal Miner*. Victoria: British Columbia Provincial Museum 1980

Kalbach, Warren E. and Wayne W. McVey. *The Demographic Basis of Canadian Society*. 2nd ed. Toronto; McGraw-Hill Ryerson 1979

Kalman, Harold, Ron Phillips, and Robin Ward. *Exploring Vancouver: The Essential Architectural Guide*. Vancouver: UBC Press 1993

Karr, Clarence G. 'James Douglas: The Gold Governor in the Context of His Times,' in E. Blanche Norcross, ed., *The Company on the Coast*, 56–78. Nanaimo: Nanaimo Historical Society 1983

Keenleyside, Hugh. *Memoirs*. 2 vols. Toronto: McClelland and Stewart 1982

Kendrick, H. Robert. 'Amor De Cosmos and Confederation,' in W. George Shelton, ed., *British Columbia & Confederation*, 67–90. Victoria: University of Victoria 1967

Kipling, Rudyard. *From Sea to Sea and Other Sketches: Letters of Travel*. London: Macmillan 1900

– *Letters of Travel, 1892–1897*. New York: Doubleday, Doran 1941

Kirkness, Verna, ed. *Khot-Law-Cha: The Autobiography of Chief Simon Baker*. Vancouver: Douglas & McIntyre 1994

Kluckner, Michael, ed. *M.I. Rogers 1869–1965*. Vancouver: privately printed 1987

Knight, Phyllis and Rolf Knight. *A Very Ordinary Life*. Vancouver: New Star 1974

Knight, Rolf. *Indians at Work: An Informal History of Native Indian Labour in British Columbia 1858–1930*. Vancouver: New Star 1978

Knight, Rolf and Maya Koizumi. *A Man of Our Times: The Life-History of a Japanese-Canadian Fisherman*. Vancouver: New Star 1976

Kopas, Cliff. *Bella Coola*. Vancouver: Douglas & McIntyre 1970

Labour Statesman. Vancouver

Lady Franklin Visits the Pacific Northwest. Victoria: Provincial Archives of British Columbia 1974

Lamb, W. Kaye, ed. *The Journals and Letters of Sir Alexander Mackenzie*. Toronto: Macmillan 1970

– *The Letters and Journals of Simon Fraser 1806–1808*. Toronto: Macmillan 1960

– *Sixteen Years in the Indian Company: The Journal of Daniel Williams Harmon 1800–1816*. Toronto: Macmillan 1957

Leacy, F.H. ed. *Historical Statistics of Canada*. 2nd ed. Ottawa: Statistics Canada 1983

Lean, Pat. 'Commemorating: William Henry Voght, "The Father of Merrit," ' *Nicola Valley Historical Quarterly* 1, no. 2 (April 1978), 1 and 4–5

– 'Coutlee,' *Nicola Valley Historical Quarterly* 6, nos. 2–3 (October 1983), 2–7

– 'The Garcia Story,' *Nicola Valley Historical Quarterly* 6, no. 4 (May 1984), 2–9

Lembcke, Jerry and William M. Tattam. *One Union in Wood*. Madeira Park: Harbour 1984

Liversedge, Ronald. *Recollections of the One to Ottawa Trek*. Toronto: McClelland and Stewart 1973

Lowther, Pat. 'Mill Town,' *Raincoast Chronicles* 6 (1977), 17

Lugrin, Nancy de Bertrand. *The Pioneer Women of Vancouver Island*. Victoria: Women's Canadian Club of Victoria 1928

Lumsden, James. *Through Canada in Harvest Time: A Study of Life and Labour in the Golden West*. London: T. Fisher Unwin 1903

Lutz, John. 'Losing Steam: The Boiler and Engine Industry as an Index of British Columbia's Deindustrialization, 1880–1915,' Canadian Historical Association, *Historical Papers 1988*, 182–202

Lyons, Cicely. *Salmon Our Heritage: The Story of a Province and an Industry.*
Vancouver: British Columbia Packers 1969

Lytton, Earl. *The Life of Edward Bulwer, First Lord Lytton, by His Grandson.* 2 vols.
London: Macmillan 1913

McAlpine, Mary. *The Other Side of Silence: A Life of Ethel Wilson.* Madeira Park:

MacDonald, Norbert. *Distant Neighbours: A Comparative History of Seattle and
Vancouver.* Lincoln: University of Nebraska Press 1987

McDonald, Robert A.J. 'Victoria, Vancouver, and the Economic Development of
British Columbia, 1886–1914,' in Alan F.J. Artibise, ed., *Town and City: Aspects of
Western Canadian Urban Development,* 31–55. Regina: Canadian Plains Research
Centre 1981

– 'Working Class Vancouver, 1886–1914: Urbanism and Class in British Columbia,'
in R.A.J. McDonald and Jean Barman, eds., *Vancouver Past: Essays in Social
History,* 33–69. Vancouver: UBC Press 1986

McEvoy, Bernard. *From the Great Lakes to the Wide West.* Toronto: William Briggs 1902

Macfie, Matthew. *Vancouver Island and British Columbia: Their History, Resources, and
Prospects.* London: Longman, Green 1865

McGeer, Patrick. *Politics in Paradise.* Toronto: Peter Martin 1972

MacGill, Elsie Gregory. *My Mother the Judge: A Biography of Helen Gregory MacGill.*
Toronto: Ryerson 1955

MacKay, Donald. *Empire of Wood: The MacMillan Bloedel Story.* Vancouver: Douglas &
McIntyre 1982

– *The Lumberjacks.* Toronto: McGraw-Hill Ryerson 1978

McLaren, Angus and Arlene Tigar McLaren. *The Bedroom and the State: The Changing
Practices and Politics of Contraception and Abortion in Canada, 1880–1980.* Toronto:
McClelland and Stewart 1986

McMicking, Thomas. *Overland from Canada to British Columbia,* ed. Joanne Leduc.
Vancouver: UBC Press 1981

McQueen Correspondence. Nicola Valley Archives, Merritt, and Provincial Archives
of British Columbia, Victoria, Add. Ms. 860

Mack, Clayton with Harvey Thommasen. *Bella Coola Man.* Madeira Park: Harbour
1994

– *Grizzlies & White Guys.* Madeira Park: Harbour 1993

Mackie, Richard. 'Colonial Land, Indian Labour and Company Capital: The
Economy of Vancouver Island, 1849–1858.' MA thesis, University of Victoria, 1984

Madill, Dennis. *British Columbia Indian Treaties in Historical Perspective.* Ottawa: Indian
and Northern Affairs 1981

Magnusson, Warren et al. *The New Reality: The Politics of Restraint in British Columbia.*
Vancouver: New Star 1984

Mair, Charles. Correspondence from the Okanagan in possession of Duane
Thomson, Okanagan College

Manuel, George and Michael Posluns. *The Fourth World: An Indian Reality.* Don Mills:
Collier-Macmillan 1974

Marchak, Patricia. *Green Gold: The Forest Industry in British Columbia*. Vancouver: UBC Press 1983

Marchak, Patricia, Neil Guppy, and John McMullan, eds. *Uncommon Property: The Fishing and Fish-Processing Industries in British Columbia*. Toronto: Methuen 1987

Marlatt, Daphne. *Steveston*. Edmonton: Longspoon 1984

Marr, William L. and Donald G. Paterson. *Canada: An Economic History*. Toronto: Gage 1980

Martin, H.S. 'The Nechaco Valley,' *British Columbia Magazine* 10, no. 8 (August 1914), 410–12

Martin, Sandra and Roger Hall, eds. *Rupert Brooke in Canada*. Toronto: Peter Martin 1978

Mason, Phyllis. 'To See Ourselves: British Columbia in *The Times* of London, 1858–1863.' Unpublished essay submitted for History 404, University of British Columbia 1985

Mayne, R.C. *Four Years in Vancouver Island and British Columbia*. London: J. Murray 1862

Mellanson, Holly, comp. *Literary Presses in Canada, 1975–1985: A Checklist and Bibliography*. Halifax: School of Library and Information Studies, Dalhousie University 1988

Merk, Frederick, ed. *Fur Trade and Empire: George Simpson's Journal*. Cambridge, Mass: Harvard University Press 1968

Miller, J.R. *Skyscrapers Hide the Heavens: A History of Indian-White Relations in Canada*. Toronto: University of Toronto Press 1989

Mitchell, David J. *Succession: The Political Reshaping of British Columbia*. Vancouver: Douglas & McIntyre 1987

– *W.A.C. Bennett and the Rise of British Columbia*. Vancouver: Douglas & McIntyre 1983

Mitchell, David and Dennis Duffy, ed. *Bright Sunshine and a Brand New Country: Recollections of the Okanagan Valley 1890–1914*. Sound Heritage 7, no. 3. Victoria: Provincial Archives of British Columbia 1979

Mitchell, M. (Hunter). 'Jessie (Olding) Hunter,' *Nicola Valley Historical Quarterly* 3, no. 4 (October 1980), 1

Mitchell, Marjorie and Anna Franklin. 'When You Don't Know the Language, Listen to the Silence: An Historical Overview of Native Women in B.C.,' in Barbara K. Latham and Roberta J. Pazdro, eds., *Not Just Pin Money: Selected Essays on the History of Women's Work in British Columbia*, 17–35. Victoria: Camosun College 1984

Money, Anton. *This Was the North*. New York: Crown 1975

Moran, Bridget. *Stoney Creek Woman: The Story of Mary John*. Vancouver: Tillicum 1988

Morton, W.L., ed. *God's Galloping Girl: The Peace River Diaries of Monica Storrs 1929–1931*. Vancouver: UBC Press 1979

Mould, Jack. *Stump Farms and Broadaxes*. Saanichton: Hancock House 1976

Mulhall, David. *Will to Power: The Missionary Career of Father Morice*. Vancouver: UBC Press 1986

Mullins, Doreen Katherine. 'Changes in Location and Structure in the Forest Industry of North Central British Columbia: 1909–1966.' MA thesis, University of British Columbia 1967

Munro, H.H. *The Short Stories of Saki*. London: Bodley Head 1930

Naylor, C. David. *Private Practice, Public Payment: Canadian Medicine and the Politics of Health Insurance 1911–1966*. Kingston: McGill-Queen's University Press 1986

The New Government Colony, British Columbia and Vancouver's Island: A Complete Hand-Book Replete with the Latest Information Concerning the Newly-Discovered Gold Fields. London: Effingham Wilson 1858

New, W.H. *A History of Canadian Literature*. London: Macmillan Education 1989

Nicola Valley Historical Quarterly. Merritt

Niehaus, Valerie. 'Mrs. Sharon McIvor Grismer,' *Nicola Valley Historical Quarterly* 1, no. 4 (October 1978), 7

Noel, Norman. *Blanket-stiff: or, a Wanderer in Canada, 1911*. London: St Catherine Press 1912

Norcross, Elizabeth. 'Mary Ellen Smith: The Right Woman in the Right Place at the Right Time,' in Barbara K. Latham and Roberta J. Pazdro, eds., *Not Just Pin Money: Selected Essays on the History of Women's Work in British Columbia*, 357–64. Victoria: Camosun College 1984

Occupational Trends in Canada, 1891–1931. Ottawa: Dominion Bureau of Statistics 1939

Okanagan History. Kelowna and Vernon

Ormsby, Margaret A. *British Columbia: A History*. Toronto: Macmillan 1958

– 'Frederick Seymour, the Forgotten Governor,' *BC Studies* 22 (Summer 1974), 3–25

– 'Introduction,' to Hartwell Bowsfield, ed., *Fort Victoria Letters 1845–1851*. Winnipeg: Hudson's Bay Record Society 1979

– 'Sir James Douglas,' *Dictionary of Canadian Biography* 10: 238–49

– ed. *A Pioneer Gentlewoman in British Columbia: The Recollections of Susan Allison*. Vancouver: UBC Press 1976

Orr, Allan D. 'The Western Federation of Miners and the Royal Commission on Industrial Disputes in 1903, with Special Reference to the Vancouver Island Coal Miners' Strike.' MA thesis, University of British Columbia 1968

Palmer, Bryan D. *Working-Class Experience: The Rise and Reconstitution of Canadian Labour, 1800–1980*. Toronto: Butterworth 1983

– ed. *A Communist Life: Jack Scott and the Canadian Workers Movement, 1927–1985*. St John's: Committee on Canadian Labour History 1988

Papers Relative to the Affairs of British Columbia. London: Queen's Printer 1859

Parkin, George R. *The Great Dominion*. London: Macmillan 1895

Patterson, II, E. Palmer. 'A Decade of Change: Origins of the Nishga and Tsimshian Land Protests in the 1880s,' *Journal of Canadian Studies* 18, no. 3 (1983), 40–54

– 'Kincolith, B.C.: Leadership Continuity in a Native Christian Village, 1867–1887,' *Canadian Journal of Anthropology* 3, no. 1 (Fall 1982), 45–55

Pattison, James with Paul Grescoe. *Jimmy: An Autobiography*. Toronto: McClelland-Bantam 1987

Pennier, Henry. *Chiefly Indian: The Warm and Witty Story of a British Columbia Halfbreed Logger*. West Vancouver: Graydonald 1972

Pethick, Derek. *First Approaches to the Northwest Coast*. Vancouver: J.J. Douglas 1976

Phillips, Paul A. 'Confederation and the Economy of British Columbia,' in W. George Shelton, ed., *British Columbia & Confederation*, 43–60. Victoria: University of Victoria 1967

– *No Power Greater: A Century of Labour in British Columbia*. Vancouver: Boag Foundation 1967

Phillipps-Wolley, Clive. *A Sportsman's Eden*. London: Richard Bentley 1888

Playfair, W.E. 'British Columbia's Fifty-Seven Varieties,' *British Columbia Magazine* 7, no. 9 (September 1911), 903–15

Prentice, Alison et al. *Women in Canada: A History*. Toronto: Harcourt Brace Jovanovich 1988

Province. Vancouver

Ralston, H.K. 'The 1900 Strike of Fraser River Sockeye Salmon Fishermen.' MA thesis, University of British Columbia 1965

– 'Theme and Pattern in British Columbia History,' in Dickson M. Falconer, ed., *British Columbia: Patterns in Economic, Political and Cultural Development*, 3–11. Victoria: Camosun College 1982

Ramsay, Bruce. *Ghost Towns of British Columbia*. Vancouver: Mitchell 1963

Rattray, Alexander. *Vancouver Island and British Columbia*. London: Smith, Elder 1862

Reid, Dennis. *A Concise History of Canadian Painting*. 2nd ed. Toronto: Oxford University Press 1988

Report from the Select Committee on the Hudson's Bay Company, 1857. London: Queen's Printer 1857

Rich, E.E. *The Fur Trade and the Northwest to 1857*. Toronto: McClelland and Stewart 1967

– ed. *The Letters of John McLoughlin, First Series, 1825–38*. Toronto: Champlain Society for the Hudson's Bay Record Society 1941

– ed. *Simpson's 1828 Journey to the Columbia*. London: Champlain Society for the Hudson's Bay Record Society 1947

Richardson, David. *Pig War Islands*. Eastsound, Washington: Orcas Publishing 1971

Richardson, Letia. *First Class: Four Graduates from the Vancouver School of Decorative and Applied Arts, 1929*. Vancouver: Floating Curatorial Gallery 1987

Robin, Martin. *The Company Province*. 2 vols. Toronto: McClelland and Stewart 1972–73

– *Radical Politics and Canadian Labour 1880–1930*. Kingston: Industrial Relations Centre, Queen's University 1968

Robinson, Harry with Wendy Wickwire. *Nature Power: In the Spirit of an Okanagan Storyteller*. Vancouver: Douglas & McIntyre 1992

– *Write it on Your Heart: The Epic World of an Okanagan Storyteller*. Vancouver: Talon 1989

Robinson, J. Lewis. 'Vancouver: Changing Geographical Aspects of a Multicultural City,' *BC Studies* 79 (Autumn 1988), 59–80

Robinson, Lara. 'Sigurd Teit Story,' *Nicola Valley Historical Quarterly* 8, nos. 1–2 (December 1985), 11–12

Robson, Ebenezer. *How Methodism Came to British Columbia*. Toronto: Methodist Young People's Forward Movement 1904

Rogers, Anthony W. 'W.P. Weston, Educator and Artist: The Development of British Ideas in the Art Curriculum of B.C. Public Schools.' PH.D. thesis, University of British Columbia 1987

Ross, A.M. 'The Romance of Vancouver's Schools,' in James M. Sandison, ed., *Schools of Old Vancouver*, 11-25. Vancouver: Vancouver Historical Society 1971

Roy, Patricia E. 'Progress, Prosperity and Politics: The Railway Policies of Richard McBride,' *BC Studies* 47 (Autumn 1980), 3–28

– *A White Man's Province: British Columbia Politicians and Chinese and Japanese Immigrants 1858–1914*. Vancouver: UBC Press 1989

Royal Commission on Dominion-Provincial Relations. *Report*. Vol. 1. Ottawa: King's Printer 1940

Rushton, Gerald A. *Echoes of the Whistle: An Illustrated History of the Union Steamship Company*. Vancouver: Douglas & McIntyre 1980

Sage, Walter. 'British Columbia Becomes Canadian, 1871–1901,' *Queen's Quarterly* 52 (1945), 168–83

Schreiner, John. *The Refiners: A Century of BC Sugar*. Vancouver: Douglas & McIntyre 1989

Schrodt, Barbara. 'A History of Pro-Rec: The British Columbia Provincial Recreation Program – 1934 to 1953.' PH.D thesis, University of Alberta, 1979

Schwantes, Carlos. *The Pacific Northwest: An Interpretive History*. Lincoln: University of Nebraska Press 1989

Scott, A.D. 'Notes on a Western Viewpoint,' *BC Studies* 13 (Spring 1972), 3–15

Selman, Gordon. 'Adult Education in Barkerville, 1863 to 1875,' *BC Studies* 9 (Spring 1971), 38–54

Servin, Manuel, P., trans. 'The Instructions of Viceroy Bucarelli to Ensign Juan Perez,' *California State Historical Quarterly* 40 (1961), 237–48

Sharpe, C.A. 'Enlistment in the Canadian Expeditionary Force: A Regional Analysis,' *Journal of Canadian Studies* 18 (1983/84), 15–29

Shelford, Cyril. *From Snowshoes to Politics: A British Columbia Adventure!* Victoria: Orca 1987

Shelford, Cyril and Arthur Shelford. *We Pioneered*. Victoria: Orca 1988

Shi, David E. 'Seward's Attempt to Annex British Columbia, 1865–1869,' *Pacific Historical Review* 47 (1978), 217–38

The Shopping Guide of the West: Woodward's Catalogue 1898–1953. Vancouver: J.J. Douglas 1977

Shrum, Gordon. *An Autobiography*. Vancouver: UBC Press 1986

Siemens, Alfred H. 'The Process of Settlement in the Lower Fraser Valley – in Its Provincial Context,' in A.J. Siemens, ed., *Lower Fraser Valley: Evolution of a Cultural Landscape*, 27–49. Vancouver: Tantalus 1968

Silver, Arnold, ed. *The Family Letters of Samuel Butler 1841–1886*. London: Jonathan Cape 1962

Simson, Joe. 'Gastown: Everybody Knew Everybody,' *Raincoast Chronicles* 9(1983), 4–11

Sinclair, Bertrand. *The Inverted Pyramid*. Toronto: Frederick Goodchild 1924

Sirotnik, Gareth. *Running Tough: The Story of Vancouver's Jack Diamond*. Vancouver: Diamond Family 1988

Sladen, Douglas. *On the Cars and Off*. London: Ward, Lock & Bowden 1895

Slater, G. Hollis. 'New Light on Herbert Beaver,' *British Columbia Historical Quarterly* 6 (1942), 13–29

Smith, Andrea B. 'The CCF, NPA, and Civic Change: Provincial Forces behind Vancouver Politics 1930–1940,' *BC Studies* 53 (Spring 1982), 45–65

Smith, Brian R.D. 'Sir Richard McBride,' *Conservative Concepts* 1 (1959), 19–27

– 'Sir Richard McBride: A Study in the Conservative Party of British Columbia.' MA thesis, Queen's University 1959

Smith, Dorothy Blakey, ed. *The Reminiscences of Doctor John Sebastian Helmcken*. Vancouver: UBC Press 1975

Smith, Robert L. 'The Kennedy Interlude, 1864–66,' *BC Studies* 47 (Autumn 1980), 66–78

Speare, Jean E., ed. *The Days of Augusta*. Vancouver: J.J. Douglas 1973

Spradley, James P. *Guests Never Leave Hungry: The Autobiography of James Sewid, a Kwakiutl Indian*. New Haven: Yale University Press 1969

Sproat, Gilbert. *Scenes and Studies of Savage Life*. London: Smith, Elder 1868

Stanwell-Fletcher, Theodora C. *Driftwood Valley*. Boston: Little, Brown 1946

Stark, Freya. *Beyond Euphrates: Autobiography 1928–1933*. London: John Murray 1951

Statistics of Industry in British Columbia, 1871–1934. Victoria: Economic Council of British Columbia 1935

Steeves, Dorothy G. *The Compassionate Rebel: Ernest E. Winch and His Times*. Vancouver: Boag 1960

Stone, Leroy O. *Urban Development in Canada*. Ottawa: Dominion Bureau of Statistics 1967

Stouck, David, ed. *Ethel Wilson: Stories, Essays and Letters*. Vancouver: UBC Press 1988

– *Major Canadian Authors: A Critical Introduction*. Lincoln: University of Nebraska Press 1984

Street, Margaret M. *Watch-fires on the Mountains: The Life and Writings of Ethel Johns*. Toronto: University of Toronto Press 1973

Struthers, James. *No Fault of Their Own: Unemployment and the Canadian Welfare State 1914–1941*. Toronto: University of Toronto Press 1983

Stursberg, Peter. *Those Were the Days: The Days of Benny Nicholas and the Lotus Eaters*. Toronto: Peter Martin 1969

Sun. Vancouver

Sutherland, Neil. *Children in English-Canadian Society: Framing the Twentieth-Century Consensus*. Toronto: University of Toronto Press 1976

Sykes, Ella C. *A Home-Help in Canada*. London: Smith, Elder 1912

Tarasoff, Koozma J. *Plakun Trava: The Doukhobors*. Grand Forks: Mir 1982

Taylor, G.W. *Mining: The History of Mining in British Columbia*. Saanichton: Hancock House 1978

Taylor, Malcolm G. *Health Insurance and Canadian Public Policy*. 2nd ed. Kingston: McGill-Queen's University Press 1987

Tennant, Paul. 'Native Indian Political Organization in British Columbia, 1900–1969: A Response to Internal Colonialism,' *BC Studies* 55 (Autumn 1982), 3–49

Thomson, Duncan Duane. 'A History of the Okanagan: Indians and Whites in the Settlement Era, 1860–1920.' PH.D thesis, University of British Columbia, 1985

Thornton, Russell. *American Indian Holocaust and Survival: A Population History since 1492*. Norman: University of Oklahoma Press 1987

The Times. London

Topping, William, ed. *A Checklist of British Columbia Post Offices*. Vancouver: privately printed 1983

Tozer, M. Anita Bennett. 'Biographies and Reminiscences,' *Okanagan History* 43 (1979), 55–7

Tratt, Grace, comp. *Check List of Canadian Small Presses; English Language*. Halifax: University Libraries, Dalhousie University 1974

Troper, Harold and Lee Palmer. *Issues in Cultural Diversity*. Toronto: Ontario Institute for Studies in Education 1976

Turnbull, Elsie G. *Trail between Two Wars: The Story of a Smelter City*. Victoria: Morriss 1980

Turner, Robert D. *West of the Great Divide: An Illustrated History of the Canadian Pacific Railway in British Columbia 1880–1986*. Victoria: Sono Nis 1987

Twigg, Alan. *Strong Voices: Conversations with Fifty Canadian Authors*. Madeira Park: Harbour 1988

Usher [Freisen], Jean. *William Duncan at Metlakatla: A Victorian Missionary in British Columbia*. Ottawa: National Museums of Canada 1974

Van Kirk, Sylvia. *'Many Tender Ties': Women in Fur-Trade Society in Western Canada. 1670–1870*. Winnipeg: Watson & Dwyer 1980

Vancouver News. Vancouver

Vital Statistics: Ottawa: Statistics Canada

Von Hesse-Wartegg, Ernst. 'A Visit to Anglo-Saxon Antipodes,' *BC Studies* 50 (Summer 1981), 29–38

Vonnegut, Mark. *The Eden Express*. New York: Praeger 1976

Waddington, Alfred Pendrell. *The Fraser Mines Vindicated or, the History of Four Months*. Victoria: P. De Garro 1858

Wade Susan. 'Helena Gutteridge: Votes for Women and Trade Unions,' in Barbara Latham and Cathy Kess, eds., *In Her Own Right: Selected Essays on Women's History in B.C.*, 187–204. Victoria: Camosun College 1980

Walkem, W.W. *Stories of Early British Columbia*. Vancouver: News-Advertiser 1914

Walker, Russell R. *Bacon, Beans 'n Brave Hearts*. Lillooet: Lillooet Publishers 1972

Warburton, Rennie and David Coburn. 'The Rise of Non-Manual Work in British Columbia,' *BC Studies* 59 (Autumn 1983) 3–27

Ward, W. Peter. 'Class and Race in the Social Structure of British Columbia,
  1870–1939,' *BC Studies* 45 (Spring 1980), 17–36
- *White Canada Forever: Popular Attitudes and Public Policy toward Orientals in British
  Columbia*. Montreal: McGill-Queen's University Press 1978
Watters, Reginald E., ed. *British Columbia: A Centennial Anthology*. Toronto:
  McClelland and Stewart 1961
The Way We Were: A Celebration of Our UBC Heritage. Vancouver: Alumni Association,
  University of British Columbia 1987
The West Shore. Portland
Westminster Hall Magazine. Vancouver
White, Brenda Lea, ed. *British Columbia: Visions of the Promised Land*. Vancouver:
  Flight Press 1986
White, Howard. 'The Bomb That Mooed: Memories of a Logging Camp Childhood,'
  Raincoast Chronicles 10 (1984), 22–7
- *A Hard Man to Beat: The Story of Bill White*. Vancouver: Pulp Press 1983
- 'Minstrel Island,' in Howard White, ed., *Raincoast Chronicles: Forgotten Villages of
  the BC Coast*, 35–50. Madeira Park: Harbour 1987
Whymper, Frederick. *Travels and Adventure in the Territory of Alaska, Formerly Russian
  America ... And in Various Other Parts of the North Pacific*. London: John Murray 1868
Wicks, Walter. *Memories of the Skeena*. Saanichton: Hancock 1976
Wickwire, Wendy. 'Jimmie Teit: Anthropologist of the People,' *Nicola Valley
  Historical Quarterly* 2, no. 2 (April 1979), 5
Williams, David R. *The Man for a New Country: Sir Matthew Baillie Begbie*. Vancouver:
  Gray's Publishing 1977
Wilson, Ethel. 'The Bridge or the Stokehold? Views of the Novelist's Art,' *Canadian
  Literature* 5 (Summer 1960), 43–7
- 'A Cat among the Falcons,' *Canadian Literature* 2 (Autumn 1959), 10–19
- *Hettie Dorval*. Toronto: Macmillan 1947
- *The Innocent Traveller*. Toronto: McClelland and Stewart 1982, orig. 1949
- *Mrs. Golightly and Other Stories*. Toronto: Macmillan 1961
- *Swamp Angel*. Toronto: McClelland and Stewart 1982, orig. 1954
- 'Tuesday and Wednesday,' in her *The Equations of Love*, London: Macmillan 1952
Wilson, J. Donald. 'The Visions of Ordinary Participants: Teachers' Views of Rural
  Schooling in British Columbia in the 1920s,' in Patricia E. Roy, ed., *A History of
  British Columbia: Selected Readings*, 239–55. Toronto: Copp Clark Pitman 1989
- and Paul J Stortz, ' "May the Lord Have Mercy on You": The Rural School
  Problem in British Columbia in the 1920s,' *BC Studies* 79 (Autumn 1988), 24–58
Wilson, Jeremy, 'Forest Conservation in British Columbia, 1935–85: Reflections on a
  Barren Political Debate,' *BC Studies* 76 (Winter 1987–88), 3–32
Wood, Colin J.B. 'Population and Ethnic Groups,' in Charles N. Forward, ed., *British
  Columbia: Its Resources and People*, 309–32. Victoria: Department of Geography,
  University of Victoria 1987
Woodcock, George. *Ravens and Prophets: An Account of Journeys in British Columbia,
  Alberta and Southern Alaska*. London: Allan Wingate 1952

Woodsworth, James S. *Strangers within Our Gates*. Toronto: Missionary Society of the Methodist Church 1909

Woodward, Frances M. 'The Influence of the Royal Engineers on the Development of British Columbia,' *BC Studies* 24 (Winter 1974–75), 3–51

Yee, Paul. *Saltwater City: An Illustrated History of the Chinese in Vancouver*. Vancouver: Douglas & McIntyre 1988

Yoshida, Ryuichi. 'An Issei Life,' *Raincoast Chronicles* 7 (1978), 3–11

Zacharias, Alexandra. 'British Columbia Women's Institute in the Early Years: Time to Remember,' in Barbara Latham and Cathy Kess, eds., *In Her Own Right: Selected Essays on Women's History in B.C.*, 55–78. Victoria: Camosun College 1980

Ziner, Freenie. *Within This Wilderness*. New York: W.W. Norton 1978

Index

Picture Credits

British Columbia Archives and Records Service: Native house at Nootka (PDP 235); James Douglas (HP 2656); settlement at Victoria in the 1850s (PDP 2898); Cariboo Wagon Road (HP 763); main street of Barkerville (HP 5191); seiner (HP 75519); 'iron chink' (HP 81162); native family placer mining (HP 70980); native packers (HP 13776); potlatch at Alert Bay (HP 95789); two young Indian women enjoying a break (HP 84161); Victoria at the time of the First World War (HP 14442); pack train leaving Hazelton 1910 (HP 61270); summertime in Kelowna (HP 2132); Bennett on the campaign trail (HP 95464)

City Archives, Vancouver: arrival of Captain Cook's ships (BO N.70 P.207); Chinese laundry on Water Street (BU N.387 P.403); first streetcar in Kitsilano (KIT N.24 P.24); grain elevators overshadowing East Vancouver (BU N.307 P.361#1)

Vancouver Public Library: East Indian workers (7641); CPR station by the docks (2536); typical wilderness enclave at Quatsino Sound (9552); ranch near Soda Creek (8334); steamship *Lady Cecilia* (8001); camping at Horseshoe Bay (4901); enforced evacuation of Japanese Canadians (1384)

Native Communications Society of British Columbia: native people protest cutbacks in education funding April 1989.

British Columbia Pavilion Corporation: Vancouver has become a major city on the Pacific Rim (Vancouver Trade and Convention Centre).